THRACE

•Dráma •Komotiní

Kavála•

Alexandroúpoli

NORTHERN GREECE
Pages 232–257

AROUND
ATHENS
•ATHENS
ATTICA
Lávrio •

ATHENS
Pages 62–135

AROUND ATHENS
Pages 140–157

EYEWITNESS *TRAVEL GUIDES*

GREECE
ATHENS & THE MAINLAND

EYEWITNESS *TRAVEL GUIDES*

GREECE
ATHENS & THE MAINLAND

Main Consultant: MARC DUBIN

A DK PUBLISHING BOOK

PROJECT EDITOR Jane Simmonds
ART EDITOR Stephen Bere
EDITORS Isabel Carlisle, Michael Ellis, Simon Farbrother,
Claire Folkard, Marianne Petrou, Andrew Szudek
DESIGNERS Jo Doran, Paul Jackson, Elly King, Marisa Renzullo
MAP CO-ORDINATORS Emily Green, David Pugh
RESEARCHERS Garifalia Boussiopoulou, Veronica Wood
PICTURE RESEARCH Ellen Root
DTP DESIGNER Adam Moore
VISUALIZER Joy Fitzsimmons
LANGUAGE CONSULTANT Georgia Gotsi
PRODUCTION David Proffit

MANAGING EDITOR Georgina Matthews
MANAGING ART EDITOR Annette Jacobs
US EDITORS Michael Wise, Mary Sutherland
DEPUTY EDITORIAL DIRECTOR Douglas Amrine
DEPUTY ART DIRECTOR Gillian Allan

CONTRIBUTORS AND CONSULTANTS
Rosemary Barron, Marc Dubin, Mike Gerrard, Andy Harris,
Lynette Mitchell, Colin Nicholson, Robin Osborne, Barnaby
Rogerson, Paul Sterry, Tanya Tsikas

MAPS
Gary Bowes, Fiona Casey, Christine Purcell (ERA-Maptec Ltd)

PHOTOGRAPHERS
Joe Cornish, John Heseltine, Rob Reichenfeld, Peter Wilson,
Francesca Yorke

ILLUSTRATORS
Stephen Conlin, Paul Guest, Steve Gyapay, Maltings Partnership,
Chris Orr & Associates, Paul Weston, John Woodcock

Text film output by Graphical Innovations (London)
Reproduced by Colourscan (Singapore)
Printed and bound by G. Canale (Italy)

First American Edition, 1997
2 4 6 8 10 9 7 5 3 1

Published in the United States by
DK Publishing, Inc.,
95 Madison Avenue, New York, New York 10016
Visit us on the World Wide Web at htttp://www.dk.com

Library of Congress Cataloging-in-Publication Data
Greece. -- 1st American ed.
p.   cm. -- (Eyewitness travel guides)
Includes index.
ISBN 0-7894-1452-X
1. Greece -- Guidebooks.
I Series.
DF716.G758 1996
914.9504'76 -- dc21   CIP 96-44381

Every effort has been made to ensure that the information in this book is as up-to-
date as possible at the time of going to press. However, details such as telephone
numbers, opening hours, prices, gallery exhibitions, and travel information are liable
to change. The publishers cannot accept responsibility for any consequences
arising from the use of this book.

We would be delighted to receive any corrections and suggestions for incorporation
in the next edition. Please write to the Managing Editor, Eyewitness Travel Guides,
Dorling Kindersley, 9 Henrietta Street, London WC2E 8PS.

THROUGHOUT THIS BOOK, FLOORS ARE REFERRED TO IN ACCORDANCE WITH EUROPEAN USAGE.
I.E, "FIRST FLOOR" IS ONE FLIGHT UP.

◁ Morning at Gýtheio harbor in the Peloponnese

CONTENTS

HOW TO USE THIS GUIDE 6

Black-figure bowl depicting
the god Dionysos

INTRODUCING ATHENS AND MAINLAND GREECE

ANCIENT GREECE

Tower houses at Vátheia, Inner Máni in the Peloponnese

Greek salad

Fresco at Varlaám monastery at
Metéora, Central Greece

View of the
Acropolis in
Athens

Reconstruction of Ancient Olympia

HOW TO USE THIS GUIDE

THIS GUIDE helps you to get the most from your visit to Mainland Greece. It provides expert recommendations and practical information. *Introducing Athens and Mainland Greece* maps the country and sets it in its historical and cultural context. *Ancient Greece* gives a background to the many remains and artifacts to be seen. The four regional chapters, plus *Athens*, describe important sights, with maps and illustrations. Restaurant and hotel recommendations can be found in *Travelers' Needs*. The *Survival Guide* has tips on everything from using a Greek telephone to transportation.

ATHENS

Athens has been divided into two sightseeing areas. Each has its own chapter, opening with a list of the sights described. All sights are numbered on an area map, and are described in detail on the following pages.

Sights at a Glance gives a categorized list of the chapter's sights: Museums and Galleries; Squares, Parks, and Gardens; Churches and Historic Buildings.

All pages relating to Athens have red thumb tabs.

A locator map shows you where you are in relation to the rest of Athens.

1 Area Map
The sights are numbered and located on a map. Sights in the city center are also shown on the Athens Street Finder *on pages 122–35.*

2 Street-by-Street Map
This gives an overhead view of the key areas in central Athens. The numbering on the map ties in with the area map and the fuller descriptions that follow.

Story boxes highlight special aspects of a particular sight.

Stars indicate the sights that no visitor should miss.

A suggested route for a walk is shown in red.

3 Detailed Information
The sights within Athens are described individually. Addresses, telephone numbers, opening hours, and information concerning admission charges and wheelchair access are given for each entry. Map references to the Athens Street Finder *are also provided for orientation.*

1 Introduction
An introduction covers the history, character, and geography of each region, showing how the area has developed over the centuries and what it has to offer the visitor today.

MAINLAND GREECE AREA BY AREA
Mainland Greece has been divided into four regions, each of which has a separate chapter. A map of these areas can be found inside the front cover of the book.

Each region can be identified by its color coding, shown on the inside front cover.

A locator map shows you where you are in relation to the other regions in the book.

2 Pictorial Map
This shows the region covered in the chapter. The main sights are numbered on the map. The major roads are marked, and there are useful tips about the best ways of getting around the area.

3 Detailed Information
All the important towns and areas to visit are described individually. They are listed in order, following the numbering on the Pictorial Map. *Within each entry there is detailed information on all the major sights.*

A Visitors' Checklist provides the practical information you will need to plan your visit.

4 Greece's Top Sights
These are given one or more full pages. Historic buildings are dissected to reveal their interiors. Many of the ancient sites are reconstructed to supplement information about the site as it is seen today.

INTRODUCING
ATHENS AND
MAINLAND GREECE

Putting Greece on the Map

Occupying the southernmost tip of the Balkan peninsula, Greece divides into over 2,000 islands stretching from the Ionian Sea in the west to the Aegean Sea and Turkey in the east. The mainland has borders with Albania, Bulgaria, Turkey, and Macedonia and is home to most of the country's 10.2 million people, with a third of these in the capital, Athens.

Key

- 🛳 Main international ferry service
- 🛫 International airport
- ═══ Divided highway
- ━━━ Major road
- ──── Railroad line
- ─ ∙ ─ International border

◁ **The fortified islet of Boúrtzi, off the coast of Methóni**

EUROPE AND
NORTH AFRICA

NORWAY   FINLAND
SWEDEN
ESTONIA
DENMARK   LATVIA   RUSSIAN
LITHUANIA   FEDERATION
RUSSIAN FED.
REPUBLIC   BELORUSSIA
OF IRELAND   UNITED   NETHERLANDS   POLAND
KINGDOM   GERMANY
BELGIUM   LUXEMBOURG
CZECH REPUBLIC
FRANCE   SLOVAKIA   UKRAINE
SWITZERLAND   AUSTRIA   HUNGARY   MOLDAVIA
SLOVENIA   ROMANIA
CROATIA   YUGOSLAVIA
BOSNIA AND
PORTUGAL   HERZEGOVINA   BULGARIA   TURKEY
SPAIN   ITALY   FYR OF
ALBANIA   MACEDONIA
GREECE   SYRIA
Athens   IRAQ
ISRAEL
TUNISIA   JORDAN
MOROCCO   SAUDI
ARABIA
ALGERIA   LIBYA   EGYPT

L'viv
E40
Dnister
E471
UKRAINE
Chernivtsi
Siret
Prut
E85
MOLDAVIA
E60
CHISINAU
E581
E85
ROMANIA
E68
Brașov
Galați
E85
Prut
E81
E60
E60
Olt
E70
Dunărea
BUCHAREST
Constanța
E87
E83
E772
Varna
Iskür
E85
E85
SOFIA
Burgas
BULGARIA
E80   E87
E79   Nestos
E90
E85   E84
Kavála   Istanbul   E80
Alexandroúpoli
Thessaloníki
E90
E90
E C E
E90
Eskişehir   ANKARA
Kızıl Irmak
E80
Aegean   Skiáthos   Lésvos
Sea
los
E87
TURKEY
Évvoia
Izmir   E90
ATHENS   Kuşadasi   Tuz Gölü
iraeús   Sámos
Tínos   Bodrum   Konya   E90
Mýkonos   Pátmos
Kos   Marmaris   İçel   E90
Santoríni   Rhodes
Kárpathos   SYRIA
Chaniá   Irákleio   Al-Lādiqiya
Crete   Agios   CYPRUS   NICOSIA
Nikólaos   Lemesós   Lárnaka
E91
LEBANON
BEIRUT
Sea
0 kilometers   200
0 miles   200
Hefa
ISRAEL
Alexandria   EGYPT

Black   Sea

A PORTRAIT OF
MAINLAND GREECE

······································

REECE IS ONE OF THE MOST VISITED *European countries, yet one of the least known. The modern Greek state dates only from 1830 and bears little relation to the popular image of ancient Greece. At a geographical crossroads, Greece combines elements of the Balkans, Middle East, and Mediterranean.*

For a relatively small country, less than 132,000 sq km (51,000 sq miles) in area, Greece possesses marked regional differences in topography. Nearly three-quarters of the land is mountainous, uninhabited, or uncultivated. Fertile agricultural land supports tobacco farming in the north, with grapes and vegetables grown in Attica and the Peloponnese. A third of the population lives in the capital, Athens, the cultural, financial, and political center, in which ancient and modern stand side by side.

Rural and urban life in contemporary Greece has been transformed this century despite years of occupation and conflict, including a bitter civil war *(see p42)* that would surely have finished off a less resilient people. The society that emerged was supported with US aid, yet Greece remained relatively under-developed until the 1960s.

Rural areas lacked paved roads and even basic utilities, prompting extensive, unplanned urban growth and emigration. It has been said, with some justice, that there are no architects in Greece, only civil engineers.

For centuries a large number of Greeks have lived abroad: currently there are over half as many Greeks outside the country as in. This

Fresco from Moní Frankavílla, Kallogriá

Backgammon players at the flea market around Plateía Monastirákiou in Athens

◁ **Leading a mule on the streets of Monemvasía**

The Píndos mountain range, from above the village of Vrysochóri

diaspora occurred in several stages, beginning during Ottoman rule in the late 17th century. Most recently, emigration has been to Africa, the Americas, and Australia.

RELIGION, LANGUAGE, AND CULTURE
During the centuries of domination by Venetians and Ottomans *(see pp38–9)* the Greek Orthodox church preserved the Greek language, and with it Greek identity, through its liturgy and schools. Today, the Orthodox church is still a powerful force, despite the secularizing reforms of the first democratically elected PASOK government of 1981–85. The query *Eísai Orthódoxos* (Are you Orthodox?) is virtually synonymous with *Éllinas eísai* (Are you Greek?). While no self-respecting couple would dispense with a church wedding and baptisms for their children, civil marriages are now equally valid in law as the traditional religious service. Sunday mass is very popular with women, who often use the services as meeting places for socializing much in the same way as men do the *kafeneía* (cafés).

Votive offerings in the Pantánassa convent

Parish priests, often recognizable by their tall stovepipe hats and long beards, are not expected to embody the divine, but to transmit it at liturgy. Many marry and have a second trade (a custom that helps keep up the numbers of entrants to the church). There has also been a

Greek priests leading a religious procession in Athens

recent renaissance in monastic life, perhaps in reaction to the growth of materialism since World War II.

Tavernas in the town of Náfplio

The subtle and beautiful Greek language, another great hallmark of national identity, was for a long time a field of conflict between *katharévousa*, an artificial, written form hastily devised around the time of Independence, and the slowly evolved *dimotikí*, or everyday speech, with its streamlined grammar and words borrowed from several other languages. The dispute acquired political overtones, with the Right tending to champion *katharévousa*, the Left, *dimotikí*, with blood even being shed at times.

Today's prevalence of the more supple *dimotikí* was perhaps a foregone conclusion in an oral culture. The art of storytelling is still as prized in Greece as in Homer's time, with conversation pursued for its own sake in *kafeneía* and at dinner parties. The bardic tradition has remained alive with poet-lyricists

such as Mános Eleftheríou and composers such as Stávros Xarchákos. The continuous efforts made to produce popular and accessible art have played a key role in helping to keep *dimotikí* alive from the 19th century until the the present day.

Both writers and singers, the natural advocates of *dimotikí,* have historically been important to the Greek public. During recent periods of censorship under the dictatorship or in times of foreign occupation, they carried out an essential role as one of the chief sources of coded news and information.

An archaeologist helping to restore the Parthenon

DEVELOPMENT AND DIPLOMACY

Compared to most of its Balkan neighbors, Greece is a wealthy and stable country, but by Western economic indicators Greece languishes at the bottom of the EU economic charts and will be a net EU beneficiary for some years to come. The persistent trade deficit is aggravated by imports of luxury goods, an expression of *xenomanía* or belief in the inherent superiority of all things foreign. Cars are most conspicuous among these, since Greece, like many other smaller European countries, does not manufacture its own.

Greece still bears the hallmarks of a developing economy, with agriculture and the service sector accounting for two-thirds of the GNP. Blurred lines

Selling fish at Vólos harbor, the Pílio

Barrels in the Achaïa Klauss winery at Pátra

between work and living space are the norm, with professional brass plates alternating with personal bell-buzzer tags in any apartment building. There is a tenacious adherence, despite repeated campaigns against it, to the long afternoon siesta. As a result, some workers have to endure commuting twice a day.

With EU membership since 1981 and a nominally capitalist orientation, Greece has now overcome its resemblance to pre-1989 Eastern Europe. The state no longer invests heavily in antiquated industries nor is the civil service of today overstaffed as part of a full-employment policy. Instead, recent years have seen a number of improvements: loss-making state enterprises have been sold off, inflation has dipped to single figures for the first time since 1973, the drachma has stablilized, and interest rates are falling; only

unemployment remains stubbornly high. Tourism ranks as the largest hard-currency earner, offsetting the depression in world shipping and the fact that Mediterranean agricultural products are duplicated within the EU. Greece's historically lenient entry requirements for refugees, and its preeminent status in the Balkans, have made it a magnet for Arabs, Africans, Kurds, Poles, and Albanians for a number of years. Now protectionist procedures, such as stringent frontier clampdowns and the deportation of all undocumented individuals, have been introduced.

The fact that the Greek state is less than 200 years old and that this century has been marked by political instability, means that there is little faith in government institutions. Life operates on networks of personal friendships and official contacts. The classic designations of Right and Left have only acquired their conventional meanings since the 1930s. The dominant political figure of the first half of the 20th century was Elenthérios Venizélos, an antiroyalist Liberal. The years following World War II have

Statue of Athena beside the Academy of Arts, Athens

Rooftops of Náfplio from the Palamídi fortress

House in the village of Psarádes, beside the Préspa lakes

been largely shaped by the influence of two men: the late Andréas Papandréou, three times premier as head of the Panhellenic Socialist Movement (PASOK), and the conservative premier Konstantínos Karamanlís.

With the Cold War over, Greece looks likely to assert its underlying Balkan identity in many ways. Relations with Albania have improved since the collapse of the Communist regime in 1990. Greece is already the biggest investor in Bulgaria, and after a recent rapprochement with Skopje, it seems poised to be a regional power, with Thessaloníki's port (the second largest in the Mediterranean) seen as the future gateway to the southern Balkans.

Man with a shepherd's crook in the village of Métsovo

HOME LIFE

The family is still the basic Greek social unit. Traditionally, one family could sow, plow, and reap its own fields, without need of cooperative work parties. Today, family-run businesses are still the norm in urban settings. Family life and social life are usually one and the same, and tend to revolve around eating out, which is done more often than in most of Europe. Arranged marriages and granting of dowries, though officially banned, persist; most single young people live with their parents or another relative until married, and outside the largest cities, few couples dare to cohabit. Despite the renowned Greek love of children, Greece has the lowest birth rate in Europe after Italy: less than half its pre-World War II levels. Partly because of recent reforms in family and inheritance law, urban Greek women have been raised in status. They are now better represented in medicine and law, and many women run their own businesses. In the country, however, traditional attitudes persist, and women often forgo the chance of a career for the sake of looking after the house and children. New notions and attitudes have crept in, especially in the larger cities, but in general tradition remains strong and no outside influence is likely to jeopardize the Greek way of life.

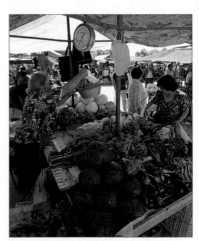

Wednesday market in Argos

Byzantine Architecture

MEDIEVAL CHURCHES are virtually all that have survived from a millennium of Byzantine civilization in Greece. Byzantine church architecture was concerned almost exclusively with a decorated interior. The intention was to carve out a holy space where the congregation would be confronted with the true nature of the cosmos, cleared of all worldly distractions. The mosaics and frescoes portraying the whole body of the Church, from Christ downward, have a dual purpose: they give inspiration to the worshiper and are windows to the spiritual world. From a mountain chapel to an urban church there is great conformity of design, with structure and decoration united to a single purpose.

THE BEST OF BYZANTINE ARCHITECTURE

① Thessaloníki *p248*
② Mount Athos *pp252–4*
③ Arta *p213*
④ Monastery of Osios Loúkas *pp222–3*
⑤ Pátra *p169*
⑥ Moní Kaisarianís *pp150–51*
⑦ Monastery of Dafní *pp152–3*
⑧ Athens *p80, p105, p108*
⑨ Mystrás *pp192–3*
⑩ Geráki *p189*

Small dome above narthex

The drum is pierced with as many as 40 windows.

The Pantokrátor, a mosaic of Christ in Judgment, is in the dome.

The iconostasis screen divides the altar from the main body of the church.

Side aisle

Four squinches support the dome.

Central apse

The three apses of the east wall often have ornamental brickwork on their curved exterior.

Colored marble flooring

Brickwork may alternate with layers of stone.

The west-facing porch may bear scenes from the life of the Virgin.

Ornamental brickwork was a 10th-century Greek invention.

Icon of Christ above the main door

TYPICAL BYZANTINE CHURCH

Each church has a covered porch (narthex) to the west and an altar behind the iconostasis in the eastern apse. The nave typically has three aisles with the dome above the central square space. In a monastery, the main church is known as the *katholikón*.

UNDERSTANDING FRESCOES IN A BYZANTINE CHURCH

The frescoes and mosaics in churches' interiors were organized according to a standard scheme. Symbolically, images descended from heaven (Christ Pantokrátor in the dome) to earth (the saints on the lowest level). The Virgin was shown in the semi-dome of the apse, with the fathers of the church below her.

Choirs of angels

Windows in drum

Christ Pantokrátor

The dome *is symbolically filled by the figure of Christ in Judgment, the Pantokrátor. Choirs of angels swirl around him, and outside them stand the Old Testament prophets. This dome comes from Moní Perivléptou in Mystrás (see p192).*

Prophets

The Virgin and Child are in the curve of the apse, symbolically between heaven (the dome) and earth (the nave).

Archangels Michael and Gabriel, dressed like courtiers of the Byzantine emperor, honor the Virgin.

The Fathers of Orthodoxy, here in their episcopal robes, defined Orthodoxy in the early centuries.

Upper register of saints

The apse *is often hidden from public view by an elaborate iconostasis screen, through whose doors only the clergy are admitted. This apse is from the Ano Mpoulárioi in the Máni (see pp194–9).*

Lower register of saints

Sand-filled tray for votive candles

The side walls *are decorated in registers. On the lowest level stand life-size portrayals of the saints, their heads illuminated with haloes. More complex scenes portraying incidents from the Gospels or the Day of Judgment fill the upper walls and vaults. This church is at Mílies in the Pílio (see pp218–20).*

THE VIRGIN MARY

Icons of the Virgin Mary abound in every Orthodox church, where she is referred to as Panagía, the All Holy. Her exceptional status was confirmed in 431 when she was awarded the title Theotókos "Mother of God," in preference to just "Mother of Christ."

Eleoúsa, *meaning "Our Lady of Tenderness," shows the Virgin Mary brushing cheeks with the Christ Child.*

The Virgin seated on a throne, *flanked by two archangels, is a depiction usually found in the eastern apse.*

Odigítria, *meaning the "Conductress," shows the Virgin with the Christ Child resting on her left arm.*

Vernacular Architecture in Mainland Greece

MOST OF THE SURVIVING masterpieces of vernacular architecture in mainland Greece date from the 18th century, when improved conditions within the Ottoman Empire permitted the rise of a non-Muslim bourgeoisie. Sumptuous mansions, or *archontiká*, relying heavily on Ottoman and Byzantine designs, were built by Orthodox Christians returning from Italy, Central Europe, and Constantinople. The stonemasons, woodworkers, and mural painters came mainly from remote mountain villages in Epirus, now a region divided between Greece and Albania.

Picturesque village in Zagória with schist-slab roofs

Decorated plasterwork

The *sachnisí* juts out on wooden buttresses.

Protective iron grille on lower windows

The Kanatsoúlis mansion in Siátista is representative of those here and in nearby Kastoriá (see p240). Lavishly decorated on their upper stories with stained glass and painted wood, they reflect the prosperity of local fur merchants in the 17th and 18th centuries.

Chatília, or bands of wood, divide masonry sections.

Main door studded with heavy nails

Arched windows with masoned lintels

Sloping roof of tiles or schist

Round turrets at the corners of the roof acted as sentry posts or *klouviá.*

The small balcony was made of wood or wrought iron.

Reversed conical supports

Arched doorway, often low

The upper floors were for sleeping, living, and guests.

Small windows for firing through

Arcadian mansions in the mountainous central Peloponnese were built of local stone. Small windows and wooden floors and ceilings were for warmth. On steep slopes, one side of the building could have two or three stories, the other up to five.

The ground floor was for storage and stabling.

Stone farmhouse

Access to the tower was often through the attached house.

Máni tower houses are found in the south-central spur of the Peloponnese. (see pp194–9) The Máni was historically occupied by feuding families who used the stone towers for both shelter and attack. The attached two-story building was occupied in peacetime.

The limestone roofing is usually dark, but here it is light.

The square chimney is hatted to exclude rain and snow.

The wooden balcony is usually south facing.

Typical arched doorway

Small windows for winter warmth

Double windows flank the fireplace.

The hooded fireplace may have a skylight in the flue.

Low divans covered in locally woven cloth are arranged around the fireplace.

Durable white limestone for the walls is closely fitted with little or no mortar.

Chamfered corners permit easy passage of pack animals.

This Zagorian mansion in the Páno Machalás region of Vitsa, near the Víkos Gorge (see p208), is typical of many in western Zagória (see p207). Wood, not abundant in this region, was embedded out of sight in the wall as an anchor for the floor planks. The ondás, or reception room, often had wall murals and coffered ceilings.

Tiled roofs with sloping ends

Narrow windows capped with pediments

Wrought iron fanlight

Stone cladding on ground floor

Secondary doors

Iron balcony supported on stone corbels

Pilasters at corners

The Neo-Classical revival style became popular in Greece in the 19th century with the rule of Bavarian King Otto. At first it was confined to public buildings such as schools, courthouses, and libraries in the capital. Later it spread to wealthy provincial towns and into domestic use. This generic Peloponnesian structure is late 19th century.

LOCAL BUILDING METHODS AND MATERIALS

Stone, usually limestone, is used across the mainland for lower stories, because of its strength in weight-bearing and fortification. *Tsatmás* and *bagdatí* (lath and plaster) suffice for upper stories, both for interior partition walls, and in *sachnisiá* (airy overhangs), which add extra space but little extra weight. Wood, in the former times when it was plentiful in Thessaly, Macedonia, and Thrace, was used for balustrades and latticework around a *chagiáti* or upstairs covered porch, window grilles, and clapboard siding. More recently, iron has been used instead of wood.

White limestone exterior wall

Wooden *sachnisí* (overhang)

Roof tiled with slates

Tsatmás (timber and rubble) wall

Ornate iron window grille

Roof of clay canal tiles

The Landscape of Mainland Greece

Gʀᴇᴇᴄᴇ ɪs ᴀ ʟᴀɴᴅ of rugged beauty. The narrow coastal belt is backed by cliffs in places while inland there are massive mountain ranges, gorges, and cliffs, the haunts of eagles and vultures. The fantastic array of vegetation, including many species of spring wild flowers, is strongly influenced by the Mediterranean climate of long, hot, and dry summers and mild, wet winters. Clearance of forests for agriculture and timber has produced a mosaic of flower-rich fields and areas of shrubs. This shrubland habitat is of two kinds: the dense aromatic bushes of *maquis* and the sparser *phrygana* with lower and more compact plants. Although the country's millions of goats destroy the vegetation with their constant grazing, one of the most romantic sights in Greece is that of flocks being herded through olive groves full of archaeological remains, as at Sparta in the Peloponnese.

Common poppy

Abandoned areas of cultivation soon revert to the wild. Larks and pipits feed and nest here, and, in spring, wildflowers and butterflies are abundant.

Phrygana often covers bare slopes and rocky outcrops.

Hilly landscapes with stately cypress trees standing tall and dark against the steep slopes are closely associated with Greece's archaeological sites. These, including the Byzantine town of Mystrás above, are worth visiting for their wildlife alone and in particular the spring wildflowers that mix rare orchids with daisies, poppies, and marigolds.

Olive trees harbor numerous birds and insects among their silvery-green foliage.

Spring flowers such as poppies and marigolds have a brief but prolific season.

Mᴀǫᴜɪs ᴀɴᴅ Pʜʀʏɢᴀɴᴀ

Maquis shrubland dominates the landscape in this view of Mycenae. It is a mixture of rock-roses and aromatic herbs. The more barren *phrygana*, in the far distance, has clumps of spiny vetches.

Olive groves are found all over Greece at low altitudes; this one is at Argalastí in the Pílio. In spring, flowers grow in profusion in the shade of trees and attract a wealth of butterflies and beetles. Lizards hunt for insects in the twisted trunks that also provide nesting places for birds such as masked shrikes.

Wetland areas, such as the margins of Lake Stymfalía in the Peloponnese, are often used for farming. Usually fairly dry underfoot, they are rich in birds, amphibians, and plants.

WILD FLOWERS OF GREECE

Greece is blessed with an extraordinary wealth of flowering plants. At least 6,000 species grow in the country, quite a few of them found nowhere else in the world. The floral richness is due in part to the country's diversity of habitats, ranging from wetlands, coastal plains, and lowland *maquis* to snow-capped mountain tops. The growing period for many plants is winter, the dampest, coolest season, and the flowering period runs from March to early June. Coastal areas of the Peloponnese are perhaps the richest in wild flowers.

The wild gladiolus has several varieties that are among the most showy spring flowers.

The tassel hyacinth is aptly named for its appearance. It grows on open ground and flowers in May.

Cytinus hypocistus is a parasite plant found growing close to the base of colorful cistus bushes (see below).

White asphodel is often seen growing on roadsides in many parts of Greece. Tall spikes of white flowers appear from April to June.

Sage-leaved cistus is widespread in *maquis* habitats. Its colorful flowers attract pollinating insects.

Areas of *maquis* provide ideal habitats for nesting birds such as warblers, serins, and hoopoes.

Between the shrubs in open areas of *maquis*, orchids, tulips, and other native flowers appear in the spring.

ORCHIDS

One of the botanical highlights of a visit to Greece is the range of wild orchid species that can be found in bloom between late February and May. All have strangely shaped, and sometimes colorful, flowers whose purpose is to attract pollinating insects.

The four-spotted orchid has spots on the flower lip. A plant of open hillsides, it flowers in April.

The naked man orchid has a dense head of pale pinkish flowers and favors open woodland.

The Greek spider orchid looks more like a bumblebee than a spider. It is found in *maquis* in early spring.

THE HISTORY OF GREECE

THE HISTORY of Greece is that of a nation, not of a land: the Greek idea of nationality is governed by language, religion, descent, and customs, not so much by location. Early Greek history is the story of internal struggles, from the Mycenaean and Minoan cultures of the Bronze Age

Alexander the Great, by the folk artist Theófilos

to the competing city-states that emerged in the 1st millennium BC.

After the defeat of the Greek army by Philip of Macedon at Chaironeia in 338 BC, Greece soon became absorbed into Alexander the Great's new Asian empire. With the defeat of the Macedonians by the Romans in 168 BC, Greece became a province of Rome. As part of the Eastern Empire she was ruled from Constantinople and in the 11th century became a powerful element within the new, Orthodox Christian, Byzantine world.

In 1453, when Constantinople fell to the Ottomans, Greece disappeared altogether as a political entity. Eventually the realization that it was the democracy of Classical Athens which had inspired so many revolutions abroad gave the Greeks themselves the courage to rebel and, in 1821, to fight the Greek War of Independence. In 1832 the Great Powers that dominated Europe established a protectorate over Greece that marked the end of Ottoman rule. Although Greece reestablished itself as a sizeable state, the "Great Idea" – to incorporate Constantinople – ended in a disastrous defeat by Turkey in 1922.

The instability of the ensuing years was followed by the dictatorship of Metaxás and then by the Civil War of 1946–9, in which half a million people were killed and one in ten was made homeless. The present borders of the Greek state have existed only since 1948, when Italy returned the Dodecanese. Now, as an established democracy and member of the European Union, Greece's fortunes seem to have come full circle after 2,000 years of foreign rule.

A map of Greece from the 1595 Atlas of Abraham Ortelius called *Theatrum Orbis Terrarum*

◁ The beginning of the 1821 Greek Revolution as shown in 1825 by Jean-Loup Charmet

Prehistoric Greece

Mycenaean gold brooch

DURING THE BRONZE AGE three separate civilizations flourished in Greece: the Cycladic, during the third millennium; the Minoan, based on Crete but with an influence that spread throughout the Aegean islands; and the Mycenaean, which was based on the mainland but spread to Crete in about 1450 BC when the Minoans went into decline. Both the Minoan and Mycenaean cultures found their peak in the Palace Periods of the second millennium, when they were dominated by a centralized religion and bureaucracy.

PREHISTORIC GREECE
Areas settled in the Bronze Age

Neolithic Head *(3000 BC)*
This figure was found on Alónnisos in the Sporades. It probably represents a fertility goddess who was worshiped by farmers to ensure a good harvest. These figures indicate a certain stability in early communities.

The town is unwalled, showing that inhabitants did not fear attack.

Cycladic Figurine
Marble statues such as this, produced in the Bronze Age from about 2800 to 2300 BC, have been found in a number of tombs in the Cyclades.

Multistory houses

Minoan Bathtub Sarcophagus
This type of coffin, dating to 1400 BC, is found only in Minoan art. It was probably used for a high-status burial.

TIMELINE

200,000 BC	5000 BC	4000 BC	3000 BC	2000
	7000 Neolithic farmers in northern Greece	**3200** Beginnings of Bronze Age cultures in Cyclades and Crete	**2000** Arrival of first Greek-speakers on mainland Greece	
200,000 Evidence of Palaeolithic civilization in northern Greece and Thessaly		*"Frying Pan." vessel from Sýros (2500–2000 BC)*	**2800–2300** Kéros-Sýros culture flourishes in Cyclades	
			2000 Building of palaces begins in Crete, initiating First Palace Period	

Mycenaean Death Mask
Large amounts of worked gold were discovered at wealthy Mycenae, the city of Agamemnon. Masks like this were laid over the faces of the dead.

Forested hills

WHERE TO SEE PREHISTORIC GREECE

The Museum of Cycladic Art in Athens *(see pp74–5)* has Greece's leading collection of Cycladic figurines. The remains at Mycenae are extensive *(pp178–80)*, and the museum at Náfplio *(p182)* displays finds from the site, as does the National Archaeological Museum, Athens *(pp68–71)*. Excavations at so-called Nestor's Palace *(p201)* uncovered tablets written in Linear B script. These earliest examples of Greek language can be seen in the museum at nearby Chóra, together with frescoes and pottery from the palace.

The inhabitants are on friendly terms with the visitors.

Cyclopean Walls
Mycenaean citadels, such as this one at Tiryns, were encircled by walls of stone so large that later civilizations believed they had been built by giants. It is unclear whether the walls were used for defense or just to impress.

Oared sailing ships

MINOAN SEA SCENE

The wall paintings on the island of Santoríni were preserved by the volcanic eruption at the end of the 16th century BC. This section shows ships departing from a coastal town. In contrast to the warlike Mycenaeans, Minoan art reflects a more stable community that dominated the Aegean through trade, not conquest.

Mycenaean Octopus Jar
This 14th-century BC vase's decoration follows the shape of the pot. Restrained and symmetrical, it contrasts with relaxed Minoan prototypes.

1750–1700 Start of Second Palace Period and golden age of Minoan culture in Crete	1525 Volcanic eruption on Santoríni devastates the region	1250–1200 Probable destruction of Troy, after abduction of Helen (see p52)	
		1450 Mycenaeans take over Knossos; use of Linear B script	Helen of Troy

1800 BC	1600 BC	1400 BC	1200 BC

1730 Destruction of Minoan palaces; end of First Palace Period		*Minoan figurine of a snake goddess, 1500 BC*	1200 Collapse of Mycenaean culture
1600 Beginning of high period of Mycenaean prosperity and dominance			1370–50 Palace of Knossos on Crete destroyed for second time

The Dark Ages and Archaic Period

Silver coin from Athens

IN ABOUT 1200 BC, Greece entered a period of darkness. There was widespread poverty, the population decreased, and many skills were lost. A cultural revival in about 800 BC accompanied the emergence of the city-states across Greece and inspired new styles of warfare, art, and politics. Greek colonies were established as far away as the Black Sea, present-day Syria, North Africa, and the western Mediterranean. Greece was defined by where Greeks lived.

Koúros *(530 BC)*
Koúroi were early monumental male nude statues (see p70). Idealized representations rather than portraits, they were inspired by Egyptian statues, from which they take their frontal, forward-stepping pose.

MEDITERRANEAN AREA, 479 BC

▪ *Areas of Greek influence*

Bronze breastplate

The double flute player kept the men marching in time.

Bronze greaves protected the legs.

Solon *(640–558 BC)*
Solon was appointed to the highest magisterial position in Athens. His legal, economic, and political reforms heralded democracy.

HOPLITE WARRIORS

The "Chigi" vase from Corinth, dating to about 750 BC, is one of the earliest clear depictions of the new style of warfare that evolved at that period. This required rigorously trained and heavily armed infantrymen called hoplites to fight in a massed formation or phalanx. The rise of the city-state may be linked to the spirit of equality felt by citizen hoplites fighting for their own community.

TIMELINE

Vase fragment showing bands of distinctive geometric line patterns

900
Appearance of first Geometric pottery

1100 BC	1000 BC	900 BC
1100 Migrations of different peoples throughout the Greek world	**1000–850** Formation of the Homeric kingdoms	

6th-Century Vase
This bowl (krater) *for mixing wine and water at elegant feasts is an early example of the art of vase painting. It depicts mythological and heroic scenes.*

Bronze helmets for protection

Spears were used for thrusting.

The phalanxes shoved and pushed, aiming to maintain an unbroken shield wall, a successful new technique.

Gorgon's head decoration

Characteristic round shields

WHERE TO SEE ARCHAIC GREECE

Examples of *koûroi* can be found in the National Archaeological Museum *(see pp68–71)* and in the Acropolis Museum *(p97)*, both in Athens. The National Archaeological Museum also houses the national collection of Greek Geometric, red-figure, and black-figure vases. The first victory over the Persians in 490 BC was commemorated by the mound of Athenian dead that still dominates the plain at Marathon *(p145)*. The museum at Sparta *(p189)* contains a bust of Leonidas, the Spartan king, who with his 300 hoplite soldiers was massacred by the Persians at Thermopylae in 480 BC.

Hunter Returning Home *(500 BC)*
Hunting for hares, deer, or wild boar was an aristocratic sport pursued by Greek nobles on foot with dogs, as depicted on this cup.

Darius I *(ruled 521–486 BC)*
This relief from Persepolis shows the Persian king who tried to conquer the Greek mainland but was defeated at the battle of Marathon in 490.

776 Traditional date for the first Olympian Games

675 Lykourgos initiates austere reforms in Sparta

580 First Doric columns built at Temple of Hera, Olympia

Doric capital

490 Athenians defeat Persians at Marathon

| 800 BC | 700 BC | 600 BC | 500 BC |

750–700 Homer records epic tales of the *Iliad* and *Odyssey*

770 Greeks start founding colonies in Italy, Egypt, and elsewhere

Spartan votive figurine

546 Persians gain control over Ionian Greeks; Athens flourishes under the tyrant, Peisistratos, and his sons

630 Poetess Sappho writing in Lesbos

480 Athens destroyed by Persians who defeat Spartans at Thermopylae; Athenian victory at Salamis

479 Persians annihilated at Plataia by Athenians, Spartans, and allies

Classical Greece

Trading amphora

THE CLASSICAL PERIOD has always been considered the high point of Greek civilization. Around 150 years of exceptional creativity in thinking, writing, theater, and the arts produced the great tragedians Aeschylus, Sophocles, and Euripides as well as the great philosophical thinkers Socrates, Plato, and Aristotle. This was also a time of warfare and bloodshed however. The Peloponnesian Wars, which pitted the city-state of Athens and her allies against the city-state of Sparta and her allies, dominated the last half of 5th century BC. In the 4th century Sparta, Athens, and Thebes struggled for hegemony only to be defeated by Philip of Macedon in 338 BC.

CLASSICAL GREECE, 440 BC
- *Athens and her allies*
- *Sparta and her allies*

Theater used in Pythian Games

Temple of Apollo

Siphnian Treasury

Fish Shop
This 4th-century BC Greek painted vase comes from Cefalù in Sicily. Large parts of the island were inhabited by Greeks who were bound by a common culture, religion, and language.

Perikles
This great democratic leader built up the Greek navy and masterminded the extensive building program in Athens between the 440s and 420s, including the Acropolis temples.

THE SANCTUARY OF DELPHI
The sanctuary *(see pp228–9),* shown in this 1894 reconstruction, reached the peak of its political influence in the 5th and 4th centuries BC. Of central importance was the Oracle of Apollo, whose utterances influenced the decisions of city-states such as Athens and Sparta. Rich gifts dedicated to the god were placed by the states in treasuries that lined the Sacred Way.

TIMELINE

Detail of the Parthenon frieze

462 Ephialtes' reforms pave the way for radical democracy in Athens

431–404 Peloponnesian War, ending with the fall of Athens and start of 33-year period of Spartan dominance

c.424 Death of Herodotus, historian of the Persian Wars

475 BC	450 BC	425 BC

478 With the formation of the Delian League, Athens takes over leadership of Aegean cities

451–429 Perikles rises to prominence in Athens and launches a lavish building program

447 Construction of the Parthenon begins

Bust of Herodotus, probably of Hellenistic origin

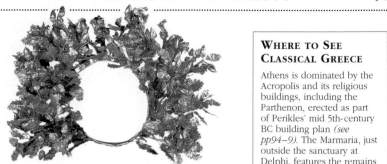

Gold Oak Wreath from Vergína
*By the mid-4th century BC, Philip II of Macedon
dominated the Greek world through diplomacy
and warfare. This wreath comes from his tomb.*

WHERE TO SEE CLASSICAL GREECE

Athens is dominated by the Acropolis and its religious buildings, including the Parthenon, erected as part of Perikles' mid 5th-century BC building plan *(see pp94–9)*. The Marmaria, just outside the sanctuary at Delphi, features the remains of the unique circular *tholos (p230)*. In the Peloponnese, the town of Messene dates from 396 BC *(p201)*; the best-preserved theater is at Epidaurus *(pp184–5)*. Philip II's tomb can be seen at Vergína in Macedonia *(p242)*.

Votive of the Rhodians

Stoa of the Athenians

Sacred Way

Athenian Treasury

Athena Lemnia
*This Roman copy of a
statue by Pheidias
(c.490–c.430 BC), the
sculptor-in-charge at
the Acropolis, depicts
the goddess protector of
Athens in an ideal
rather than realistic
way, typical of the
Classical style in art.*

Slave Boy *(400 BC)*
*Slaves were funda-
mental to the Greek
economy and were
used for all types of
work. Many slaves
were foreign; this
boot boy came from
as far as Africa.*

387 Plato founds
Academy in Athens

*Sculpture
of Plato*

337 Foundation of the the League of
Corinth legitimizes Philip II's control
over the Greek city-states

359 Philip II becomes
King of Macedonia

400 BC	375 BC	350 BC

399 Trial and
execution of Socrates

371 Sparta defeated by
Thebes at Battle of Leuktra,
heralding a decade of Theban
dominance in the area

338 Greeks defeated by Philip II of
Macedonia at Battle of Chaironeia

336 Philip II is assassinated at Aigai and is
succeeded by his son,
Alexander

Hellenistic Greece

ALEXANDER THE GREAT of Macedon
fulfilled his father Philip's plans
for the conquest of the Persians. He
went on to create a vast empire that
extended to India in the east and Egypt
in the south. The Hellenistic period
was extraordinary for the dispersal of
Greek language, religions and culture
throughout the territories conquered
by Alexander. It lasted from after Alexander's
death in 323 BC until the Romans began to
dismantle his empire in the mid-2nd century BC.
For Greece, Macedonian domination was
replaced by that of Rome in AD 168.

Alexander the Great

Relief of Hero-worship *(c.200 BC)*
*The worship of heroes after death
was a feature of Greek religion.
Alexander, however, was worshiped as
a god in his lifetime.*

Pélla was the birthplace of Alexander
and capital of Macedonia.

The Mausoleum of
Halicarnassus was
one of the Seven
Wonders of the
Ancient World.

Issus, in modern Turkey, was
the site of Alexander's victory
over the Persian army in 333 BC.

BLACK SEA

• Pélla

• Athens

ASIA
MINOR

**Mausoleum of
Halicarnassus**

• Issus

MEDITERRANEAN SEA

**Ishtar Gate
Babylon**

Ammon • **Lighthouse at
Alexandria**

Alexander died in
Babylon in 323 BC.

EGYPT

RED SEA

ARABIA

**The Ammon
oracle** declared
Alexander to
be divine.

Alexandria, founded by
Alexander, replaced Athens as
the center of Greek culture.

Alexander Defeats Darius III
*This Pompeian mosaic shows the
Persian leader overwhelmed at
Issus in 333 BC. Macedonian
troops are shown carrying their
highly effective long pikes.*

Terracotta Statue
*This 2nd-century BC
statue of two women
gossiping is typical
of a Hellenistic
interest in private
rather than public
individuals.*

KEY

– – – Alexander's route

Alexander's empire

Dependent regions

TIMELINE

333 Alexander the Great defeats
the Persian king, Darius III, and
declares himself king of Asia

323 Death of Alexander,
and of Diogenes

301 Battle of Ipsus, between
Alexander's rival successors,
leads to the break-up of his
empire into three kingdoms

268–261
Chremonidean War,
ending with the
capitulation of
Athens to Macedonia

325 BC	300 BC	275 BC	250 BC

322 Death
of Aristotle

287–275 "Pyrrhic
victory" of King
Pyrros of Epirus
who defeated the
Romans in Italy but
suffered heavy losses

331 Alexander founds
Alexandria after
conquering Egypt

*Diogenes, the
Hellenistic philosopher*

Fusing Eastern and Western Religion
This plaque from Afghanistan shows the Greek goddess Nike and the Asian goddess Cybele in a chariot pulled by lions.

Susa, capital of the Persian Empire, was captured in 331 BC. A mass wedding of Alexander's captains to Asian brides was held in 324 BC.

Alexander chose his wife, Roxane, from among Sogdian captives in 327 BC.

WHERE TO SEE HELLENISTIC GREECE

The royal palace at Pélla (*see p243*), capital of Macedonia and birthplace of Alexander, and the palace of Palatítsia (*p242*) are exceptional. Pélla has outstanding mosaics, one of which depicts Alexander. Goldwork and other finds are in the museum at Pélla and the Archaeological Museum at Thessaloníki (*pp244–5*). In Athens, the Stoa of Attalos (*pp90–91*) in the Greek Agora was given by Attalos of Pergamon (ruled 159 to 138 BC). The Tower of the Winds (*pp86–7*) in the Roman Agora, built by the Macedonian astronomer Andronikos Kyrrestes, incorporates a water clock.

ROXANE
• Alexandropolis

SOGDIANA

CASPIAN SEA

BACTRIA

• Taxil

PERSIA

• Susa

Sculpture from Persepolis

War elephant

GEDROSIA

INDIA

Beas

PERSIAN GULF

ARABIAN SEA

Battle elephants were used against the Indian King Poros in 326 BC.

Alexander's army turned back at the River Beas.

The Persian religious center of Persepolis, in modern Iran, fell to Alexander in 330 BC.

Alexander's army suffered heavy losses in the Gedrosia desert.

ALEXANDER THE GREAT'S EMPIRE
In forming his empire Alexander covered huge distances. After defeating the Persians in Asia he moved to Egypt, then returned to Asia to pursue Darius, and then his murderers, into Bactria. In 326 his troops revolted in India and refused to go on. Alexander died in 323 in Babylon.

The Death of Archimedes
Archimedes was the leading Hellenistic scientist and mathematician. This mosaic from Renaissance Italy shows his murder in 212 BC by a Roman.

227 Colossus of Rhodes destroyed by earthquake

Colossus of Rhodes

197 Romans defeat Philip V of Macedon and declare Greece liberated

146 Romans sack Corinth and Greece becomes a province of Rome

225 BC	200 BC	175 BC	150 BC

222 Macedonia crushes Sparta

217 Peace of Naupaktos: a call for the Greeks to settle their differences before "the cloud in the west" (Rome) settles over them

168 Macedonians defeated by Romans at Pydna

Roman coin (196 BC) commemorating Roman victory over the Macedonians.

Roman Greece

Mark Antony

After the romans gained control of Greece with the sack of Corinth in 146 BC, Greece became the cultural center of the Roman Empire. The Roman nobility sent their sons to be educated in the schools of philosophy in Athens *(see p57)*. The end of the Roman civil wars between leading Roman statesmen was played out on Greek soil, finishing in the Battle of Actium in Thessaly in 31 BC. In AD 323 the Emperor Constantine founded the new eastern capital of Constantinople; the empire was later divided into the Greek-speaking East and the Latin-speaking West.

ROMAN PROVINCES, AD 211

Bema, or raised platform, where St. Paul spoke

Roman basilica

Mithridates
In a bid to extend his territory, this ruler of Pontus, on the Black Sea, led the resistance to Roman rule in 88 BC. He was forced to make peace three years later.

Bouleuterion

Springs of Peirene, the source of water

Notitia Dignitatum *(AD 395)*
As part of the Roman Empire, Greece was split into several provinces. The proconsul of the province of Achaia used this insignia.

RECONSTRUCTION OF ROMAN CORINTH
Corinth *(see pp162–6)* was refounded and largely rebuilt by Julius Caesar in 46 BC, becoming the capital of the Roman province of Achaia. The Romans built the forum, covered theater, and basilicas. St. Paul visited the city in AD 50–51, working as a tent maker.

Baths of Eurycles

TIMELINE

A coin of Cleopatra, Queen of Egypt

49–31 BC Rome's civil wars end with the defeat of Mark Antony and Cleopatra at Actium, in Greece

AD 49–54 St. Paul preaches Christianity in Greece

AD 124–131 Emperor Hadrian oversees huge building program in Athens

100 BC	AD 1	AD 10

86 BC Roman commander, Sulla, captures Athens

46 BC Corinth refounded as Roman colony

St. Paul preaching

AD 66–7 Emperor Nero tours Greece

Mosaic *(AD 180)*
This highly sophisticated Roman mosaic of Dionysos riding on a leopard comes from the House of Masks, on Delos.

Temple of Octavia

Odeion or Roman covered theater

Greek open-air theater

Archaic Greek Temple of Apollo

WHERE TO SEE ROMAN GREECE

In Athens the Roman Agora, Hadrian's library nearby *(see p85)*, and the Arch of Hadrian, which leads from the Roman into the old Greek city, *(pp90–1)*, are examples of Roman architecture. The Temple of Olympian Zeus *(p111)* and the Theater of Herodes Atticus *(p100)* are also in Athens. The triumphal arch of Galerius in Thessaloníki *(p244)* commemorates the Emperor Galerius's victories over the Persians in AD 297. The museum at Corinth *(p166)* contains fine Roman mosaics and other artifacts.

Arch of Galerius
This arch at Thessaloníki commemorates the Emperor Galerius's victory over the Persians. The carved panel shows Galerius in his chariot.

Apollo Belevedere
Much Greek sculpture is known to us only through Roman copies of Greek originals, like this statue of Apollo.

170 Pausanias completes guide to Greece for Roman travelers

323 Constantine becomes sole emperor of Roman Empire and establishes his capital in Constantinople

395 Goths devastate Athens and Peloponnese

267 Goths pillage Athens

381 Emperor Theodosius I makes Christianity state religion

AD 200

AD 300

Coin of the Roman Emperor Galerius

293 Under Emperor Galerius, Thessaloníki becomes second city to Constantinople

393 Olympian games banned

395 Death of Theodosius I; formal division of Roman Empire into Latin west and Byzantine east

Byzantine and Crusader Greece

Byzantine court dress arm band

U NDER THE BYZANTINE EMPIRE, which at the end of the 4th century succeeded the old Eastern Roman Empire, Greece became Orthodox in religion and was split into administrative *themes*. When the capital, Constantinople, fell to the Crusaders in 1204, Greece was again divided, mostly between the Venetians and the Franks. Constantinople and Mystrás were recovered by the Byzantine Greeks in 1261, but the Turks' capture of Constantinople in 1453 marked the final demise of the Byzantine Empire. It left a legacy of hundreds of churches and a wealth of religious art.

BYZANTINE GREECE IN THE 10TH CENTURY

Chapel

Watch-tower of Tsimiskís

Refectory

Two-Headed Eagle
In the Byzantine world, the emperor was also patriarch of the church, a dual role represented in this pendant of a two-headed eagle.

GREAT LAVRA
This monastery is the earliest (AD 963) and largest of the religious complexes on Mount Athos *(see pp252–4)*. Many parts of it have been rebuilt, but its appearance remains essentially Byzantine. The monasteries became important centers of learning and religious art.

Defence of Thessaloníki
The fall of Thessaloníki to the Saracens in AD 904 was a blow to the Byzantine Empire. Many towns in Greece were heavily fortified against attack from this time on.

TIMELINE

	578–86 Avars and Slavs invade Greece	*Gold solidus of the Byzantine Empress Irene, who ruled AD 797–802*

400	600	800
529 Aristotle's and Plato's schools of philosophy close as Christian and Orientalized culture supplants Classical thought	**680** Bulgars cross Danube and establish empire in northern Greece	**726** Iconoclasm introduced by Pope Leo III (abandoned in 843) **841** Parthenon becomes a cathedral

Constantine the Great

The first eastern emperor to recognize Christianity, Constantine founded the city of Constantinople in AD 324. Here he is shown with his mother, Helen.

WHERE TO SEE BYZANTINE AND CRUSADER GREECE

In Athens, both the Benáki *(pp78–9)* and the Byzantine *(p76)* museums contain sculpture, icons, metalwork, and textiles. The medieval city of Mystrás *(pp192–3)* has a castle, palaces, houses, and monasteries. The churches of Thessaloníki *(p248)* and the monasteries of Dafní *(pp152–3)*, and Osios Loúkas *(pp222–3)* contain fine Byzantine mosaics and frescoes, as do the monasteries of Mount Athos *(pp252–4)*. Chlemoútsi *(p169)*, built in 1223, is one of Greece's oldest Frankish castles. There are important fortresses at Acrocorinth *(p166)* and Monemvasía *(pp186–8)*.

Cypress tree of Agios Athanásios

Christ Pantokrátor

This 14th-century fresco of Christ as ruler of the world is in the Byzantine city and monastic center of Mystrás.

Fortified walls

Chapel of Agios Athanásios, founder of Great Lávra

Combined library and treasury

The katholikón, the main church in Great Lávra, has the most magnificent Byzantine murals on Mount Athos.

1054 Patriarch of Constantinople and Pope Leo IX excommunicate each other	*Frankish Chlemoútsi Castle* **1081–1149** Normans invade Greek islands and mainland		**1354** Ottoman Turks enter Europe, via southern Italy and Greece **1390–1450** Turks gain power over much of mainland Greece
1000	**1200**		**1400**
Basil the Bulgar Slayer, Byzantine emperor (lived 956–1025)	**1204** Crusaders sack Constantinople. Break-up of Byzantine empire as result of occupation by Franks and Venetians	**1210** Venetians win control over Crete	**1261** Start of intellectual and artistic flowering of Mystrás **1389** Venetians in control of much of Greece and the islands

Venetian and Ottoman Greece

Venetian lion of St. Mark

FOLLOWING THE OTTOMANS' momentous capture of Constantinople in 1453 and their conquest of almost all the remaining Greek territory by 1460, the Greek state effectively ceased to exist for the next 350 years. Although Athens became the capital of the vast Ottoman Empire, it remained the principal center of Greek population and the focus of Greek dreams of resurgence. The small Greek population of what today is modern Greece languished in an impoverished and under-populated backwater, but even there rebellious bands of brigands and private militias were formed. The Ionian islands, Crete, and a few coastal enclaves were seized for long periods by the Venetians – an experience more intrusive than the inefficient tolerance of the Ottomans, but one that left a rich cultural and architectural legacy.

GREECE IN 1493

Areas occupied by Venetians

Areas occupied by Ottomans

Battle of Lepanto *(1571)*
The Christian fleet, under Don John of Austria, decisively defeated the Ottomans off Náfpaktos, halting their advance westward (see p200).

Cretan Painting
This 15th-century icon is typical of the style developed by Greek artists in the School of Crete, active until the Ottomans took Crete in 1669.

ARRIVAL OF TURKISH PRINCE CEM ON RHODES

Prince Cem, Ottoman rebel and son of Mehmet II, fled to Rhodes in 1481 and was welcomed by the Christian Knights of St. John. In 1522, however, Rhodes fell to the Ottomans after a siege.

TIMELINE

1453 Mehmet II captures Constantinople, which is re-named Istanbul and made capital of the Ottoman Empire

1503 Ottoman Turks win control of the Peloponnese apart from Monemvasía

1571 Venetian and Spanish fleet defeats Ottoman Turks at the Battle of Lepanto

1500

1550

1600

1460 Turks capture Mystrás

Cretan chain mail armor from the 16th century

1456 Ottoman Turks occupy Athens

1522 The Knights of St. John forced to cede Rhodes to the Ottomans

Shipping

Greek merchants traded throughout the Ottoman Empire. By 1800 there were merchant colonies in Constantinople and as far afield as London and Odessa. This 19th-century embroidery shows the Turkish influence on Greek decorative arts.

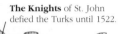

The Knights of St. John defied the Turks until 1522.

The massive fortifications eventually succumbed to Turkish artillery.

The Knights supported Turkish rebel Prince Cem.

WHERE TO SEE VENETIAN AND OTTOMAN ARCHITECTURE

Náfplio contains many examples of the Venetian presence, especially the Naval Warehouse (now a museum) and the Palamídi fortress *(see p183).* Following a pattern familiar throughout the Balkan states, enormous efforts were made after Independence to remove or disguise all Ottoman buildings. However, in Athens there are small but well-preserved Ottoman quarters in the Pláka district, and the Tsistaráki mosque (now the Ceramics Museum, *p86)* is also Ottoman. The White Tower in Thessaloníki *(p244)* was rebuilt by the Turks in the 15th century. In Kavála *(p255),* there is an aqueduct built in the reign of Suleiman the Magnificent, and in Ioánnina *(p210)* the Aslan Pasha mosque.

Dinner at a Greek House in 1801

Nearly four centuries of Ottoman rule profoundly affected Greek culture, ethnic composition, and patterns of everyday life. Greek cuisine incorporates Turkish dishes still found throughout the old Ottoman empire.

1687 Parthenon seriously damaged during Venetian artillery attack on Turkish magazine

1715 Turks reconquer the Peloponnese

Ali Pasha (1741–1822), a governor of the Ottoman empire

1814 Britain gains possession of Ionian islands

1650	1700	1750	1800

1684 Venetians reconquer the Peloponnese

Parthenon blown up

1778 Ali Pasha becomes Vizier of Ioánnina and establishes powerful state in Albania and northern Greece

1801 Frieze on Parthenon removed by Lord Elgin

1814 Foundation of *Filikí Etaireía,* Greek liberation movement

The Making of Modern Greece

Flag with the symbols of the *Filikí Etaireía*

T HE GREEK WAR of Independence marked the overthrow of the Ottomans and the start of the "Great Idea," an ambitious project to bring all Greek people under one flag *(Enosis)*. The plans for expansion were initially successful, and during the 19th century the Greeks succeeded in doubling their national territory and reasserting Greek sovereignty over many of the islands. However, an attempt to take the city of Constantinople by force after World War I ended in disaster: in 1922 millions of Greeks were expelled from Smyrna in Turkish Anatolia, ending thousands of years of Greek occupation in Asia Minor.

THE EMERGING GREEK STATE

	Greece in 1832
	Areas gained 1832–1923

Klephts (mountain brigands) were the basis of the Independence movement.

Massacre at Chíos
This detail of Delacroix's shocking painting Scènes de Massacres de Scio *shows the events of 1822, when Turks took savage revenge for an earlier killing of Muslims.*

Weapons were family heirlooms or donated by philhellenes.

Declaration of the Constitution in Athens
Greece's Neo-Classical parliament building in Athens was the site of the Declaration of the Constitution in 1843. It was built as the Royal Palace for Greece's first monarch, King Otto, in the 1830s.

TIMELINE

1824 The poet Lord Byron dies of a fever at Mesolóngi

1831 President Kapodístrias assassinated

1832 Great Powers establish protectorate over Greece and accept Otto, Bavarian prince, as king

1834 Athens replaces Náfplio as capital

German archaeologist Heinrich Schliemann

1830	1840	1850	1860	18

1827 Battle of Navaríno

1828 Ioánnis Kapodístrias becomes first President of Greece

King Otto (ruled 1832–62)

1862 Revolution drives King Otto from Greece

1874 Heinrich Schliemann begin excavation o Mycenae

1821 Greek flag of independence raised on March 25; Greeks massacre Turks at Tripolitsá in Morea

1864 New constitution makes Greece a "crowned democracy"; Greek Orthodoxy made the state religion

Life in Athens

By 1836 urban Greeks still wore a mixture of Greek traditional and Western dress. The Ottoman legacy had not totally disappeared and is visible in the fez worn by men.

FLAG RAISING OF 1821 REVOLUTION
In 1821, the Greek secret society *Filikí Etaireía* was behind a revolt by Greek officers, which led to anti-Turk uprisings throughout the Peloponnese. Tradition credits Archbishop Germanós of Pátra with raising the rebel flag near Kalávryta *(see p168)* on March 25. The struggle for independence had begun.

WHERE TO SEE 19TH-CENTURY GREECE
Independence was proclaimed at the Moní Agías Lávras, near Kalávryta *(see p168)*. Lord Byron died at Mesolóngi *(p225)*. Ioánnis Kapodístrias was assassinated at the church of Agios Spyrídon in Náfplio *(p182)*. Pýlos is the site of the battle of Navaríno *(p200)*.

Corinth Canal
This spectacular link between the Aegean and Ionian seas opened in 1893 (see p167).

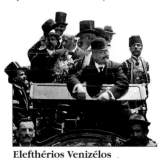

Elefthérios Venizélos
This great Cretan politician and advocate of liberal democracy doubled Greek territory during the Balkan Wars (1912–13) and joined the Allies in World War I.

				1921 Greece launches offensive in Asia Minor	1922 Turkish burning of Smyrna signals end of the "Great Idea"
1893 Opening of Corinth Canal	1896 First Olympics of modern era, held in Athens	1908 Crete united with Greece	1917 King Constantine resigns; Greece joins World War I		
1880	**1890**	**1900**	**1910**		**1920**
Spyrídon Louis, Marathon winner at the first modern Olympics	1899 Arthur Evans begins excavations at Knossos	1912–13 Greece extends its borders during the Balkan Wars	1920 Treaty of Sèvres gives Greece huge gains in territory		
		1923 Population exchange agreed between Greece and Turkey at Treaty of Lausanne. Greece loses previous gains			

Twentieth-Century Greece

T HE YEARS after the 1922 defeat by Turkey were terrible ones for the Greek people. The influx of impoverished refugees contributed to the political instability of the interwar years. The dictatorship of Metaxás was followed by invasion in 1940, then Italian, German, and Bulgarian occupation and, finally, the bitter Civil War, between 1946 and 1949, with its legacy of division. After experiencing the Cyprus problem of the 1950s and the military dictatorship of 1967 to 1974, Greece is now an established democracy and a member of the European Union.

1947 Internationally acclaimed Greek artist, Giánnis Tsaroúchis, holds his first exhibition of set designs, in the Romvos Gallery, Athens

1938 Death of sculptor Giannoúlis Chalepás, best known for his *Sleeping Girl* funerary statue

1946 Government institutes "White Terror" against Communists

1945 Níkos Kazantzákis publishes *Zorba the Greek*, later made into a film

1958 USSR threatens Greece with economic sanctions if NATO missiles installed

1957 Mosaics found by chance at Philip II's 300 BC palace at Pélla

1925	1935	1945	1955

1925	1935	1945	1955

1933 Death of Greek poet, Constantine (C P) Cavafy

1932 Aristotle Onassis purchases six freight ships, the start of his shipping empire

1939 Greece declares neutrality at start of World War II

1951 Greece enters NATO

1955 Greek Cypriots start campaign of violence in Cyprus against British rule

1948 Dodecanese becomes part of Greece

1925 Birth of Chatzidákis, who wrote music for the 1960 film *Never on Sunday*

ΟΙ ΗΡΩΙΔΕΣ ΤΟΥ 1940

1946–9 Civil War between Greek government and the Communists who take to the mountains

1960 Cyprus declared independent

1944 Churchill visits Athens to show his support for Greek government against Communist Resistance

1940 Italy invades Greece. Resistance fighters defend northern Greece. Greece enters World War II

1963 Geórgios Papandréou's center-left government voted into power

1967 Right-wing colonels form Junta, forcing King Constantine into exile

1993 Andréas Papandréou wins Greek general election for the third time

1981 Melína Merkoúri appointed Minister of Culture. Start of campaign to restore Elgin Marbles to Greece

1990 New democracy voted into power; Konstantínos Karamanlís becomes President

1994 Because of the choking smog *(nefos)* central Athens introduces traffic restrictions

1975 Death of Aristotle Onassis

1965	1975	1985	1995

1965	1975	1985	1995

1981 Andréas Papandréou's left-wing PASOK party forms first Greek Socialist government

1971 Nobel poet laureate George Seféris dies

1974 Fall of Junta; Konstantínos Karamanlís elected Prime Minister

1996 Andréas Papandréou dies; Kóstas Simítis succeeds him and wins September election

1973 Greek bishops give their blessing to the short-lived presidency of Colonel Papadópoulos

1988 Eight million visitors to Greece; tourism continues to expand

1994 European leaders meet in Corfu under Greek presidency of the EU

ATHENS AND MAINLAND GREECE THROUGH THE YEAR

PREDOMINANTLY RURAL, Greece is deeply attached to its locally produced food and wine, and chapels dotting the countryside serve as the focus for culinary as well as religious celebrations. Festivals of the Orthodox church are deeply identified with Greekness, no more so than on March 25, a date that

May Day wild-flower wreath

commemorates both the Feast of the Annunciation and the start of the Independence uprising in 1821. Summer festivals are celebrated widely in rural villages, and expatriate Greeks return from across the globe. Organized arts events are a more recent phenomenon, paralleling the rise of tourism.

SPRING

SPRING is a glorious time in Greece. The lowland landscape, parched for much of the year, luxuriates in a carpet of green, and wild-flowers abound. But the weather does not stabilize until late spring, with rainy or blustery days common in March and April. Artichokes ripen in March, and May sees the first strawberries. The fishing season lasts to the end of May, overlapping with the start of the tourist season. Spring festivities focus on Easter.

March 25, Independence Day

MARCH

Apókries, Carnival Sunday *(first Sun before Lent)*. Carnivals take place for three weeks leading up to this climax of pre-Lenten festivities. There are parades and costume balls in many large cities, and the port of Pátra *(see p169)* hosts one of the most exuberant celebrations.

Katharí Deftéra, Clean Monday *(immediately after "Cheese Sunday" – seven Sundays before Easter)*. Kites are flown in the countryside.

Independence Day/ Evangelismós *(Mar 25)* is a national holiday, with parades and dances nationwide celebrating the 1821 revolt against the Ottoman empire. The religious festival, one of the most important for the Ortho-dox church, marks the Angel Gabriel's announcement to the Virgin Mary that she was to become the Holy Mother.

CELEBRATING EASTER IN GREECE

Greek Orthodox Easter can fall up to three weeks either side of Western Easter. It is the most important religious festival in Greece, and Holy Week is a time for Greek families to reunite. It is a also a good time to visit Greece, to see the processions and church services, and to sample the Easter food. The ceremony and symbolism are a direct link with Greece's Byzantine past, as well as with earlier and more primitive beliefs. The festivities reach a climax at midnight on Easter Saturday. As priests intone "Christ is risen," fireworks are lit, the explosions ushering in a Sunday devoted to feasting, music, and dance. The smaller, more isolated towns, such as Andrítsaina and Koróni in the Peloponnese, and Polýgyros (the capital of Chalkidikí), are particularly worth visiting during the Holy Week for the Friday and Saturday night services.

Priests in their richly embroidered Easter robes

Christ's bier, decorated with flowers and containing his effigy, is carried in solemn procession through the streets at dusk on Good Friday.

Candle lighting takes place at the end of the Easter Saturday mass. In pitch darkness, a single flame is used to light the candles held by worshipers.

Banners raised during a workers' May Day rally in Athens

APRIL

Megáli Evdomáda, Holy Week *(Apr or May)*, including *Kyriakí ton Vaíon* (Palm Sunday), *Megáli Pémpti* (Maundy Thursday), *Megáli Paraskeví* (Good Friday), *Megálo Savváto* (Easter Saturday), and the most important date in the Orthodox calendar, *Páscha* (Easter Sunday).
Agios Geórgios, St. George *(Apr 23)*. One of the most important feast days in the Orthodox calendar, commemorating the patron saint of shepherds, and traditionally marking the start of the grazing season. Celebrations are nationwide and are particularly festive at Aráchova, near Delphi *(see p221)*.

MAY

Protomagiá, May Day, *(May 1)*. Also known as Labor Day, this is given over to a national holiday. Traditionally, families go to the countryside and pick wildflowers, which are made

Firewalkers in a Macedonian village, May 21

into wreaths with garlic. These are then hung on doors, balconies, fishing boats, and even hoods of cars to ward off evil. In major towns and cities across the country, there are also parades and workers' rallies to mark Labor Day, usually led by the Communist Party.
Agios Konstantínos kai Agía Eléni *(May 21)*. A celebration throughout Greece for Constantine and his mother, Helen, the first Orthodox Byzantine rulers *(see p37)*. Firewalking ceremonies may be seen in some Macedonian villages.
Análipsi, Ascension *(40 days after Easter; usually May)*. This is another important religious feast day.

The procession of candles in the very early hours of Easter Day, here at Lykavittós Hill in Athens, celebrates Christ's resurrection.

Easter biscuits celebrate the end of Lent. Another Easter dish, magerítsa *soup, is made of lamb's innards and is eaten in the early hours of Easter Sunday.*

Egg loaves, made of sweet braided dough, contain eggs with shells dyed red to symbolize the blood of Christ. Red eggs are also given separately as presents.

Lamb roasting is traditionally done in the open air on giant spits over charcoal, for lunch on Easter Sunday. The first retsina wine from the previous year's harvest is opened. After lunch young and old join hands to dance, Greek-style.

SUMMER

WARM DAYS in early June signal the first sea-baths for Greeks (traditionally after Análipsi, Ascension Day). The peak tourist season begins, and continues until late August; after mid-July it can be difficult to find hotel vacancies in the more popular resorts. June sees the arrival of cherries, plums, and apricots, and honey can begin to be collected from hives. The last green leaf vegetables are soon totally replaced by tomatoes, melons, and cucumbers. By July much of the Aegean is buffeted by the notorious *meltémi*, a high-pressure northerly wind that – though more severe on the islands – can be felt along the mainland coast.

Various cultural festivals – programmed with an eye on the tourist audience, but no less impressive for that – are hosted in major cities and resorts. Outdoor cinemas are also well attended *(see p119)*. Urban Greeks retreat to mountain villages, often the venues for musical and religious fairs.

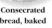

Consecrated bread, baked for festivals

JUNE

Pentikostí, Pentecost or Whitsunday *(seven weeks after Orthodox Easter)*. This important Orthodox feast day is celebrated throughout Greece.

Beehives for summer honey production, near Mount Parnassus

Agíou Pnévmatos, Feast of the Holy Spirit or Whitmonday *(the following day)*. A national holiday.
Athens Festival *(mid-Jun to mid-Sep)*. A cultural festival encompassing a mix of modern and ancient theater, ballet, opera, classical music, and jazz. It takes place at various venues, including the Herodes Atticus Theater *(see p119)* and the Lykavittós Theater *(see p72)*. The Herodes Atticus Theater, on the slopes of the Acropolis, hosts performances of ancient tragedies, concerts by international orchestras, and ballet. The Lykavittós Theater, spectacularly situated on Lykavittós Hill, with extensive views across Athens, hosts performances of modern music – jazz and folk – as well as drama and dance.

Epidaurus Festival *(Jun–Aug)*. Affiliated with the Athens Festival, though sited 150 km (90 miles) from the capital at the Epidaurus Theater *(see p184)* in the Peloponnese, this festival includes open-air performances of Classical drama.
Agios Ioánnis, St. John's Day *(Jun 24)*. A day celebrated throughout Greece commemorating the birth of St. John the Baptist. However, it is on the evening of the 23rd that bonfires are lit in most areas, and May wreaths consigned to the flames. Older children jump over the fires. This is an equivalent celebration to midsummer's eve.
Agioi Apóstoloi Pétros kai Pávlos, Holy Apostles Peter and Paul *(Jun 29)*. A widely celebrated name day for Pétros, Pávlos, and Apóstolos.

JULY

Agía Marína *(Jul 17)*. This day is widely celebrated in rural areas, with feasts to honor the saint, an important protector of crops.
Ioánnina's Cultural Summer *(through Jul and Aug)*. A wide range of music, arts and cultural events.
Profítis Ilías, the Prophet Elijah *(Jul 18–20)*. This is widely celebrated at hilltop shrines. The best known of these is on Mount Taÿgetos, near the town of Spárti.
Agía Paraskeví *(July 26)*. There are many big village festivals on this day, but it is particularly celebrated in the Epirus region.

Concert at Herodes Atticus Theater during the Athens Festival

Agios Panteleïmon
(Jul 27). As a doctor-saint, he is celebrated as the patron of many hospitals, and as a popular rural saint he is celebrated in the countryside. Name day for Pantelís and Panteleímon.

AUGUST

Metamórfosi, Transfiguration of Christ *(Aug 6).* For the Orthodox church

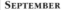
Girl in National dress for August 15 festivities

this is an important feast day. Name day for Sotíris and Sotiría.
Koímisis tis Theotókou, Assumption of the Virgin Mary *(Aug 15).* A national holiday, and an important and widely celebrated feast day. This is traditionally a day when Greeks return to celebrate in their home villages. It is also a name day for Mary, María, Pános and Panagiótis.

Pátra Summer Festival
(Aug–Sep). This festival offers events such as Classical drama and art exhibitions, as well as concerts in the Roman theater.
Vlachopanagiá *(Aug 23),* Epirus. A day for celebrations in the villages of the mountainous Epirus region.
Apotomí Kefalís Ioánnou Prodrómou, beheading of John the Baptist *(Aug 29).* The occasion for festivals at the many country chapels that bear his name.

Strings of tomatoes hanging out to dry in the autumn sunshine

AUTUMN

BY SEPTEMBER most village festivals have finished. The sea is at its warmest for swimming and, though the crowds have gone, most facilities are still available. There is a second, minor blooming of wild flowers, and the fine, still days of October are known as the "little summer of St. Dimitrios,"

randomly punctuated by stormy weather. Grapes, and the fat peaches *germádes*, are virtually the only fruit to ripen since the figs of August, and strings of onions, garlic, and tomatoes are hung up to dry for the winter. The hills echo with the sound of the September quail shoot and dragnet fishing resumes.

SEPTEMBER

Génnisis tis Theotókou, birth of the Virgin Mary *(Sep 8).* An important religious feast day in the calendar of the Orthodox church.
Ypsosis tou Timíou Stavroú, Exaltation of the True Cross *(Sep 14),* an important Orthodox feast day. This end-of-season celebration is the last of Greece's summer festivals.

OCTOBER

Agios Dimítrios *(Oct 26).* This traditionally marks the end of the grazing season, when sheep are brought down from the hills. Celebrations for Dimítrios are particularly lively in Thessaloníki, where he is the patron saint. Name day for Dimítris, and Dímitra.
Ochi Day *(Oct 28).* A national holiday, with patriotic parades and plenty of dancing. The day commemorates the reply to the 1940 ultimatum from Mussolini, calling for Greek surrender: an emphatic "no" *(óchi).*

Ceromonial dress on Ochi Day

NOVEMBER

Ton Taxiarchón Archangélou Michaïl kai Gavriíl *(Nov 8).* Ceremonies at the many rural monasteries and churches named after Archangels Gabriel and Michael. Name day for Angelos, Angéla, Michális.
Eisódia tis Theotókou, Presentation of the Virgin in the Temple *(Nov 21).* An important feast day in the Orthodox calendar, celebrated throughout Greece.
Agios Andréas, St. Andrew *(Nov 30)*, Pátra. A long liturgy is recited for Pátra's patron saint in the opulent cathedral named after him.

Parade in Thessaloníki for Agios Dimítrios, October 26

View over a snow-covered Herodes Atticus Theater, Athens

MAIN PUBLIC HOLIDAYS

These are the dates when museums and public sites are closed nationwide.

Agios Vasíleios (Jan 1)
Independence Day (Mar 25)
Protomagiá (May 1)
Paraskeví (Good Friday)
Páscha (Easter Sunday)
Chistoúgenna (Dec 25)
Sýnaxis tis Theotókou (Dec 26)

WINTER

MANY MOUNTAIN VILLAGES assume a ghostly aspect in winter, with their seasonal inhabitants returned to the cities. Deep snow accumulates at higher altitudes and skiing can begin; elsewhere, rain falls several days of the week. Fishing is in full swing, and at the markets kiwi fruits and exotic greens abound. Cheese shops display a full range of goat and sheep products, and olives are pressed for oil. The major festivals cluster on either side of the solstice. New Year's and Epiphany are the most fervently celebrated festivals during winter.

Branch of olives

DECEMBER

Agios Nikólaos, St. Nicholas (*Dec 6*). The patron saint of seafarers, travelers, children, and orphans is celebrated at seaside churches. Name day for Nikólaos and Nikolétta.

Christoúgenna, Christmas (*Dec 25*). A national holiday and, though less significant than Easter, it still constitutes an important religious feast day.

Sýnaxis tis Theotókou, meeting of the Virgin's entourage (*Dec 26*). A religious celebration and national holiday.

JANUARY

Agios Vasíleios, also known as *Protochroniá,* or New Year (*Jan 1*). A national holiday. Gifts are exchanged on this day and the traditional new year greeting is *Kalí Chroniá*.
Theofánia, or Epiphany (*Jan 6*). A national holiday and an important feast day. Blessing of the waters ceremonies take place by rivers and coastal locations throughout Greece. Youths dive to recover a cross that is thrown into the water by a priest.

Gynaikokratía (*Jan 8*), Thrace. Matriarchy is celebrated by women and men swapping roles for the day in some villages of Thrace.

FEBRUARY

Ypapantí, Candlemas (*Feb 2*). An Orthodox feast day all over Greece, at a quiet time, prior to pre-Lenten carnivals.

Diving for a cross at a blessing of the waters ceremony, January 6

Women playing cards on Gynaikokratía day, Thrace

NAME DAYS

Most Greeks do not celebrate birthdays past the age of about 12. Instead they celebrate their name days, or *giortí*, the day of the saint after whom they were named when baptized. Children are usually named after their grandparents, though in recent years it has become fashionable to give children names derived from Greece's history and mythology. When someone celebrates their name day you may be told, *Giortázo símera* (I'm celebrating today), to which the traditional reply is *Chrónia pollá* (many years). Friends tend to drop in, bearing small gifts, and are given cakes and sweet liqueurs in return.

The Climate of Mainland Greece

Summer visitors

THE MAINLAND CLIMATE varies most between the coastal lowlands and the mountainous inland regions. The mountains of western Greece and the Peloponnese get heavy snow in winter, rain during autumn and spring, and hot days in summer. The Ionian coast has milder temperatures, but is the wettest part of Greece. In Macedonia and Thrace rainfall is spread more evenly across the year, with the North Aegean exerting a moderating influence on coastal temperatures. Around Athens, temperatures are hot in summer and rarely drop below freezing in winter, when rainfall is at its greatest.

NORTHERN GREECE

°F			
79	100	82	
39	63	45	61
			25

☀	8 hrs	12 hrs	6 hrs	4 hrs
☂	1.6 in	.9 in	2.2 in	1.7 in
month	Apr	Jul	Oct	Jan

CENTRAL AND WESTERN GREECE

°F			
81	104	91	
36	59	41	61
			21

☀	8 hrs	11 hrs	5 hrs	3 hrs
☂	3.1 in	.7 in	3.1 in	3.3 in
month	Apr	Jul	Oct	Jan

NORTHERN GREECE

CENTRAL AND WESTERN GREECE

ATHENS AND AROUND ATHENS

THE PELOPONNESE

ATHENS

THE PELOPONNESE

°F			
77	97	82	
34	52	39	59
			25

☀	8 hrs	12 hrs	7 hrs	4 hrs
☂	2.4 in	.8 in	3.2 in	5.0 in
month	Apr	Jul	Oct	Jan

ATHENS AND AROUND ATHENS

Average monthly maximum temperature

Average monthly minimum temperature

Average daily hours of sunshine

Average monthly rainfall

°F			
79	102	86	
43	66	52	64
			34

☀	8 hrs	12 hrs	7 hrs	4 hrs
☂	.9 in	.2 in	2.0 in	2.4 in
month	Apr	Jul	Oct	Jan

ANCIENT GREECE

Gods, Goddesses, and Heroes

THE GREEK MYTHS that tell the stories of the gods, goddesses, and heroes date back to the Bronze Age when they were told aloud by poets. They were first written down in the early 6th century BC and have lived on in Western literature. Myths were closely bound up with Greek religion and gave meaning to the unpredictable workings of the natural world. They tell the story of the creation and the "golden age" of gods and mortals, as well as the age of semidivine heroes, such as Theseus and Herakles, whose exploits were an inspiration to ordinary men. The gods and goddesses were affected by human desires and failings and were part of a divine family presided over by Zeus. He had many offspring, both legitimate and illegitimate, each with a divine role.

Hades and Persephone were king and queen of the Underworld (land of the dead). Persephone was abducted from her mother Demeter, goddess of the harvest, by Hades. She was then only permitted to return to her mother for nine months each year.

Zeus was the father of the gods and ruled over them and all mortals from Mount Olympos.

Clymene, a nymph and daughter of Helios, was mother of Prometheus, creator of mankind.

Eris was the goddess of strife.

Poseidon, one of Zeus's brothers, was given control of the seas. The trident is his symbol of power, and he married the sea-goddess Amphitrite, to whom he was not entirely faithful. This statue is from the National Archaeological Museum in Athens (see pp68–71).

Hera, sister and wife of Zeus, was famous for her jealousy.

Athena was born from Zeus's head in full armor.

Paris was asked to award the golden apple to the most beautiful goddess.

Paris's dog helped him herd cattle on Mount Ida, where the prince grew up.

Dionysos, god of revelry and wine, was born from Zeus's thigh. In this 6th-century BC cup painted by Exekias he reclines in a ship whose mast has become a vine.

A DIVINE DISPUTE

This vase painting shows the gods on Mount Ida, near Troy. Hera, Athena, and Aphrodite, quarreling over who was the most beautiful, were brought by Hermes to hear the judgment of a young herdsman, the Trojan prince, Paris. In choosing Aphrodite, he was rewarded with the love of Helen, the most beautiful woman in the world. Paris abducted her from her husband Menelaos, King of Sparta, and thus the Trojan War began (see pp54–5).

◁ **Frieze from the Archaeological Museum, Delphi**

Artemis, the virgin goddess of the hunt, was the daughter of Zeus and sister of Apollo. She can be identified by her bow and arrows, hounds, and group of nymphs with whom she lived in the forests. Although sworn to chastity, she was, in contrast, the goddess of childbirth.

Happiness, here personified by two goddesses, waits with gold laurel leaves to garland the winner. Wreaths were the prizes in Greek athletic and musical contests.

Helios, the sun god, drove his four-horse chariot (the sun) daily across the sky.

Hermes was the gods' messenger.

Aphrodite, the goddess of love, was born from the sea. Here she has her son Eros (Cupid) with her.

Apollo, son of Zeus and brother of Artemis, was god of healing, plague, and also music. Here he is depicted holding a lyre. He was also famous for his dazzling beauty.

THE LABORS OF HERAKLES

Herakles (Hercules to the Romans) was the greatest of the Greek heroes, and the son of Zeus and Alkmene, a mortal woman. With superhuman strength he achieved success, and immortality, against seemingly impossible odds in the "Twelve Labors" set by Eurystheus, King of Argos. For his first task he killed the Nemean lion, and wore its hide ever after.

Killing the Lernaean hydra was the second labor of Herakles. The many heads of this venomous monster, raised by Hera, grew back as soon as they were chopped off. As in all his tasks, Herakles was helped by Athena.

The huge boar that ravaged Mount Erymanthus was captured next. Herakles brought it back alive to King Eurystheus, who was so terrified that he hid in a storage jar.

Destroying the Stymfalian birds was the sixth labor. Herakles rid Lake Stymfalia of these man-eating birds, which had brass beaks, by stoning them with a sling, having first frightened them off with a pair of bronze castanets.

The Trojan War

Ajax carrying
the body of the
dead Achilles

THE STORY of the Trojan War,
narrated in the *Iliad*, Homer's
8th-century BC epic poem, tells
how the Greeks sought to avenge
the capture of Helen, wife of
Menelaos, King of Sparta, by the
Trojan prince, Paris. The Roman
writer Virgil takes up the story in the
Aeneid, where he tells of the sack of
Troy and the ancestry of Rome. Archaeological
evidence of the remains of a city identified with ancient
Troy in modern Turkey suggests that the myth may
have a basis in fact. Many of the ancient sites in the
Peloponnese, such as Mycenae and Pylos, are thought
to be the cities of some of the heroes of the Trojan War.

Achilles binding up the battle
wounds of his friend Patroklos

GATHERING OF THE HEROES

WHEN PARIS *(see p52)*
carries Helen back
to Troy, her husband King
Menelaos summons an army
of Greek kings and heroes to
avenge this crime. His brother, King Agamemnon of
Mycenae, leads the force; its
ranks include young Achilles,
destined to die at Troy.

At Aulis their departure is
delayed by a contrary wind.
Only the sacrifice to Artemis
of Iphigeneia, the youngest
of Agamemnon's daughters,
allows the fleet to depart.

FIGHTING AT TROY

THE ILIAD OPENS with the
Greek army outside Troy,
maintaining a siege that has
already been in progress for
nine years. Tired of fighting, yet still

hoping for a decisive victory,
the Greek camp is torn apart
by the fury of Achilles over
Agamemnon's removal of his
slave girl Briseis. The hero
takes to his tent and refuses
adamantly to fight.

Deprived of their greatest
warrior, the Greeks are driven
back by the Trojans. In des-
peration, Patroklos persuades
his friend Achilles to let him
borrow his ar-
mor. Achilles
agrees and
Patroklos leads
the Myrmidons,
Achilles's troops,
into battle. The
tide is turned, but
Patroklos is killed
in the fighting by
Hector, son of
King Priam of
Troy, who mistakes him for
Achilles. Filled with remorse at
the news of his friend's death,
Achilles returns to battle, finds
Hector, and kills him
in revenge.

King Priam begging Achilles
for the body of his son

PATROKLOS AVENGED

REFUSING HECTOR'S dying
wish to allow his body
to be ransomed, Achilles
instead hitches it up to his
chariot by the ankles and
drags it round the walls of
Troy, then takes it back to
the Greek camp. In contrast,
Patroklos is given the most
elaborate funeral possible
with a huge pyre, sacrifices
of animals and Trojan prisoners, and funeral games.
Still unsatisfied, for 12 days
Achilles drags
the corpse
of Hector
around
Patroklos's
funeral mound
until the gods
are forced to
intervene over
his callous
behavior.

PRIAM VISITS ACHILLES

ON THE INSTRUCTIONS of
Zeus, Priam sets off for
the Greek camp holding a
ransom for the body of his
dead son. With the help of
the god Hermes he reaches
Achilles' tent undetected.
Entering, he pleads with
Achilles to think of his own
father and to show mercy.
Achilles relents and allows
Hector to be taken back to
Troy for a funeral and burial.

Although the Greek heroes
often seem superhuman,
they were portrayed as
fallible beings with human
emotions who had to face
universal moral dilemmas.

Greeks and Trojans, in bronze armor, locked in combat

ACHILLES KILLS THE AMAZON QUEEN

PENTHESILEIA WAS the Queen of the Amazons, a tribe of warlike women reputed to cut off their right breasts to make it easier to wield their weapons. They come to the support of the Trojans. In the battle, Achilles finds himself face to face with Penthesileia and deals her a fatal blow. One version of the story has it that as their eyes meet at the moment of her death, they fall in love. The Greek idea of love and death would be explored 2,000 years later by the psychologists Jung and Freud.

An early image of the Trojan Horse, from a 7th-century BC clay vase

Achilles killing the Amazon Queen Penthesileia in battle

THE WOODEN HORSE OF TROY

AS WAS FORETOLD, Achilles is killed at Troy by an arrow from Paris's bow. With this weakening of their military strength, the Greeks resort to guile.

Before sailing away they build a great wooden horse, in which they conceal some of their best fighters. The rumor is put out that this is a gift to the goddess Athena and that if the horse enters Troy, the city can never be taken. After some doubts, but swayed by supernatural omens, the Trojans drag the horse inside the walls. That night, the Greeks sail back, the soldiers creep out of the horse, and Troy is put to the torch. Priam, with many others, is murdered. Among the Trojan survivors is Aeneas, who escapes to Italy and founds the race of Romans: a second Troy. The next part of the story (the *Odyssey*) tells of the heroes' adventures on their way home to Greece.

DEATH OF AGAMEMNON

KLYTEMNESTRA, the wife of Agamemnon, had ruled Mycenae in the ten years that he had been away, in the company of Aigisthos, her lover. Consumed with vengeance for the death of her daughter Iphigeneia, Klytemnestra receives her husband with a triumphal welcome and then brutally murders him, trapping him ignominiously in a net. Agamemnon's fate was a result of a curse laid on his father, Atreus, which was finally worked out by the murder of Klytemnestra and Aigisthos by her son Orestes and daughter Elektra. In myths, the will of the gods both shapes and overrides that of heroes and mortals.

GREEK MYTHS IN WESTERN ART

From the Renaissance onward, the Greek myths have been a powerful inspiration for artists and sculptors. Kings and queens have often had themselves portrayed as gods and goddesses, invested with their symbolic attributes of love or war. Myths have also been an inspiration for artists to paint the nude or Classically draped figure. This was true of the 19th-century artist Lord Leighton, whose depiction of the human body reflects the Classical ideals of beauty. His tragic figure of Elektra is shown here.

Elektra mourning the death of her father Agamemnon at his tomb

Greek Writers and Philosophers

Playwrights Aristophanes and Sophocles

THE LITERATURE OF GREECE began with long epic poems, accounts of war and adventure, which established the relationship of the ancient Greeks to their gods. The tragedy and comedy, history and philosophical dialogues of the 5th and 4th centuries BC became the basis of Western literary culture. Much of our knowledge of the Greek world is derived from Greek literature. Pausanias's *Guide to Greece*, written in the Roman period and used by Roman tourists, is a key to the physical remains.

Hesiod with the nine Muses who inspired his poetry

EPIC POETRY

As FAR BACK as the 2nd millennium BC, before even the building of the Mycenaean palaces, poets were reciting the stories of the Greek heroes and gods. Passed on from generation to generation, these poems were never written down but were changed and embellished by successive poets, called *rhapsodes*. The oral tradition culminated in the *Iliad* and *Odyssey* (*see pp54–5*), composed around 700 BC. Both works are traditionally ascribed to the same poet, Homer, of whose life

nothing reliable is known. Hesiod, whose most famous poems include the *Theogony*, a history of the gods, and the *Works and Days*, on how to live an honest life, also lived around 700 BC. Unlike Homer, Hesiod is thought to have written down his poems, although there is no firm evidence available to support this theory.

PASSIONATE POETRY

FOR PRIVATE OCCASIONS, and particularly to entertain guests at the cultivated drinking parties known as *symposia*, shorter poetic forms were developed. These poems were often full of passion, whether love or hatred, and could be personal or, often, highly political. Much of this poetry, by writers such as Archilochus, Alcaeus, Alcman, Hipponax, and Sappho, survives only in quotations by later writers or on scraps of papyrus that have been preserved by chance from private libraries in Hellenistic and Roman Egypt. Through these fragments we can gain glimpses

of the life of a very competitive elite. Since *symposia* were an almost exclusively male domain, there is a strong element of misogyny in much of this poetry. In contrast, the fragments of poems discovered by the poetess Sappho, who lived on the island of Lésvos, are exceptional for showing a woman competing in a literary area in the male-dominated society of ancient Greece, and for describing with great intensity her passions for other women.

HISTORY

UNTIL THE 5th century BC little Greek literature was composed in prose – even early philosophy was in verse. In the latter part of the 5th century, a new tradition of lengthy prose histories, looking at recent or current events, was established with Herodotus's account of the great wars between Greece and Persia (490–479 BC). Herodotus put the clash between Greeks and Persians into a context and included an ethnographic account of the vast Persian Empire. He attempted to record objectively what people said about the past.

Herodotus, the historian of the Persian wars

Thucydides took a narrower view in his account of the long years of the Peloponnesian Wars between Athens and Sparta (431–404 BC). He concentrated on the political history, and his aim was to work out the "truth" that lay behind the events of the war. The example of Thucydides dominated the later writing of Greek history, though few could match his acute insight into human nature.

An unusual vase-painting of a *symposion* for women only

The orator Demosthenes in a Staffordshire figurine of 1790

ORATORY

PUBLIC ARGUMENT was basic to Greek political life even in the Archaic period. In the later part of the 5th century BC, the techniques of persuasive speech began to be studied in their own right. From that time on some orators began to publish their speeches. In particular, this included those wishing to advertise their skills in composing speeches for the law courts, such as Lysias and Demosthenes. The texts that survive give insights into both Athenian politics and the seamier side of Athenian private life. The verbal attacks on Philip of Macedon by Demosthenes, the 4th-century BC Athenian politician, became models for Roman politicians seeking to defeat their opponents. With the 18th-century European revival of interest in Classical times, Demosthenes again became a political role model.

DRAMA

ALMOST ALL the surviving tragedies come from the hands of the three great 5th-century BC Athenians: Aeschylus, Sophocles, and Euripides. The latter two playwrights developed an interest in individual psychology (as in Euripides's *Medea*). While 5th-century comedy is full of direct references to contemporary life and dirty jokes, the "new" comedy developed in the 4th century BC is essentially situation comedy employing character types.

Vase painting of two costumed actors from around 370 BC

GREEK PHILOSOPHERS

The Athenian Socrates was recognized in the late 5th century BC as a moral arbiter. He wrote nothing himself, but we know of his views through the "Socratic dialogues," written by his pupil, Plato, examining the concepts of justice, virtue, and courage. Plato set up his academy in the suburbs of Athens.

His pupil, Aristotle, founded the Lyceum to teach subjects from biology to ethics and helped to turn Athens into one of the first university cities. In 1508–11 Raphael painted this vision of Athens in the Vatican.

Plato saw "the seat of ideas" in heaven.

Aristotle, author of the *Ethics*, had a genius for scientific observation.

Euclid laid the rules of geometry in around 300 BC.

Epicurus advocated moderation in all things.

Socrates taught by debating his ideas.

Diogenes, the Cynic, lived like a beggar.

Temple Architecture

Temples were the most important public buildings in ancient Greece, largely because religion was a central part of everyday life. Often placed in prominent positions, temples were also statements about political and divine power. The earliest temples, in the 8th century BC, were built of wood and sun-dried bricks. Many of their features were copied in marble buildings from the 6th century BC onward.

Pheidias, sculptor of the Parthenon, at work

TEMPLE CONSTRUCTION

This drawing is of an idealized Doric temple, showing how it was built and used.

The cella, or inner sanctum, housed the cult statue.

The cult statue was of the god or goddess to whom the temple was dedicated.

The pediment, triangular in shape, often held sculpture.

A ramp led up to the temple entrance.

The stepped platform was built on a stone foundation.

The column drums were initially carved with bosses for lifting them into place.

Fluting on the columns was carved *in situ*, guided by that on the top and bottom drums.

TIMELINE OF TEMPLE CONSTRUCTION

700 First temple of Poseidon, Ancient Isthmia (Archaic; *see p167*) and first Temple of Apollo, Corinth (Archaic; *see p163*)	**550** Second temple of Apollo, Corinth (Doric; *see p163*)	**520** Temple of Olympian Zeus, Athens, begun (Doric; completed Corinthian 2nd century AD; *see p111*)	*Detail of the Parthenon pediment*
		6th century Temple of Artemis, Ancient Brauron (Doric; *see pp146–7*)	

700 BC	600 BC	500 BC	400 BC	300 BC
		460 Temple of Zeus, Olympia (Doric; *see p171*)		**4th century** Temple of Apollo, Delphi (Doric; see *p229*); Temple of Athena Alea, Tegéa (Doric and 1st Corinthian capital; *see p177*)
7th century Temple of Hera, Olympia (Doric; *see p170*)		**447–405** Temples of the Acropolis, Athens: Athena Nike (Ionic), Parthenon (Doric), Erechtheion (Ionic) (*see pp94–9*)		**440–430** Temple of Poseidon, Soúnio (Doric; *see pp148–9*)
445–425 Temple of Apollo, Bassae (Doric with Ionic; *see p177*)				

The gable ends of the roof were surmounted by statues, known as *akroteria*, in this case of a Nike or "Victory." Almost no upper portions of Greek temples survive.

The roof was supported on wooden beams and covered in rows of terra-cotta tiles, each ending in an upright antefix.

Stone blocks were smoothly fitted together and held by metal clamps and dowels: no mortar was used in the temple's construction.

The ground plan was derived from the megaron of the Mycenaean house: a rectangular hall with a front porch supported by columns.

Caryatids, *or figures of women, were used instead of columns in the Erechtheion at Athens' Acropolis. In Athens' Agora (see pp90–91), tritons (half-fish, half-human creatures) were used.*

THE DEVELOPMENT OF TEMPLE ARCHITECTURE

Greek temple architecture is divided into three styles, which evolved chronologically, and are most easily distinguished by the column capitals.

Doric temples were surrounded by sturdy columns with plain capitals and no bases. As the earliest style of stone buildings, they recall wooden prototypes.

Triangular pediment filled with sculpture

Guttae imitated the pegs for fastening the wooden roof beams.

Triglyphs resembled the ends of cross beams.

Metopes could contain sculpture.

Doric capital

Ionic temples differed from Doric in their tendency to have more columns, of a different form. The capital has a pair of volutes, like rams' horns, front and back.

The frieze was a continuous band of decoration.

The Ionic architrave was subdivided into projecting bands.

Akroteria, at the roof corners, could look Persian in style.

The Ionic frieze took the place of Doric triglyphs and metopes.

Ionic capital

Corinthian temples in Greece were built under the Romans and only in Athens. They feature columns with slender shafts and elaborate capitals decorated with acanthus leaves.

Akroterion in the shape of a griffin

The cella entrance was at the east end.

The entablature was everything above the capitals.

The pediment was decorated with a variety of moldings.

Acanthus leaf capital

Vases and Vase Painting

Donkey cup

T HE HISTORY OF GREEK vase painting continued without a break from 1000 BC to Hellenistic times. The main center of production was Athens, which was so successful that by the early 6th century BC it was sending its high-quality black- and red-figure wares to every part of the Greek world. The Athenian potters' quarter of Kerameikós can still be visited today *(see pp88–9)*. Beautiful works of art in their own right, the painted vases are the closest we can get to the vanished paintings with which ancient Greeks decorated the walls of their houses. Although vases could break during everyday use (for which they were intended), a huge number still survive intact or in reassembled pieces.

This 6th-century BC black-figure vase shows pots being used in an everyday situation. The vases depicted are hydriai. *It was the women's task to fill them with water from springs or public fountains.*

The white-ground lekythos was developed in the 5th century BC as an oil flask for grave offerings. They were usually decorated with funeral scenes, and this one, by the Achilles Painter, shows a woman placing flowers at a grave.

The naked woman holding a *kylix* is probably a flute-girl or prostitute.

THE SYMPOSION

These episodes of mostly male feasting and drinking were also occasions for playing the game of *kottabos*. On the exterior of this 5th-century BC *kylix* are depictions of men holding cups, ready to flick out the dregs at a target.

THE DEVELOPMENT OF PAINTING STYLES

Vase painting reached its peak in 6th- and 5th-century BC Athens. In the potter's workshop, a fired vase would be passed to a painter to be decorated. Archaeologists have been able to identify the varying styles of many individual painters of both black-figure and red-figure ware.

The body of the dead man is carried on a bier by mourners.

The geometric design is a prototype of the later "Greek-key" pattern.

Chariots and warriors form the funeral procession.

Geometric style characterizes the earliest Greek vases, from around 1000 to 700 BC, in which the decoration is in bands of figures and geometric patterns. This 8th-century BC vase placed on a grave as a marker is over 1 m (3 ft) high and depicts the bier and funeral rites of a dead man.

Eye cups *were given an almost magical power by the painted eyes. The pointed base suggests that they were passed around during feasting.*

This *kylix* **is being** held by one handle by another woman feaster, ready to flick out the dregs at a *kottabos* target.

The rhyton, *such as this one in the shape of a ram's head, was a drinking vessel for watered-down wine. The scene of the symposion around the rim indicates when it would have been used.*

This drinker holds aloft a branch of a vine, symbolic of Dionysos's presence at the party.

Striped cushions made reclining more comfortable.

The drinking horn shape was copied in the pottery *rhyton*.

VASE SHAPES

Almost all Greek vases were made to be used; their shapes are closely related to their intended uses. Athenian potters had about 20 different forms to choose from. Below are some of the most commonly made shapes and their uses.

The amphora *was a two-handled vessel used to store wine, olive oil, and foods pre-served in liquid such as olives. It also held dried foods.*

This krater *with curled handles or "volutes" is a wide-mouthed vase in which the Greeks mixed water with their wine before drinking it.*

The hydria *was used to carry water from the fountain. Of the three handles, one was vertical for holding and pouring, two horizontal for lifting.*

The lekythos *could vary in height from 3 cm (1 in) to nearly 1 m (39 in). It was used to hold oil both in the home and as a funerary gift to the dead.*

The oinochoe, *the standard wine jug, had a round or trefoil mouth for pouring, and just one handle.*

The kylix, *a two-handled drinking cup, was one shape that could take in-terior decoration.*

Black-figure style *was first used in Athens around 630 BC. The figures were painted in black liquid clay onto the iron-rich clay of the vase that turned orange when fired. This vase is signed by the potter and painter Exekias.*

Red-figure style *was introduced in c.530 BC. The figures were left in the color of the clay, silhouetted against a black glaze. Here a woman pours from an oinochoe (wine-jug).*

ATHENS
AREA BY AREA

Athens at a Glance

ATHENS HAS BEEN A CITY for 3,500 years, but its
greatest glory was during the Classical period
of ancient Greece from which so many buildings
and artifacts still survive. The 5th century BC in
particular was a golden age, when Perikles oversaw
the building of the Acropolis. Within the Byzantine
Empire and under Ottoman rule, Athens played
only a minor role. It returned to prominence in
1834, when it became the capital of Greece. Today
it is a busy and modern metropolitan center.

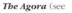

The Kerameikós *quarter
(see pp88–9) was once the potters'
district of ancient Athens and site
of the principal cemetery,
whose grave monuments
can still be seen.
Tranquil and
secluded, it lies
off the main
tourist track.*

SEE ALSO

- ***Where to Stay*** pp264–7

- ***Where to Eat*** pp286–9

- ***Getting Around Athens*** pp322–5

The Agora *(see
pp90–91), or market
place, was the ancient
center of commercial
life. The Stoa of Attalos
was reconstructed in
1953–6 on its original,
2nd-century BC foun-
dations. It now houses
the Agora Museum.*

The Tower of the Winds
*(see pp86–7) stands in the
Roman forum, but this
small, octagonal building
is Hellenistic in style. The
tower – built as a water
clock, with a compass,
sundials, and weather vane
– has a relief on each side
depicting the wind from
that direction.*

The Acropolis *(see pp94–101)
has dominated Athens for over
2,000 years. From the scale of the
Parthenon to the delicacy of the
Erechtheion, it is an extraordinary
achievement.*

0 meters	500
0 yards	500

◁ **The Parthenon on the Acropolis, viewed from the Hephaisteion**

The National Archaeological Museum (see pp68–71) *houses some of the treasures from one of the greatest Western civilizations. This is the Plaque of Ninnion, a stele from the Kerameikós, dating from c.370–350 BC.*

CENTRAL ATHENS NORTH
(see pp66–81)

The Museum of Cycladic Art (see pp74–5) *holds an unrivaled collection of Cycladic artifacts. This marble figurine with crossed-arm pose is typical of the style.*

CENTRAL ATHENS SOUTH
(see pp82–113)

The Benáki Museum (see pp78–9), *formed from a private collection, is a treasure house of antiquities, Egyptian and Islamic art, icons, folk costumes, and Byzantine relics, such as this gold-plated incense boat.*

The Panagía Gorgoepíkoös (see p105), *or Little Cathedral, is one of the best-preserved Byzantine buildings in Athens. You can spot ancient carved reliefs reused in the walls of this tiny church.*

CENTRAL ATHENS NORTH

INHABITED FOR 7,000 YEARS, Athens was the birthplace of European civilization. It flourished in the 5th century BC when the Athenians controlled much of the eastern Mediterranean. The buildings from this era, including those in the ancient Agora and on the Acropolis, lie largely in the southern part of the city. The northern half has grown since the early 1800s, when King Otto made Athens the new capital of Greece. When the king's architects planned the new, European-style city, they included wide, tree-lined avenues, such as Panepistimíou and Akadimías, that were soon home to many grand

Icon of the Archangel Michael, from the Byzantine Museum

Neo-Classical public buildings and mansions. Today, these edifices still provide elegant homes for all the major banks, embassies, and public institutions, such as the University and the Library.

The chic residential area of Kolonáki is located in the north of the city center, as is the cosmopolitan area around Patriárchou Ioakeím and Irodótou. These streets have excellent shopping and entertainment venues. Most of Athens' best museums, including the National Archaeological Museum, are also found in this area of the city. For information on getting around Athens, see pages 322–5.

SIGHTS AT A GLANCE

Museums and Galleries
Benáki Museum pp78–9 ⑩
Byzantine Museum ⑦
City of Athens Museum ⑫
Museum of Cycladic Art pp74–5 ⑧
National Archaeological Museum pp68–/1 ①
National Gallery of Art ⑤
National Historical Museum ⑬
Theatrical Museum ⑪
War Museum ⑥

Squares, Parks and Gardens
Exarcheía and Stréfi Hill ②
Lykavittós Hill ③
Plateía Kolonakíou ⑨

Churches
Kapnikaréa ⑭

Historic Buildings
Gennádeion ④

KEY

M	Metro station
P	Parking
i	Tourist information

◁ The elegant façade of the Neo-Classical University building (see p81)

National Archaeological Museum ❶
Εθνικό Αρχαιολογικό Μουσείο

Hellenistic bronze head from Delos

OPENED IN 1891, this superb museum, often known simply as the National Museum, brought together a collection that had previously been stored all over the city. New wings were added in 1939. The priceless collection was then dispersed and buried underground during World War II to protect it from possible damage. The museum reopened in 1946, but it has taken 50 years of renovation and reorganization finally to do justice to its formidable collection. With the combination of such unique exhibits as the Mycenaean gold, along with the unrivaled amount of sculpture, pottery, and jewelry on display, this is without doubt one of the world's finest museums.

Neo-Classical entrance to the National Archaeological Museum on Patission

GALLERY GUIDE

On the ground floor, Mycenaean, Neolithic, and Cycladic finds are followed by Geometric, Archaic, Classical, Roman, and Hellenistic sculpture. Smaller collections of bronzes, Egyptian artifacts, the Eléni Stathátou jewelry collection, and the Karapános collection are also on the ground floor. The first floor houses pottery and the Thíra frescoes.

Dipylon Amphora
This huge Geometric vase was used to mark an 8th-century BC woman's burial and shows the dead body surrounded by mourning women. It is named after the location of its discovery near the Dipylon Gate in Athens' Kerameikós (see pp88–9).

Bronze collection

Sculpture garden

Main entrance hall

Harp Player
The minimalist Cycladic style of sculpture flourished in the third millennium BC and originated in the Cyclades. The simple lines and bold forms of the marble figurines influenced many early 20th-century artists, including the British sculptor Henry Moore.

Entrance

Ground floor

★ **Thíra Frescoes**
These fine wall paintings (c.1500 BC) were found on the island of Thíra (Santoríni). This one is known as The Fisherman.

Egyptian collection

Eléni Stathátou jewelry collection

The pottery collection contains a vast display of vases.

Karapános collection

Stairs to first floor

★ **Mask of Agamemnon**
Found at Mycenae by Schliemann, this gold death mask was originally thought to have belonged to the legendary king, Agamemnon. It dates from c.1500 BC.

The courtyard has stairs leading to a basement café and shop.

KEY TO FLOOR PLAN

☐ Neolithic and Cycladic art
☐ Mycenaean art
☐ Geometric and Archaic art
☐ Classical sculpture
☐ Roman and Hellenistic sculpture
☐ Other collections
☐ Thíra frescoes
☐ Pottery collection
☐ Temporary exhibitions
☐ Nonexhibition space

STAR EXHIBITS

★ **Thíra Frescoes**

★ **Mask of Agamemnon**

★ **Youth of Antikýthira**

★ **Youth of Antikýthira**
This fine Hellenistic bronze statue was discovered off the island of Antikýthira in 1900. Larger than life, it is approximately 2m (7 ft) tall.

Exploring the National Archaeological Museum's Collection

DISPLAYING ITS TREASURES in chronological order, the museum presents an impressive and thorough overview of Greek art through the centuries. Beginning with early Cycladic figurines and continuing through the Greek Bronze Age, the exhibits end with the glories of Hellenistic period bronzes and a collection of busts of Roman emperors. High points in between include the numerous gold artifacts found at Mycenae, the elegant Archaic *koúroi* statues, and the many examples of fine Classical sculpture.

Mycenaean head of a sphinx

NEOLITHIC AND CYCLADIC ART

THE DAWNING of Greek civilization (3500–2900 BC) saw primitive decorative vases and figures. This collection also contains terra-cotta figurines, jewelry, and a selection of weapons.

Neolithic clay vases with simple painted decoration

The vibrant fertility gods and goddesses, such as the *kourotróphos* (nursing mother) with child, are particularly well preserved. Of exceptional importance are the largest known Cycladic marble figurine, from Amorgós, and the earliest known figures of musicians – the *Flute Player* and *Harp Player*, both from Kéros. Later finds from Mílos, such as the painted vase with fishermen, reveal the changes in pot shapes and color that took place in the late Cycladic Bronze Age.

MYCENAEAN ART

IT IS NOT DIFFICULT to understand the allure of the museum's most popular attraction, the Hall of Mycenaean Antiquities, with its dazzling array of 16th-century BC gold treasures. Other exhibits in the collection include frescoes, ivory sculptures, and seal rings made out of precious stones.

From the famous shaft graves *(see p180)* came a procession of daggers, cups, seals, and rings, as well as a number of regal death masks, including the justly famous *Mask of Agamemnon*. Two superb *rhytons*, or wine jugs, are also on display: one in the shape of a bull's head, made in silver with gold horns, and one in gold shaped like a lion's head. Equally rich finds from sites other than Mycenae have since been made. These include two gold bull cups found at Vafeió, in Crete, a gold phial entwined with dolphins and octopuses (excavated from a royal tomb at Déntra), clay tablets with the early Linear B script from the Palace of Nestor *(see p201)*, and a magnificent sword from the Tomb of Stáfylos on the island of Skópelos.

Mycenaean bronze dagger, inlaid with gold

THE DEVELOPMENT OF GREEK SCULPTURE

Sculpture was one of the most sophisticated forms of Greek art. We are able to trace its development from the early *koúroi* to the great works of named sculptors such as Pheidias and Praxiteles in Classical times. Portraiture only began in the 5th century BC; even then most Greek sculptures were of gods and goddesses, heroes and athletes, and idealized men and women. These have had an enormous influence on Western art down the centuries.

The Sounion Koúros *(600 BC) was an offering dedicated to either Poseidon or Athena at Soúnio (see p148). The highly stylized koúroi (statues of nude youths) first appear in the mid-7th century BC. Derived from Egyptian art, these figures share a common pose and proportions. Clothed kórai are the female counterpart.*

The Marathon Boy *(340 BC), like many other Greek bronzes, was found on the sea floor. The dreamy expression and easy pose of the figure are characteristic of the works of Praxiteles, the leading late Classical sculptor. An example of the "heroic nude," it shows a great naturalism and perfect balance.*

GEOMETRIC AND ARCHAIC ART

FAMED FOR ITS monumental burial vases, such as the *Dipylon Amphora*, the Geometric period developed a more ornate style in the 7th century BC, introducing mythological and plant and animal motifs. By the 6th century BC the full artistry of the black-figure vases had developed. Two rare examples from this period include a *lekythos* depicting Peleus, Achilles, and the centaur Cheiron, and the sculptured heads *'aryballoi'*.

Warrior from Boiotia, early 7th century BC

CLASSICAL SCULPTURE

THE COLLECTION OF Classical sculpture contains both fine statues and a selection of grave monuments, mostly from the Kerameikós. These include the beautiful stele (c.410 BC) of Hegeso *(see p88)*. Classical votive sculpture on display includes parts of a statue of the goddess

This "valedictory stele" *(mid-4th century BC) shows a seated woman bidding farewell to her family. The figures express a dignified suffering found in many Greek funerary reliefs.*

Hera, from the Heraion at Argos in the Peloponnese, and many statues of the goddess Athena, including the *Varvakeion Athena*, a reduced copy of the original ivory and gold statue from the Parthenon *(see p99)*.

ROMAN AND HELLENISTIC SCULPTURE

ALTHOUGH A LARGE number of Greek bronzes were lost in antiquity, as metal was melted down in times of emergency for making weapons, the museum has some excellent pieces on display. These include the famous bronzes *Poseidon* and the *Horse with the Little Jockey*, both found at Cape Artemision on Evvoia, and the *Youth of Antikythira*, found in the sea off that island. Another of the best known sculptures is the *Marathon Boy*.

OTHER COLLECTIONS

THE MUSEUM also houses several smaller collections, many donated by private individuals. Among these is the glittering **Eléni Stathátou jewelry collection**, which covers the Bronze Age through to the Byzantine period. The **Karapános collection**, which is composed mainly from discoveries made at the site at Dodóni *(see p211)*, contains many fine bronzes, including *Zeus Hurling a Thunderbolt*. Also on display are small decorative and votive pieces, and strips of lead inscribed with questions for the oracle at Dodóni.

Other collections include the recently opened **Egyptian collection**, and the **Bronze collection**, which comprises many small pieces of statuary and decorative items discovered on the Acropolis.

Hellenistic bronze known as the *Horse with the Little Jockey*

THIRA FRESCOES

THESE COLORFUL frescoes, discovered at Akrotíri on the island of Thíra (Santoríni) in 1967, were originally thought to be from the mythical city of Atlantis. They confirm the sophistication of late Minoan civilization. The frescoes, dating from 1500 BC, depict images of a naval expedition, elegant women, children, naked fishermen, animals, and flowers. Now restored, they are a highlight of the museum.

POTTERY COLLECTION

THE STRENGTH of this vast collection lies not only in its size, but in the quality of specific works, representing the flowering of Greek ceramic art. The real gems belong to the 5th century BC, when red-figure vases and white-ground *lekythoi* became the established style *(see p60)* and were produced in vast numbers. Expressive painting styles and new designs characterize this period. The most poignant pieces are by the "Bosanquet painter" and the "Achilles painter," who portrayed young men by their graves.

Gold Hellenistic ring from the Eléni Stathátou collection

View northeast to Lykavittós Hill from the Acropolis

Exárcheia and Stréfi Hill **2**

Εξάρχεια
Λόφος του Στρέφη

Map 2 F2 & 3 A2. **M** *Omónoia.*

UNTIL RECENTLY, the area around Plateía Exarcheíon was renowned as a hotbed of student anarchist activity. Prior to the student invasion, Exárcheia was a very attractive area, and the 19th-century Neo-Classical buildings still stand as testament to this. Today, the area is picking up again and has a mixed atmosphere of student squalor and new gentrification, which has brought many fashionable cafés, bars, and *ouzerí* to the area. Themistokléous, which leads off the square down to Omónoia, is pleasant to wander along; the local food stores and small boutiques make a refreshing change from the noisy bars. Plateía Exarcheíon is especially lively at night, when the *rempétika* music clubs and the open-air cinema, the Riviera, in the streets that climb toward Stréfi, attract many visitors.

Every year a demonstration takes place on November 17, marking the date in 1973 when many students were killed by the Junta *(see p43)* during a sit in.

The nearby park of Stréfi Hill, with its intriguing maze of paths, is quiet and peaceful by day but comes to life at night, when its cafés are full. Stréfi Hill is one of the many green areas in Athens that provide welcome relief from the noise and grime of the city, particularly in the oppressive heat of summer.

The restaurant on Lykavittós Hill, overlooking Athens

Lykavittós Hill **3**

Λόφος του Λυκαβηττός

Map 3 C3. **Funicular:** *from Ploutárchou, 8:45am–12:45pm Mon–Wed & Fri–Sun, 10:30am–12:45pm Thu.*

THE PEAK of Lykavittós (also known as Lycabettus) reaches 277 m (910 ft) above the city and is its highest hill. It can be climbed on foot by various paths or by the easier, albeit vertiginous, ride in the funicular from the corner of Ploutárchou. On foot, it should take about 45 minutes. The hill derives its name from the popular belief that wolves *(lýkoi)* lived here. The ancient Greeks believed that this was the rock once destined to be the Athenian citadel, accidentally dropped by the city's patron goddess, Athena. Although it is without doubt the most prominent hill in Athens, surprisingly little mention is made of Lykavittós in Classical literature; the one exception is a passing reference in Aristophanes's play, *Clouds.* This landmark is a favorite haunt for many Athenians, who come for the panoramic views of the city from the observation decks that rim the summit.

The small whitewashed chapel of **Agios Geórgios** crowns the top of the hill. It was built in the 19th century on the site of an older Byzantine church, dedicated to Profitis Ilías (the Prophet Elijah). Both are celebrated on their name days (Profitis Ilías on July 20 and Agios Geórgios on April 23). On the eve of Easter Sunday a spectacular candlelit procession winds down the peak's wooded slopes *(see p45).*

Lykavittós Hill is also home to a summit restaurant, some cafés, and the open-air **Lykavittós Theater**, where contemporary jazz, pop, and dance performances are held annually during the Athens Summer Festival *(see p46).*

Gennádeion ➍
Γεννάδειον

American School of Classical Studies,
Souidías 61, Kolonáki. **Map** 3 C4.
[01 721 0536. **🚌** 3, 7, 8, 13.
◐ 9am–5pm Mon, Tue & Fri,
9am–8pm Wed & Thu, 9am–2pm Sat.
● Aug, main public hols.

T HE GREEK DIPLOMAT and
bibliophile Ioánnis
Gennádios (1844–1932)
spent a lifetime accumulat-
ing rare first editions and
illuminated manuscripts. In
1923, he donated his collection to the American School
of Classical Studies. The
Gennádeion building, named
after him, was designed and
built between 1923 and 1925
by the New York firm Van
Pelt and Thompson to house
the collection. Above its
façade of Ionic columns is an
inscription which translates as
"They are called Greeks who
share in our culture" – from
Gennádios's dedication speech
at the opening in 1926.

Researchers need special
permission to gain access to
over 70,000 rare books and
manuscripts, and no items are
allowed to be removed from
the library. Casual visitors
may look at selected exhibits,
and books, posters, and
postcards are for sale at the
souvenir stand.

The exhibits in the main
reading room include a set
of 192 Edward Lear sketches
purchased in 1929 and an
eclectic mix of Byron memorabilia, including the last
known portrait of the poet
made before his death in
1824 *(see p149)*.

**The imposing Neo-Classical
façade of the Gennádeion**

National Gallery of Art ➎
Εθνική Πινακοθήκη

Vasiléos Konstantínou 50, Ilísia.
Map 7 C1. **[** 01 723 5937. **🚌** 3,
13. **◐** 9am–3pm Mon, Wed–Sat,
10am–2pm Sun. **●** main public
hols. **📷** **♿**

O PENED IN 1976, the National
Gallery of Art is housed
in a modern low-rise building
that contains a permanent
collection of European and
Greek art. The ground floor
stages traveling exhibitions
and opens out onto a sculpture garden. The first floor,
with the exception of five
impressive works by El Greco
(1541–1614), is devoted to a
minor collection of non-Greek,
European art. Alongside
works of the Dutch, Italian,
and Flemish schools, there
are studies, engravings, and
paintings by Rembrandt,
Dürer, Brueghel, Van Dyck,
Watteau, Utrillo, Cézanne, and
Braque, among others. These
include Caravaggio's *Singer*

(1620), Eugène Delacroix's
Greek Warrior (1856), and
Picasso's Cubist-period *Woman
in a White Dress* (1939).

A changing display of Greek
modern art from the 18th to
the 20th century forms the
majority of the collection on
the second floor. The 19th
century is represented mainly
by numerous depictions of
the War of Independence and
seascapes, enlivened by portraits such as Nikólaos Gýzis's
The Loser of the Bet (1878), and
Waiting (1900) and *The Straw
Hat* (1925), both by Nikifóros
Lýtras. There are many fine
examples of works by major
Greek artists including Chatzi-
michaíl, Chatzikyriákos-Gkíkas,
Móralis, and Tsaroúchis.

War Museum ➏
Πολεμικό Μουσείο

Corner of Vasilíssis Sofías & Rizári,
Ilísia. **Map** 7 C1. **[** 01 729 0543.
🚌 3, 7, 8, 13. **◐** 9am–2pm
Tue–Sun. **●** main public hols. **♿**

T HE WAR MUSEUM, housed in
a modern building, was
opened in 1975
after the fall of
the military dic-
tatorship *(see
p43)*. The first
nine galleries
are chronologi-
cally ordered,
and contain
battle scenes,
armor, and
plans from as far   **Spartan**
back as ancient   **bronze**
Mycenaean times   **helmet**
through to the
German occupation of 1941.
Other galleries contain a
miscellany of items including
a selection of uniforms and
Turkish weapons.

There is a fine display of
paintings and prints of leaders
from the Greek War of Independence *(see pp40–41)*,
such as general Theódoros
Kolokotrónis (1770–1843).
The death mask of the famous
general can also be seen in
the museum. A sizable collection of fine sketches and oils
by the artists Florás-Karavías
and Argyrós vividly captures
the hardships of the two
world wars.

Modern sculpture outside the National Gallery of Art

Museum of Cycladic Art 8

Μουσείο Κυκλαδικής και Αρχαίας Ελληνικής Τέχνης

OPENED IN 1986, this modern museum offers the world's finest collection of Cycladic art. It was initially assembled by Nikólas and Dolly Goulandrí and has expanded with donations from other wealthy Greeks. The museum now has an excellent selection of ancient Greek art, the earliest from about 5,000 years ago.

The Cycladic figurines, dating from the 3rd
Cycladic marble head millennium BC, have never enjoyed quite the same level of popularity as Classical sculpture.

However, the haunting simplicity of these marble statues has inspired many 20th-century artists and sculptors, including Picasso, Modigliani, and Henry Moore.

LOCATOR MAP

The third floor houses temporary exhibitions.

Second floor

Red-figure Kylix
This 5th-century BC drinking cup depicts a boxing match between two young male athletes, supervised by their instructor.

First floor

Main entrance

Ground floor

Violin-shaped Figurine
This 13-cm (5-in) high, Cycladic, white marble statuette is thought to be a stylized human figure. Most figurines of this shape come from Páros and Antíparos.

Stairs to rest rooms and café

Walkway leading to Stathátos Mansion

GALLERY GUIDE
In the main building, the Cycladic collection is on the first floor. Ancient Greek art is on the second, and the third shows temporary exhibitions. The fourth floor houses the Charles Polítis collection. In the Stathátos Mansion is the Greek art collection of the Athens Academy.

STAR EXHIBITS

★ **Cycladic Figurine**

★ **White Lekythos**

★ Cycladic Figurine
This "Folded Arm" type statue of a woman is 39 cm (15 in) tall. It has only four toes on each foot and a swollen abdomen, indicating pregnancy.

Terra-cotta Figurine
This elegant figure of a woman is one of many found at Tanágra, in Boiotia, central Greece. It dates from 330–320 BC.

KEY

- ▢ Shop and ticket office
- ▢ Cycladic art
- ▢ Ancient Greek art
- ▢ Temporary exhibitions
- ▢ Charles Polítis collection

Fourth floor

Stairs and elevator to all floors

★ **White Lekythos**
This fine clay lekythos (funerary vase) is an example of white-ground vase-painting (see p60) and was used to contain embalming oil. It depicts a mourning woman taking offerings to a grave and dates from c.450 BC.

Bronze Askos
This elegant Hellenistic bronze wine jar dates from the 2nd century BC. The jar is so named because of its resemblance to the shape of a wineskin, or askos.

Entrance to main building via walkway

The first floor houses temporary exhibitions.

The original porch is the entrance to the Stathátos Mansion.

The ground floor is home to the Greek art collection of the Athens Academy. The glass, greenhouse-style roof at the back makes this a very light and airy floor.

STATHATOS MANSION
The "new" wing of the Museum of Cycladic Art was opened in 1992. It is housed in this elegant Neo-Classical building, once the home of Otho and Athiná Stathátos. It was designed and built by the architect Ernst Ziller in 1885.

The lower ground floor houses a café.

A 14th-century icon of St. Michael in the Byzantine Museum

Byzantine Museum ⓞ
Βυζαντινό Μουσείο

Vasilíssis Sofías 22, Plateía Rigílis, Kolonáki. **Map** 7 B1. █ 01 721 1027. ▄▄ 3, 8, 7, 13. ◯ 8:30 am–2:45pm Tue –Sun. ● main public hols. ▨ █ ground floor only.

ORIGINALLY CALLED the Villa Ilissia, this elegant, Florentine-style mansion was built between 1840 and 1848 by Stamátis Kleánthis for the Duchesse de Plaisance (1785–1854). This eccentric woman, wife of one of Napoleon's generals, was a key figure in Athens' society during the mid-19th century and a dedicated philhellene.

Collector Geórgios Sotírou converted the house into a museum in the 1930s with the help of architect Aristotélis Záchos. They transformed the entrance into a monastic court, incorporating a copy of a fountain from a 4th-century AD mosaic in Dafní *(see pp152–3).* A modern annex (which is currently under construction) will soon enable the whole collection of icons and mosaics, sculptures and frescoes, and ecclesias-tical silverware to be on permanent display in the museum.

Spanning over 1,500 years of Byzantine art and architecture from the Greek diaspora, the ground floor exhibits run in chronological order. Three rooms have been cleverly created from fragments of now lost Byzantine churches. They are of three different periods: an early 5th-century three-aisled basilica, an 11th-century domed cruciform structure, and a post-Byzantine church. Icons are on display in these rooms. Elsewhere on the ground floor, the exhibits range from early Christian 4th-century basilica fragments from the Acropolis to ornate 15th-century sculptures from the Frankish occupation of Greece. Fine pieces to watch out for include a 4th–5th-century BC funerary stele from Aígina, depicting Orpheus surrounded by wild animals, and an unusual 10th–11th-century marble plaque of three apostles from Thessaloníki.

Funerary stele showing Orpheus with his lyre

The first floor is devoted to ecclesiastical objets d'art, including the *Epitaphios of Salonika*, an intricate 14th-century gold-threaded embroidery. There are also some magnificent frescoes that have been res-cued from churches in Náxos, Oropós, and Delphi. In addition, the first floor houses an unsurpassed collec-tion of icons from the Greek diaspora. Two of the most stunning icons are the *Galaktotrophousa* (Virgin and Child), painted in 1784 by Makários of Galatísta, a monk from Mount Athos, and the famous 14th-century mosaic icon, the *Episkepsis,* from Bithynia.

The *Episkepsis*, from the Byzantine Museum, depicting the Virgin and Child

ICONS IN THE ORTHODOX CHURCH

The word icon simply means "image" and has come to signify a holy image through associa-tion with its religious use. Subjects range from popular saints such as St. Andrew and St. Nicholas to lesser known martyrs, prophets, and archangels. The image of the Virgin and Child is easily the most popular and exalted. Icons are a prominent feature in the Greek Orthodox faith and appear in many areas of Greek life. You will see them in taxis and buses, on boats and in restaurants, as well as in homes and churches. An icon can be in fresco, a mosaic, or made from bone or metal. The most common form is a portable paint-ing in wax-based paints applied to wooden boards treated with gesso. The figures are arranged so that the eyes are clearly depicted and appear to be looking directly at the viewer of the icon. These works, often of great artistic skill, are unsigned, undated, and share a rigid conformity, right down to details of color, dress, gesture, and expression *(see pp18–19).* The icon painter is careful to catch every detail of a tradition that stretches back hundreds of years.

Puppet Theater from the Theatrical Museum

Museum of Cycladic Art ❽

See pp74–5.

Plateía Kolonakíou ❾
Πλατεία Κολονακίου

Kolonáki. **Map** 3 B5. 🚌 3, 7, 8,13.

Kolonaki square and its neighboring side streets are the most chic and sophisticated part of Athens. The area is often missed by those who restrict themselves to the ancient sites and the popular flea markets of Monastiráki. Also known as Plateía Filikís Etaireiás, the square is named after a small ancient column *(kolonáki)* found in the area. Celebrated for its designer boutiques and fashionable bars and cafés, stylish antique shops and art galleries, sumptuous *zacharoplastéia* (pastry shops) and *ouzerí*, it revels in its status as the city's most fashionable quarter *(see p116)*. The lively sidewalk cafés around the square each attract a particular devoted clientele. At one there may be rich kids drinking *frappé* (iced coffee) perched on their Harley-Davidson motorcycles. Another, such as the *Likovríssi*, will be full of an older crowd of intellectuals sipping coffee and discussing the ever popular subject of politics.

Benáki Museum ❿

See pp78–9.

Theatrical Museum ⓫
Μουσείο και Κέντρο Μελέτης του Ελληνικού Θεάτρου

Akadamías 50, Kéntro. **Map** 2 F4. 📞 01 362 9430. 🚌 3, 8, 13. 🕐 9am–2:30pm Mon–Fri. 🔴 Aug, Nov 17, main public hols. 🈺 ♿ limited. 🎫

Housed in the basement of a fine Neo-Classical building, this small museum traces Greek theatrical history from Classical times to the present. There are displays of original posters and programs, costumes, and designs from productions by influential directors such as Károlos Koun. There is also a colorful puppet theater. The dressing rooms of famous Greek actresses such as Eléni Papadáki and Elli Lampéti have been recreated to give an insight into their lives.

Perikles, from the Theatrical Museum

City of Athens Museum ⓬
Μουσείο της Πόλεως των Αθηνών

Paparrigopoúlou 7, Plateía Klafthmónos, Syntágma. **Map** 2 E5. 📞 01 324 6164. 🚌 1, 2, 4, 5, 9, 11, 12, 15, 18. 🕐 9am–1:30pm Mon–Wed, Fri & Sat. 🔴 main public hols. 🈺

King otto and Queen Amalia *(see p40)* lived in this modest mansion for seven years from 1831, until their new palace, today's Voulí parliament building *(see p112)*, was completed in 1838. It was joined to the neighboring house to create what was known as the Old Palace.

The palace was restored in 1980 as a museum devoted to royal memorabilia, furniture, and family portraits, maps, and prints. It offers a delightful look at life during the early years of King Otto's reign.

Exhibits include the manuscript of the 1843 Constitution, coats of arms from the Frankish (1205–1311) and Catalan (1311–88) rulers of Athens, and a scale model of the city as it was in 1842, made by architect Giánnis Travlós (1908–1985).

The museum also has a fine art collection, including Nikólaos Gýzis's oil painting *The Carnival in Athens* (1892) and a selection of watercolors by the English artists Edward Dodwell (1767–1832), Edward Lear (1812–88), and Thomas Hartley Cromek (1809–73).

Upstairs sitting room recreated in the City of Athens Museum

Benáki Museum ⑩
Μουσείο Μπενάκη

THIS OUTSTANDING MUSEUM was founded in 1931 by Antónis Benákis (1873–1954), the son of Emmanouil, a wealthy Greek who made his fortune in Egypt. Housed in an elegant Neo-Classical mansion, which was once the home of the Benáki family, the collection contains a diverse array of Greek arts and crafts, paintings and jewelry, local costumes, and political memorabilia that spans over 2,000 years, from the 3rd century BC to the 20th century.

Flag of Ydra
The spear and cross represent the instruments of Christ's crucifixion and the devout nature of the people of Ydra.

Lecture hall

Bridal Cushion
This ornate embroidered cushion comes from Epirus and dates from the 18th century. It depicts a bridal procession, with ornamental flowers in the background.

Roof garden

Second floor

Auditorium

Ship Pendant
This early 18th-century gold pendant is enameled with blue and green and set with pearls. It comes from the island of Pátmos and is thought to be Venetian.

Atrium

★ **El Faiyúm Portrait**
This Egyptian portrait of a young man, painted on linen, dates from the 3rd century AD.

Chatzikyriákos-Gkíkas gallery

Entrance

KEY TO FLOOR PLAN

- ☐ Ground floor
- ☐ First floor
- ☐ Second floor
- ☐ Third floor
- ☐ Nonexhibition space

Third floor

Silver Ciborium
Used to contain consecrated bread, this elegant piece of ecclesiatical silverware is dated 1667 and comes from Edirne, in Turkey.

★ Detail of Wood Decoration
This intricately painted and carved piece of wooden paneling comes from a mansion in Siátista, in western Macedonia. It dates from the 18th century.

GALLERY GUIDE
The museum is currently undergoing a reorganization, but the contents of each floor will remain largely unchanged. The ground floor collection is arranged into different periods and ranges from Neolithic to late Byzantine art. The first floor exhibits are organized geographically and are from Asia Minor, mainland Greece, and the islands. There is also a collection of ecclesiastical silverware and jewelry. The second floor has items relating to Greek spiritual life, economy, and social life, and the third floor concentrates on the liberation of Greece. The Chatzikyriákos-Gkíkas gallery, a few streets away, houses works by the late artist and sculptor.

Ground floor

First floor

Bowl from Paphos
Dating from the 13th century AD, this colorful bowl originates from Cyprus. The dancing figure is holding rattles.

★ Icon of St. Anne
The icon of St. Anne was painted in the 17th century. She is carrying the Virgin Mary as a child, who is holding a white lily, symbol of purity.

STAR EXHIBITS

★ El Faiyúm Portrait

★ Icon of St. Anne

★ Detail of Wood Decoration

Neo-Classical façade of the National Historical Museum

National Historical Museum ⑬
Εθνικό Ιστορικό Μουσείο

Stadíou 11, Syntágma. **Map** 2 F5. 🛈 *01 323 7617*. 🚃 *1, 2, 4, 5, 9, 10, 11, 18*. ◗ *9am–1:30pm Tue–Sun.* ◕ *main public hols.* 🎫

DESIGNED BY French architect François Boulanger (1807–75), this museum was originally built as the first home of the Greek parliament. Queen Amalía laid the foundation stone in 1858, but it was 13 years later that it became the first permanent site of the Greek parliament. The country's most famous prime ministers have sat in the imposing chamber of the Old Parliament of the Hellenes, including Charílaos Trikoúpis and Theodóros Diligiánnis, who was assassinated on the steps at the front of the building in 1905. The parliament moved to its present-day site in the Voulí building on Plateía Syntágmatos *(see p112)* after the Voulí was renovated in 1935.

In 1961, the building was opened as the National Historical Museum, owned by the Historical and Ethnological Society of Greece. Founded in 1882, the purpose of the society is to collect objects that illuminate the history of modern Greece. The museum covers all the major events of Greek history from the Byzantine period to the 20th century in a chronological display. Venetian armor, traditional regional costumes and jewelry, and figureheads from the warships used during the Revolution in 1821 are just some examples of the many exhibits on display.

The collection also focuses on major parliamentary figures, philhellenes, and leaders in the War of Independence, displaying such items as Byron's sword, the weapons of Theódoros Kolokotrónis (1770–1843), King Otto's throne, and the pen that was used by Elefthérios Venizélos to sign the Treaty of Sèvres in 1920. The revolutionary memoirs of General Makrigiánnis (1797–1864) can also be seen. Among the numerous paintings on view is a fine rare woodcut of the Battle of Lepanto (1571), the work of Bonastro.

Outside the building is a copy of Lázaros Sóchos's statue of Kolokotrónis on horseback, made in 1900, the original of which is in Náfplio *(see pp182–3)*, the former capital of Greece. There is a dedication on the statue in Greek, which reads "Theódoros Kolokotrónis 1821. Ride on, noble commander, through the centuries, showing the nations how slaves may become free men."

Statue of General Theódoros Kolokotrónis

Kapnikaréa ⑭
Καπνικαρέα

Corner of Ermoú & Kalamiótou, Monastiráki. **Map** 6 D1. 🛈 *01 322 4462*. Ⓜ *Monastiráki.* ◗ *8am–2pm daily, 4:30–9:30pm Tue, Thu & Fri.* ◕ *main public hols.*

THIS CHARMING 11th-century Byzantine church was rescued from demolition in 1834, thanks to the timely intervention of King Ludwig of Bavaria. Stranded in the middle of a square between Ermoú and Kapnikaréa streets, it is surrounded by the modern office buildings and shops of Athens' garment district.

Traditionally called the Church of the Princess, its foundation is attributed to Empress Irene, who ruled the Byzantine empire from AD 797 to 802. She is revered as a saint in the Greek church for her efforts in restoring icons to the empire's churches.

The true origins of the name "Kapnikaréa" are unknown, although according to some sources, the church was named after its founder, a "hearth-tax gatherer" *(kapnikaréas)*. Hearth tax was imposed on buildings by the Byzantines. Restored by the University of Athens in the 1950s, the dome of the church is supported by four Roman columns. Frescoes by Fótis Kóntoglou (1895–1965) were painted during the restoration, including one of the Virgin and Child. Much of Kóntoglu's work is also on display in the National Gallery of Art *(see p73)*.

The dome and main entrance of the Byzantine Kapnikaréa

Athenian Neo-Classical Architecture

NEO-CLASSICISM flourished in the 19th century, when the German architects commissioned by King Otto to build the capital in the 1830s turned to this fashionable European style. Among those commissioned were the von Hansen brothers, Christian and Theophil, and also Ernst Ziller. As a result of their planning, within 50 years a modern city had emerged, with elegant administrative

National Bank, built in the 1890s

buildings, squares, and tree-lined avenues. In its early days Neo-Classicism had imitated the grace of the buildings of ancient Greece, using marble columns, sculptures, and decorative detailing. In later years, it evolved into an original Greek style. Grand Neo-Classicism is seen at its best in the public buildings along Panepistimíou; its domestic adaptation can be seen in the houses of Pláka.

Schliemann's House (also known as Ilíou Mélathron, the Palace of Ilium, or Troy) was built in 1878 by Ziller. The interior is decorated with frescoes and mosaics of mythological subjects. It is now home to the Numismatic Museum (**Map** 2 F5).

The National Theater was built between 1882 and 1890. Ernst Ziller used a Renaissance-style exterior with arches and Doric columns for George I's Royal Theater. Inspired by the Public Theater of Vienna, its interior was very modern for its time (**Map** 2 D3).

The National Library was designed by Theophil von Hansen in 1887 in the form of a Doric temple with two side wings. Built of Pentelic marble, it houses over half a million books, including many illuminated manuscripts and rare first editions (**Map** 2 F4).

Athens Academy was designed by Theophil von Hansen and built between 1859 and 1887. Statues of Apollo and Athena, and seated figures of Socrates and Plato, convey a Classical style, as do the Ionic capitals and columns. Inside the building, the Academy hall has beautiful frescoes that depict scenes from the myth of Prometheus (**Map** 2 F4).

The University of Athens was designed by Christian von Hansen. This fine building, completed in 1864, has an Ionic colonnade and a portico frieze depicting the resurgence of arts and sciences under the reign of King Otto. A symbol of wisdom, the Sphinx is connected with Athens through the Oedipus legend (see p221). Having solved the riddle of the Sphinx, Oedipus was later befriended by the Athenians. Other statues on the façade include Patriarch Gregory V, a martyr of the War of Independence (**Map** 2 F4).

CENTRAL ATHENS SOUTH

SOUTHERN ATHENS is dominated by the Acropolis and is home to the buildings that were at the heart of ancient Athens. Pláka and Monastiráki still revel in their historical roots as the oldest inhabited areas of the city and are full of Byzantine churches and museums. Nestling among the restored Neo-Classical houses are grocery stores,

Relief from Panagía Gorgoepíkoös

icon painters, and open-air tavernas. In the busy streets of Monastiráki's flea market, food vendors, gypsies, and street musicians pro-vide the atmosphere of a middle eastern bazaar. Southeast of Plateía Syntág-matos are the National Gardens, the city center's tree-filled park. For infor-mation on getting around Athens, see pages 322–5.

SIGHTS AT A GLANCE

Museums and Galleries
Greek Folk Art Museum **16**
Jewish Museum of Greece **17**
Kanellópoulos Museum **8**
Kyriazópoulos Folk Ceramic
 Museum **1**
Municipal Art Gallery **4**
Museum of Greek Popular
 Musical Instruments **10**
University of Athens
 Museum **9**

Ancient Sites
Acropolis pp94–101 **7**
Ancient Agora pp90–91 **6**
Kerameikós pp88–9 **5**
Temple of Olympian Zeus **18**
Tower of the Winds pp86–7 **2**

Churches
Agios Nikólaos Ragavás **13**
Mitrópoli **12**
Panagía Gorgoepíkoös p105 **11**
Russian Church of
 St. Nicodemus **19**

Historic Districts
Anafiótika **14**

Markets
Flea Market **3**

Squares and Gardens
National Gardens **21**
Plateía Lysikrátous **15**
Plateía Syntágmatos **20**

**Historic Buildings
and Monuments**
Kallimármaro Stadium **23**
Presidential Palace **22**

Cemeteries
First Cemetery of Athens **24**

KEY

Street-by-Street:
Monastiráki *pp84–5*

Street-by-Street:
Pláka *pp102–103*

M   Metro

P   Parking

0 meters   500
0 yards   500

◁ **The remaining columns of the ancient Temple of Olympian Zeus**

Street-by-Street: Monastiráki

THIS OLD AREA OF THE CITY takes its name from the
little sunken monastery in Plateía Monastirakíou.
The former heart of Ottoman Athens, Monastiráki is still
home to the bazaar and market stalls selling everything
from junk to jewelry. The Fethiye Mosque and the
Tsistaráki Mosque, home of the Kyriazópoulos
Museum, stand as reminders of the area's
eastern past. Roman influences are also
strong in Monastiráki. The area borders
the Roman Agora and includes the
remains of Emperor Hadrian's library
and the unique Tower of the Winds,
a Hellenistic water clock. Monastiráki
mixes the atmospheric surroundings
of ancient ruins with the excitement
of bargaining in the bazaar.

Flea Market
*Plateía Avissynías is the heart
of the flea market, which extends
through the surrounding streets. It is
particularly popular on Sundays* ❸

Ifaístou is named after
Hephaistos, the god of fire and
metal craftmanship. Areos is
named after Ares, the war god.

**Monastiráki
metro station**

KEY

− − − Suggested route

STAR SIGHT

★ **Tower of the Winds**

0 meters		50
0 yards		50

**The Fethiye
Mosque** is situa-
ted in the corner
of the Roman
agora. It was built
by the Turks in
the late 15th cen-
tury to celebrate
their occupation
of Athens.

Ancient Agora
(see pp90–91)

LOCATOR MAP
*See Athens Street Finder
maps 2, 6*

Pantánassa church is the "little monastery" *(monastiráki)* that gave the area its name. Also known as the church of the Dormition of the Virgin, it is thought to have been built in the 10th century. It is situated opposite the metro station, on the east side of Plateía Monastirakíou.

Kyriazópoulos Folk Ceramic Museum
Housed in the old Tsistaráki Mosque, this museum is part of the Museum of Greek Folk Art. Originally opened in 1974, it contains around 800 fine ceramics originating from all over Greece ❶

Pláka *(see pp102–3)* →

Hadrian's Library was built in the years following AD 132. It measured 120 m (390 ft) by 80 m (260 ft). Smaller rooms and a garden with a pool were contained in the complex, in addition to the vast library itself.

★ **Tower of the Winds**
An unusual, octagonal design, this tower was built as a water clock and weather vane by the architect Andronikos Kyrrestes in the 1st century BC ❷

Kyriazópoulos Folk Ceramic Museum ❶
Μουσείο Ελληνικής Λαϊκής Τέχνης, Συλλογή Κεραμεικών Β. Κυριαζόπουλου

Tsistaráki Mosque, Areos 1, Monastiráki. **Map** 6 D1. [☎] *01 324 2066.* Ⓜ *Monastiráki.* ◷ *9am–2:30pm Mon & Wed–Sun.* ◉ *main public hols.* ▨

THIS COLORFUL collection of ceramics was donated to the Greek Folk Art Museum in 1974 by Professor Vasíleios Kyriazópoulos. Now an annex of the Folk Art Museum, the Kyriazópoulos Folk Ceramic Museum is housed in the imposing Tsistaráki Mosque (or the Mosque of the Lower Fountain). Of the hundreds of pieces on display, many are of the type still used today in the traditional Greek kitchen, such as terra-cotta water jugs from Aígina, earthenware oven dishes from Sífnos, and storage jars from Thessaly and Chíos. There are also some ceramic figures and plates, based on mythological and folk stories, crafted by Minás Avramídis and Dimítrios Mygdalínos, who came from Asia Minor in the 1920s.

The mosque itself is of as much interest as its contents. It was built in 1759 by the newly appointed Turkish *voivode* Tsistaráki. The *voivode* was the civil

Ceramic of a young girl from Asia Minor

governor who possessed complete powers over the law courts and the police. He collected taxes for his own account, but also had to pay for the sultan's harem and the treasury. His workmen dynamited the 17th column of the Temple of Olympian Zeus *(see p11?)* in order to make lime to be used for the stucco work on the mosque. Destruction of ancient monuments was forbidden by Turkish law, and this act of vandalism was the downfall of Tsistaráki. He was exiled the same year. The mosque has now been well restored after earthquake damage in 1981.

Tower of the Winds ❷
Αέρηδες

Within Roman Agora ruins, Pláka. **Map** 6 D1. [☎] *01 324 5220.* Ⓜ *Monastiráki.* ◷ *8:30am–3pm Tue–Sun.* ◉ *main public hols.* ▨ [♿]

THE REMARKABLE Tower of the Winds is set within the ruins of the Roman Agora. Constructed from marble in the 2nd century BC by the Syrian astronomer Andronikos Kyrrestes, it was built as a combined weather vane and water clock. The name comes from the external friezes, personifying the eight winds. Sundials are etched into the walls beneath each relief.

The tower is well preserved, standing today at over 12 m (40 ft) high with a diameter of 8 m (26 ft). Still simply called Aérides ("the winds") by Greeks today, in the Middle Ages it was thought to be either the school or prison of Socrates, or even the tomb of Philip II of Macedon *(see p240)*. It was at last correctly identified as the Horologion (water clock) of Andronikos in the 17th century. All that remains today of its elaborate water clock are the origins of

a complex system of water pipes and a circular channel cut into the floor that can be seen inside the tower.

The west and southwest faces of the Tower of the Winds

NORTH

Northwest entrance

Relief carving of mythological wind

Metal rod casting shadow

Lines of sundial carved into wall of tower

N NE NW E W SW SE S Reservoir

This floor plan of the tower shows the compass direction of the building's eight sides. External friezes personify each of the eight winds.

NORTHWEST

Boreas blows the cold north wind through a large conch shell.

Skiron scatters glowing ashes from a bronze vessel.

WEST

Zephyros is a seminaked youth scattering flowers.

Flea Market 3
Παζάρι

From Plateía Monastirakíou to
Plateía Avyssinías, Pláka. **Map** 5 C1.
M *Thiseío.* ◯ *8am–2pm Sun.*

A BANNER WELCOMES visitors to Athens' famous flea market, past the ubiquitous tourist trinket shops of Adrianoú and Pandrósou streets. For the locals, the true heart of the market lies just west of Plateía Monastirakíou, in Plateía Avyssinías and its warren of surrounding streets.

On Sunday mornings when stores are closed, the market itself bursts into action. Traders set out their bric-a-brac on stalls and the pavement and many bargains can be found,

Shoppers browsing in Athens' lively flea market

especially the colorful handwoven woolen cloths and the many bangles and beads sold by hippies. More expensive items are also on sale, including brassware, leatherware, and silverware.

During the week the shops in the surrounding area are

open and filled with much the same as the Sunday stalls. Individual shops each have their own specialties, so hunt around before making a purchase. You can buy almost anything, from antiques and old books to taverna chairs and army surplus gear.

*The **southwest wind**, Lips, heralds a swift voyage. The reliefs show that each wind was given a personality according to its characteristics, and each promises different conditions. Gentle Zephyros and chilly Boreas, mentioned in Western literature and represented in art and sculpture, are the best known of these.*

Whirling dervishes used the tower as a monastery in the mid-18th century. The dervishes were a Muslim order of ascetics. The tower's occupants became a popular attraction for Grand Tour visitors who came to witness the weekly ritual of a hypnotic dance, which is known as the sema.

The east- and north-facing sides each contain a hole that lets light into the otherwise dark interior of the tower.

SOUTHWEST	SOUTH	SOUTHEAST	EAST	NORTHEAST

Lips holds the *aphlaston* (or stern ornament) of a ship as he steers.

Notos is the bearer of rain, emptying a pitcher of water.

Euros is a bearded old man, warmly wrapped in a cloak.

Apeliotes is a young man bringing fruits and grain.

Kaikias empties a shield full of icy hailstones on those below.

Déspoina T K, by Giánnis Mitarákis, in the Municipal Art Gallery

Municipal Art Gallery ❹
Πινακοθήκη του Δήμου Αθηναίων

Plateía Koumoundoúrou, Omónoia.
Map 1 C4. 📞 *01 324 3023*.
Ⓜ *Omónoia.* ⭕ *Jul–Aug: 9am–1pm Sun–Fri; Sep–Jun: 9am–1pm, 5–8:30pm Mon–Fri, 9am–1pm Sun.* ⚫ *Oct 3, main public hols.* 🎫

THIS LITTLE-VISITED museum has one of the finest archive collections of modern Greek art. Designed by architect Panagíotis Kálkos in 1872, the home of the museum is the old Neo-Classical Foundling Hospital. It was built to cope with the city's population explosion toward the end of the 19th century; unwanted babies were left outside the main entrance to be cared for by hospital staff.

The Municipality of Athens has been amassing the collection since 1923. It now offers a fine introduction to the diverse styles of modern Greek artists. Many paintings are passionate reflections on the Greek landscape, such as Dímos Mpraésas's (1878–1967) landscapes of the Cyclades, or Konstantínos Parthénis's (1882–1964) paintings of olive and cypress trees.

There are also portraits by Giánnis Mitarákis and still lifes by Theófrastos Triantafyllídis. Paintings such as Nikólaos Kartsonákis's *Street Market* (1939) also reveal the folk roots that are at the heart of much modern Greek art.

Kerameikós ❺
Κεραμεικός

THIS ANCIENT CEMETERY has been a burial ground since the 12th century BC. The Panathenaic procession, which took place every four years, passed through the Sacred Gate, and along the Sacred Way to Eleusis *(see pp156–7)*. Most of the graves remaining today are along the Street of the Tombs. The sculptures excavated in the early 1900s are in the National Archaeological Museum *(see pp68–71)* and the Oberlander Museum; however, plaster copies of the originals can be seen in situ.

Grave Stele of Hegeso
This is from the family burial plot belonging to Koroibos of Melite. It shows his wife, Hegeso, admiring her jewels with a servant and dates from the late 5th century BC.

Precinct of Aristion

STREET OF THE TOMBS

The Precinct of the Lysimachides contains a marble dog, originally one of a pair.

The Sanctuary of Hekate was sacred to the ancient goddess of the underworld. It contained an altar and votive offerings.

Oberlander Museum

South terrace

★ **Tomb of Dionysios of Kollytos**
This fine tomb belongs to a rich treasurer. A bull often represents the god Dionysos.

STAR MONUMENTS

★ **Tomb of Dionysios of Kollytos**

★ **Stele of Demetria and Pamphile**

STREET OF THE TOMBS

Most of the monuments in the Street of the Tombs date from the 4th century BC. The different styles, from the lavish stelae (relief sculptures) to the simple *kioniskoi* (small columns), all reveal the dignity that is typical of Greek funerary art.

LOCATOR MAP

This tumulus was the burial place of an old Attic family dating from the 6th century BC.

Tomb of Hipparete

Eridanos River

The Sacred Way
led from the Acropolis (see pp94–7) to ancient Eleusis (see pp156–7).

Sacred Gate, Acropolis

South Hill

Stele of Dexileos
Dexileos was a young man killed in 394 BC during the Corinthian War. The son of Lysanias, he is seen on the relief slaying an enemy.

Loutrophoros of Hegetor
The farewell scene on this two-handled vase, used to contain embalming oil, is typical of the less ornate style of commemorative funerary art.

★ **Stele of Demetria and Pamphile**
This moving sculpture shows the seated Pamphile with her sister Demetria behind her. This was one of the last ornate stelae to be made in the late 4th century BC.

VISITORS' CHECKLIST

Ermou 148, Thiseio. **Map** 1 B5.
[C] 01 346 3552. [M] *Thissio*.
[○] 8:30am–3pm Tue–Sun.
[●] Jan 1, Mar 25, Easter Sun,
May 1, Dec 25, 26. [&] [&] [○]

[○] Oberlander Museum
This museum, opened in 1961, is named after Gustav Oberlander (1867–1936), a German-American industrialist whose donations helped fund excavations in the 1930s. In Gallery 1, there are some large fragments from grave stelae found incorporated into the Dipylon and Sacred Gates. These include a marble sphinx (c.550 BC) that once crowned a grave stele. Galleries 2 and 3 offer an array of huge Proto-Geometric and Geometric amphorae and black-figure *lekythoi* (funerary vases). The most moving exhibits come from children's graves and include pottery toy horses and terra-cotta dolls. There are also examples of some of the 7,000 *ostraka* (voting tablets) (see pp90–91) found in the bed of the Eridanos River. Among the superb painted pottery, there is a red-figure *hydria* (water vase) of Helen of Troy and a *lekythos* of Dionysos with satyrs.

Winged sphinx from grave stele

Geometric funerary amphora from the Oberlander Museum

Ancient Agora ⑥
Αρχαία Αγορά

Voting lot

THE AGORA, or market-place, formed the political heart of ancient Athens from 600 BC. Democracy was practiced in the *Bouleuterion* (Council) and the law courts, and in open meetings. Socrates was indicted and executed in the state prison here in 399 BC. The theater, schools, and stoas filled with shops also made this the center of social and commercial life. Even the city mint that produced Athens' silver coins was here. The American School of Classical Studies began excavations of the ancient Agora in the 1930s, and since then the vast remains of a complex array of public buildings have been revealed.

View across the Agora from the south, showing the reconstructed Stoa of Attalos on the right

The Panathenaic Way was named after the Great Panathenaia festival, which took place every four years.

Library of Pantainos

Monopteros temple

Triton statues

Temple of Ares

Altar of the twelve gods

Stoa of Zeus Eleutherios

Hellenistic temple

Temple of Apollo Patroös

Odeion of Agrippa
This statue of a triton (half god, half fish) once adorned the façade of the Odeion of Agrippa. It dates from AD 150 and is now in the Agora museum.

RECONSTRUCTION OF THE ANCIENT AGORA
This shows the Agora as it was in c.AD 200, viewed from the northwest. The main entrance to the Agora at this time was via the Panathenaic Way, which ran across the site from the Acropolis in the southeast to the Kerameikos in the northwest.

0 meters

0 yards   50

Stoa of Attalos
This colonnaded building was reconstructed in the mid-20th century as a museum to house finds from the ancient Agora.

Statue of Hadrian
Hadrian was Emperor of Rome from AD 117–38. Athens was under his authority. The statue dates from the 2nd century AD.

VISITORS' CHECKLIST

Main entrance at Adriánou, Monastiráki. **Map** 5 C1.
[C] 01 321 0185. [M] *Thiseío, Monastiráki.* **Museum & site**
[ ] 8:30am–2:30pm Tue–Sun, noon–3pm Good Fri. ● *Jan 1, Mar 25, Easter Sun, May 1, Dec 25, 26.* limited.

Ostrakon condemning Hippokrates to exile

Southeast temple

The middle stoa housed shops.

Altar of Zeus

Southwest temple

Heliaia

Southwest fountain

Latrines

The Tholos was the Council headquarters.

Bouleuterion, or Council chamber

Monument of the Eponymous Heroes

Oil flask in the Archaic style

Metroön

Arsenal

Hephaisteion
This temple, also known as the Theseion, is the best-preserved building on the site. It was built c.449–440 BC.

Stoa of Attalos

This fine building was rebuilt between 1953 and 1956, helped by a huge donation from John D. Rockefeller, Jr. An impressive two-story stoa, or roofed arcade, founded by King Attalos of Pergamon (ruled 159–138 BC), it dominated the eastern quarter of the Agora until it was burned down by the Heruli tribe in AD 267. Reconstructed using the original foundations and ancient materials, it now contains a museum whose exhibits reveal the great diversity and sophistication of ancient life. Artifacts include rules from the 2nd-century AD Library of Pantainos, the text of a law against tyranny from 337 BC, bronze and stone lots used for voting, and a *klepsydra* (water clock) used for timing speeches. *Ostraka* (voting potsherds on which names were inscribed) bear such famous names as Themistokles and Aristeides the Just, the latter banished, or ostracized, in 482 BC. More everyday items, such as terra-cotta toys and portable ovens, and hobnails and sandals found in a shoemaker's shop, are equally fascinating. Also on display are some beautiful black-figure vases and an unusual oil flask molded into the shape of a kneeling boy.

Acropolis **❼**

Ακρόπολη

I N THE MID-5TH CENTURY BC, Perikles persuaded the Athenians to begin a grand program of new building work in Athens that has come to represent the political and cultural achievements of Greece. The work transformed the Acropolis with three contrasting temples and a monumental gateway. The Theater of Dionysos on the south slope was developed further in the 4th century BC, and the Theater of Herodes Atticus was added in the 2nd century AD.

LOCATOR MAP

★ Porch of the Caryatids
These statues of women were used in place of columns on the south porch of the Erechtheion. The originals, four of which can be seen in the Acropolis Museum, have been replaced by casts.

An olive tree now grows where Athena first planted her tree in a competition against Poseidon.

The Propylaia was built in 437–432 BC to form a new entrance to the Acropolis *(see p96)*.

★ Temple of Athena Nike
This temple to Athena of Victory is on the west side of the Propylaia. It was built in 427–424 BC (see p96).

The Beule Gate was the first entrance to the Acropolis *(see p96)*.

Pathway to Acropolis from ticket office

STAR SIGHTS

- **★ Parthenon**
- **★ Porch of the Caryatids**
- **★ Temple of Athena Nike**

Theater of Herodes Atticus
Also known as the Odeion of Herodes Atticus, this superb theater was originally built in AD 161. It was restored in 1955 and is used today for outdoor concerts (see p100).

◁ **The Porch of the Caryatids on the Erechtheion**

★ **Parthenon**
Although few sculptures are left on this famous temple to Athena, some can still be admired, such as this one from the east pediment (see pp98–9).

Acropolis Museum *(p97)*

The Monument of Thrasyllos was one of many *choregic* monuments erected by sponsors of successful dramatic performances *(see p100)*.

Panagíai Spiliótissa is a chapel cut into the Acropolis rock itself *(see p100)*.

Shrine of Asklepios

Stoa of Eumenes

The Acropolis rock was an easily defended site. It has been in use for nearly 5,000 years.

Theater of Dionysos
This figure of the comic satyr Seilenos can be seen here. The theater visible today was built by Lykourgos in 342–326 BC (see p100).

TIMELINE

3000 BC First settlement on the Acropolis during Neolithic period

AD 51 St. Paul delivers sermon on the Areopagos hill

480 BC All buildings of Archaic period destroyed by the Persians

AD 267 Germanic Heruli tribe destroy Acropolis

St. Paul

3000 BC	2000 BC	1000 BC	AD 1	AD 1000

1200 BC Cyclopean wall built to replace original ramparts

510 BC Delphic Oracle declares Acropolis a holy place of the gods, banning habitation by mortals

447–432 BC Construction of the Parthenon under Perikles

AD 1687 Parthenon damaged by Venetians

Perikles (495–429 BC)

AD 1987 Restoration of the Erechtheion completed

Exploring the Acropolis

Statue of
Mourning
Athena

O NCE THROUGH the first entrance, the Beule Gate, straight ahead is the Propylaia, the grand entrance to the temple complex. Before going through here, it is worth exploring the Temple of Athena Nike, on the right. Beyond the Propylaia are the Erechtheion and the Parthenon *(see pp98–9)*, which dominate the top of the rock. There are also stunning views of Athens itself from the Acropolis. Since 1975, access to all the temple precincts has been banned to prevent further damage. Buildings located at the foot of the Acropolis and the hills immediately to the west are covered on pages 100–101.

View of the Acropolis from the southwest

⌂ Beule Gate

The gate is named after the French archaeologist Ernest Beulé, who discovered it in 1852. It was built in AD 267 after the raid of the Heruli, a Germanic people, as part of the Roman Acropolis fortifications. It incorporates stones from the choregic monument *(see p109)* of Nikias that was situated near the Stoa of Eumenes. Parts of the original monument's dedication are still visible over the architrave. There is also an inscription identifying a Roman, Flavius Septimius Marcellinus, as

The eastern end of the Erechtheion

donor of the gateway. In 1686, when the Turks destroyed the Temple of Athena Nike, they used the marble to build a bastion for artillery over the gate.

⌂ Temple of Athena Nike

This small temple was built in 427–424 BC to commemorate the Athenians' victories over the Persians. The temple frieze has representative scenes from the Battle of Plataia (479 BC). Designed by Kallikrates, the temple stands on a 9.5-m (31-ft) bastion. It has been used as both observation post and an ancient shrine to the goddess of Victory, Athena Nike, of whom there is a remarkable sculpture situated on the balustrade. Legend records the temple site as the place from which King Aegeus threw himself into the sea, believing that his son Theseus had been killed in Crete by the Minotaur. Built

of Pentelic marble, the temple has four Ionic columns 4 m (13 ft) high at each portico end. It was reconstructed in 1834–8, after being destroyed in 1686 by the Turks. On the point of collapse in 1935, it was again dismantled and reconstructed according to information resulting from more recent research.

⌂ Propylaia

Work began on this enormous entrance to the Acropolis in 437 BC. Although the outbreak of the Peloponnesian War in 432 BC curtailed its completion, its architect Mnesikles created a building admired throughout the ancient world. The Propylaia comprises a rectangular central building divided by a wall into two porticoes. These were punctuated by five entrance doors, rows of Ionic and Doric columns, and a vestibule with a blue-coffered ceiling decorated with gold stars. Two wings flank the main building. The north wing was home to the *pinakothíki*, an art gallery.

During its checkered history – later as archbishop's residence, Frankish palace, and Turkish fortress and armory – parts of the temple have had destructive accidents; it even suffered the misfortune of a lightning strike in 1656 and the explosion of the Turkish gunpowder *(see p98)*.

⌂ Erechtheion

Built between 421 and 406 BC, the Erechtheion is situated on the most sacred site of the Acropolis. It is said to be where Poseidon left his trident marks in a rock and Athena's olive tree sprouted in their battle for possession of the city. Named after Erechtheus, one of the mythical kings of Athens, the temple was a sanctuary to both Athena Polias and Erechtheus-Poseidon.

Famed for its elegant and extremely ornate Ionic architecture and caryatid columns in the shape of women, this extraordinary monument is built on different levels. The large rectangular cella was divided into three rooms. One contained the holy olive wood statue of Athena Polias. The cella was bounded by north, east, and south porticoes. The south is the Porch of the Caryatids, the maiden statues that are now in the Acropolis Museum.

The Erechtheion complex has been used for a range of purposes, including a harem for the wives of the Turkish *disdar* (commander) in 1463. It was almost completely destroyed by a Turkish shell in 1827 during the War of Independence *(see pp40–41)*. Recent restoration has caused heated disputes: holes have been filled with new marble, and copies have been made to replace original features that have been removed to the safety of the museum.

A youth leading a cow to sacrifice, from the Parthenon's north frieze

Acropolis Museum

Built below the level of the Parthenon, this museum is located in the southeast corner of the site. Opened in 1878, it was reconstructed after World War II to accommodate a collection devoted to finds from the Acropolis. Treasures include fine statues from the 5th century BC and well-preserved segments of the Parthenon frieze.

The collection begins chronologically in **Rooms I, II**, and **III** with 6th-century BC works. Fragments of painted pedimental statues include mythological scenes of Herakles grappling with various monsters, ferocious lions devouring calves, and the more peaceful votive statue of the *Moschophoros*, or Calf-Bearer, portraying a young man carrying a calf on his shoulders (c.570 BC).

Room V houses a pediment from the old Temple of Athena showing part of a battle where the figures of Athena and Zeus against the Giants represent the Greek triumph over primitive forces. **Rooms IV** and **VI** contain a unique collection of *kórai* from c.550–500 BC. These were votive statues of maidens offered to Athena. They represent the development of ancient Greek art, depicting the move from the formal bearing of the *Peplos Kóre* to the more natural body movement of the *Kóre of Euthydikos* and *Almond-Eyed Kóre*. Other representative statues of this later period are the *Mourning Athena*, head of the *Blond Boy*, and the *Kritios Boy*.

Rooms VII and **VIII** contain, among other exhibits, fragments from the Erechtheion frieze and a well-preserved metope from the south side of

The *Moschophoros* (Calf-Bearer), a sculpture from the Archaic period

the Parthenon showing the battle between the Lapiths and centaurs. The remaining parts of the Parthenon frieze depict the Panathenaic procession, including the chariot and *apobates* (slaves riding the chariot horses), the *thallophoroi* (bearers of olive branches), and a sacrificial cow being led by youths.

Room IX ends the collection with four caryatids from the Erechtheion south porch. They are the only ones that remain in Athens and are carefully kept in a temperature-controlled environment.

THE ELGIN MARBLES

These famous sculptures from the Parthenon frieze, now in the British Museum in London, were acquired by Lord Elgin in 1801–3 from the occupying Turkish authorities. He sold them to the British nation for £35,000 in 1816. There is great controversy surrounding the Marbles. While some argue that it is better that they are carefully preserved in the British Museum, the Greek government does not accept the legality of the sale, and many agree with this, believing their true home is in Athens. A famous supporter of this cause was the Greek actress and politician, Melína Merkoúri, who died in 1994.

The newly arrived Elgin Marbles at the British Museum, in a painting by A Archer

The Parthenon
Ο Παρθενώνας

ONE OF THE WORLD'S most famous buildings, this temple was begun in 447 BC. It was designed by the architects Kallikrates and Iktinos, primarily to house the 12 m (40 ft) high statue of Athena Parthenos (Maiden), sculpted by Pheidias. Taking fifteen years to complete, the temple was dedicated to the goddess in 438 BC. Over the centuries, it has been used as a church, a mosque, and an arsenal and has suffered severe damage. Built as an expression of the glory of ancient Athens, it remains the city's emblem to this day.

View of the Parthenon today, from the west

Akroterion

The west cella was used as a treasury.

The external frieze consisted of triglyphs and metopes.

Marble walls concealed the cellas, or inner rooms.

Each column was constructed from fluted drums of marble. The fluting was added once the columns were in place.

The Elgin Marbles (see p97) were taken largely from the internal frieze.

Parthenon Frieze
The frieze, designed by Pheidias, ran around the inner wall of the Parthenon. The metopes (sections of the frieze) depicted myths and the Great Panathenaia festival, honoring Athena.

RECONSTRUCTION OF THE PARTHENON
This reconstruction, from the southeast, shows the Parthenon as it was in the 5th century BC. It was 70 m (230 ft) long and 30 m (100 ft) wide. The entablature of this peripteral temple (with a single row of columns around the edge) was painted in blue, red, and gold.

VEDUTA DEL CAST: D'ACROPOLIS DALLA PARTE DI TRAMONTANA.

Explosion of 1687
During the Venetian siege of the Acropolis, General Francesco Morosini bombarded the Parthenon with cannon-fire. The Turks were using the temple as an arsenal at the time, and the ensuing explosion demolished much of it, including the roof, the inner structure, and 14 of the outer columns.

Statue of Athena
The huge chryselephantine (ivory and gold) statue of Athena, patron goddess of Athens, was the focus of the Parthenon. This Roman copy is in the National Archaeological Museum (see pp68–71). During the Great Panathenaia festival the statue was adorned in a new robe made by the women of the city.

The internal columns were in two rows and Doric in style.

THE ILLUSION OF PERFECTION

Every aspect of the Parthenon was built on a 9:4 ratio to make the temple completely symmetrical. The sculptors also used visual trickery to counteract the laws of perspective. The illustration below is exaggerated to show the techniques they employed.

The base of the temple is higher in the middle than at the edges.

Entasis (a bulge in the middle) makes each column look straight.

Each column leans slightly inward.

The roof was made from Pentelic marble tiles supported on wooden rafters.

Entrance

The steps curved upward slightly at the center to make them appear level from a distance.

Southeast Corner
This corner shows the remains of the pediment sculptures and the vertical carvings of the triglyphs alternating with the faded metope carvings.

View of the East Cella
The cella was the inner room of the temple. In the case of the Parthenon, there were two – east and west. The east cella contained the enormous cult statue of Athena and the offerings bestowed upon it. The west cella was the back room, reserved for the priestess.

Around the Acropolis

Throne from the Theater of Dionysos

THE AREA AROUND THE ACROPOLIS was the center of public life in Athens. In addition to the Agora in the north *(see pp90–91)*, there were the two theaters on the south slope, used for drama festivals in honor of the god Dionysos. Political life was largely centered on the Pnyx and the Areopagos, the hills lying to the west of the Acropolis: the Assembly met on the former and murder trials were heard by a council of ex-magistrates on the latter. Other ancient remains and the Acropolis Study Center provide a fascinating insight into daily life in ancient Athens.

The remains of the Theater of Dionysos

⋔ Theater of Herodes Atticus

This small Roman theater seats 5,000 spectators and is still in use today. Built by the Roman consul Herodes Atticus between AD 161 and 174, in memory of his wife, the shape was hollowed out of the rocks on the southern slope of the Acropolis. The semicircular orchestra in front of the stage was repaved with alternating blue and white marble slabs in the 1950s. Behind the stage, its distinctive colonnade once contained statues of the nine Muses. The whole theater was originally enclosed by a cedarwood roof that gave better acoustics and allowed for all-weather performances. Today it is used for a range of entertainment, including plays and concerts, both classical and popular *(see p119)*.

⋔ Theater of Dionysos

Cut into the southern cliff face of the Acropolis, the Theater of Dionysos is the birthplace of Greek tragedy and was the first theater built of stone. Aeschylus, Sophocles,

Euripides, and Aristophanes all had their plays performed here, during the dramatic contests of the annual City Dionysia festival, when it was little more than a humble wood-and-earth affair. The theater was rebuilt in stone by the Athenian statesman Lykourgos between 342–326 BC, but the ruins that can be seen today are in part those of a much bigger structure, built by the Romans, that could seat 17,000. They used it as a gladiatorial arena and

added a marble balustrade with metal railings to protect spectators. In the 1st century AD, the Emperor Nero added the marble mosaic flooring depicting Dionysos's life, and the front row of thrones reserved for dignitaries, still in situ.

Other remains around the theater include two large Corinthian columns, all that is left of the *choregic* monument of Thrasyllos erected in 320 BC to celebrate the benefactor's team winning a drama festival. There is also a cave sacred to the goddess Artemis. This was converted into a chapel in the Byzantine era, dedicated to **Panagía i Spiliótissa** (Our Lady of the Cave), and was the place where mothers brought their sick children. The Sanctuary of Asklepios to the west, founded in 420 BC, was dedicated to the god of healing. Worshipers seeking a cure had to take part in purification rites before they could enter the temple precincts.

🔲 Acropolis Study Center

Makrygiánni 2–4, Makrygiánni.
📞 01 923 9381. 🕐 9am–2:45pm daily. ● main public hols. 🔳
This handsome Neo-Classical building acts as a research center and storehouse of historical information on the Acropolis. Exhibitions on permanent display include a scale model of the Parthenon and a complete representation of its frieze using plaster casts. On the upper floor there is a fascinating account of how and where the famous white Pentelic marble was quarried and brought to the Parthenon.

Interior of the chapel of Panagía i Spiliótissa, above the Theater of Dionysos

Areopagos Hill

There is little left to see on this low hill today, apart from the rough hewn, slippery steps and what are thought to be seats on its summit. The Areopagos was used by the Persians and Turks during their attacks on the Acropolis citadel and played an important role as the home of the Supreme Judicial Court in the Classical period. It takes its name, meaning the "Hill of Ares," from a mythological trial that took place here when the god Ares was acquitted of murdering the son of Poseidon. The nearby **Cave of the Furies** inspired the playwright Aeschylus *(see p57)* to set Orestes' trial here in his play *Eumenides* (The Furies). The hill also achieved renown in AD 51, when St. Paul delivered his sermon "On an unknown God" and gained his first convert, Dionysios the Areopagite, who subsequently became the patron saint of Athens.

Cross from Agios Dimítrios church

Pnyx Hill

Today's role for the Pnyx, as outdoor theater for multilingual sound-and-light performances, seems a sad fate for the home of 4th- and 5th century BC democracy. This is where the *Ekklesia* (citizens' assembly) met to discuss and vote upon all but the most important matters of state, until it lost its powers during Roman rule. In its heyday, 6,000 Athenians gathered 40 times a year to listen to speeches and make vital political decisions. Themistokles, Perikles, and Demosthenes all spoke from the *bema* (speaker's platform) that is still visible today. Carved out of the rock face, it formed the top step of a platform that doubled as a primitive altar to the god Zeus. There are also the remains of the huge retaining wall that was built to support the semicircular terraces that placed citizens on a level with the speakers. It completely surrounded the auditorium, which was 110 m (358 ft) high.

Agios Dimítrios

Dionysiou Areopagítou, south slope of Acropolis. ◯ *daily.* except Sun.
This Byzantine church is often called Agios Dimítrios Loumpardiáris, after an incident in 1656. The Turkish *disdar* (commander) at the time, Yusuf Aga, laid plans to fire a huge cannon called Loumpardiáris, situated by the Propylaia *(see p96)*, at worshipers in the church as they celebrated the feast day of Agios Dimítrios. However, the night before the feast, lightning struck the Propylaia, miraculously killing the commander and his family.

Filopáppos Hill

The highest summit in the south of Athens, at 147 m (482 ft), offers spectacular views of the Acropolis. It has always played a decisive defensive role in Athens' history – the general Demetrios Poliorketes built an important fort here overlooking the strategic Piraeus road in 294 BC, and Francesco Morosini bombarded the Acropolis from here in 1687. Popularly called

The Monument of Philopappus AD 114–116

The Asteroskopeíon on the Hill of the Nymphs

Filopáppos Hill after a monument still on its summit, it was also known to the ancient Greeks as the Hill of Muses or the Mouseion, because the tomb of Musaeus, a disciple of Orpheus, was traditionally held to be located here.

Built between AD 114–16, the Monument of Philopappus was raised by the Athenians in honor of Gaius Julius Antiochus Philopappus, a Roman consul and philhellene. Its unusual concave marble façade, 12 m (40 ft) high, contains niches with statues of Philopappus and his grandfather, Antiochus IV. A frieze around the monument depicts the arrival of Philopappus by chariot for his inauguration as Roman consul in AD 100.

Hill of the Nymphs

This 103-m (338-ft) high, treeclad hill takes its name from dedications found carved on rocks in today's Observatory Garden. The Asteroskopeíon (Observatory), built in 1842 by the German architect Theophil von Hansen, with funds from philanthropist Baron Sína, occupies the site of a sanctuary to nymphs associated with childbirth. The modern church of Agía Marína nearby has similar associations of childbirth; pregnant women used to slide effortlessly down a smooth rock near the church, in the hope of an equally easy labor.

Street-by-Street: Central Pláka

PLÁKA IS THE HISTORIC HEART of Athens. Even though only a few houses date back farther than the Ottoman period, it remains the oldest continually inhabited area of the city. One explanation of its name comes from the word *pliaka*, which was used to describe the area by Albanian soldiers in the service of the Turks who settled here in the 16th century. Despite the crowds of tourists and the many Athenians, who come to eat in the tavernas or browse in antique shops, it still retains the feel of a residential neighborhood.

Mitrópoli
Athens' cathedral was built in the second half of the 19th century ⑫

Thoukidídou
is named after the historian Thucydides (c.460– 400 BC).

★ **Panagía Gorgoepíkoös**
This tiny 12th-century church, also known as the Little Cathedral, has some beautiful carvings ⑪

Museum of Greek Popular Musical Instruments
A range of folk instruments is displayed in this museum, which was opened in 1991 ⑩

Monastiráki
(see pp84–5)

Acropolis
(see pp94–101)

University of Athens Museum
Occupying the university's original home, this museum has memorabilia from the university's early days, including these old medical artifacts ⑨

Ancient Agora
(see pp90–1)

Kanellópoulos Museum
Privately owned, this museum has exquisite works of art from all areas of the Hellenic world ⑧

Greek Folk Art Museum
Offering the best of Greek folk art,
this has everything from shadow
puppets to terra-cotta ornaments **16**

Plateía
Syntágmatos
(see p112)

LOCATOR MAP
See Street Finder maps 5–6

CENTRAL ATHENS NORTH

CENTRAL ATHENS SOUTH

0 meters 50
0 yards 50

**Agios Nikólaos
Ragavás**
*This 11th-century,
Byzantine chapel is
a popular location
for weddings* **13**

Plateía Lysikrátous
*Named after the monu-
ment in its center, this
square was a favorite
haunt of the poet Byron* **15**

KEY
– – – Suggested route

STAR SIGHT
★ **Panagía
Gorgoepíkoös**

Anafiótika
*The whitewashed houses and winding
streets resembling a Cycladic village
were built in the 19th century by
settlers from the island of Anáfi* **14**

Rempétika musicians, Museum of Greek Popular Musical Instruments

Kanellópoulos Museum ⑧

Μουσείο Κανελλόπουλου

Corner of Theorías & Panós, Pláka.
Map 6 D2. 📞 *01 321 2313.*
Ⓜ *Monastiráki.* ◯ *8:30am–3pm
Tue–Sun, noon–3pm Good Fri.*
● *Jan 1, Mar 25, Easter Sun, Dec 25,
26.* 🖼 📷

I
N AN IMMACULATELY restored
Neo-Classical town house,
this museum contains what
was the private collection of
wealthy collectors Pávlos and
Alexándra Kanellópoulos. A
varied collection of artifacts
from all over the Hellenistic
world, the three floors of exhibits include a selection of
coins, 6th-century BC helmets,
5th-century BC gold Persian
jewelry, and Attic vases. There
are also Cycladic
figurines, some

**Sculpture of a triton
from the Kanellópoulos Museum**

unusual terra-cotta figures of
actors in their theatrical masks,
and a fine 2nd-century AD El
Faiyúm portrait of a woman.
   A huge block of stone that
fell from the walls of the
Acropolis, so heavy that the
museum was built around it,
can be still be seen as an
exhibit on the ground floor.

University of Athens Museum ⑨

Μουσείο Ιστορίας του
Πανεπιστημίου Αθηνών

Thólou 5, Pláka. **Map** 6 E2.
📞 *01 324 0861.* Ⓜ *Monastiráki.*
◯ *Oct–May: 2:30–7pm Mon &
Wed, 9:30am–2:30pm Tue, Thu & Fri;
Jun–Sep: 5–9pm Mon & Wed.*
● *Aug & main public hols.*

T
HIS THREE-STORY house
was the first home of the
University of Athens. It
opened on May 3, 1837 with
52 students and 33 professors
in its first year. In
November 1841
the University
moved to its
new quarters,
and from 1922
the building was
home to many immigrant
families. While they were

there, a taverna known as
"The Old University" was
opened on the ground floor.
   In 1963 the building was
declared a National Monument.
Later reacquired by the university, the old building was
opened as a museum in 1974.
Today, the "Old University,"
as it is still known, has an
eclectic collection of memorabilia such as corporeal body
maps, anatomical models,
scientific instruments, and
medicine jars. There is also a
display about the university's
past professors and students.

Museum of Greek Popular Musical Instruments ⑩

Μουσείο Ελληνικών
Λαϊκών Μουσικών
Οργάνων

Diogénous 1–3, Aérides. **Map** 6 D1
📞 *01 325 0198.* Ⓜ *Monastiráki.*
◯ *10am–2pm Tue, Thu–Sun, noon–
7pm Wed (summer), noon–6pm Wed
(winter).* ● *Nov 17, main public hols.*

C
RETAN MUSICOLOGIST ROÍVOS
Anogianákis donated over
1,200 musical instruments from
his impressive collection to the
Greek State in 1978. In 1991
this study center and museum
was opened, devoted to the
history of popular Greek
music, including Anogianákis's
collection. The museum traces
the development of different
styles of island music and the
arrival of *rempétika* (Greek
"blues") from Smyrna in 1922.
   Instruments from all over
Greece are displayed on the
three floors, with recordings
and headphones available at
every exhibit. The basement
contains a selection of church
and livestock bells, as well
as water whistles, wooden
clappers, and flutes, which
are sold during pre-Lenten
carnival celebrations. The
ground floor has wind instruments on display including
tsampoúna, bagpipes made
from goatskin. On the first
floor, there is a selection of
string instruments, such as the
bouzouki, the *santoúri*, and
the Cretan *lýra*. There is also
a beautiful 19th-century ivory
and tortoiseshell lute.

Panagía Gorgoepíkoös ⓫
Παναγία η Γοργοεπήκοός

Bas-relief from south façade

THIS DOMED CRUCIFORM CHURCH is built entirely from Pentelic marble, now weathered to a rich wheat-colored hue. Dating from the 12th century, it measures only 7.5 m (25 ft) long by 12 m (40 ft) wide. The size of the church is in scale with Athens when it was just a village in the 12th century. Adorned with friezes and bas-reliefs taken from earlier buildings, the exterior is a mix of styles from Classical to Byzantine. Although dedicated to Panagía Gorgoepíkoös (the Madonna who Swiftly Hears) and Agios Elefthérios (the saint who protects women in childbirth), it is often affectionately known as the Mikrí Mitrópoli (Little Cathedral).

VISITORS' CHECKLIST

Plateía Mitropóleos, Pláka.
Map 6 E1. **M** *Monastiráki.*
☐ *7am–7pm daily.* ✝

The south façade of the church, dwarfed by the giant Mitrópoli

Allegorical Animals
This 12th century bas-relief detail is one of a pair from the west façade.

Four brick pillars
replaced the original marble ones in 1834.

The floor
is lower than ground level by about 30 cm (12 in).

Fragments of Classical buildings made from Pentelic marble were combined with new Byzantine sections in the style of a Classical frieze.

Main entrance

Lintel Frieze
This relief depicting the seasons dates from the 4th century BC. The cross at the center was added in the 12th century.

Modern mosaics above the main entrance to Athens' cathedral, Mitrópoli

Mitrópoli ⓬
Μητρόπολη

Plateía Mitropóleos, Pláka. **Map** 6 E1.
📞 *01 322 1308.* Ⓜ *Monastiráki.*
🕐 *7am–7pm daily.*

WORK BEGAN in 1840 on this huge cathedral, using marble from 72 demolished churches for its walls. The cornerstone was laid in a ceremony by King Otto and Queen Amalia on Christmas Day, 1842. It took another 20 years to finish the building, using three different architects (Franz Boulanger, Theophil von Hansen, and Dimítrios Zézos), which may account for its slightly ungainly appearance. On May 21, 1862, it was formally dedicated to Evangelismós Theotókou (the Annunciation of the Virgin) by the king and queen. At 40 m (130 ft) long, 20 m (65 ft) wide, and 24 m (80 ft) high, it is the largest church in Athens.

The cathedral is the official seat of the Bishop of Athens and remains a popular city landmark that has been used for ceremonial events from the coronations of kings to the weddings and funerals of the rich and famous.

Inside, there are the tombs of two saints murdered by the Ottoman Turks: Agía Filothéi and Gregory V. The bones of Agía Filothéi, who died in 1589, are still visible in a silver reliquary. Her charitable works included the ransoming of Greek women enslaved in Turkish harems. Gregory V, Patriarch of Constantinople, was hanged and thrown into the Bosphorus in 1821. His body was rescued by Greek sailors and taken to Odessa. It was eventually returned to Athens by Black Sea (Pontic) Greeks 50 years later.

Agios Nikólaos Ragavás ⓭
Αγιος Νικόλαος ο Ραγαβάς

Corner of Prytaneíou & Epichármou, Pláka. **Map** 6 E2. 📞 *01 322 8193.* Ⓜ *Monastiráki.* 🚌 *1, 2, 4, 5, 9, 10, 11, 12, 15, 18.* 🕐 *7am–noon, 3:30–7:30pm daily.* ♿ *limited.*

THIS TYPICAL 11th-century Byzantine church, rebuilt in the 18th century and restored to some of its former glory in the late 1970s, incorporates marble columns and other remains of ancient buildings in its external walls. It is one of the favorite parish churches of Pláka, frequently used for colorful Greek weddings that spill out onto the street on weekends. It was the first church in Athens to have a bell after the War of Independence (1821), and the first to ring out after the city's liberation from the Germans on October 12, 1944.

Anafiótika ⓮
Αναφιώτικα

Map 6 D2. Ⓜ *Monastiráki.*

NESTLING BENEATH the northern slopes of the Acropolis, this area is one of the oldest settlements in Athens. Today, its whitewashed houses, cramped streets, lazy cats, and pots of basil on windowsills still give

Looking down on Agios Nikólaos Ragavás church from Anafiótika

◁ View from Anafiótika toward the ancient Agora

it the atmosphere of a typical Cycladic village. Its first residents were refugees from the Peloponnesian War *(see p30)*. By 1841, it had been colonized by workmen from Anáfi, in the Cyclades, who eventually gave the area its name. Part of the influx of island craftsmen helped construct the new city following Independence. They ignored an 1834 decree declaring the area an archaeological zone, completed their houses overnight, and installed their families by morning; by Ottoman law, this meant the authorities were powerless to tear the new houses down.

The area is bounded by two 17th-century churches: Agios Geórgios tou Pétrou to the east, which has a tiny courtyard filled with flowers, and Agios Symeón to the west, which contains a copy of a miraculous icon originally brought from Anáfi.

Terra-cotta sphinxes, or *akroteria*, on a roof in Anafiótika

Plateía Lysikrátous ⓯
Πλατεία Λυσικράτους

Lysikrátous, Sélley & Epimenídou, Pláka. **Map** 6 E2. 🚋 *1, 5, 9, 18.*

SITUATED IN THE EAST of the Pláka district, this square is named after the monument of Lysikrates that dominates it. Despite Lord Elgin's attempts to remove it to England, the elegant structure is the city's only intact choregic monument. These monuments were built to commemorate the victors at the annual choral and dramatic festival at the Theater of Dionysos *(see p100)*. They take their name from the rich sponsor *(choregos)* who produced the winning team. Built in 334 BC, this is the earliest known example where Corinthian

capitals are used externally. Six columns rise in a circle to a marble dome, decorated with an elegant finial of acanthus leaves that supported the winner's bronze trophy. It bears the inscription "Lysikrates of Kikynna, son of Lysitheides, was choregos; the tribe of Akamantis won the victory with a chorus of boys; Theon played the flute; Lysiades, an Athenian, trained the chorus; Evainetos was archon." The Athenians elected nine magistrates known as archons each year, and referred to the year by the name of one of them, the "eponymous archon." A frieze above this inscription, probably the theme of the winners' performance, depicts a battle between Dionysos, the god of theater, and Tyrrhenian pirates. Surrounded by satyrs, the god transforms the pirates into dolphins and their ship's mast into a sea serpent.

Capuchin friars converted the monument into a library. Grand tour travelers, such as Chateaubriand (1768–1848) and Byron *(see p149)*, stayed at their convent, which was founded on the site in 1669.

The monument of Lysikrates, named after the *choregos* of the winning team of actors

Byron was inspired while staying there and wrote some of his poem *Childe Harold* sitting in the monument during his final visit to Athens in 1810.

Not far from the monument is the beautifully restored 11th-century Byzantine church of Agía Aikateríni (St. Catherine). In 1767 it was given to the monastery of St. Catherine of Mount Sinai. It was renovated, but in 1882 the monastery was forced to exchange it for land elsewhere, and it became a local parish church.

ICON PAINTERS IN PLAKA

Pláka is littered with small artists' studios where icons are still painted using traditional methods. The best are situated just south of Plateía Mitropóleos, among the ecclesiastical shops selling vestments and liturgical objects, on Agías

Filothéis and Apóllonos streets. In some workshops, painters still use the Byzantine method of painting in egg-based tempera on specially treated wood. Customers of all religions can order the saint of their choice in a variety of different sizes. A medium-sized icon depicting a single saint, 25 cm by 15 cm (10 in by 6 in), and copied from a photograph, takes about one day to complete.

Ornate embroidery from Ioánnina, Epirus, on display in the Greek Folk Art Museum

Greek Folk Art Museum ⑯
Μουσείο Ελληνικής Λαϊκής Τέχνης

Kydathinaíon 17, Pláka. **Map** 6 E2.
📞 01 322 9031. 🚌 2, 4, 9, 10, 11, 12, 15. 🚋 1, 5. ◗ 10am–2pm Tue–Sun. ● main public hols. 📷 ♿ limited. 📷

GREEK FOLK ART, including some unrivaled regional embroidery and costumes from the mainland and Aegean islands, fills five floors in this fascinating museum. The collection also covers the renaissance of decorative crafts in the 18th and 19th centuries, to reveal a rich heritage of traditional techniques in skills such as weaving, woodcarving, and metalwork.

The ground floor has an extensive collection of fine embroidery work, showing a wide range of techniques.

Displays on the mezzanine floor include ceramics, metalwork, and woodcarving. The ceramics range from architectural works, such as chimneys, to decorative or practical pieces such as household pots. Made from terra-cotta

Decorative plate from Rhodes

and faïence, they include both glazed and unglazed pieces. The metalwork on display includes examples made from copper, bronze, iron, steel, and pewter. Many are covered with intricate decoration. The woodcarving products are equally impressive in their decoration, often being inlaid with mother-of-pearl, ivory, or silver. The wood used varies widely, from walnut to fragrant cedar and wild olive. Also on the mezzanine are disguise costumes. Their origin is thought to be in the ancient Greek drama festivals in honor of Dionysos that made use of overtly expressive masks. The puppets from the Karagkiózis theater (see p151) amused the audience by satirizing topical political and social life.

The first floor houses popular paintings, including works by Theófilos Chatzimichaïl (see p218). There is an excellent collection of silverware on the second floor of the museum, with displays of various ecclesiastical items such as chalices and crosses, as well as secular pieces, such as ornate weaponry, and delicate jewelry. Examples of traditional weaving and stone-carving can be found on the third floor. The range of materials used for weaving includes lamb's wool, goat's hair, silk, and plant fibers. Traditional costumes are also displayed on this floor. The decorations and design, which are frequently elaborate, vary according to the geographical region. Costumes from many different areas are on display.

Jewish Museum of Greece ⑰
Εβραϊκό Μουσείο της Ελλάδος

Amalías 36, Pláka. **Map** 6 F2.
📞 01 322 5582. 🚌 1, 2, 4, 5, 9, 10, 11, 12, 15, 18. ◗ 9am–1pm Mon–Fri & Sun. ● Greek & Jewish public hols. ♿ 📷 📷

THIS SMALL MUSEUM fills just one floor of an apartment. It traces the history of Greece's Jewish communities, which date back to the 3rd century BC. The exhibits present a revealing portrait of the Sephardic Jews, who fled Spain and Portugal in the 15th century to settle throughout Greece in the religiously tolerant years of the Ottoman Empire.

Reconstruction of the ark from Pátra

Among the examples of traditional Jewish costumes and religious ceremonial instruments, one exhibit of particular interest is the reconstruction of the *ehal*. This is the ark containing the Torah from the inside of the Pátra synagogue, which dates from the 1920s. It was rescued by Nikólaos Stavrolákis, founder of the museum, who has also written several books about the Greek Jews, on sale in the museum book store.

Moving displays of documentation record the German occupation of Greece during World War II, when 87 percent of the Jewish population here was wiped out. Over 45,000 Greeks from Thessaloníki alone were sent to Auschwitz and other concentration camps during a period of three months in 1943.

Hadrian's Arch, next to the Temple of Olympian Zeus

Temple of Olympian Zeus ⑱
Ναός του Ολυμπίου Διός

Corner of Amalías & Vasilíssis Olgas, Pláka. **Map** 6 F3. [01 922 6330. 2, 4, 11. 8:30am–3pm Tue–Sun. main public hols. limited.

T HE TEMPLE of Olympian Zeus is the largest in Greece, exceeding even the Parthenon in size. Work began

on this vast edifice in the 6th century BC, in the reign of the tyrant Peisistratos, who allegedly initated the building work to gain public favor. Although there were several attempts over many years to finish the temple, it was not completed until 650 years later.

The Roman Emperor Hadrian dedicated the temple to Zeus Olympios during the Panhellenic festival of AD 132, on his second visit to Athens. He also set up a gold and ivory inlaid statue of the god inside the temple, a copy of the original by Pheidias at Olympia *(see pp170–72).* Next to it he placed a huge statue of himself. Both these statues have since been lost.

Only 15 of the original 104 Corinthian columns remain, each 17 m (56 ft) high – but enough to give a sense of the enormous size of this temple, which would have been approximately 96 m (315 ft) long and 40 m (130 ft) wide. Corinthian capitals were added to

the columns by a Roman architect in 174 BC in place of the original, simple Doric columns.

The temple is situated next to Hadrian's Arch, built in AD 131. It was positioned deliberately to mark the boundary between the ancient city and the new Athens of Hadrian.

The Russian Church of St. Nicodemus

Russian Church of St. Nicodemus ⑲
Σωτείρα του Λυκοδήμου

Filellínon 21, Pláka. **Map** 6 F2. [01 323 1090. 1, 2, 4, 5, 9, 10, 11, 12, 15, 18. 7:30–10am Mon–Fri, 7–11am Sat & Sun. main public hols. limited.

S TILL IN USE BY the Russian community, this was once the largest church in the city. Built in 1031 by the Lykodímou family (also called Nikodímou), it was ruined by an earthquake in 1701. In 1780 the Turkish *voivode* (governor), Hadji Ali Haseki, partly demolished the church to use its materials for the defensive wall that he built around the city. During the siege of the city in 1827, it received more damage from Greek shells fired from the Acropolis.

The church remained derelict until the Russian government restored it 20 years later. It was then reconsecrated as the Church of the Holy Trinity.

A large cruciform building, its most unusual feature is a wide dome, 10 m (33 ft) in diameter. Its interior was decorated by the Bavarian painter Ludwig Thiersch. The bell tower, a separate building, was also built in the 19th century, its bell a gift from Tsar Alexander II.

The remaining Corinthian columns of the Temple of Olympian Zeus

The Tomb of the Unknown Soldier in Plateía Syntágmatos

Plateía Syntágmatos ⑳
Πλατεία Συντάγματος

Syntágma. **Map** 6 F1. 🚌 *1, 5, 9, 10, 12, 15, 18.* Ⓜ *Syntágma.*

THIS SQUARE (also known as Syntágma Square) is home to the Greek parliament, in the Voulí building, and the Tomb of the Unknown Soldier, decorated with an evocative relief depicting a dying Greek hoplite. Unveiled on March 25, 1932 (National Independence Day), the tomb is flanked by texts from Perikles famous funeral oration. The other walls enclosing the square are covered in bronze shields celebrating military victories since 1821.

The National Guard (*évzones*) are on continuous patrol in front of the tomb, dressed in their famous uniform of kilt and pom-pom clogs. They are best seen at the changing of the guard, every Sunday at 11am.

National Gardens ㉑
Εθνικός Κήπος

Borders Eleftheríou Venizélou, Iródou Attikoú, Vasilíssis Olgas & Vasilíssis Amalías, Syntágma. **Map** 7 A1. 🚌 *1, 3, 5, 7, 8, 10, 13, 18.* 🕐 *dawn–dusk.* **Botanical Museum, zoo, cafés** 🕐 *7:30am–3pm daily.*

BEHIND THE VOULI parliament building, this 40-acre park, cherished by all Athenians and formerly known as the "Royal Gardens," was renamed the National Gardens by decree in 1923. Queen Amalía ordered the creation of the park in the 1840s; she even used the fledgling Greek Navy to bring 15,000 seedlings from Italy. The gardens were landscaped by the Prussian horticulturalist Friedrich Schmidt, who traveled the world in search of rare plants.

Although the gardens have lost much of their original grandeur, they remain one of the most peaceful spots in the city. Shady paths meander past small squares, park benches, and ponds filled with goldfish. A huge feral cat population is also resident in the park. Remains of Roman mosaics excavated in the park and an old aqueduct add atmosphere. Modern sculptures of writers, such as Dionýsios Solomós, Aristotélis Valaorítis, and Jean Moreas, can be found throughout the park. There is also a small **Botanical Museum** to visit, a ramshackle zoo, and cafés.

South of the park lies the **Záppeion**

exhibition hall, an impressive building used today as a conference center. It was donated by Evángelos and Konstantínos Záppas, two wealthy Greek-Romanian cousins. Built by von Hansen, architect of the University (*see p81*), between 1874 and 1888, it also has its own gardens. The elegant café next door to the Záppeion is a pleasant place to relax after a walk around these charming, peaceful gardens.

The tranquil National Gardens

Presidential Palace ㉒
Προεδρικό Μέγαρο

Iródou Attikoú, Syntágma. **Map** 7 A2. 🚌 *3, 7, 8, 13.* ⚫ *to the public.*

THIS FORMER royal palace was designed and built by Ernst Ziller (*see p81*) in 1878. It was occupied by the Greek Royal Family from 1890 until the hasty departure of King Constantine in 1973. It is still guarded by the *évzones* whose barracks are at the top of the street. It has been the seat of the Greek parliament since 1935, and following the abolition of the monarchy it also became the official residence of the President of Greece. Its well-maintained gardens can just be glimpsed through the iron railings.

Voulí parliament building in Plateía Syntágmatos, guarded by *évzones*

Panathenaic Stadium ㉓
Παναθεναϊκό Στάδιο

Archimídous 16, Pagkráti. **Map** 7 B3.
☎ *01 723 5930*. 🚎 *3, 4, 11.*
◯ *8:30am–1pm, 3pm–7pm daily.* ♿

THIS HUGE marble structure set in a small valley by Ardittós Hill occupies the exact site of the Panathenaic Stadium built by Lykourgos in 330–329 BC. Not to be confused with the Panathinaïkós Stadium in north Athens *(see p120)*, it was first reconstructed for gladiatorial contests during Hadrian's reign (AD 76–138), then rebuilt in white marble by the wealthy Roman benefactor Herodes Atticus for the Panathenaic games in AD 144. Neglected for many years, its marble was gradually quarried for use in new buildings or burned down to make lime.

In 1895 Geórgios Averof gave four million drachmas in gold for the restoration of the stadium in time for the start of the first modern Olympic Games on April 5, 1896. Designed by Anastásios Metaxás,

Some of the ornate tombs in the First Cemetery of Athens

the present structure is a faithful replica of Herodes Atticus's stadium, as described in the *Guide to Greece* by Pausanias *(see p56)*. Built in white Pentelic marble, it is 204 m (669 ft) long and 83 m (272 ft) wide and can seat up to 60,000 spectators. Metaxás was also helped by the plans of Ziller, who excavated the site. Among his finds was a double-headed statue of Apollo and Hermes, one of many that divided the stadium's running track down its length. It is on display in the National Archaeological Museum *(see pp68–71)*.

First Cemetery of Athens ㉔
Πρώτο Νεκροταφείο Αθηνών

Entrance in Anapáfseos, Goúva.
Map 7 A4 ☎ *01 923 6118*. 🚎 *2, 4.* ◯ *7am–7pm daily.* ♿ *limited.*

ATHENS' MUNICIPAL cemetery, which is not to be confused with the Kerameikós, the ancient cemetery *(see p88–9)*, is a peaceful place, filled with pine and olive trees and the scent of incense burning at the well-kept tombs.

Fine examples of 19th-century funerary art range from the flamboyance of some of the marble mausoleums to the simplicity of the Belle Epoque *Kimimeni* or *Sleeping Maiden (see p42)*. Created by Giannoúlis Chalepás, this beautiful tomb is found to the right of the main cemetery avenue where many of Greece's foremost families are buried.

Among the notable 19th- and 20th-century figures with tombs here are Theodóros Kolokotrónis *(see p80)*, British philhellene historian George Finlay (1799–1875), German archaeologist Heinrich Schliemann *(see p180)*, the Nobel prize-winning poet Giórgos Seféris (1900–71), and the actress and politician Melína Mercoúri (1922–94).

In addition to the large number of tombs for famous people that are buried here, the cemetery contains a moving, single memorial to the 40,000 Athenians who died of starvation during World War II.

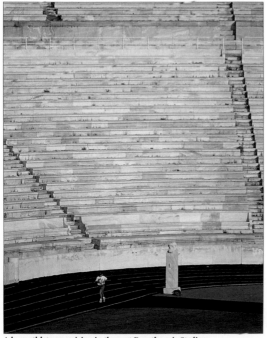
A lone athlete exercising in the vast Panathenaic Stadium

SHOPPING IN ATHENS

SHOPPING IN ATHENS offers many delights. There are open-air street markets, quiet arcades, traditional arts and crafts shops, and designer fashion boutiques to rival Paris and New York. Most Athenians go to the triangle formed by Omónoia, Sýntagma, and Monastiráki squares to buy everyday household items, clothes, and shoes. For leather goods, bargain hunters should head for Mitropóleos, Ermoú, Aiólou, and nearby streets. Along the smarter Stadíou and Panepistimíou, there are world-class jewelers and large clothing stores. The maze of arcades in the center also houses chic leather goods shops, booksellers, cafés, and *ouzerís*. The most stylish shopping is to be found in Kolonáki, where some of the city's most expensive art galleries and antique shops are clustered among the foreign and Greek designer outlets selling the latest fashions. Around Athinás, Monastiráki, and Pláka there is an eclectic mix of aromatic herb and spice stores, religious retailers selling icons and church candlesticks, second-hand bookstores with rare posters and prints, and catering stores packed with household goods such as pots and pans.

Colorful shadow puppet

OPENING HOURS

SHOPS GENERALLY open from 8am–2pm or 9am–3pm, Monday to Saturday. On Tuesdays, Thursdays, and Fridays there is late shopping from 5:30–8:30pm. Exceptions are department stores, tourist shops, supermarkets, florists, and *zacharoplasteía* (cake shops), which often open for longer. Many shops also close throughout August every year.

DEPARTMENT STORES AND SUPERMARKETS

THE MAIN STORES are **Minión** and **Lambrópoulos**. They stock a wide range of beauty products, clothes, gifts, and electrical and household goods. Minión is the larger,

Miníon department store is one of the largest in Athens

with an excellent bookstore, restaurant, and departments specializing in music and camping equipment. **Marinópoulos**, **Prisunic**, **Continent**, and **AB Vassilópoulos** are all supermarket chains in the city center. Continent and AB Vassilópoulos also have hyperstores next to the airport, for last-minute food and drink purchases.

MARKETS

ATHENS IS FAMOUS FOR its flea markets. **Monastiráki** market starts early in the morning every Sunday, when dealers set out their wares along Adrianoú and neighboring streets. Hawkers of *salépi* (a drink made from sesame seeds) and gypsy clarinet players weave through the crowds. The commercial tourist and antique shops of Pandrósou and Ifaístou, which collectively refer to themselves as "Monastiráki Flea Market," are open every day. Friday, Saturday, and Sunday mornings are the best times to visit Plateía Avissynías, when dealers arrive with piles of bric-a-brac. For food, the **Central Market** is excellent, as are the popular *laïkés agorés* (street markets) selling fruit and vegetables, which occur daily in different areas. Centrally located *laïkés agorés* include one on **Xenokrátous** in Kolonáki which takes place each Friday.

ART AND ANTIQUES

AS AUTHENTIC GREEK antiques become increasingly hard to find, many shops import furniture, glassware, and porcelain from around the globe. Fortunately, however, there are still reasonable buys in old Greek jewelry, brass

Shoppers in Adrianoú at the center of Monastiráki flea market

and copperware, carpets and embroidery, engravings and prints. Some can be found at **Antiqua**, just off Plateía Syntágmatos. Kolonáki is a prime area for small, exclusive stores around Sólonos, Skoufá, and their side streets. Try **Anthes** for interesting furniture and paintings or **Tiffany** for clocks and Art Deco items. The **Collectors Gallery** for early Greek advertising posters and **Serafetinídis**, excellent for antique kilims and carpets, are both on Charítos. Kolonáki is also the art center, with well-established galleries selling paintings and prints. The premier **Zoumpouláki Galleries** specialize in art and antiques.

Monastiráki also has an abundance of antique shops. Look out for **Giórgios Koútis**'s two stores selling 19th-century jewelry and costumes, **Digran Serapian** for popular art and glassware, and **Vergína** for copperware, in particular nautical items. **Martinós** has some beautiful, ornate icons and silverware.

Antique jewelry and ornaments in Giórgios Koútis

TRADITIONAL FOLK ART AND CRAFTS

AFFORDABLE POPULAR folk art, crafts, and souvenirs are plentiful in Monastiráki and Pláka. There are innumerable stores filled with ecclesiastical ephemera and cramped icon painters' studios. In addition, there are more unusual shops offering unique services. **Stávros Melissinós**, a self-styled poet sandalmaker, makes a wide

The famous shoemaker and poet Stávros Melissinós

variety of sturdy sandals and leather goods and is famous for handing out translations of his work as a parting gift. Many shops stock elegant wood carvings, rustic painted wooden trays, and richly colored *flokáti* rugs *(see p209).* **Amorgós** is packed with fine wood carvings and puppets from the Karagkiózis theatre in Maroúsi *(see p151).*

The **National Welfare Organization** offers an excellent selection of different goods including tapestries, rugs, and needlepoint cushions. Beautiful carved shepherds' crooks from Epirus as well as a large variety of finely crafted ceramics can be found at the fascinating **Center of Hellenic Tradition**.

JEWELRY

ATHENS IS JUSTLY FAMED for its jewelry stores. There is no shortage in Monastiráki and Pláka, which is full of small shops selling gold and silver. But the best-known are to be found in Voukourestíou, which is packed with such exclusive jewelers as **Anagnostópoulos** and **Vourákis**. Window displays also dazzle at the designer of world class fame, **Zolótas**, whose own pieces copy museum treasures. Another famous name is that of the designer Ilías Lalaoúnis, whose collections, inspired by Classical and other

archaeological sources, such as the gold of Mycenae, are eagerly sought by the rich and famous. At the **Ilías Lalaoúnis Jewelry Museum** over 3,000 of his designs are exhibited, and there is also a workshop and where you can watch the craftsmen demonstrate the skills of the goldsmith and buy some of the jewelry.

MUSEUM COPIES

MUSEUM SHOPS provide some of the better buys in the city. Well-crafted, mostly tasteful copies draw on the wide range of ancient and Byzantine Greek art. They come in all shapes and sizes, from a life-size Classical statue to a simple Cycladic marble bowl. Many fine reproductions of the exhibits in the **Benáki Museum** *(see pp78–9)* can be bought from a collection of silverware, ceramics, embroidery, and jewelry in the museum shop.

The **Museum of Cycladic Art** *(see pp74–5)* has some fine Tanagran and Cycladic figurines, bowls, and vases for sale. There is a large selection of reproduction statues and pottery at the **National Archaeological Museum** *(see pp68–71)* souvenir shop. Apart from the museums, the Monastiráki shop **Orféas** offers good quality marble and pottery copies of Classical Greek works as well as glittering Byzantine icons.

Display of red- and black-figure reproduction vases for sale

Períptero in Kolonáki selling English and Greek newspapers

BOOKS, NEWSPAPERS, AND MAGAZINES

ALL THE PERIPTERA (kiosks) in the city center sell foreign newspapers and magazines. English publications include the daily *Athens News*, the weekly *Greek Times*, and the monthly magazines, *The Athenian* and *Odyssey*. Athens' wealth of bookstores includes many selling foreign language publications. **Raÿmóndos** offers the best selection of foreign magazines, but for foreign books, go to the huge branch of **Eleftheroudákis** on Panepistimíou, with seven floors of English and Greek books. Try **Androméda Books** for classical and archaeological subjects and **Ekdotikí Athinón** for history and guide books.

The DKNY store, one of the many designer shops in Athens

CLOTHES

ALTHOUGH THERE are some famous Greek designers, such as **Aslánis**, who produces colorful *prêt-à-porter* party dresses, and **Parthénis**, whose hallmark is black and white minimalism, the majority of fashion stores concentrate on imported clothes.

However, there is no shortage of high-quality clothes: every designer label can be found in Kolonáki, the city's main fashion center. There are branches of such internationally famous names as **DKNY**, **Emporio Armani**, **Max Mara**, and **Ralph Lauren**. Such upscale stores as **Sotíris**, **Helen B**, and **Mohnblumchen** typify the urban chic of the area.

KITCHENWARE

CAVERNOUS CATERING stores in the side streets around the Central Market specialize in classic Greek kitchen- and tableware. There are tiny white cups and copper saucepans used to make Greek coffee, long rolling pins for making filo pastry, and metal olive oil pourers. **Kotsópoulos** in Evripídou has a huge range of cheap and cheerful equipment, including traditional *kantária* (wine-measuring jugs), used to serve retsina in restaurants, round *tapsiá* (metal roasting dishes), and *saganákia* (two-handled pans) used for frying cheese. More stylish products can be found at **Méli Interiors** in Kolonáki. A good selection of tinware is on display, as well as traditional Greek pottery and miniature taverna chairs.

FOOD AND DRINK

THERE ARE MYRIAD gourmet treats in Athens, including unusual *avgotáracho* (smoked cod roe preserved in beeswax), herbs and spices, cheeses and wines. The bakeries and *zacharoplasteía* (pastry shops) are irresistible, brimming with delicious breads and biscuits, homemade ice cream, and yogurt. **Aristokratikón**, off Plateía Syntágmatos, sells luxurious chocolate and marzipan confections. One of Athens' finest patisseries, **Asimakópouloi**, is crammed with decadent baklava and crystallized fruits.

The colorful Central Market on Athinás is one of the most enticing places for general food shopping. It is surrounded by stores packed with cheeses, pistachio nuts, dried fruits, and legumes like *fáva* (yellow peas) and *gígantes* (butter beans). You will find over 20 different types of olive and pickle at **Papalexandrís**, and a range of herbs and spices at **Bakar**, in particular dried savory and sage, lemon verbena, and saffron. Two enterprising *cáves* (wine merchants), **Cellier** in Kriezótou and **Oino-Pneúmata** in Irakleítou, offer a broad range of wines and spirits from the new generation of small Greek wineries. **Brettós** in Pláka has an attractive and varied display of house-label spirits and liqueurs *(see p308)*.

A crammed Athenian kitchenware store

DIRECTORY

DEPARTMENT STORES AND SUPERMARKETS

AB Vassilópoulos
Stadíou 19, Sýntagma.
Map 2 F5.
☎ 01 322 2405.
One of several branches.

Continent
Palaistínis 1, Alimos.
☎ 01 988 0986.

Lambrópoulos
Aiólou 99 and Lykoúrgou 26, Omónoia. **Map** 2 E4.
☎ 01 324 5811.

Marinópoulos Prisunic
Kanári 9, Kolonáki.
Map 3 A5.
☎ 01 362 4907.
One of several branches.

Minión
28 Oktovríou 13, Omónoia. **Map** 2 E3.
☎ 01 523 8909.

MARKETS

Central Market
Athinás, Omónoia.
Map 2 D4.

Monastiráki
Adrianoú & Pandrósou, Pláka.
Map 6 E1

Xenokrátous
Xenokrátous, Kolonáki.
Map 3 C5.

ART AND ANTIQUES

Anthes
Pindárou 24, Kolonáki.
Map 3 A5.
☎ 01 363 6951.

Antiqua
Amaliádos 4, Sýntagma.
Map 4 F2.
☎ 01 324 1700.

Collectors Gallery
Cháritos 27, Kolonáki.
Map 3 B5.
☎ 01 723 9400.

Digran Serapian
Ifaístou 6, Monastiráki.
Map 5 C1.
☎ 01 321 0169.

Giórgos Koútis
Pandrósou 40 & 47, Pláka. **Map** 6 D1.
☎ 01 321 3212.

Martinós
Pandrósou 50, Pláka.
Map 6 D1.
☎ 01 321 3110.

Serafetinídis
Cháritos 29, Kolonáki.
Map 3 B5.
☎ 01 721 4186.

Tiffany
Sólonos 28, Kolonáki.
Map 3 A5.
☎ 01 751 0494.

Vergína
Adrianoú 37, Pláka.
Map 6 E1.
☎ 01 321 7065.

Zoumpouláki Galleries
Kriezótou 7, Kolonáki.
Map 2 F5.
☎ 01 363 4454.
One of three branches.

TRADITIONAL FOLK ART AND CRAFTS

Amorgós
Kódrou 3, Monastiráki.
Map 6 E1.
☎ 01 324 3836.

Center of Hellenic Tradition
Mitropóleos 59 (Arcade) - Pandrósou 36, Monastiráki. **Map** 6 D1.
☎ 01 321 3023.

National Welfare Organization
Ypatías 6 and Apóllonos, Monastiráki. **Map** 6 E1.
☎ 01 325 0524.

Stávros Melissinós
Pandrósou 89, Monastiráki. **Map** 6 D1.
☎ 01 321 9247.

JEWELRY

Anagnostópoulos
Voukourestíou 13, Kolonáki. **Map** 2 F5.
☎ 01 324 9697.

Ilías Lalaoúnis Jewelry Museum
Kallispéri 12, Pláka.
Map 6 D3.
☎ 01 922 1044.

Vourákis
Voukourestíou 11, Kolonáki. **Map** 2 F5.
☎ 01 361 5489.

Zolótas
Panepistimíou 10, Kolonáki. **Map** 2 F5.
☎ 01 361 3782.

MUSEUM COPIES

Orféas
Pandrósou 28B, Pláka.
Map 6 D1.
☎ 01 324 5034.

BOOKS, NEWSPAPERS, AND MAGAZINES

Androméda Books
Mavromicháli 46–50, Exárcheia. **Map** 2 F3.
☎ 01 630 0825.

Ekdotikí Athinón
Omírou 11, Kolonáki.
Map 2 F5.
☎ 01 360 8911.

Eleftheroudákis
Panepistimíou 17, Kolonáki. **Map** 2 F5.
☎ 01 331 4180.

Raymóndos
Voukourestíou 18, Kolonáki. **Map** 2 F5.
☎ 01 364 8189.

CLOTHES

Aslánis
Anagnostopoúlou 16, Kolonáki. **Map** 3 A4.
☎ 01 360 0049.

DKNY
Tsakálof & Dimokrítou 34, Kolonáki. **Map** 3 A5.
☎ 01 363 6188.

Emporio Armani
Milióni 3, Kolonáki.
Map 3 A5.
☎ 01 360 3388.

Helen B
Anagnostopoúlou 48, Kolonáki.
Map 3 A4.
☎ 01 363 5751.

Max Mara
Kanári 19 & Sólonos, Kolonáki. **Map** 3 A5.
☎ 01 360 2142.

Mohnblumchen
Plateía Dexamenís 7, Dexaméni. **Map** 3 B5.
☎ 01 723 6960.

Parthénis
Dimokrítou 20, Kolonáki.
Map 3 A5.
☎ 01 363 3158.

Ralph Lauren
Kassavéti 19, Kifisiá.
☎ 01 808 5902.
One of two branches.

Sotíris
Anagnostopoúlou 30, Kolonáki. **Map** 3 A4.
☎ 01 363 9281.
One of two branches.

KITCHENWARE

Kotsópoulos
Evripídou 44, Omónoia.
Map 2 D4.
☎ 01 321 2866.

Méli Interiors
Tsakálof 33, Kolonáki.
Map 3 A5.
☎ 01 361 8512.

FOOD AND DRINK

Aristokratikón
Karagiórgi Servías 9, Sýntagma. **Map** 2 E5.
☎ 01 322 0546.

Asimakópouloi
Chariláou Trikoúpi 82, Exárcheia. **Map** 3 A3.
☎ 01 361 0092.

Bakar
Evripídou 31, Omónoia.
Map 2 D4.
☎ 01 321 7225.

Brettós
Kydathinaíon 41, Pláka.
Map 6 E2.
☎ 01 323 2110.

Cellier
Kriezótou 1, Kolonáki.
Map 3 A5.
☎ 01 361 0040.

Oino-Pneúmata
Irakleítou 7, Kolonáki.
Map 3 A5.
☎ 01 361 2644.

Papalexandrís
Sokrátous 9, Omónoia.
Map 2 D4.
☎ 01 321 1461.

ENTERTAINMENT IN ATHENS

ATHENS EXCELS in the sheer variety of its open-air summer entertainment. Visitors can go to outdoor showings of the latest film releases, spend lazy evenings in garden bars heady with the aroma of jasmine, or try a concert in the atmospheric setting of the Herodes Atticus Theater, which sits beneath the Acropolis.

Two Athens listings magazines

The Mégaron Athens Concert Hall has given the city a first-class classical concert venue and draws some of the best names in the music world. For most Athenians, however, entertainment means late-night dining in tavernas, followed by bar- and club-hopping until the early hours. There is also an enormous number of large discotheques, music halls, and intimate *rempétika* clubs, playing traditional Greek music, throughout Athens. Whatever your musical taste, there is something for everyone in this lively city. Sports and outdoor facilities are also widely available, in particular water sports, which are within easy reach of Athens along the Attic coast.

LISTINGS MAGAZINES

THE MOST comprehensive Greek weekly listings magazines are *Athinorama*, published on Thursdays and *Downtown*, published on Fridays. Both list events and concerts and the latest fashionable music bars and clubs. English language publications such as the daily *Athens News*, weekly *Greek News* and *Athenscope*, monthly *The Athenian* and *Athina*, and the bimonthly *Odyssey* also have listings sections. All are widely available at kiosks.

BOOKING TICKETS

ALTHOUGH IT IS NECESSARY to book tickets in advance for the summer Athens Festival *(see p46)* and for concerts at the Mégaron Concert Hall, most theaters and music clubs sell tickets at the door on the day of performance. However, there is also a central ticket office, open daily from 10am to 4pm, located near Plateía Syntágmatos, where tickets can be purchased for concerts at both the Mégaron Concert Hall and for the summer Athens Festival.

THEATER AND DANCE

THERE ARE MANY FINE theaters scattered around the city centre, often hidden in converted Neo-Classical mansion houses or arcades. Numerous popular revues that combine an entertaining mixture of contemporary political satire and comedy are regularly performed in theaters such as the **Metropolitan**.

Some excellent productions of 19th-century Greek and European plays are staged at

Ibsen at the Evros Theatre, Psýrri

the **National Theater**. Playhouses such as the **Evros**, **Athínaion**, **Alfa**, and **Vrettánia** also mount Greek-language productions of works by well-known 19th- and 20th-century playwrights such as Ibsen.

The major classical venues, including the National Theater, put on contemporary dance and ballet as well as plays and operas. The **Dóra Strátou Dance Theater** on Filopáppos Hill performs traditional regional Greek dancing nightly between May and September.

The Dóra Strátou Dance Theater performing traditional Greek dancing outdoors

The doorway to the outdoor Refresh Dexamení theater

THE MOVIES

ATHENIANS LOVE GOING to the movies, especially from late May to September when the warm weather means that local open-air theaters are open. All foreign-language movies are subtitled, with the exception of children's films, which are usually dubbed. The last showing is always at 11pm, which makes it possible to dine before seeing a movie.

The city center has several excellent, large screen theaters showing the latest international releases. **Ideál**, **Embassy-Heineken**, and **Pallás** are large, comfortable, indoor theaters equipped with with Dolby Stereo sound systems. The **Alphaville-Bar-Cinema** and **Aavóra** tend to show a comprehensive range of art-house and cult movies.

Athenians like to hang out at the bars and tavernas next to open-air theaters, such as **Refresh Dexamení** and **Athinaía** in Kolonáki or the **Riviéra** in Exárcheía, before catching the last performance. The acoustics are not always perfect, but the relaxed atmosphere, in the evening warmth, with street noises dominated by cats and cars invading the soundtrack, is an unforgettable experience. These theaters seem more like clubs, with tables beside the seats for drinks and snacks. The outdoor

Thiseíon theater comes with the added attraction of a stunning view of the Acropolis.

CLASSICAL MUSIC

THE ANNUAL Athens Festival, held throughout the summer, attracts the major international ballet and opera companies, orchestras, and theatrical troupes to the open-air **Herodes Atticus Theater**, which seats 5,000 people, and to other venues around the city. This has always been the premier event of the classical music calendar. In 1991, the **Mégaron Athens Concert Hall** was inaugurated, providing a year-round venue for opera, ballet, and classical music performances. This majestic marble building contains two recital halls with exceptional acoustics, an exhibition space, a shop, and

Accordionist
in Plateía
Kolonakíou

a restaurant. The Olýmpia Theater is home to the **Lyrikí Skiní** (National Opera) and stages excellent ballet productions as well as opera.

Details of concerts held at cultural centers such as the **French Institute** can be found in listings magazines and newspapers.

TRADITIONAL GREEK MUSIC

THE LIVELY GREEK music scene thrives in a variety of venues throughout central Athens. The large music halls of Syngróu advertise on omnipresent billboards around the city. **Diogénis Palace**, **Bio-Bio**, and **The Tunnel Club** attract the top stars and their loyal fans. The more old-fashioned venues in Pláka, such as **Zoom** and **Esmerálda**, offer more intimate surroundings for the haunting sounds of *rempétika* music, which draws its inspiration and defiant stance from the lives of the urban poor. **Rempétiki Istoría** and **Taksími** are two of the places at which you can hear genuine bouzouki (Greek mandolin) music. Both bars have well-known bouzouki players and reasonable prices. **Mpoémissa** attracts a much younger crowd, more concerned with dancing the night away than with the authenticity of the music.

A classical concert at the Herodes Atticus Theater

ROCK AND JAZZ MUSIC

INTERNATIONAL ACTS usually perform at large stadiums or the open-air **Lykavittós Theater** as part of the annual Athens Festival. The **Ródon**, a successfully converted movie house, also attracts the cream of foreign and Greek rock bands. **Lollapalooza** often features visiting salsa or country and western bands. Greek bands can be seen at **Ach María**, and at the **Skyládiko** club, which offers Greek rock 'n' roll dinner dancing.

The city's premier jazz venue is the **Half Note Jazz Club**. Housed in a former stone mason's workshop, opposite the First Cemetery, this intimate club presents the best of foreign contemporary jazz. Next to the Hilton Hotel, the **Public** restaurant and bar has live jazz and blues bands. Alternatively, for an evening of ethnic Afro-Latin sounds, head for **Café Asante**, or **La Joya**, which features lively Cuban bands.

Live music in the Ródon, one of the city's popular rock clubs

NIGHTCLUBS

ATHENS IS A HIVE of bars and nightclubs that come and go at an alarming rate. Most offer special DJ nights that attract the paparazzi and the dedicated followers of fashion. Many large dance clubs, such as **La Mamoúnia**, **+Soda**, and the **Camel Club**, offer a hedonistic atmosphere and dancing until the early hours. Also worth trying are the designer sleek **Kalúa**, **Wild Rose**, and **Lobby**, all with a sophisticated crowd.

Marathon runner in Athens retracing the path of his ancestors

SPORTS

MOST TAXI DRIVERS will reel off their favorite soccer team to passengers before they have had a chance to mention their destination. Such is the Athenian passion for soccer that the two main rival teams, Panathinaïkós and Olympiakós, are always the subject of fervent debate. Each team is backed by a consortium of private companies, each of which also owns a basketball team of the same name. Soccer games are played every Wednesday and Sunday during the September to May season. The basketball teams play weekly in what is the latest popular national sport.

Lack of adequate parkland within the city means that joggers are a rare sight, despite the annual **Athens Open Marathon** every October. The athletes run from Marathon to the Panathenaic Stadium in the center of Athens *(see p113)*. The **Olympiakó Stadium** in Maroúsi seats 80,000 spectators and was built in 1982. The Panathenaïkós soccer team is based here. It has excellent facilities for all sports and includes an indoor sports hall and tennis courts in its 250 acres of grounds. The **Karaïskáki Stadium** in Piraeus is the home of the Olympiakós soccer team. There are also facilities there for many other sports including volleyball and basketball.

Another famous event is the **Acropolis Rally**, a celebration of vintage cars, held around the Acropolis every spring. It attracts between 50 and 100 cars.

Outside the city center, there are more facilities available, including bowling at the **Bowling Center of Piraeus** and golf at the fine 18-hole **Glyfáda Golf Course**, which is located close to the airport. Tennis courts are available for players to rent at various places, including the **Glyfáda Tennis Club**.

Proximity to the Attic coast means that a large variety of water sports is available. Windsurfing and water-skiing facilities are widely available on most beaches. The **Karageorgíou Water-Skiing School** offers instruction in Vouliagméni, and there are several scuba-diving clubs, including the **Piraeus Kartelías School,** that offer diving lessons to beginners as well as more advanced divers.

Basketball, an increasingly popular national sport among the Greeks

DIRECTORY

THEATER AND DANCE

Alfa
Patisíon & Stournára 37,
Exárcheia. **Map** 2 E2.
[01 523 8742.

Athínaion
Voukourestíou 10,
Kolonáki. **Map** 2 E5.
[01 323 5524.

Dóra Strátou Dance Theater
Filopáppou Hill,
Filopáppou. **Map** 5 B4.
[01 324 4395.

Lampéti
Leof Alexándras 106,
Avérof. **Map** 8 D1.
[01 646 3685.

Metropolitan
Leof Alexándras 16,
Avérof. **Map** 1 A1.
[01 822 3333.

National Theater
Agíou Konstantínou 22,
Omónoia. **Map** 1 D3.
[01 523 3322.

Vrettánia
Panepistimíou 7,
Sýntagma. **Map** 2 E4.
[01 322 1579.

MOVIES

Aavóra
Ippokrátous 180,
Neápolis. **Map** 2 E4.
[01 646 2253.

Alphaville-Bar-Cinema
Mavromicháli 168,
Neápolis. **Map** 2 F4.
[01 646 0521.

Athinaía
Cháritos 50,
Kolonáki. **Map** 3 B5.
[01 721 5717.

Embassy-Heineken
Patriárchou Ioakeím 5,
Kolonáki. **Map** 3 B5.
[01 722 0903.

Ideál
Panepistimíou 46,
Omónoia. **Map** 2 E4.
[01 382 6720.

Pallás
Voukourestíou 1,
Kolonáki. **Map** 3 A5.
[01 322 4434.

Refresh Dexamení
Plateía Dexamenís,
Dexamení. **Map** 3 B5.
[01 362 3942.

Riviéra
Valtetsioú 46,
Exárcheia. **Map** 2 F3.
[01 363 7716.

Thiseíon
Apostólou Pávlou 7,
Thiseío. **Map** 5 B2.
[01 342 0864.

CLASSICAL MUSIC

French Institute
Sina 29–31, Pefkákia.
Map 3 A4.
[01 362 4301.

Herodes Atticus Theater
Dionysíou Areopagítou,
Acropolis. **Map** 6 C2.
[01 323 2771.

Lyrikí Skiní, Olympia Theater
Akadimías 59,
Omónoia. **Map** 2 E4.
[01 361 2461.

Mégaron Athens Concert Hall
V Sofías & Kókkali,
Stégi Patrídos. **Map** 4 E4.
[01 728 2333.

TRADITIONAL GREEK MUSIC

Bio-Bio
Leof A Syngroú 137,
Kallithéa.
[01 942 9580.

Diogénis Palace
Leof A Syngroú 259,
Kallithéa.
[01 942 5755.

Esmerálda
Kefallinías 50,
Kypséli.
[01 867 1290.

Mpoémissa
Solomoú 19,
Exárcheia. **Map** 2 D2.
[01 384 3836.

Rempétiki Istoria
Ippokrátous 181,
Neápoli. **Map** 3 C2.
[01 642 4937.

Taksími
C Trikoúpi & Isávron 29,
Neápoli. **Map** 3 A2.
[01 363 9919.

Tunnel Club
Leof A Syngroú 123,
Kallithéa.
[01 934 6311.

Zoom
Kydathinaíon 37,
Pláka. **Map** 6 E2.
[01 322 5920.

ROCK AND JAZZ MUSIC

Ach María
Solomoú 20,
Exárcheia. **Map** 2 E2.
[01 383 0086.

Café Asante
Damáreos 78,
Goúva. **Map** 8 E3.
[01 726 0102.

Half Note Jazz Club
Trivonianoú 17,
Stádio. **Map** 6 F4.
[01 921 3310.

La Joya
Isócha 43,
Stégi Patrídos. **Map** 6 F3.
[01 644 0030.

Lollapalooza
Vouliagménis 63 & Kélsou,
Kynosárgous. **Map** 6 F5.
[01 924 7317.

Lykavittós Theater
Lykavittós Hill.
Map 3 B4.
[01 722 7209.

Public
Chatzigiánni Méxi 6,
Ilísia. **Map** 4 D5.
[01 721 6258.

Ródon
Márni 24,
Váthis. **Map** 1 C3.
[01 524 7427.

Skyládiko
Formiónos 102,
Pagkráti. **Map** 8 D2.
[01 766 9903.

NIGHTCLUBS

Camel Club
Vouliagménis 268,
Agios Dimítrios.
[01 971 6145.

Kalúa
Amerikís 6,
Sýntagma. **Map** 2 F5.
[01 360 8304.

La Mamoúnia
Vouliagménis 22,
Kynosárgous. **Map** 6 F5.
[01 923 3165.

Lobby
Ermoú 110 & Avlitón 6–8,
Monastiráki. **Map** 1 C5.
[01 323 6975.

+Soda
Ermoú 161,
Thiseío. **Map** 1 A5.
[01 345 6187.

Wild Rose
Panepistimíou 10,
Sýntagma. **Map** 2 E4.
[01 364 2160.

SPORTS

Bowling Center of Piraeus
Profítis Ilías,
Kastélla.
[01 412 7077.

Glyfáda Golf Course
Glyfáda.
[01 894 6820.

Glyfáda Tennis Club
Diadóchou Pávlou,
Glyfáda.
[01 806 6162.

Karageorgíou Water-Skiing School
Vouliagméni.
[01 894 7413.

Karaïskáki Stadium
Néo Fáliro.
[01 481 2763.

Olympiakó Stadium
Leof. Kifisías 37, Maroúsi.
[01 683 4000.

Piraeus Kartelías School
Karageórgi Servias 3,
Kastélla.
[01 412 2047.

ATHENS STREET FINDER

MAP REFERENCES given for sights in Athens refer to the maps on the following pages. References are also given for Athens hotels *(see pp264–7)*, Athens restaurants *(see pp286–9)*, and for useful addresses in the *Survival Guide* section *(see pp296–325)*. The first figure in the reference tells you which Street Finder map to turn to, and the letter and number refer to the grid reference. The map below shows the area of Athens covered by the eight Street Finder maps (the map numbers are shown in black). The symbols used for sights and features are listed in the key below.

SCALE OF KEY

0 kilometers   1

0 miles   0.5

KEY

■ Major sight	🚖 Taxi stand	═ Railroad line
■ Place of interest	P Parking	← One-way street
■ Other sight	ℹ Tourist information	▬ Pedestrianized street
M Metro station	✚ Hospital with emergency room	**Note** that the full metro network is due to open in 1998 *(see p324–5)*.
🚆 Railroad station	🚓 Police station	
🚌 Main coach or bus station	✝ Church	SCALE OF MAP PAGES
🚎 Trolleybus terminus	✡ Synagogue	0 meters 250
🚠 Funicular	⊠ Post office	0 yards 250

Street Finder Index

Abbreviations

Ag	Agios, Agía (saint)
Leof	Leofóros (avenue)
Pl	Plateía (square)

Note: Squares and avenues are indexed by their name followed by Plateía or Leofóros.

MAINLAND GREECE
AREA BY AREA

Mainland Greece at a Glance

T HE UNIQUE ATTRACTION of the mainland lies in the wealth of ancient remains, set in landscapes of great natural beauty. Classical sites are most notable in the south, around Athens, and the coasts of Attica and the Peloponnese, while Macedonian ruins can be seen in the temperate northeast. Byzantine monasteries and churches are found all over the country, particularly on the holy peninsula of Mount Athos, which is governed by its 20 monasteries.

The Metéora area *(see pp216–17) combines extraordinary sandstone pinnacles with some of the first medieval monasteries in Greece, perched on the rocky peaks.*

NORTHERN GREECE
(see pp232–57)

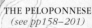

Delphi *(see pp228–31) is home to the evocative ruins of an ancient religious complex and theater situated on Mount Parnassus.*

CENTRAL AND WESTERN GREECE
(see pp202–31)

Ancient Olympia *(see pp170–73) was, from the 11th to the 1st centuries BC, the site of the Panhellenic Games, the forerunner of today's Olympics. One of the best-preserved buildings is the Temple of Hera (left), dating from around the 6th century BC.*

THE PELOPONNESE
(see pp158–201)

Mystrás *(see pp192–3) is one of the best-preserved Byzantine complexes in Greece, exemplified in this church of Agía Sofía. It is a medieval city, and held out against the Ottomans until 1460.*

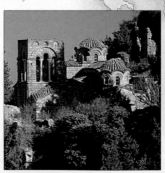

0 kilometers	50
0 miles	25

The Máni peninsula *(see pp194–9)* is dotted with tower houses.

◁ **Moní Spiliótissa, near the Zagorian village of Arísti in Western Greece**

Thessaloníki's Archaeological Museum (see pp246–7) has spectacular gold finds from the tombs of the Macedonian kings, and this bronze head from around AD 235 of Alexander Severus.

Osios Loúkas monastery (see pp222–3) is beautifully set in a flowering orchard. The octagonal design of the 11th-century dome was widely copied. Its plain exterior conceals the gold-ground mosaics inside.

Mount Athos has, since 1060, been entirely occupied by monks *(see pp252–5)*.

Ancient Corinth (see pp162–6), capital of the Roman province of Achaia, was renowned for its luxury and elegance, exemplified by this ornate capital.

AROUND ATHENS *(see pp140–57)*

The Monastery of Dafní (see pp152–3) is a famous work of Byzantine architecture with outstanding medieval mosaics decorating the interior of the church.

Athens

Mycenae (see pp178–80), one of Greece's oldest sites, dates back to 1550 BC; the Lion Gate was the entrance to the citadel. Mycenae was possibly ruled by Agamemnon.

Epidaurus *(see pp184–5)* has one of the best-preserved theaters in Greece.

Monemvasía (see pp186–8) means "one way in," a reference to the strategic advantage of this heavily fortified Byzantine sea port. Its former role as the main port of Byzantine Greece is reflected in the buildings of the old town.

AROUND ATHENS

ATTICA

THE AREA AROUND ATHENS, *known as Attica, is the spiritual heart-land of ancient and modern Greece. Its archaeological sites have attracted generations of scholars and plunderers alike, and its mountains and coastline have provided important refuge in times of strife. Today the golden beaches along the eastern coast attract those simply wishing to escape the bustle of modern Athens.*

The land of Attica was the basis of Athenian wealth. The fine marble from the quarries on Mount Ymittós and Mount Pentéli was used for the temples and sculptures of ancient Athens. The silver from Lávrio financed their construction, and the produce from the local agricultural areas fed the population.

Waiting for a ferry in Piraeus

Attica has witnessed many significant historical events. The plain of Marathon was the site of one of the greatest battles in Greek history. Piraeus, now Greece's largest and busiest port, was also the port of ancient Athens. The Classical temples at less-known archaeological sites around the countryside, such as Eleusis, Rhamnoús, and Brauron, offer a rural retreat from the overcrowding and

pollution of the city. At Soúnio, the majestic, well-preserved Temple of Poseidon on the cape has been a beacon for mariners for centuries.

The Byzantine era also left a great legacy of fine architecture to the region. Two of the best examples of this are the imposing monasteries of Dafní and Kaisarianí, with their ornate mosaics and elegant stonework.

South of Athens, the summer heat of the Attic plain is ideal for growing crops. Grapes are a specialty in the Mesógeia (Midland) region, which produces some of the finest retsina in the country. North of Athens, the pine-forested Mount Párnitha provides interesting walks and offers superb views of the city from the summit.

The peaceful ruins of the Parthenon of the Bear Maidens at Ancient Brauron

◁ **The Christ Pantokrátor figure in the dome of the *katholikón* of the Monastery of Dafní**

Around Athens

BEYOND THE ENDLESS urban sprawl of Athens, the region around the city, known as Attica, offers the diversity of wild mountains, Byzantine monasteries and churches, evocative archaeological sites, and sandy beaches. Not surprisingly, such easy accessibility to the coast and countryside has led to overcrowding in Athens' suburbs and pollution around Piraeus and Ancient Eleusis. The hills of Mount Párnitha and Ymittós are rich in wildlife, with deserted trails, caves, and icy spring water. In the summer months, Athenians move out to the Attic Coast, where the well-kept beaches have every kind of water sport facility, and there are bars and clubs. Toward the cape at Soúnio there are countless fish tavernas by the sea and quiet rocky coves ideal for snorkeling.

Boats moored in Mikrolímano harbor, Piraeus

Lárisa, Ioánnina, Préveza, Vólos, Thessaloníki

Chalkída

Thebes

MOUNT PARNITHA

ANCIENT ELEUSIS 16

MEGARA

MONASTERY 14
OF DAFNI

PIRAEUS 15

Corinth, Trípoli, Pátra, Kalamáta

ANCIENT OROPOS

ATH

ACHA

PALAIO FA

SEE ALSO

KEY

▬▬	Divided highway
▬	Major road
▬	Minor road
▬	Scenic route
➥	River
☼	Viewpoint

GETTING AROUND

Athens' international airport, Ellinikón, serves the region. There are two routes out of Athens to southeast Attica: the popular coastal road from Piraeus to Soúnio, and the inland road, via Korópi and Markópoulo, to the east coast towns of Pórto Ráfti and Lávrio. This is also the way for the turn-off to the port of Rafína, where there are ferry connections to Evvoia and the Cyclades. Frequent buses from Athens link all the towns in the area. Mount Párnitha and northern Attica are best reached by taking the E75 national road.

The Temple of Poseidon on the cape at Soúnio

LOCATOR MAP

SIGHTS AT A GLANCE

0 kilometers   10

0 miles   5

The *katholikón* of Moní Kaisarianís

View of the Enkimitirion at Oropós

Ancient Oropós **❶**
Ωρωπός

Kálamos, Attica. **Road map** D4.
0295 62144. Kálamos.
daily. main public hols.

THE PEACEFUL SANCTUARY of Oropós nestles on the left bank of the Cheímarros, a small river surrounded by pine trees and wild thyme bushes. It is dedicated to Amphiaraos, a hero credited with healing powers whom, according to mythology, Zeus rescued when he was wounded in battle. It is said that the earth swallowed up Amphiaraos while he was riding his chariot, and that he then miraculously reappeared through the sacred spring at this site. In ancient times visitors would throw coins into the spring in the hope of being granted good health.

The Amphiaraion sanctuary came to prominence as a healing center in the 4th century BC, when its Doric temple and sacrificial altar were built, attracting the sick from all over Greece. Houses erected during the Roman period, when the area became a popular spa center, are still visible on the right bank of the river. The Enkimitirion was the site's most interesting building. It was a long stoa, the remains of which are still visible today, where the patients underwent treatment by *enkimisis*. This gruesome ritual entailed the sacrifice of a goat in whose bloody hide the patient would then spend the night. The next morning, priests would prescribe medicines based on their interpretations of the dreams of the patient.

Above the Enkimitirion are the remains of an impressive theater, which has a well-preserved *proskenion* (stage) and five sculpted marble thrones, once reserved for the use of priests and guests of honor. On the right bank of the valley, opposite the altar, is a water clock dating from the 4th century BC.

Marble throne from the theater at Oropós

Ramnoús **❷**
Ραμνούς

Attica. **Road map** D4. 0294 63477.
daily (Sanctuary of Nemesis only). main public hols.

RAMNOUS is a remote but beautiful site, overlooking the gulf of Evvoia. It is home to the only Greek sanctuary dedicated to the goddess of vengeance, Nemesis. The sanctuary was demolished when the Roman emperor Arcadius decreed in AD 399 that all temples left standing should be destroyed. Thus only the remains of this sanctuary can be seen today.

Within its compound, two temples are preserved side by side. The smaller and older Temple of Themis dates from the 6th century BC. Used as a treasury and storehouse in ancient times, its impressive polygonal walls are all that now survive.

Within the cella, some important statues of the goddess and her priestess, Aristonoë, were uncovered. They can now be seen in the National Archaeological Museum (see pp68–71).

The larger Temple of Nemesis dates from the mid-5th century BC. It is very similar in design to the Hephaisteion in Athens' Agora (see pp90–91) and the Temple of Poseidon at Soúnio (see p148). Built in the Doric style, the temple contained a

The remains of the Temple of Nemesis at Ramnoús

statue of Nemesis by Agora-kritos, a disciple of Pheidias *(see p98)*. The statue has recently been partially reconstructed from shattered fragments, and the head is now in the British Museum.

The dockside at the port of Rafína

Marathónas ❸
Μαραθώνας

Attica. **Road map** D4. 0294 55155. **Site & Museum** *Tue–Sun.* main public hols.

THE MARATHON PLAIN is the site of the great Battle of Marathon, where the Athenians defeated the Persians. The burial mound of the Athenians lies 4 km (2.5 miles) from the modern town of Marathónas. This tumulus is 180 m (590 ft) in circumference and 10 m (32 ft) high. It contains the ashes of the 192 Athenian warriors who died in the battle. The spot was marked by a simple stele of a fallen warrior by the sculptor Aristion. The original is now in the National Archaeological Museum *(see pp68–71)* in Athens. There is a copy at the site, inscribed with an epigram by the ancient poet Simonides: "The Athenians fought first among the Greeks at Marathon, defeating the gold-bearing Persians and stealing their power."

In 1970 the burial mound of the Plataians and royal Mycenaean tombs were found nearby in the village of Vraná. The Plataians were the only other Greeks who sent warriors in time to assist the Athenians already at the battle. The **Marathon Museum** displays archaeological finds from these local sites. There are also some beautiful

Plate discovered in the tomb of Plataians

Egyptian-style statues from the 2nd century AD, found on the estate of Herodes Atticus, on the Marathon Plain. This wealthy benefactor was born and bred in this area. He is known for erecting many public buildings in Athens, including the famous theater located on the southern slope of the Acropolis *(see p100)* that was named in his honor.

ENVIRONS: Just 8 km (5 miles) west of Marathónas is **Lake Marathon**, which is crossed by a narrow causeway. This vast expanse of water is man-made. The impressive dam, made from white Pentelic marble, was built in 1926. It created an artificial lake that was Athens' sole source of water up until 1956. The lake is fed by the continuous streams of the Charádras and Varnávas, which flow down from Mount Párnitha *(see p151)* and makes a good setting for a picnic.

Rafína ❹
Ραφήνα

Attica. **Road map** D4. 8,600

THE CHARM OF RAFINA is its lively fishing port, packed with caïques and ferries. After Piraeus it is the main port in Attica. Frequent buses from Athens bring passengers for the regular hydrofoil and ferry connections to the Cyclades and other Aegean islands.

One of the administrative *demes* (regions) of ancient Athens, Rafína is a long-established settlement. Although there is little of historical or archaeological interest, the town offers a selection of excellent fish restaurants and tavernas. Choose one by the waterside to sit and watch the hustle and bustle of this busy port.

ENVIRONS: North of Rafína, a winding road leads to the more picturesque resort of **Máti**. Once a quiet hamlet, it is packed today with trendy cafés and bars, apartment houses, and summer homes owned by Athenians.

THE BATTLE OF MARATHON

When Darius of Persia arrived at the Bay of Marathon with his warships in 490 BC, it seemed impossible that the Greeks could defeat him. Heavily outnumbered, the 10,000 Greek hoplites had to engage 25,000 Persian warriors. Victory was due to the tactics of the commander Miltiades, who altered the usual battle phalanx by strengthening the wings with more men. The Persians were enclosed on all sides and driven back to the sea. Around 6,000 Persians died and only 192 Athenians. The origins of the marathon run also date from this battle. News of the victory was relayed by a runner who covered the 41 km (26 miles) back to Athens in full armor before dying of exhaustion.

Vase showing Greek hoplites fighting a Persian on horseback

Ancient Brauron 🔾

Βραυρώνα

SITUATED NEAR MODERN VRAVRONA, Brauron is one of the most evocative sites near Athens. Although little remains of its former architectural glory, finds in the museum reveal its importance as the center of worship of Artemis, goddess of childbirth and protectress of animals *(see p53)*. Legend relates that it was founded by Orestes and Iphigeneia, the children of Agamemnon, who introduced the cult of Artemis into Greece. Evidence of Neolithic and Mycenaean remains have been found on the hill above the site, but the tyrant Peisistratos brought Brauron its fame in the 6th century BC when he made the worship of Artemis Athens' official state religion.

0 meters 30

0 yards 30

KEY TO THE SANCTUARY OF ARTEMIS

① Temple of Artemis
② Chapel of Agios Geórgios
③ Sacred House
④ Tomb of Iphigeneia
⑤ Parthenon of the Bear Maidens
⑥ Dormitories
⑦ Stoa
⑧ Stone Bridge

The Parthenon of the Bear Maidens at Brauron

Exploring Ancient Brauron
The center of this compact site lies just north of the recently excavated prehistoric acropolis. The 5th-century BC Doric **Temple of Artemis**, of which only the foundations remain, formed the focal point of the sanctuary to the goddess. Beside the temple stands a late Byzantine chapel, dedicated to **Agios Geórgios**. From here a path leads southeast to the oldest cult site in the sanctuary. This is said to

be the **Tomb of Iphigeneia**, the high priestess of Artemis. Next to it are the foundations of the **Sacred House**, which was used as a home by the cult's priestesses. The most extensive remains at the site are to the northeast, at the **Parthenon of the Bear Maidens**. This courtyard was where young girls performed

the bear dance. Surrounded by a late 5th-century BC **stoa**, the courtyard had rooms behind that were used as dining areas and **dormitories**. Only the foundations remain, but the stone sleeping couches and bases of statues can still be seen. There are also fragments of a 5th-century BC **stone bridge** to the west.

The small Byzantine chapel of Agios Geórgios

BRAURONIA CEREMONY

Held every four years in the spring, the Brauronia festival was celebrated in atonement for the killing of one of Artemis's sacred pet bears. Little is known about the mysterious rites today, but Aristophanes mentions the "bear dance" that initiates had to perform in his play *Lysistrata*. Disguised as bears and adorned with saffron-colored robes, young girls, between 5 and 10 years of age, performed a dance honoring this sacred animal.

Relief showing pilgrims approaching the altar of Artemis at the Brauronia ceremony

**Mycenaean vase from the
Brauron Museum, 1200–1100 BC**

Brauron Museum
This fascinating museum
has a wealth of finds
from the site. In
Room 1, there are
cases filled with
assorted votive
offerings such as
miniature vases and
jewelry. In Room 2
are the serene statues
of *árktoi* ("bear
maidens"). Room 3
has a fine votive
relief of the gods
Zeus, Leto, Apollo,
Statue of   and Artemis, and
a bear   the remains of an
maiden   altar. Rooms 4 and
5 offer a variety of
prehistoric and Mycenaean
finds, including some ornate
Geometric vases.

RETSINA

Although many Greeks prefer drinking whisky to wine
these days, retsina is still favored by millions of tourists.
Around 16 million bottles were drunk in 1994, and 50 percent of them were exported around the
world. The unique, distinctive flavor comes
from the Aleppo pine resin that is added in
small quantities to the grape juice during
fermentation. This method has been used
since antiquity to preserve and flavor wine
in Greece. Since entry into the EEC in
1981, traditional production areas have
had their own appellations. Aficionados
agree that some of the best retsina comes
from the Mesógeia appellation in Attica,
where the Savatiano grape is cultivated.
Kourtákis, the largest producers of
retsina, have their vineyards in
Markópoulo and Koropí.

**Collection
of pine
resin**

Pórto Ráfti 6
Πόρτο Ράφτη

Attica. **Road map** D4. 3,300.

PÓRTO RÁFTI takes its name
from Ráfti island, which is
visible just off the headland.
On the island is a colossal
marble statue of a seated
female, known as "the tailor"
(ráftis). It was most likely
built to be used as a beacon
for shipping and would have
lit up the harbor. Pórto Ráfti
has one of the best natural
harbors in Greece, although
the town itself has never
developed into an important
seafaring port. In April 1941,
during World War II, 6,000
New Zealand troops were
successfully evacuated from
the beach. Today it is primarily
a pleasant vacation resort, with
tavernas and bars. The area is

rich in archaeological history.
Many Mycenaean tombs have
been found south of the bay
of Pórto Ráfti, at **Prasiés**, a
port that flourished in the 7th
and 6th centuries BC.

ENVIRONS: The remains of a
fortress built during the
Chremonidean War (265– 261
BC) between Egypt and
Macedonia can be seen on
the southern **Koróni** headland. The northern coastline
of **Peráti** is pockmarked with
unexplored caves and attracts
many people who come to
swim in the clear water and
fish off the craggy rocks.
Markópoulo, a thriving
market town and viticultural
center 8 km (5 miles) inland,
is famous for its tavernas.
Spicy sausages are for sale
in the butchers' shops, and
the bakeries are fragrant with
the smell of fresh bread.

Pórto Ráfti harbor with Ráfti island in the background

One of the many 19th-century Neo-Classical buildings in Lávrio

Lávrio **7**
Λαύριο

Attica. **Road map** D4. 🏘 8,800.
🚌 🚢 🚇 Thu.

LAVRIO WAS FAMOUS for its silver mines in ancient times. They were used as a source of revenue for the Athenian state and financed Perikles' program of grand public building in Athens in the 5th century BC (see p30). They also enabled the general Themistokles to construct a fleet capable of beating the Persians at the Battle of Salamis in 480 BC. It was this excellent naval fleet that established Athens as a naval power. Before their closure in the 19th century, the mines were further exploited by French and Greek companies for other minerals such as manganese and cadmium.

Originally worked by slaves, over 2,000 mine shafts have been discovered in the surrounding hills, and some are now open to visitors as the **Mineralogical Museum**. It is the only such museum in Greece. Traces of ore and minerals in the rock face can be seen on tours of the old mines. Since their closure the area has suffered high unemployment. The old Neo-Classical houses and empty waterfront warehouses are an indication of the former prosperity of the town. Makrónisos, the long, narrow island opposite the port, was used as a prison for political detainees during the Civil War (see p42).

🏛 **Mineralogical Museum**
Leof Andréa Kordelá. 📞 0292 26270. ☐ Wed, Sat & Sun. 🎫 🚹

Soúnio **8**
Σούνιο

9 km (5.5 miles) S of Lávrio, Attica.
Road map D4. 📞 0292 39363.
🚌 to Lávrio. ☐ daily. 🎫

THE TEMPLE OF POSEIDON, built on a site set back from sheer cliffs tumbling into the Aegean Sea at Soúnio (Cape Sounion), was ideally located for worship of the powerful god of the sea. Its brilliant white marble columns have been a landmark for ancient and modern mariners alike.

The present temple, built in 444 BC, stands on the site of older ruins. An Ionic frieze, made from 13 slabs of Parian marble, is located on the east side of the temple's main approach path. It is very eroded but is known to have depicted scenes from the mythological battle of the Lapiths and centaurs, and also the adventures of the hero Theseus, who was said in some legends to be the son of Poseidon.

The Doric columns of the Temple of Poseidon

Local marble, taken from quarries at nearby Agriléza, was used for the temple's 34 slender Doric columns, of which 15 survive today. The temple also possesses a

The ruins of the Temple of Poseidon on Soúnio

unique design feature that helps combat the effects of sea-spray erosion: the columns were cut with only 16 flutings instead of the usual 20, thus reducing the surface area exposed to the elements.

When Byron carved his name on one of the columns in 1810, he set a dangerous precedent of vandalism at the temple, which is now covered with scrawling signatures.

A waterside restaurant at Várkiza, along the Attic coast

Attic Coast ⑨
Παραλία

Attica. **Road map** D4.

THE COASTAL STRIP from Piraeus to Soúnio is often called the "Apollo Coast" after a small Temple of Apollo discovered at Vouliagméni. It is covered with beaches and resort towns that are always very busy on weekends, and particularly so in the summer vacation season.

One of the first places along the coast from Piraeus is the tiny seaside resort of **Palaío Fáliro**, which is home to the Phaleron War Cemetery. In this quiet spot is the Athens Memorial, erected in May 1961 to 2,800 British soldiers who died in World War II.

Noisy suburbs near Athens airport, like **Glyfáda** and **Alimos** (famous as the birthplace of the ancient historian Thucydides), are very commercialized with a large number of marinas, hotels, and shopping malls.

At chic **Vouliagméni**, with its large yacht marina, luxury

hotels line the promontory. A short walk northward away from the coast, beside the main road, is the enchanting Vouliagméni Lake. This unusual freshwater lake lies beneath low limestone cliffs. The stunning stretch of warm, sulfurous water has been used for years to bring relief to arthritis sufferers. There are changing rooms and a café close by.

At **Várkiza**, the wide bay is filled with windsurfers. By the main road there are two massive gin-mill music halls, *On the Rocks* and *Riba's*, where popular Greek singers perform throughout the summer season. From Várkiza, a road snakes inland to **Vári**, renowned for its

restaurants serving meat dishes. The Vári cave is located about 2 km (1 mile) north of the village. Inside are a freshwater spring and some fine stalactites. Some minor Classical ruins remain in the caves, although many have been removed. There is unrestricted access and no admission charge.

From Várkiza to Soúnio, the coastal road is lined with quiet swimming coves, fish tavernas, and luxury villas. **Anávyssos** is a thriving market town surrounded by vineyards and fields. In its harbor, caïques sell locally caught fish every day, and there is a small street market every Saturday, with stalls piled high with seasonal fruit and vegetables.

Colorful stall of local produce in Anávyssos

Sculpture in the gardens of the Vorre Museum

Paianía ⑩
Παιανία

Attica. **Road map** D4. ⚇ *9,700.* 🚌
🚆 *Tue.*

JUST EAST OF ATHENS, Paianía is a town of sleepy streets and cafés. In the main square, the church of **Zoödóchou Pigís** has some fine modern frescoes by the 20th-century artist Fótis Kóntoglou. The birthplace of the orator Demosthenes (384–322 BC), Paianía is more famous today for the **Vorre Museum**. Set in beautiful gardens, this features private collector Ian Vorre's eclectic array of ancient and modern art. The museum is divided into two sections, encompassing 3,000 years of Greek history and heritage. The first is housed in what was the collector's private home: two traditional village houses filled with ancient sculptures, folk artifacts, ceramics, Byzantine icons, seascapes, and furniture. The second section, housed in a specially built modern building, offers a unique overview of contemporary Greek art since the 1940s, with many excellent works by more than 300 different painters and sculptors, encompassing every major art movement from Photo-Realism to Pop Art.

🏛 Vorre Museum
Diadóchou Konstantínou 1. ☎ *01 664 4771.* ☐ *Sat & Sun.* ● *Aug & main public hols.* 🖼 ⛔

ENVIRONS: Above Paianía, the **Koutoúki Cave** is hidden in the foothills of Mount Ymittós. It was found in 1926 by a shepherd looking for a goat that had fallen into the 12,200 sq m (130,000 sq ft) cave. There are tours every half hour, with *son-et-lumière* effects lighting up the stalagmites and stalactites. The temperature inside is 17˚C (62˚F).

🏛 Koutoúki Cave
4 km (2.5 miles) W of Paianía. ☎ *01 664 2108.* ☐ *daily.* ● *main public hols.* 🖼

Moní Kaisarianís ⑪
Μονή Καισαριανής

5 km (3 miles) E of Athens, Attica. **Road map** D4. ☎ *01 723 6619.* 🚌 *to Kaisarianís.* ☐ *8:30am–3pm Tue–Sun.* ● *main public hols.* 🖼

LOCATED IN A WOODED valley of Mount Ymittós, Moní Kaisarianís was founded in the 11th century. In 1458, when Sultan Mehmed II conquered Athens, the monastery was exempted from taxes in recognition of the abbot's gift to the sultan of the keys of the city. This led to great prosperity until 1792, when it lost these privileges and went into decline. The complex was used briefly as a convent after the War of Independence, until 1855. Its buildings were eventually restored in 1956.

The small *katholikón* is dedicated to the Presentation of the Virgin. All the frescoes date from the 16th and 17th centuries. The

Decorative stonework on Moní Kaisarianís

finest are those in the narthex, painted by the Peloponnesian artist Ioánnis Ypatos in 1682.

The large, peaceful gardens in the monastery are owned by the Athens Friends of the Tree Society, who planted them after all the trees were cut down during World War II. Just above the monastery, the source of the River Ilissós has

Moní Kaisarianís, hidden in the hills around Mount Ymittós

been visited since antiquity for its sacred Kylloú Péra spring, whose water is reputed to cure sterility; water still gushes from an ancient marble ram's head fountain on the eastern side of the monastery. Before the Marathon dam was built *(see p145)*, the spring was Athens' main source of water.

Kifisiá 🄬
Κηφισιά

12 km (7.5 miles) NE of Athens, Attica.
Road map D4. 🐾 40,000. 🚇
Ⓜ *Kifisiá.*

The tiny chapel of Agía Triáda on the hillside of Mount Párnitha

KIFISIÁ HAS BEEN a favorite summer retreat for many Athenians since Roman times. Once the exclusive domain of rich Greeks, it is congested today with apartment houses and shopping malls. Traces of its former tranquillity can still be seen by taking a ride in a horse-drawn carriage. These wait by the metro station offering drives down shady streets lined with mansions and villas, built in a bizarre variety of hybrid styles such as Alpine chalet and Gothic Neo-Classicism.

The **Goulándris Natural History Museum**, which opened in 1974, is housed in one of these villas. Its large collection covers all aspects of Greece's varied wildlife and minerals. There are 200,000 varieties of plants and over 1,300 examples of taxidermy; the stuffed creatures are carefully displayed in their natural habitats.

Clamshell outside the Goulándris Natural History Museum, Kifisiá

🅸 Goulándris Natural History Museum
Levidou 13. 🄲 *01 808 6405.*
⭘ *Tue–Thu, Sat & Sun.*
⬤ *main public hols.* 🈂

ENVIRONS: In Kifisiá's suburb Maroúsi is the small **Spathári Museum of Shadow Theater**. Opened in 1995, it is devoted to the fascinating history of the Karagkiózis puppet theater. Shadow theater originally came to Greece from the Far East, via players who used to travel throughout the Ottoman Empire performing for the aristocracy in the 18th century. It was soon transformed into a popular folk art by entertainers who would travel around Greece with their makeshift theaters. The name Karagkiózis refers to the indomitable and impoverished Greek character who is tormented by the other standard theatrical characters such as the rich Pasha and tough guy Stávrakas. The museum displays the history of two generations of the Spathári family, who were the leading exponents of this dying art, along with a collection of colorful home-made sets and the various puppets that were used in their past performances.

Puppet from the Museum of Shadow Theater

🅸 Spathári Museum of Shadow Theater
Plateía Kastalías. 🄲 *01 612 7206.*
⭘ *Tue–Sun.* ⬤ *main public hols.*

Mount Párnitha 🄬
Όρος Πάρνηθα

Attica. **Road map** D4. 🚌 *to Acharnés, Thrakomakedónes & Agía Triáda.*

IN ANCIENT TIMES, Mount Párnitha sheltered wild animals. Today, this rugged range, which extends nearly 25 km (16 miles) from east to west, is rich in less dangerous fauna. Tortoises can be seen in the undergrowth, and birds of prey circle the summit of Karampóla at 1,413 m (4,635 ft). Wildflowers are abundant, particularly in autumn and spring when cyclamen and crocus carpet the mountain. There are spectacular views of alpine scenery, all within an hour's drive of the city. At the small town of **Acharnés**, a cable car ascends to a casino perched at over 900 m (3,000 ft).

Still little used by hikers, the mountain has plenty of demanding trails. The most popular walk leads from Thrakomakedónes, in the foothills of the mountain, to the Vafí refuge. This uphill march takes about two hours and offers superb views of the surrounding mountain scenery. Starting with thorny scrub typical of the Mediterranean *maquis*, it follows well-worn paths to end among alpine firs and clear mountain air. Once at the Vafí refuge, it is worth walking on to the Flampoúri refuge, which has some dramatic views.

Monastery of Dafní ⓮
Μονή Δαφνίου

THE MONASTERY OF DAFNI was founded in the 5th century AD. Named after the laurels *(dáfnes)* that used to grow here, it was built with the remains of an ancient sanctuary of Apollo that had occupied this site until it was destroyed in AD 395. In the early 13th century, Otto de la Roche, the first Frankish Duke of Athens, bequeathed it to Cistercian monks in Burgundy. Greek Orthodox monks took the site in the 16th century, erecting the elegant cloisters just south of the church. Today, the beautiful gold-leaf Byzantine mosaics in the *katholikón* (main church) are the principal attraction of the monastery *(see pp18–19)*.

Fresco detail

Aerial view of the monastery complex

The Gothic exonarthex was built almost 30 years after the main church.

Cloisters
This arcade was built in the 16th century. On the other side of the courtyard, above a similar arcade, are the monks' cells.

The symmetry of the design makes Dafní one of the most attractive examples of Byzantine architecture in Attica.

Esonarthex

Exonarthex

Entrance

Entrance

KEY TO MOSAICS IN THE KATHOLIKON

WALLS
 1 Resurrection
 2 Adoration of the Magi
 4 Archangel Gabriel
 5 Archangel Michael
 6 Nativity of the Virgin
 8 St. John the Theologian
 9 Entry into Jerusalem
 12 Dormition of the Virgin
 13 Last Supper
 14 Washing of the Feet
 15 Betrayal by Judas
 16 Prayer of Sts. Anne and Joachim
 17 Blessing of the Priests
 18 Presentation of the Virgin
 20 St. Thomas

CEILING AND DOME
 3 Nativity
 7 Annunciation
 10 Christ Pantokrátor
 11 Transfiguration
 19 Baptism

★ **Christ Pantokrátor**
The Pantokrátor ("Almighty") gazes sternly down from the dome of the katholikón. Around the central figure are images of the 16 prophets.

VISITORS' CHECKLIST

10 km (6 miles) NW of Athens, Attica. **Road map** D4. 01 581 1558. 8:30am–3pm daily. main public hols. limited.

The dome is 8 m (26 ft) in diameter and 16 m (52 ft) high at the center.

Nave

The Transfiguration
This is in the northwest corner under the dome. Elijah and Moses are on either side of Christ, and the apostles Peter, James, and John are below.

The Windows
Elaborate three-tiered brickwork surrounds each of the windows.

Ticket office and museum

STAR MOSAICS

★ **Christ Pantokrátor**

★ **Esonarthex Mosaics**

★ **Esonarthex Mosaics**
These mosaics include depictions of the Last Supper *and the* Washing of the Feet. *The finest is the* Betrayal of Judas. *Christ stands unmoved as Judas kisses him.*

Piraeus ⑮
Πειραιάς

Waiting for a ferry

ONE OF THE BIGGEST Mediterranean ports, Piraeus is also one of the largest cities in Greece. It has been the port of Athens since ancient times. The Long Walls between Piraeus and Athens were started in 480 BC by Themistokles. However, Sulla destroyed the walls in 86 BC, and by the Middle Ages Piraeus was little more than a fishing village. When Athens became the Greek capital in 1834, Piraeus was once again revitalized, with Neo-Classical buildings and modern factories. In 1923, 100,000 refugees came here from Asia Minor, bringing their culture and contributing to the cosmopolitan feel of this port city.

View across Kentrikó Limáni with ferries in the foreground

Small boats moored in peaceful Tourkolímano harbor

Little Harbor) houses many colorful fishing caïques. It is popular for its waterside fish restaurants and has a more relaxing ambience than the larger harbors.

On the coastal road between Pasalimáni and Tourkolímano, stylish bars and clubs inhabit the renovated Neo-Classical mansions in the gentrified Kastélla neighborhood. Even the traditional working-class neighborhood of Drapetsóna has been cleaned up. The most important manufacturing center of the country, Drapetsóna is also popular for its late-night restaurants.

🎭 Municipal Theater
Agíou Konstantínou 2. **(** 01 417 8351. **☐** Mon–Fri.
The Neo-Classical façade of this imposing building is one of the delights of Piraeus. Designed by Ioánnis Lazirímos (1849–1913), who based his plans on the Opéra Comique in Paris, it has seating for 800, making it one of the largest modern theaters in Greece. It took nearly 10 years to complete and was finally

Exploring Piraeus
After the Junta (see p43) razed many irreplaceable public buildings in the town center in the early 1970s, civic pride reemerged with a vengeance. Besides the Municipal Theater, there are elegant open-air restaurants and fountains in the shade of Neo-Classical façades. On the streets behind the main banks and ticket offices that rim the **Kentrikó Limáni** (the main ferry port), there are stylish restaurants and shops, as well as some fine examples of Neo-Classical architecture, such as the **Town Hall**. For information on ferry departures from Kentrikó Limáni, see page 321.

South of the railroad station around Navarínou lies the lively market area, including fishmongers, fruit and vegetable stalls, ships' chandlers, and hardware stores. On Sunday mornings there is also a bustling flea market, which

is centered on the antique shops around Plateía Ippodámeias, and also on Alipédou and Skylítsi streets.

There are three harbors in Piraeus, all situated east of Kentrikó Limáni. **Pasalimáni** (Pasha's port, also known as Limín Zéas) was once used to harbor the Ottoman fleet. Today it is filled with luxurious yachts. Once known as Zéa, Pasalimáni was also formerly used as one of Themistokles' major naval ports, with dry docks for 196 triremes. **Marína Zéas** is situated to the south of Pasalimáni and is a jetty used as a dock for hydrofoils to the Argo-Saronic islands. **Tourkolímano** (also known as Mikrolímano, or

Façade of the Municipal Theater

inaugurated on April 9, 1895. Today, it is the home of both the **Municipal Art Gallery** and also the **Pános Aravantinoú Museum of Stage Decor**. The Museum of Stage Decor has displays of set designs by the stage designer Pános Aravantinoú (who worked with the Berlin opera in the 1920s), as well as general ephemera from the Greek opera.

Archaeological Museum

Chariláou Trikoúpi 31. **C** 01 452 1598. **○** Tue–Sun. **●** main public hols.

This museum is home to some stunning bronzes. Found by workmen in 1959, these large statues of Artemis with her quiver, Athena with her helmet decorated with owls, and Apollo reveal the great expressiveness of Greek sculpture. The Piraeus *koúros* of Apollo, dating from 520 BC, is the earliest full-size bronze

Statue of Athena in the Archaeological Museum

to be discovered. There is also a seated cult statue of the earth goddess Cybele and a fine collection of Greek and Roman statues and grave stelae. Near the museum are the remains of the 2nd-century BC **Theater of Zéa**; the remains include a well-preserved orchestra.

Hellenic Maritime Museum

Aktí Themistókleous, Freatýda. **C** 01 451 6822. **○** Tue–Sun. **●** main public hols, Aug.

On the dockside of Marína Zéas, an old submarine marks the entrance to this fascinating museum. Its first room is built around an original section of Themistokles's Long Walls. More than 2,000 exhibits, such as models of triremes, ephemera from naval battleships, and paintings of Greek *trechantíri* (fishing caïques), explore the world of Greek seafaring. From early voyages around

the Black Sea by trireme, to 20th-century emigration to the New World by transatlantic liner, the museum unravels the complexities of Greek maritime history. Exhibits include models of ships, maps, flags, uniforms, and pictures. The War of Independence is well documented with information and memorabilia about the generals who served in it. The old naval ship *Averof*, which was the flagship of the Greek fleet up until 1951, has been fully restored and is berthed nearby. As part of the museum, the ship is also open to visitors.

PIRAEUS CITY CENTER

- Archaeological Museum ④
- Hellenic Maritime Museum ⑥
- Municipal Theater ②
- Pasalimáni ③
- Theater of Zéa ⑤
- Town Hall ①

0 meters 150
0 yards 150

KEY

Ferry service
Tourist information
Church

Ancient Eleusis ⓰
Αρχαία Ελευσίνα

ELEUSIS was an ancient center of religious devotion that culminated in the annual Eleusinian Mysteries. These attracted thousands of people from around the Greek-speaking world, for whom the only initial requirement for becoming a *mystes* (or initiate) was to be neither a murderer nor a barbarian. Both men and women were freely admitted. Existing from Mycenaean times, the sanctuary was closed by the Roman Emperor Theodosius in AD 392 and was finally abandoned when Alaric, king of the Goths, invaded Greece in AD 396, bringing Christianity in his wake.

Anaktoron
This small, rectangular stone edifice had a single entrance. It was considered the holiest part of the site. Meaning "palace," it existed long before the Telesterion, which was built around it.

Telesterion
Designed by Iktinos, this temple was built in the 5th century BC. It was constructed to hold several thousand people at a time.

4th-century BC shops and bouleuterion (council chamber)

Temple of Kore hewn out of rock

Roman houses

THE ELEUSINIAN MYSTERIES

Perhaps established by 1500 BC and continuing for almost 2,000 years, these rites centered on the myth of the grieving goddess Demeter, who lost her daughter Persephone (or Kore) to Hades, god of the Underworld, for three months each year *(see p52)*. Participants were sworn to secrecy, but some evidence of the details of the ceremony does exist. Sacrifices were made before the procession from the Kerameikós *(see pp88–9)* to Eleusis. Here the priestesses would reveal the vision of the holy night, thought to have been a fire symbolizing life after death for the initiates.

A priestess with a *cista mystica* (basket)

ANCIENT ELEUSIS

This reconstruction is of Eleusis as it was in Roman times (c.AD 150), when the Mysteries were still flourishing. The view is from the east. Although there is little left today, it is still possible to sense the awe and mystery that the rites of Eleusis inspired.

Ploutonion
This cave is said to be where Persephone was returned to earth. It was a sanctuary to Hades, or Pluto, god of the underworld and the abductor of Persephone.

Greater Propylaia
Built from Pentelic marble in the 2nd century AD by the Roman Emperor Antoninus Pius, this was modeled on the Propylaia of Athens' Acropolis.

One of a pair of triumphal arches

Temple of Artemis Propylaia

Well of Kallichoron
Demeter is believed to have grieved for Persephone here.

Lesser Propylaia
This fragment shows sheaves of grain and poppies, which were used to make kykeon, the drink of the initiates.

Relief from the Telesterion, now in the museum

📷 Eleusis Museum
This small museum, south of the Telesterion, has five rooms. The entrance hall contains a copy of the famous relief from the Telesterion showing Triptolemos receiving grain from Demeter. Also in this room are a large 7th-century BC amphora and a copy of the Ninnion votive painting, one of the few remaining representations of the Eleusinian Mysteries. The other rooms are arranged on the left of the hall. In the first of these there is an elegant 6th-century BC *koúros* and a 2nd-century BC Roman statue of Dionysos. In the second room there are two reconstruction models of the site. The third room has a Classical period terra-cotta sarcophagus and a large caryatid carrying a *cista mystica* basket on her head from the Lesser Propylaia. The last room has a variety of pottery fragments, including examples of unusual terra-cotta fire containers, known as *kernoi*, which were used to carry lights in the annual sacred procession.

Fleeing maiden

THE PELOPONNESE

PELOPONNESE

O NE OF THE PRIMARY *strongholds and battlefields of the 1821–31 Revolution, the Peloponnese is the kernel from which the modern Greek state grew. This enormous peninsula, which falls short of being an island by the mere 6-km (4-mile) width of the Corinth isthmus, also has some of the most spectacularly varied scenery and monuments on the mainland.*

The name "Peloponnese" means "island of Pelops," who in legend was fed to the gods by Tantalos, his father. Resurrected, he went on to sire the Atreid line of kings, whose semimythical adventures and brooding citadels were given substance by the discovery of ruins at Mycenae. Today the ancient and medieval sites of the Argolid region, south of Corinth, contrast with the elegantly Neo-Classical town of Náfplio.

Leonidas statue, Spárti town

In the west lies ancient Olympia, the athletic and religious nexus of the ancient world and inspiration for the games' revival in modern times. The lush coastal plain of Ilía, heart of an early medieval Crusader principality, spawned Frankish-Byzantine architecture, most famously at Chlemoútsi.

More purely Byzantine art adorns the churches of Mystrás, Geráki, and the remote Máni region, whose warlike medieval inhabitants claimed to be descended from the warriors of ancient Sparta. Imposing Venetian fortifications at the beach-fringed capes of Methóni, Koróni, and Monemvasía allowed the Venetians to play a role here after most of their other Aegean possessions were lost to the Ottomans.

In Arcadia, at the center of the Peloponnese, lushly cultivated valleys rise to conifer-draped mountains and deep gorges such as the Loúsios; cliffside monasteries and somber hill towns like Stemnitsa are a world apart from the popular Mediterranean image of Greece.

Restaurant terrace overlooking the ocean, Monemvasía

◁ Náfplio, seen from the stairs leading to the town's Venetian citadel, Palamídi

Exploring the Peloponnese

ANCIENT AND MEDIEVAL ruins are abundant on the Peloponnese and provide the main focus of sightseeing. Though there are few highly developed resorts away from the Argolid, such areas as the Loúsios Gorge and Kalogriá attract thousands of hikers and naturalists. A rural economy is still paramount inland, with Pátra being the only large city. The landscape is dominated by forested mountains, and the west coast, between Pátra and Methóni, boasts some of the finest beaches in the Mediterranean.

Kariténa village, Loúsios Gorge

GETTING AROUND

Major roads link Athens and Pátra via Corinth, and also connect Corinth to Trípoli. Secondary roads are more interesting and mostly paved, if dangerously narrow. Public transportation consists of the bus service between major towns and a rather creaky rail system. One line runs slowly around the north and west coasts, and the other cuts diagonally through the middle via Trípoli, both lines converging at Kalamáta. Ferries and hydrofoils (see p321) serve various points on the east coast, such as Monemvasía and Neápoli. There is also an airport at Kalamáta.

SIGHTS AT A GLANCE

Gýtheio harbor, Inner Máni

HERAION OF
PERACHORA

3

CORINTH CANAL

2

8

LOCATOR MAP

ANCIENT CORINTH 1

ANCIENT NEMEA

4

MYCENAE

15

ARGOLID

ANCIENT
TIRYNS

ARGOS 14 16

17

NAFPLIO

18 EPIDAURUS

19

ANCIENT TROEZEN

TRIPOLI

13

ANCIENT
TEGEA

E65

70

31

SPARTI

22

23

MYSTRAS

21 GERAKI

Evrotas

24 OUTER MANI

86

MONEMVASIA 20

25

INNER MANI

NEAPOLI

SEE ALSO

• *Where to Stay* pp269–71

• *Where to Eat* pp291–2

KEY

▬▬	Divided highway
▬	Major road
▬	Minor road
▬	Unpaved road
▬	Scenic route
~~	River
☼	Viewpoint

0 kilometers   20

0 miles   20

Ancient Corinth **❶**
Αρχαία Κόρινθος

ANCIENT CORINTH derived its prosperity from its position on a narow isthmus between the Saronic and Corinthian gulfs. Transporting goods across this isthmus, even before the canal *(see p167)* was built, provided the shortest route from the eastern Mediterranean to the Adriatic and Italy. Founded in Neolithic times, the town was razed in 146 BC by the Romans, who rebuilt it a century later. Attaining a population of 750,000 under the patronage of the emperors, the town gained a reputation for licentious living that St. Paul attacked when he came here in AD 52. Excavations have revealed the vast extent of the city, destroyed by earthquakes in Byzantine times. The ruins constitute the largest Roman township in Greece.

LOCATOR MAP

The *bema* (platform), was where St. Paul was accused of sacrilege by the Jews of Corinth.

Bouleuterion

The agora was the hub of Roman civic life.

South stoa

★ Lechaion Way
This marble-paved road linked the port of Lechaion with the city, ending at a still-surviving stairway and an imposing propylaion *(entrance).*

The Peirene fountain's springs still supply the local modern village.

Basilica

RECONSTRUCTION OF ANCIENT CORINTH (C.AD 100)

Bouleuterion

South stoa

Bema

Agora

Peirene fountain

Basilica

Lechaion Way

Temple of Octavia

Odeion

Theater

Glauke fountain

North stoa

Temple of Apollo

Temple of Octavia

These three ornate Corinthian columns, overarched by a restored architrave, are all that remain of a temple, standing on a platform, dedicated to the sister of the Emperor Augustus.

VISITORS' CHECKLIST

7 km (4 miles) SW of modern Corinth, Peloponnese. **Road map** C4. ☎ *0741 31207.* 🚌 **Site & Museum** ◻ *Apr–Oct: 8am–7pm Mon–Fri, 8am–6pm Sat & Sun; Nov–Mar: 8am–5pm Mon–Fri, 8am–6pm Sat & Sun.* ● *Mon am (museum only), Jan 1, Mar 25, Good Fri am, Easter Sun, May 1, Dec 25, 26.* 🎫 📷 ♿ *limited.* **Acrocorinth:** 4 km (2.5 miles) S of Ancient Corinth. ◻ *unrestricted access.* 🍴

Acrocorinth
(see p166)

The museum contains artifacts from the site *(see p166).*

Odeion

This was one of several buildings endowed by Herodes Atticus, the wealthy Athenian and good friend of the Emperor Hadrian.

The theater was modified in the 3rd century AD so water could be piped in and mock sea battles staged.

The Glauke fountain's four cisterns were hewn from a cubic monolith and filled by an aqueduct from the hills.

The north stoa was a large market terrace. A single vaulted structure remains.

★ Temple of Apollo

The most striking structure of the lower city, this temple was one of the few buildings preserved by the Romans when they rebuilt the site in 44 BC. At the southeast corner an ingenious stepped ramp leads to the temple terrace.

STAR SIGHTS

★ Temple of Apollo

★ Lechaion Way

The surviving Doric columns of the Temple of Apollo, Ancient Corinth ▷

Exploring Acrocorinth and the Museum

EXCAVATIONS OF RECENT YEARS have yielded numerous artifacts now on view in the museum and have revealed the vast extent of the ancient city, which included the summit of Acrocorinth. Altogether, the ruins constitute the largest Roman township in Greece, since few earlier structures were restored after the Romans destroyed the town in 146 BC. Acrocorinth became one of medieval Greece's most important fortresses and can now be reached by a road that climbs the western face of the hill from the lower town.

⋔ Acrocorinth

Acrocorinth, 4 km (2.5 miles) beyond the main city, has been held and refortified by every occupying power in Greece since Roman times. Entry is on the west, where the peak's natural defenses are weakest, through three successive gateways from different eras. The lowest is mostly Turkish; the middle, Frankish; and the third and highest, Byzantine, though it and two adjacent towers incorporate abundant ancient masonry. Beyond sprawls a (60-acre) terraced wilderness of minaret stumps, Muslim tombs, and lonely mosques or chapels – all that remains of the town abandoned more than a century ago, when its last defenders, the Turks, were defeated.

The lower elevation at the southwest corner of the 5-km (3-mile) circuit of walls sports a Venetian tower, while the true, northeast summit bears the scant foundations of an Aphrodite temple, attended in antiquity by 1,000 sacred

Mosaic of Bacchus (Dionysos), 2nd century AD, in the museum

prostitutes. It was against such practices that St. Paul wrote his two letters to the Corinthians. Today its attraction is one of the most sweeping views in the whole of Greece, up to 60 km (37 miles) in all directions from the Geráneia range in the northeast to the peaks of Zíria in the southwest. Toward Zíria, a prominent nearby hill, Penteskoúfi, was fortified by the Franks during the 13th century.

Acrocorinth could withstand lengthy sieges because of the presence of the upper Peirene spring, on the southeast side of the ramparts. A right-angled stairway descends to a vaulted, subterranean chamber pool; in dry seasons the water recedes to expose a carved column supporting an ornate Hellenistic pediment.

🏛 Museum

The site museum, just south of the odeion, ranks among Greece's best provincial collections, despite an unsolved burglary in 1990. All periods of the ancient town's history are represented, though the Roman gallery in the west wing is particularly rich. Here the top attraction is the 2nd-century AD mosaics lifted from the floors of nearby villas: a head of Bacchus (Dionysos) set in a circular geometric pattern, a nude shepherd playing his flute to three cows, and a goat napping under a tree. The north doorway is flanked by two columns in the shape of Phrygian prisoners, shown with their arms crossed, their tunics and long hair seeming to prefigure medieval art. The east gallery features older artifacts. Attic ware from the 5th century BC (see pp60–61), including the famous "Owl" vase, is rarer than the 7th- and 6th-century BC pottery, some painted with fantastic beasts, for which Corinth was noted.

At the shrine of Asklepios, just within the northern boundary of the ancient city walls, votive offerings in the shape of afflicted body parts were found and are on display here, the precursors of the *támmata* or metal *ex votos* left in modern Orthodox churches. Other oddities include a startling 6th-century marble sphinx and Hellenistic pediments with lion-head spouts, whose brilliant pigmentation has unusually survived.

Stone reliefs in the central courtyard include depictions of the Labors of Herakles (see p53), one of which was performed nearby at the sanctuary of Neméa.

The entrance to Acrocorinth, with its three gateways

Ships passing through the Corinth Canal with the road bridge overhead

Corinth Canal ❷
Διώρυγα Κορίνθου

Peloponnese. **Road map** C4.
Loutráki.

STORMY CAPE MATAPAN, or Taínaro *(see p199)*, the southernmost point of the Peloponnese, was one of the dreaded capes of antiquity; rather than risk sailing around it, boats would be unloaded on one shore of this isthmus, dragged the 6 km (4 miles) across on the *diolkós* (paved slipway), and then refloated and reloaded.

The traffic enriched Corinth and inspired plans for a canal. Emperor Nero began construction, but the project was only completed between 1882 and 1893. The 23-m (75-ft) wide canal is obsolete in an age of giant container ships that easily weather the cape, but small freighters squeezing through are regularly seen from the road bridge above.

ENVIRONS: Near the southern end of the canal is the site of **Ancient Isthmia**, once the major local religious center (devoted to Poseidon) and

View of the Sanctuary of Hera at Perachóra, Cape Melangávi

location of the quadrennial Isthmian Games. Today only foundations of Poseidon's temple (7th century BC) are traceable, though adjacent lie the remains of a starting gate used for track events in the vanished stadium.

The site museum stresses finds from Kenkreai, Corinth's eastern port; unique exhibits include panels of painted glass or stone embedded in a resin matrix. They were intended to decorate an Isis temple but were never used because of an earthquake in AD 375.

� Ancient Isthmia
Southern end of Corinth Canal. **Site & Museum** 0741 37244. Tue–Sun. main public hols.

Heraion of Perachóra ❸
Ηραίον της Περαχώρας

13 km (8 miles) W of Loutráki, Peloponnese. **Road map** C4.

PROBABLY FOUNDED during the 8th century BC, the Heraion of Perachóra (a near-by village) was, like Ancient Isthmia, primarily a religious center. Only foundations and column stumps remain of the Archaic temple of Hera Limeneia, plus an altar and a Classical stoa, but the site has an incomparable setting, above a tiny cove on the south shore of Cape Melangávi, close to a 19th-century lighthouse.

Scenic Vouliagénis Lake, 3 km (2 miles) east, is fringed by Aleppo pines, with the best swimming and a selection of tavernas at its west end.

Ancient Neméa ❹
Αρχαία Νεμέα

5 km (3 miles) NE of Neméa, Peloponnese. **Road map** C4.
0746 22739 **Site & Museum**
Tue–Sun main public hols.

EVOCATIVELY OCCUPYING an isolated rural valley, the site of Ancient Neméa is a local landmark with the three Doric columns of its 4th-century Zeus temple plainly visible from afar. Below them lie the broken remains of column drums toppled by vandals between the 4th and 13th centuries AD. At the west end of the temple's complete floor, the deep *adyton* (underground crypt) has been exposed.

A short walk to the south-west, under a giant modern shelter, a Hellenistic bathhouse is being excavated; so far only the plunge-pool and feed system have been revealed. Recent digs have uncovered the Byzantine village that took root here in the 4th century, including graves, kilns, a basilica built above the ancient pilgrims' inn, and a baptistry

The **museum** merits a visit for illuminating reconstructions and displays of old engravings. The Hellenistic stadium, 400 m (1,312 ft) southeast, has the earliest known vaulted entrance tunnel.

Three Doric columns of the Temple of Zeus, Ancient Neméa

The peaks of Mount Chelmós, seen from the southeast at dawn

Mount Chelmós ❺
Όρος Χελμός

Peloponnese. **Road map** C4.
to Kalávryta.

Rising to 2,355 m (7,729 ft), Mount Chelmós is the third highest point of the Peloponnese, its foothills cloaked in extensive forests and divided by deep gorges. The most famous of these is Mavronéri, where the waterfall cascading from the remote north face of the summit is claimed to be the source of the mythical river Styx.

Overlooking the wooded Feneoú valley, on the southeastern slopes, stands the remote monastery of **Agíou Georgíou Feneoú**, originally founded in 1693, though mostly dating to the mid-18th century. The *katholikón*, with its high dome and transept, offers unusual frescoes. A stairway leads to a secret school, which functioned during the Ottoman years.

Moní Agías Lávras, 6 km (4 miles) from Kalávryta, played a pivotal role in the Greek Revolution. The archbishop of Pátra raised the standard of revolt here on March 25, 1821, the banner now being the centerpiece of a nationalist shrine in the upstairs treasury *(see pp40–41)*.

Founded in 961, the monastery has been rebuilt after its destruction by the Germans in 1943. On the day before their arrival, the Germans had set fire to the town of Kalávryta, where they perpetrated one of their worst occupation atrocities, massacring 1,436 men and boys in reprisal for local resistance. The cathedral clock is permanently stopped at the time the killing began.

The **Cave of the Lakes**, near Kastriá, was known in ancient times but was lost until its rediscovery in 1964. It is arranged on three levels, and groups can visit the first 350 m (1,150 ft) of the cave, down to the second of 15 lakes. The massive stalactite-hung caverns were formed by an underground river, which still flows during the winter.

Cave of the Lakes
16 km (10 miles) S of Kalávryta.
0692 31633. daily.

Old steam locomotive at Diakoftó

Kalávryta–Diakoftó Railroad ❻
Οδοντωτός Σιδηρόδρομος Καλάβρύτων–Διακοφτού

Peloponnese. **Road map** C4. 0691 41205. daily Kalávryta–Diakoftó.

The most enjoyable narrow-gauge railroad in Greece was engineered between 1889 and 1896 to bring ore down from the Kalávryta area. Over 22 km (14 miles) of track were laid, over 6 km (4 miles) of which relies on a third rail (a rack and pinion system) engaged both uphill and downhill where grades are up to one in seven. Two of the original steam locomotives, replaced in 1959, are displayed at Diakoftó. For a good view of the mechanism, travel at the front, by the engineer.

En route there are 14 tunnels and many bridges over the Vouraïkós gorge. The single station of Mégalo Spilaíou, with two modest hotels, is roughly halfway. The station is the start of a 45-minute trail up to **Moní Megálo Spilaíou**. Though its age is uncertain, this is believed to be the oldest monastery in Greece.

Pátra
Πάτρα

Peloponnese. **Road map** C4.
🏛 231,000. 🚢 🚉 🚌
ℹ *Filepimonos 26 (0616 20353).*

GREECE'S THIRD LARGEST city and second port is no beauty. High rises dominate the few elegantly arcaded streets of this planned Neo-Classical town. Where Pátra excels is in its celebration of Carnival – the best in Greece – when the city's large gay community and student body both turn out in force.

On the ancient acropolis the originally Byzantine kástro bears marks of every subsequent era. The vast bailey, filled with gardens and orchards, often hosts public events, as does the nearby brick Roman odeion.

At the southwest edge of town, the mock-Byzantine basilica of **Agios Andréas** stands where St. Andrew was supposedly martyred and houses his skull and a fragment of his cross.

ENVIRONS: Founded in 1861, the **Achaïa Klauss Winery** was Greece's first commercial winery and is now one of the largest vintners in Greece. It produces 30 million liters (8 million gallons) a year, with grapes gathered from across the country. Tours include a visit to the Imperial Cellar, where Mavrodaphne, a fortified (15 percent) dessert wine, can be tasted.

🏭 Achaïa Klauss Winery
8 km (5 miles) SE of Pátra.
📞 *0613 25051.* ⬤ *daily.* ⬤ *main public hols.* ♿ 🎫

Kalogriá
Καλογριά

Peloponnese. **Road map** B4.
🚌 *to Lápas.* ℹ *Lápas town hall (0693 31234).*

THE ENTIRE lagoon-speckled coast, from the Araxos River mouth to the Kotýchi lagoon, ranks as one of the largest wetlands in Europe. Incorporating the Strofiliá marsh and a 5,000-acre

Sandy beaches of Kalogriá

umbrella pine dune-forest, the area is now a protected nature preserve. Resort development is confined to a zone between the Prokópos lagoon and the excellent 7-km (4-mile) beach of Kalogriá. The dunes also support Aleppo pines and valonea oaks, and bass, eels, and water snakes swim in the marsh channels.

Migratory populations of ducks, including pintails and coots, live at Kotýchi, while marsh harriers, owls, kestrels, and falcons can be seen all year round. A new **Visitor Center** at Lápas runs nature trails through the nearby dunes.

🏛 Visitor Center
Kotichion Strofiliás, Lápas 27052. ⬤
Mon–Fri. ⬤ *main public hols.* ♿ 🎫

Chlemoútsi Castle
Κάστρο Χλεμούτσι

Kástro, Peloponnese. **Road map** B4.
⬤ *daily.*

THE MOST FAMOUS Frankish castle in Greece, known also as "Castel Tornesi" after the gold *tournois* coin minted here in medieval times, was erected between 1219 and 1223 to defend thriving Glaréntza port (Kyllíni) and the principality capital of Andreville (Andravída). To bolster the weak natural defenses, exceptionally thick walls and a massive gate were built; much of the rampart catwalk can still be followed. The magnificent hexagonal keep has echoing, vaulted halls; a plaque by the entry commemorates the 1428–32 residence of Konstantinos Palaiológos, the last Byzantine emperor, while he was governor of Ileía.

Steps lead to a roof for views of the Ionian islands and the coastal plain. Chlemoútsi is now being reconstructed, with the enormous fan-shaped courtyard already used for summer concerts.

The modern Byzantine-style basilica of Agios Andréas, Pátra

Ancient Olympia ⑩

Αρχαία Ολυμπία

AT THE CONFLUENCE of the rivers Alfeiós and Kládeos, the Sanctuary of Olympia enjoyed 2,000 years of esteem as a religious and athletic center. Though the sanctuary flourished in Mycenaean times (see pp26–7), its historic importance dates to the coming of the Dorians and their worship of Zeus, after whose abode on Mount Olympos the site was named. More elaborate temples and secular buildings were erected as the sanctuary acquired a more Hellenic character, a process completed by 300 BC. By the end of the reign of Roman Emperor Hadrian (AD 117–38), the sanctuary had ceased to have religious or political significance.

Aerial view south over the Olympia site today

The Temple of Hera, begun in the 7th century BC, is one of the oldest temples in Greece.

The Philippeion, commissioned by Philip II, honors the dynasty of Macedonian kings.

Olympia Museum (see p172)

Main entrance

Pheidias's Workshop
A huge statue of Zeus (see p241) was made here. The ruins include those of a 5th-century AD basilica.

The Heroön housed an altar dedicated to an unknown hero.

0 meters		50
0 yards		50

Palaestra
This was a training center for wrestlers, boxers, and long-jumpers. Much of the colonnade surrounding the central court has been reconstructed.

Stadium Entrance
Late in the 3rd century BC the stadium entrance acquired a vaulted ceiling, part of which survives. The existing stadium was the third laid out at Olympia.

The treasuries, which stored votive offerings from their donor city-states, looked like miniature temples.

The Metroön was a Doric shrine to the pre-Olympian goddess Rhea.

South Hall

Altar of Oaths

The Bouleuterion, or council house, was the seat of the Olympian senate.

Sanctuary entrance

The Leonidaion, with its clover-shaped water garden, accommodated distinguished guests.

RECONSTRUCTION OF OLYMPIA (AD 100)

This shows Olympia as it was under the Romans. At that time the worship of Zeus predominated; the games were dedicated to him, and his temple (containing a huge statue of the god) was at the heart of the Olympian enclosure.

Temple of Zeus
Though only column bases and tumbled sections remain, they clearly indicate the grandeur of this 5th-century BC Doric temple.

Exploring the Olympia Archaeological Museum

Archaic clay head of Hera

THE OLYMPIA ARCHAEOLOGICAL MUSEUM, built opposite the excavation site to display its many treasures, officially opened in 1982 and is one of the richest museums in Greece. Except for the central hall, devoted solely to the pediment and metope sculptures from the Zeus temple, and the corner room dedicated to the games, the exhibit galleries are arranged chronologically, proceeding clockwise from the entrance hall from prehistory, through the Classical period, to the Romans.

Prehistoric, Geometric, and Archaic Galleries

To the left of the entrance hall, the first of these rooms has as a centerpiece a 9th-century BC bronze horse; other contemporary finds include a bronze tripod cauldron and elongated male figures upholding cauldron handles. The second gallery contains an excellent exhibition of Asian-influenced bronze work molded with imaginary beings. Griffin-headed cauldron ornaments were popular in the 7th-century BC: a hammered-metal relief of a mother griffin nurses her young. Winged monsters serve as two shield devices, and a one-winged harpy retains eyes of inlaid bone.

Classical Galleries

Weapons, especially helmets, were a favorite offering to Zeus made by pilgrims and athletes at Olympia. Two famous ones were booty from the Persian Wars (see p29), shown together in the Classical gallery: an Assyrian helmet, and that of Miltiades, victor at the Battle of Marathon (see p145). The same room contains a 5th-century Corinthian terra-cotta of Zeus and Ganymede, the most humanized of the portrayals of Zeus.

The central hall houses surviving relief statuary from the Temple of Zeus. Unusually, both pediments survive, their compositions carefully balanced, though not precisely symmetrical. The more static east pediment tells of the chariot race between local king Oinomaos and Pelops, suitor for the hand of the king's daughter Hippodameia. Zeus stands between the two contestants; a soothsayer on his left foresees Oinomaos's defeat, and the two local rivers are personified in the corners. The western pediment, a metaphor of the tension between barbarism and civilization, portrays the mythological Battle of the Lapiths and the Centaurs. The centaurs, invited to the wedding of Lapith king Peirithous, attempt,

Zeus and Ganymede, in terra-cotta

while drunk, to abduct the Lapith women. Apollo, god of reason, is central, laying a reassuring hand on Peirithous's shoulder as the latter rescues his bride from the clutches of the centaur chief. Theseus is seen to the left of Apollo preparing to dispatch another centaur, while other women watch from the safety of the corners. The interior metopes, far less intact, depict the Twelve Labors of Herakles, a hero mythically associated with the sanctuary.

In its own niche, the fragmentary 5th-century BC Nike, by the sculptor Paionios, was a thanks-offering from Messene and Naupaktos, following their victory over Sparta during the Peloponnesian Wars (see p30). A plaster reconstruction allows visualization of the winged goddess on the back of an eagle as she descends from heaven to proclaim victory.

The more complete Hermes, by Praxiteles, also has a room to itself, and shows the nude god carrying the infant Dionysos to safety, away from jealous Hera. The arm holding the newborn deity rests on a tree trunk hung with Hermes's cape; Dionysos reaches for a bunch of grapes in the elder god's now-vanished right hand.

Statue of Hermes by Praxiteles

Roman and Olympic Galleries

The penultimate room is devoted to a series of statues of Roman emperors and generals and a marble bull dedicated by Regilla, wife of Herodes Atticus.

The final gallery displays objects relating to the games. A 5th-century BC bronze statuette of a runner at the starting position is dedicated to Zeus by an athlete, as evidenced by an inscription on the runner's thigh. A set of halteres (jumping weights) are also on display, next to a bronze discus and part of a starting block.

The Origins of the Olympian Games

THE ESTABLISHMENT of the Olympian Games in 776 BC is traditionally treated as the first certain event in Greek history. Originally, men's sprinting was the only event, and competitors were local; the first recorded victor was Koroibos, a cook from nearby Elis. During the 8th and 7th centuries BC, wrestling, boxing, equestrian events, and boys' competitions were added. The elite of

Title page of 1896 Games brochure

many cities came to compete and provided victory trophies although, until the Romans took charge in 146 BC, entry was restricted to Greeks. Local cities disputed control of the games, but a sacred truce guaranteed safe conduct to spectators and competitors. Part of a pagan festival, the Christians did not approve of the games, which died out in AD 393.

The ancient pentathlon consisted of sprinting, wrestling, javelin- and discus-throwing, and the long jump (assisted by swinging weights). From 720 BC, athletes competed naked and women were excluded from spectating

Wrestling and boxing are depicted on this 6th-century BC amphora. The boxers are shown wearing himantes, an early type of boxing glove made of leather straps wrapped around the hands and wrists.

The Olympic revival came in 1896, when the first modern games were held in Athens (see p113). They were organized by the Frenchman Baron Pierre de Coubertin.

TIMELINE

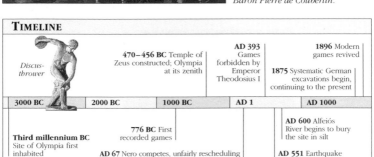

Discus-thrower

3000 BC	2000 BC	1000 BC	AD 1	AD 1000

470–456 BC Temple of Zeus constructed; Olympia at its zenith

AD 393 Games forbidden by Emperor Theodosius I

1896 Modern games revived

1875 Systematic German excavations begin, continuing to the present

Third millennium BC Site of Olympia first inhabited

776 BC First recorded games

AD 67 Nero competes, unfairly rescheduling the games, and "wins" most prizes

AD 600 Alfeiós River begins to bury the site in silt

AD 551 Earthquake destroys much of site

Loúsios Gorge ⓫
Φαράγγι του Λουσίου

Walkers in the gorge

ALTHOUGH MERELY A TRIBUTARY of the Alfeiós River, the Loúsios stream in its upper reaches boasts one of the most impressive canyons in Greece. Scarcely 5 km (3 miles) long, the Loúsios Gorge is almost 300 m (984 ft) deep at the narrowest, most spectacular portion. Because of its remote mountain setting near the very center of the Peloponnese, the Loúsios region was one of the strongholds of the revolutionaries during the Greek War of Independence *(see pp40–41)*. Medieval monasteries and churches cling to the steep cliffs of the gorge, and hiking trails have recently been marked, connecting some of the area's highlights. The picturesque villages *(see p176)* of the canyon's east bank make suitable touring bases.

TRIPOLI

Dimitsána is the best place to join the path.

ZATUNA

Palaiochóri

LOÚSIOS GORGE

Loúsios

Moní Néa Filosófou
Situated on the west bank amid the narrows, this 17th-century monastery was recently renovated and restaffed by a caretaker monk. Frescoes in the church date from 1693 and illustrate many seldom-depicted biblical episodes, such as the Gadarene Swine.

★ Ancient Gortys
The Asklepieion, or therapeutic center, of ancient Gortys occupies a sunken excavation on the west bank. It includes the foundations of a 4th-century BC temple to Asklepios, the god of healing.

Agios Andréas, an 11th-century chapel, stands just below the Loúsios narrows.

Kokkorás Bridge
This restored medieval bridge once carried the age-old road linking the regions of Arcadia and Ileía. Anglers fish for trout here in the icy river water.

STAR SIGHTS

★ Moní Aimyalón

★ Ancient Gortys

★ Moní Agíou Ioánnou Prodrómou

Wooded flanks of the Loúsios Gorge, viewed from the south

VISITORS' CHECKLIST

Peloponnese. **Road map** C4.
Dimitsána. **All monasteries**
dawn–dusk. **Moní
Aimyalón** 2–5pm daily.
Moní Néa Filosófou: daily.
Ancient Gortys daily.
main public hols.

ZIGOVISTI

Paleoú Filosófou,
dating to 960, is
the oldest monastery
of the area. It is
now in ruins.

★ **Moní Aimyalón**
*Founded in 1605, Moní Aimyalón
is tucked into a side canyon, above
garden plots. A passage partly hewn
through the rock leads to its barrel-
vaulted church with excellent
frescoes from 1608.*

KEY

P	Parking
▬	Minor road
– –	Footpath

TRIPOLI

Stemnítsa *(see p176)* is
a charming village and
a good place to hike
out to, having passed
through the gorge.

ELLINIKO

★ **Moní Agíou Ioánnou
Prodrómou**
*Wedged into a palisade on
the canyon's east flank, this
11th-century monastery is the
most spectacular sight of the
Loúsios. There is room for only
a dozen monks in the tiny,
frescoed church whose shape
is dictated by the cliff face.*

0 kilometers   1

0 miles   0.5

Exploring Around the Loúsios Gorge

OVERLOOKING the gorge are some of the most beautiful hill towns in the Arcadia region, each making a good base from which to explore the area. Dimitsána has two bus services daily to Trípoli, one of these via Stemnítsa, and two weekday buses between Andrítsaina and Trípoli can be picked up just below Karítaina. Getting around by car is best, although taxis are available in most towns. Winters can be chilly and wet, with snow chains often required.

Bridge over the Alfeiós River, below Karítaina, complete with chapel

The narrow streets of Dimitsána

Dimitsána

Spread attractively along an airy ridge with the Loúsios River on three sides and glorious views down the valley, Dimitsána stands on the Classical site of ancient Teuthis. The town boasts four belfries; that of **Agía Kyriakí** is illuminated at night; the three-level **Pyrsogiannítiko** bell tower was erected by skilled Epirot masons in 1888.

Two clerics involved in the 1821 Revolution against Turkish rule *(see pp40–41)* were born here. The birthplace of Bishop Germanós of Pátra, who helped instigate the Revolution, is marked by a plaque near the summit of westerly Kástro hill. A plaque dedicated to Patriarch Grigórios V stands lower down in the market; he was hanged in Istanbul when news of the revolt reached the Sultan.

Dimitsána's three- and four-story mansions date from its heyday as a trade center in the 18th century. There were 14 powder factories here during the War of Independence.

Stemnítsa

Situated in a large hollow, the village of Stemnítsa forms a naturally hidden fortress. Like Dimitsána, it, too, has a venerable history, though the revival of its ancient name, Ypsoús, has not been locally accepted. In medieval times, Stemnítsa was one of Greece's main metalworking centers, but today only one silversmith continues the tradition. A **Folk Museum** recreates workshops of indigenous craftsmen and local house interiors, and also hosts a top-floor gallery of weaponry, textiles, and ceramics belonging to the Savvopoúlou family.

Among a number of magnificent medieval churches, those of **Treis Ierárches**, near the Folk Museum, and 10th-century **Profítis Ilías**, up on Kástro hill, have frescoes in excellent condition. Also at Kástro, the 12th-century **Panagía Mpaferó**, has an unusual portico, while the **Moní Zoödóchou Pigís**, on the northerly hillside, was where the revolutionary chieftains held their first convention during the War of Independence; it is for this reason that Stemnítsa was called the first capital of Greece.

⬚ Folk Museum

Stemnítsa. (*0795 81252.*
🔲 *Wed–Mon.* ⬤ *main public hols.*

Karítaina

In a strategic position on a bend of the Alfeiós, Karítaina is now almost a ghost town of less than 200 inhabitants. It has a 13th-century **Kástro**, dating to the time when the town was the seat of a Frankish barony. The castle was the hideout of Theódoros Kolokotrónis, who survived a long Turkish siege here in 1826. Nearby, the **Panagía tou Kástrou** boasts restored 11th-century column capitals with intricate reliefs.

ENVIRONS: East of Karítaina, a bridge over the Alfeiós dates to 1439; four of six original arches survive, with a tiny chapel built into one pier. The bridge appears on one side of the 5,000-drachma bill.

The town of Dimitsána, seen from the east

Andrítsaina ⑫
Ανδρίτσαινα

Peloponnese. **Road map** C4.
🏠 *900.* 🚌

DESPITE ITS CURRENT role as the gateway to the Temple of Bassae, the sleepy town of Andrítsaina is hardly touched by tourism. Tavernas and shops around its central square, home to a lively morning produce market, make few concessions to modernity in either their cuisine or their vivid displays of merchandise. These are echoes of the 18th century, when this was a major market center. Downhill from the 18th-century fountain of Traní, a **Folk Museum** features local rag-rugs, traditional dress, and metalware.

🏛 Folk Museum
Andrítsaina. 📞 *0626 22197.*
⬜ *daily.* ⬛ *main public hols.*

ENVIRONS: The 5th-century BC **Temple of Bassae** graces a commanding knoll, occupying the most remote site of any major ancient sanctuary. Today it hides under an enormous tent, until 12 billion Dr ($22 million) can be raised to re-install the architraves. Without them, winter cold damages the temple's colonnades, now reinforced by scaffolding.

Below Bassae lies the modern village of Figaleía, named after the ancient town to the west. The citizens of ancient Figaleía built the temple in thanks to Apollo Epikourios for stopping a plague. A path descends to the gorge of the Néda River.

⋔ Temple of Bassae
14 km (9 miles) S of Andrítsaina.
📞 *0626 22254.* ⬜ *daily.* 🏞 ♿

Ancient Tegea ⑬
Τεγέα

Peloponnese. **Road map** C4.
📞 *0715 56540.* 🚌 Site ⬜ *daily.*
Museum ⬜ *Tue–Sun.* ⬛ *main public hols.* ♿

SOUTH OF modern Trípoli, the remains of the ancient city of Tegea lie near the village of Aléa. The most impressive

Typical street-café scene at the traditional town of Andrítsaina

ruin is the 4th-century BC Doric temple of Athena Alea, the massive column drums of which are the Peloponnese's second largest, after Olympia's Temple of Zeus *(see p171)*. The site **museum** features sculpture from the city, including a number of fragments of the temple pediment.

Argos ⑭
Άργος

Peloponnese. **Road map** C4.
🏠 *20,000.* 🚌

ALTHOUGH ONE of the oldest settlements in Greece, modern Argos is a busy, rather shabby market town, with its open-air fairground next to a restored Neo-Classical marketplace. To the east of the central square, the **Archaeological Museum** exhibits local finds from all eras. Highlights include a Mycenaean bronze helmet and breastplate and an Archaic pottery fragment showing Odysseus blinding Polyphemos, as well as a *krater* (bowl) from the 7th-century BC.

The most visible traces of ancient Argos lie on the way to Trípoli, where Roman baths and an amphitheater are dwarfed by one of the largest and most steeply raked theaters in the Greek world. From here a path climbs Lárisa hill, one of Argos's two ancient acropolises.

🏛 Archaeological Museum
E of Plateía Agíou Pétrou. 📞 *0751 47597.* ⬜ *Tue–Sun.* ⬛ *main public hols.* 🏞 ♿

ENVIRONS: Heading south of ancient Argos, past the theater, a minor road leads to **Ellinikó** village, on the outskirts of which stands the lower half of an enormous ancient pyramid. Of uncertain date, the structure is thought to have been a tomb or fort guarding the road to Arcadia.

Lérna, further south, is a 2200 BC palace dubbed the "House of the Tiles" for its original terra-cotta roofing. It now shelters under a modern protective canopy. Adjacent Neolithic house foundations and two Mycenaean graves, inside the palace foundations, suggest two millennia of habitation. Settlers were attracted by springs that powered watermills and still feed a deep seaside pond. This was the home of the legendary nine-headed serpent Hydra, which Herakles killed as one of his labors *(see p53)*.

Seating in the ancient theater of Argos, seen from the stage

Mycenae **⑮**
Μυκήναι

T HE FORTIFIED PALACE complex of Mycenae, uncovered by the archaeologist Heinrich Schliemann *(see p180)* in 1874, is one of the earliest examples of sophisticated citadel architecture. The term "Mycenaean," more properly late Bronze Age, applies to an entire culture spanning the years 1700–1100 BC. Only the ruling class inhabited this hilltop palace, with artisans and merchants living just outside the city walls. It was abandoned in 1100 BC after a period of great disruption in the region.

Secret Stairway
A flight of 99 steps drops to a cistern deep beneath the citadel. Connected by pipes to a spring outside, the cistern was added to protect the water supply in times of siege.

Northeast gate

Lion Gate
The Lion Gate was erected in the 13th century BC, when the walls were re-aligned to enclose Grave Circle A. It takes its name from the lions carved above the lintel.

Artisans' workshops

The megaron was the social heart of the palace.

MYCENAE TODAY

Secret Stairway

Royal Palace

Klytemnestra's Tomb

Grave Circle A

Lion Gate

Path to the Treasury of Atreus

Grave Circle B

Bastion

RECONSTRUCTION OF MYCENAE
This illustration shows Mycenae as it was in the time of the House of Atreus and the 1250 BC Trojan War *(see pp54–5)*. Most tombs lie outside the walls *(see p180)*.

Royal Palace
Situated at the acropolis summit, only the floors remain of this central structure. Burn-marks dating to its destruction in 1200 BC are still visible on the stone.

The "Cyclopean" walls, up to 14 m (46 ft) wide, were unbreachable. Later Greeks imagined that they had been built by giants.

The houses of Mycenae yielded a number of tablets inscribed with an archaic script, known as Linear B, deciphered by Michaïl Ventrís in 1952.

The House of Tsoúntas, named after its discoverer, was a minor palace.

Great ramp

Grave Circle A
This contained six royal family shaft-graves containing 19 bodies. The 14 kg (31 lb) of gold funerary goods are on display in Athens (see p70).

VISITORS' CHECKLIST

2 km (1 mile) N of Mykínes, Peloponnese. **Road map** C4.
📞 0751 76585. 🚌 to Mykínes. ⏰ Apr: 8am–6pm daily; May–Oct: 8am–7pm daily; Nov–Mar: 8am–5pm daily.
🚫 Jan 1, Mar 25, Good Fri am, Easter Sun, May 1, Dec 25, 26.
📷 📹 ♿ Treasury of Atreus only. 🅿️

Klytemnestra, after murdering her husband, Agamemnon

THE CURSE OF THE HOUSE OF ATREUS

King Atreus slaughtered his brother Thyestes's children and fed them to him; for this outrage the gods laid a curse on Atreus and his descendants *(see p180)*. Thyestes's surviving daughter, Pelopia, bore her own father a son, Aigisthos, who murdered Atreus and restored Thyestes to the throne of Mycenae. But Atreus also had an heir, the energetic Agamemnon, who seized power.

Agamemnon raised a fleet to punish the Trojan Paris, who had stolen his brother's wife, Helen. He sacrificed his daughter to obtain a favorable wind. When he returned he was murdered by his wife, Klytemnestra, and her lover – none other than Aigisthos. The murderous pair were in turn disposed of by Agamemnon's children, Orestes and Elektra.

Exploring the Tombs of Mycenae

MYCENAE'S NOBLES were entombed in shaft graves, such as Grave Circle A *(see p179)* or, later, in *tholos* ("beehive") tombs. The ten *tholos* tombs, found outside the palace walls, were built using successive circles of masonry, each level nudged inward to narrow the diameter until the top could be closed with a single stone. The entire structure was then buried, save for an entrance approached by a *dromos* or open-air corridor.

The entrance to Klytemnestra's Tomb, with a gap over its lintel

Treasury of Atreus

The Treasury of Atreus *(see p179)* is the most outstanding of the *tholos* tombs. Situated at the southern end of the site, the tomb dates from the 14th century BC and is one of only two double-chambered tombs in Greece. It has a 36-m (120-ft) *dromos* flanked by dressed stone and a small ossuary (the second chamber) that held the bones from previous burials. A 9-m (30-ft) long lintel stone stands over the entrance; weighing almost 265,000 pounds it is still not known how it was hoisted into place, and it is a tribute to Mycenaean building skills.

The treasury is also known as the Tomb of Agamemnon. However, the legendary king and commander of the Trojan expedition *(see pp54–5)* could not have been buried here, as the construction of the tomb predates the estimated period of the Trojan Wars by more than 100 years.

Tomb of Klytemnestra

Of the other *tholos* tombs only the so-called Tomb of Klytemnestra, which is situated just west of the Lion Gate, is as well preserved as that of Atreus. It is a small, single-chambered sepulcher with narrower and more steeply inclined walls, but the finely masoned *dromos* and triangular air hole over the entrance (which also relieved pressure on the lintel) date it to the same period.

HEINRICH SCHLIEMANN

Born in Mecklenburg, Germany, Heinrich Schliemann (1822–90) was self-educated and by the age of 47 had become a millionaire, expressly to fund his archaeological digs. Having discovered Troy and demonstrated the factual basis of Homer's epics, he came to Mycenae in 1874 and commenced digging in Grave Circle A. On discovering a gold death mask that had preserved the skin of a royal skull he proclaimed: "I have gazed upon the face of Agamemnon!" Although archaeologists have since dated the mask to 300 years earlier than any historical Trojan warrior, the discovery corroborated Homer's description of "well-built Mycenae, rich in gold."

TREASURY OF ATREUS

Unlike their Greek contemporaries who would cremate their dead, the Mycenaeans buried their deceased in tombs. In the Treasury of Atreus, a Mycenaean king was buried with his weapons and enough food and drink for his journey to the Underworld.

Tholos, made of 33 rows of stone

Doorway

Resting place of the king's body

Ossuary

Dromos, with walls lined with waterproofing clay

Earth mound covering the entire chamber

Ancient Tiryns
Τίρυνθα

4 km (2 miles) NW of Náfplio,
Peloponnese. **Road map** C4.
☎ 0752 22657. 🚌 ◻ daily.
⬤ main public hols. 🈳

THE 13TH-CENTURY BC citadel of Tiryns confirms Homer's epithet "mighty-walled." A 700-m (2,300-ft) circuit of Cyclopean walls (named after the giants who could be imagined maneuvering the huge blocks into place) attains a thickness of 8 m (26 ft). The fortifications, over double their present height, were necessarily stronger than those of Mycenae since Tiryns was not on a naturally strong site.

Excavated ruins of the Cyclopean walls, Tiryns

The bluff on which it stood was only 18 m (59 ft) higher than the surrounding plain, which, in ancient times, was a salt marsh.

An inclined ramp to the east, designed with sharp turns to expose attackers' unshielded sides, leads to the massive middle gate, the lintel of which has long been missing. At the southern end of the complex, beyond and beneath the vanished inner gate, a gallery with a pointed corbel ceiling has had its walls polished by the fleeces of sheep that have sheltered here for centuries. On the west side, a stone stairway between inner and outer walls, leading to a pos-tern gate, has been completely preserved. The lower, northern acropolis was the last to be enclosed and was used to protect commoners, animals, and (as at Mycenae) a water supply.

ENVIRONS: The early 13th-century Byzantine church of the Panagías rears up startlingly in the cemetery at **Agía Triáda**, a village which is 5 km (3 miles) north of Tiryns. The walls are constructed of ancient masonry to shoulder height; above that, at the southeast corner of the building, the builders have inserted an entire Classical grave stele.

Farther north, the **Argive Heraion** was the Archaic and Classical religious center of the Argolid. The most impressive remains are those of a late 5th-century BC temple. Home to the priest-esses of Hera, and a huge chrsyselephantine cult statue of the goddess, the temple was flanked by stoas, identi-fiable by remaining column stumps. Above the temple is the ledge where the leaders swore loyalty to Agamemnon before sailing for Troy. To the west, complete with drain-gutter, stands the Peristyle Building, where *symposia* were hosted.

⋔ Argive Heraion
10 km (6 miles) N of Tiryns.
◻ variable.

Náfplio

See pp182–3.

Epidaurus

See pp184–5.

Tower of Theseus, ancient Troezen

Ancient Troezen
Τροιζήνα

60 km (37 miles) E of Náfplio,
Peloponnese. **Road map** D4.
◻ unrestricted access.

NEAR THE MODERN village of Troizína are the sparse ruins of ancient Troezen, the legendary birthplace of the hero Theseus and the setting for Euripides' incestuous tra-gedy *Hippolytus*. Remains from many eras are scattered over a wide area; most conspicuous are three Byzantine chapels known as *Episkopí*, from the time when this was the seat of the Bishops of Damála.

The town was built on a high bluff isolated by two ravines; the westerly Damála Gorge is sheer, and half an hour's walk up it a natural rock arch called the Devil's Bridge spans the canyon. Near the lower end of the gorge stands the Tower of Theseus, Hellenistic at its base, medieval higher up.

Foundations of the Argive Heraion, seen at dawn

Náfplio ⑰
Ναύπλιο

With its marble pavements, looming castles, and remarkably homogenous architecture, Náfplio is the most elegant town in mainland Greece. It emerged from obscurity in the 13th century and endured many sieges during the struggles between Venice and Turkey for the ports of the Peloponnese. The medieval quarter, to the west, is mostly a product of the second Venetian occupation (1686–1715). From 1829 until 1834, the town was the first capital of liberated Greece.

View over Náfplio from the stairway to the Palamídi fortress

Exploring Náfplio

Defended to the south by the Akronafplía and Palamídi fortresses and to the north by Bourtzi castle, Náfplio occupies the northern side of a peninsula at the head of the Argolic Gulf. Since the Venetian period, **Plateía Syntágmatos** has been the hub of public life, and still looks much as it did three centuries ago when a couple of mosques were erected by the victorious Ottomans. One stands at the east end of the square and now houses a cinema;

President Kapodístrias

Vouleftikó Mosque, to the south, was where the Greek parliament *(voulí)* first met. West of the bus station, **Agios Geórgios** cathedral was built as a mosque during the first Ottoman occupation (1540–1686). Also converted is the **Catholic church**, another early mosque near the top of Potamianoú, which contains a monument honoring fallen philhellenes, including George Washington's nephew. Four Turkish fountains survive from the second Turkish occupation (1715–1822). The most famous are the scroll-arched one behind the "Cinema" Mosque and another opposite **Agios Spyrídon** on Kapodistríou; this is near where President Kapodístrias was assassinated on October 9, 1831. There are less elaborate Ottoman fountains up the steps at number 9 Tertsétou, and at the corner of Potamianoú and Kapodistríou.

🔍 Archaeological Museum

Plateia Syntágmatos. **☎** *0752 27502.*
○ *Tue–Sun.* **●** *main public hols.*
Exhibits, housed in a Venetian warehouse, largely center on pre-Mycenaean artifacts from various local sites, including Tiryns *(see p181)*. Noteworthy are a Neolithic *thylastro* (baby-bottle), a late Helladic octopus vase, and a full set of bronze Mycenaean armor. Strangest of all the exhibits are the female votive figurines from Mycenae (2300–2000 BC). Up to one-third life size, they could be hung on hooks like modern Orthodox *ex votos*.

🔍 Folk Art Museum

Ypsilántou 1. **☎** *0752 28379.*
○ *Mon & Wed–Sun.* **●** *Feb, main public hols.* 🅿
This award-winning museum, established in a former mansion by the Peloponnesian Folklore Foundation, is devoted to textile crafts. The ground floor describes the cultivation and life cycle of fiber-bearing plants and animals, and then focuses on milling, spinning, and loom-weaving, accompanied by examples of finished products. The upper floor displays numerous regional costumes, concluding with a high-quality gift shop. The exhibits on display change periodically, since there is not enough space to show the entire collection at once.

♣ Bourtzi

NW of harbor. **ℹ** *Xenia Pallas Hotel, Akronafplia (0752 28981).*
This island fortress acquired its present appearance during the second Venetian occupation, and until 1930 served as the local executioner's residence.

The fortified isle of Bourtzi, north of Náfplio harbor

It defended the only navigable passage in the bay; the channel could be closed off by a chain extending from the fortress to the town.

⚓ Akronafplía
W of Palamídi.
🚫 *unrestricted access.*
Akronafplía, also known as Its Kale ("Inner Castle" in Turkish), was the site of the Byzantine and early medieval town and contains four Venetian castles built in sequence from west to east. The most interesting relic is the Venetian Lion of St. Mark relief over the 15th-century gate just above the Catholic church. The westernmost "Castle of the Greeks" was Náfplio's ancient acropolis, now home to the clock tower, a major landmark.

⚓ Palamídi
Polyzoïdou. 📞 *0752 28036.*
🚫 *daily.* ⚫ *main public hols.* 📷
Palamídi, named after the legendary inventor Palamedes, born here in the 13th century BC, is a huge Venetian citadel built between 1711 and 1714. It was designed to withstand

Palamídi fortress seen from the isle of Bourtzi

all contemporary artillery, though it fell to the Ottomans in 1715 after a mere one-week siege, and to the Greek rebels lead by Staïkos Staïkopoulos on November 30, 1822, after an 18-month campaign.

The largest such complex in Greece, Palamídi consists of a single curtain wall enclosing seven self-sufficent forts, now named after Greek heroes; the gun slits are aimed at each other as well as outward, in case an enemy managed to penetrate the

Detail above fountain, Agía Moní

VISITORS' CHECKLIST

Peloponnese. **Road map** C4.
🏛 *12,000.* 🚌 *corner of Polyzoïdou.* 🚊 *Syngroú.*
ℹ️ *Ikostispémptis Martiou 2 (0752 24444).* 🎭 *Náfplio Cultural Festival: July.*

defenses. Fort Andréas was the Venetian headquarters, with a Lion of St. Mark in relief over its entrance. The Piazza d'Armi, from where Náfplio assumes toy-town dimensions below you, offers arguably the best views in the country. At the summit, an eighth fort, built by the Ottomans, looks south towards the Karathóna beach.

ENVIRONS: The 12th-century convent of **Agía Moní** nestles 4 km (2 miles) outside Náfplio; the octagonal dome-drum rests on four columns with Corinthian capitals. Just outside the walls, in an orchard, the Kánathos fountain still springs from a niche decorated with animal reliefs; this was ancient Amymone, where the goddess Hera bathed each year to renew her virginity.

NAFPLIO TOWN CENTER

Akronafplía ⑦
Archaeological Museum ①
Agios Spyrídon ④
Agios Geórgios ⑤
Catholic Church ⑥
Folk Art Museum ③
Plateía Syntágmatos ②

KEY

🚌	Bus station
🚢	Ferry service
ℹ️	Tourist information
✚	Church
▬	Fortifications

0 meters   200
0 yards   200

Epidaurus ®
Επίδαυρος

THOUGH MOST RENOWNED for its magnificent theater, the Sanctuary of Epidaurus was an extensive therapeutic and religious center, dedicated to the healing god Asklepios. A mortal physician deified by Zeus after his death for retrieving a patient from the underworld, Asklepios was depicted in his temple here clutching a staff and flanked by a dog and a serpent – common symbols of natural wisdom. This sanctuary was active from the 6th century BC until at least the 2nd century AD, when the traveler-historian Pausanias recorded a visit.

Dusk over Epidaurus during a modern production at the theater

The Theater
Designed by Polykleitos the Younger late in the 4th century BC, the theater is well known for near-perfect acoustics that are endlessly demonstrated by tour group leaders. Owing to the sanctuary's relative remoteness, its masonry was never pilfered, remaining unrestored until only recently. It has the only circular *orchestra* (stage) to have survived from antiquity, though the altar that once stood in the center is now gone. Two side corridors, or *paradoi*, gave the actors access to the stage; each had a monumental gateway whose pillars have

now been reerected. Behind the *orchestra* and facing the auditorium stand the remains of the *skene*, the main reception

Foundations of the *tholos* building in the Asklepieion

hall, and the *proskenion*, which was used by performers as an extension of the stage. Today, the theater is still the site for a popular summer festival of ancient drama.

The Asklepieion
Most of the Asklepieion, or Sanctuary of Asklepios, is being reexcavated, and many of its monuments are off-limits. One of the accessible sites is the *propylaia*, or monumental gateway, at the north edge of the sanctuary, its original entrance. Also preserved are a ramp and some buckled pavement from the Sacred Way, which led north from the gateway to the coastal town of ancient Epidaurus. At the

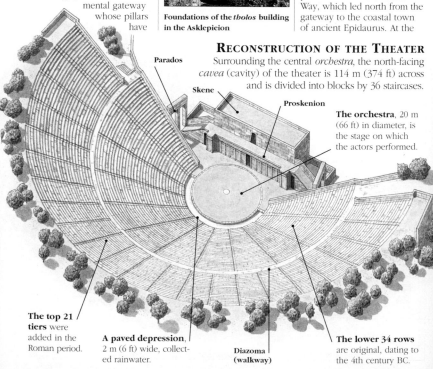

RECONSTRUCTION OF THE THEATER
Surrounding the central *orchestra*, the north-facing *cavea* (cavity) of the theater is 114 m (374 ft) across and is divided into blocks by 36 staircases.

Parados

Skene

Proskenion

The orchestra, 20 m (66 ft) in diameter, is the stage on which the actors performed.

The top 21 tiers were added in the Roman period.

A paved depression, 2 m (6 ft) wide, collected rainwater.

Diazoma (walkway)

The lower 34 rows are original, dating to the 4th century BC.

Overview of today's site showing the stadium at the bottom (north)

VISITORS' CHECKLIST

30 km (19 miles) E of Náfplio, Peloponnese. **Road map** C4.
📞 0753 22009. 🚌 **Site & Museum** ⏰ Apr–Sep: 7:30am–7pm daily; Oct–Mar: 8am–5pm daily. ⚫ Mon (museum only), Jan 1, Mar 25, Good Fri am, Easter Sun, May 1, Dec 25, 26.
🎫 📷 ♿ limited. 🎫 🛍

northeastern end of the sanctuary stand the remains of the *tholos* (a circular building of uncertain function, also designed by Polykleitos) whose concentric passages are thought to have been used either as a pit for sacred serpents, or possibly as the locale for rites by the cult's priests. Patients slept in the *enkoimitiria* – a hall north of the *tholos* where they would await a diagnostic dream or a visit from the harmless serpents. Therapeutic mineral springs, which are still on tap beside the museum, also played a part in the curing of patients who were brought here. Only the foundations of Asklepios's temple have survived, lying to the east of the *tholos*.

Another undisturbed point is the late Classical stadium south of the *tholos*. With intact rows of stone benches and a starting line still visible, this was used during the quadrennial festival in honor of Asklepios. The Romans built an odeion inside the Hellenistic gymnasium to host the festival's musical contests.

ENVIRONS: The adjacent village of Lygourió reflects the importance of the region during Byzantine times. There are three Byzantine churches, the most distinguished being the 14th-century **Koímisis tis Theotókou**, which has superb early medieval frescoes.

THE ORIGINS OF GREEK DRAMA

Greek drama developed from ritual performance at festivals of Dionysos *(see p52)*. First came group dancing – 6th century BC Athenian vases show groups elaborately costumed, often as animals. In the late 6th century BC, the first Greek theaters appeared: rectangular (later round) spaces with seats on three sides. Singing and dancing choruses were joined by individual actors, whose masks made visible at a distance the various character roles, all played by just three male actors. The depiction of animal choruses on vases suggests humorous presentation, but the earliest plays in Athens were tragedies, staged in sets of three by a single writer *(see p57)*, in which episodes from epic poems and mythology were acted out. Historical events were rarely dramatized as they were politically sensitive. Comedy became part of the dramatic festival at Athens only in the 480s BC.

Masks were worn by actors to express the personality of the characters they played.

Theater was mass entertainment and had to cater to large numbers – during the Roman period, the theater at Epidaurus could hold 13,000 people – but it is uncertain whether women were permitted to attend the performances.

Souvenir statuettes, such as this terra-cotta figurine of a sinister character from one of the later comedies, could be bought as mementos after performances.

The chorus, though chiefly an impersonal commentator, often spoke directly to the characters, questioning them on the wisdom of their actions.

Monemvasía ⑳

Μονεμβασία

Mural above the main entrance to Agía Sofía

A FORTIFIED town built on two levels on a rock rearing 350 m (1,150 ft) above the sea, Monemvasía well deserves its nickname, "the Gibraltar of Greece." A town of 50,000 in its 15th-century prime, Monemvasía enjoyed centuries of existence as a semiautonomous city-state, living off the commercial acumen (and occasional piracy) of its fleets and its strategic position astride the sea lanes from Italy to the Black Sea. Exceptionally well defended, it was never taken by force but fell only through protracted siege *(see p188)*. Though the upper town is in ruins, most of the lower town is restored.

Upper Town
A paved stair-street zigzags up the cliff face from the lower town to the tower gate of the upper town (see p188).

★ Agía Sofía
Standing at the summit of Monemvasía, this beautiful 13th-century church is the only intact remnant of the upper town (see p188).

Giánnis Rítsos's House
Immediately next to the gate, the birthplace of prominent poet and communist Giánnis Rítsos (1909–90) is marked by a plaque and a bust at the front.

Western gate

The mosque has been refurbished as a museum to display local finds, including some fine marble works.

Panagía Myrtidiótissa
The façade of this 18th-century church sports a Byzantine inscription and a double-headed eagle from an earlier Byzantine church.

STAR SIGHTS

★ **Agía Sofía**

★ **Walls**

VISITORS' CHECKLIST

Peloponnese. **Road map** C5.
800. Main square.
Géfira. 0732 61210. **Mosque**
Museum: 0732 61403.
Tue–Sun. main public hols.

"The Gibraltar of Greece"

Monemvasía was severed from the mainland by an earthquake in AD 375, remaining an island until the causeway was built in the 6th century.

Agios Nikólaos, begun in 1703, resembles Myrtidiótissa in its masonry, cruciform plan, and cement-covered dome.

★ Walls

The 16th-century walls are 900 m (2,953 ft) long and up to 30 m (98 ft) high. Much of the parapet can be walked.

The east gate opens onto a former burial ground known as Lípsoma.

Panagía Chrysafítissa has its bell hanging from a cypress tree.

The sea gate gave access to the sea when the main port was threatened.

Christós Elkómenos

Restored in 1697, this 13th-century cathedral with its Venetian belfry is stark inside; the only decoration is the plaque of two peacocks above the door.

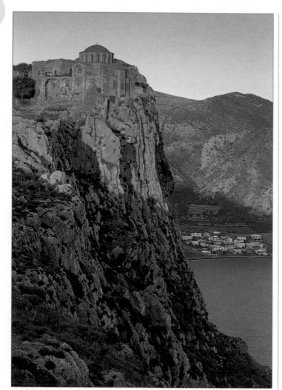

The cliff-top church of Agía Sofía, at dawn, Monemvasía upper town

Exploring the Upper Town

First fortified in the 6th century as a refuge from raiding Avars, the upper town is the oldest part of Monemvasía. Largely in ruins, the area is now under the protection of the Greek archaeological service. Though in medieval times it was the most densely populated part of the peninsula,

Ruins of Monemvasía's 13th-century fortress

the upper town is deserted today, the last resident having departed in 1911.

A path climbs the cliff face above the town's north-western corner, leading to an entrance gate that still has its iron slats. Directly ahead a track leads to the summit's best-preserved building, the church of **Agía Sofía**. It was founded by Emperor Andronikos II (1282–1328) in emulation of Dafní monastery (see pp152–3) near Athens. With its 16-sided dome, the church perches on the brink of the northerly cliff and is visible from a considerable distance inland. The west portico is Venetian, while the niche on the south wall dates from its use as a mosque. A few frescoes surviving from the early 14th century are badly faded, but the *Ancient of Days* can be discerned in the sanctuary's vault, as can the *Birth of John the Baptist* in the north vault. Carved ornamentation has fared better, such as the

THE SIEGE OF MONEMVASIA

The siege of Monemvasía by the Greeks, early in the War of Independence (see pp40–41), began on March 28, 1821. Because of a Greek ruse, the town's Turkish garrison was badly supplied with food, and reinforcements failed to arrive. By late June, both Christians and Muslims were forced to eat weeds, cats, and mice, some even resorting to cannibalism. Turkish civilians in the lower town urged surrender, but the garrison of the upper town refused. The besiegers also seemed set to give up, but one night, the Greek commander inside the town convinced three messengers to swim from the Portello Gate to the revolutionary forces on the mainland, giving them word to persevere. They did, and on August 1 the Turks surrendered, handing over the keys of the city to the Greek Prince Kantakouzinós.

The taking of Monemvasía by Prince Kantakouzinós

marble capitals flanking the south windows, depicting mythical monsters and a richly dressed woman.

To the west are the remains of a 13th-century **fortress**, amid the debris of former barracks, guardrooms, and a gunpowder magazine from the Venetian period. A vast **cistern** recalls the times of siege when great quantities of water had to be stored. Food supplies, entirely imported, were more of a problem, as was demonstrated by the siege of 1821.

Agía Paraskeví, viewed from Byzantine Geráki

Geráki 🔞
Γεράκι

Peloponnese. **Road map** C5.
🏠 *2,000.* 🚏

OCCUPYING A SPUR of Mount Párnonas, Geráki is like a miniature Mystrás with its kástro overlooking the frescoed Byzantine churches on the slopes below. The polygonal **kástro** was built in 1254–5 by the Frank Jean de Nivelet, though it was ceded in 1262 to the Byzantines, together with Monemvasía and Mystrás. Inside, 13th-century **Agios Geórgios** is a hybrid Franko-Byzantine church, the third

aisle and narthex added after 1262; a carved marble screen and varied frescoes decorate its interior.

Below the west gate, 13th-century **Zoodóchou Pigís** sports a complete Gothic door and south window, while inside later frescoes include *Christ on the Road to Calvary.*

At the base of the hill, the domeless, 14th-century church of **Agía Paraskeví** has a fine *Nativity* in its cross vault, plus a painting of the donor family on the west wall.

ENVIRONS: Four more churches stand a short drive to the west in **Geráki** village. Both 12th-century Agios Athanásios and 13th-century Agios Sózon share a cross-in-square plan, with a high dome on four piers. Market edicts of the Roman Emperor Diocletian, inscribed on stone, flank the doorway of barrel-vaulted, 14th-century Agios Ioánnis Chrysóstomos, covered inside with scenes from the life of Christ and the Virgin. Tiny Evangelístria has a Pantokrátor fresco in its dome.

7th-century BC clay head of a woman, from Sparta acropolis

Sparta 🔞
Σπάρτι

Peloponnese. **Road map** C5.
🏠 *20,000.* 🚌 🛈 *Town Hall, Plateía Kentriki (0731 26517).*

THOUGH ONE of the most powerful of the Greek city-states, ancient Sparta was unfortified and has few ruins dating to its heyday. The acropolis lies 700 m (2,300 ft) northwest of the modern town center which in itself has little of interest. On the western side of the acropolis is the cavity of the Roman theater, its masonry largely pilfered to build Mystrás, while directly east stands the long, arcaded stoa that once held shops. Of the Artemis Orthia sanctuary just east of town, where Spartan youths were made men by testing strength, only some Roman seating remains. The most interesting finds are on display in the museum.

Highlights in the rich **Archaeological Museum** are 4th- and 5th-century Roman mosaics, including two lions rampant over a vase, Arion riding his dolphin, Achilles disguised as a woman on Skýros, and a portrait of Alkibiades. A Classical marble head of a warrior, possibly Leonidas I *(see p224)*, was found on the acropolis, while bas-reliefs of the Underworld serpent-deities hail from a sanctuary of Apollo at Amyklés, 8 km (5 miles) south of Spárti. Bizarre ceramic masks are smaller replicas of those used in dances at the Artemis Orthia sanctuary.

🏛 **Archaeological Museum**
Agios Níkon. 📞 *0731 28575.*
🕐 *Tue–Sun.* ⬛ *main public hols.*
📷 ♿

LIFE IN ANCIENT SPARTA

Rising to prominence around 700 BC, Sparta became one of the most powerful city-states of ancient Greece. Its power was based on rigid social and military discipline, as well as suspicion of foreigners, which eventually led to its downfall as it had no natural allies. The "city" was made up of five villages, where the male citizens lived communally in constant readiness for war. Warriors were selected at the age of seven and subjected to rigorous training – whipping contests, with young boys as the victims, were held in the sanctuary of Artemis Orthia. Sparta was able to support its citizens as professional soldiers because it had conquered neighboring Messenia, and the enslaved population provided all the food required. Sparta led the Greek forces against the Persians, but ceased to be a major power after defeat by Thebes in 371 BC.

5th-century BC bronze figurine of a Spartan warrior

Mystrás ⑳
Μυστράς

MAJESTIC MYSTRAS occupies a panoramic site on a spur of the rugged Taÿgetos range. Founded by the Franks in 1249 to replace medieval Spárti, it soon passed to the Byzantines, under whom it became a town of 20,000 and, after 1348, the seat of the Despots of Morea. The despotate acted semiindependently and had become the last major Byzantine cultural center by the 15th century, attracting scholars and artists from Italy and Serbia as well as Constantinople. One result was the uniquely cosmopolitan decoration of the Mystrás churches – their pastel-colored frescoes, crowded with detail, reflect Italian Renaissance influence.

Double-eagle marble plaque, mitrópolis

VISITORS' CHECKLIST

5 km (3 miles) W of Spárti, Peloponnese. **Road map** C5.
🚌 0731 83377. 🚍 to Néos Mystrás. ⏰ May–Oct: 8:00am–7pm daily; Nov–Apr: 8:30am–3pm daily. ⬤ Jan 1, Mar 25, Good Fri, Easter Sun, May 1, Dec 25, 26. 🎫 📷

PLAN OF MYSTRAS

0 meters ___ 100
0 yards ___ 100

KASTRO
UPPER TOWN
LOWER TOWN
Spárti & Néos Mystrás

KEY TO PLAN

① Lower town entrance
② Mitrópolis
③ Moní Perivléptou
④ Moní Pantánassas
⑤ Vrontóchion
⑥ Monemvasía Gate
⑦ Despots' Palace
⑧ Agía Sofía
⑨ Upper town entrance
⑩ Kástro

Exploring Mystrás

Now in ruins, Mystrás consists of a lower and upper town, linked by the Monemvasía Gate. The site can be entered from the castle at the top of the upper town or from the base of the lower town. Allow half a day for exploring the monasteries, churches, palaces, and houses that line the narrow, winding streets. An unusual northwest-to-southeast alignment of the churches is dictated by the site's steep topography.

◁ *Healing of the Paralytic* fresco, Moní Pantánassas, Mystrás

🔒 Mitrópolis

The mitrópolis, situated by the lower town entrance, is the oldest church in Mystrás. It is approached through a

The 14th-century fresco of the *Nativity* in the south vault of Moní Perivléptou

double courtyard. Like many Balkan cathedrals, it began in 1291 as a barrel-vaulted nave flanked by two aisles. The domes were added early in the 1400s in a clumsy attempt to equal the architecture of the Pantánassas and Afentikó churches. Frescoes, mostly early 14th-century, show the martyrdom of the church's patron (Agios Dimítrios) in the northeast vaulting, while Christ's miracles begin next to these with the *Healing of the Lepers* and continue on the southwest aisle in such scenes as the *Wedding at Cana.* In the narthex is the *Preparation of the Throne of Judgment,* flanked by angels, a theme repeated in the southwest diaconicon (sacristy). Constantine XI Palaiológos, the last Byzantine emperor, was crowned here in 1449; a double-eagle plaque marks the spot.

🔒 Moní Perivléptou

Squeezed against the rock face, the 14th-century monastery of Perivléptou has a compact, three-aisled church. Its small dome retains a fresco of the Pantokrátor, flanked by the Virgin and prophets, arranged in diminishing order of importance. The 14th-century frescoes, the most refined in Mystrás, focus on the 12 major church feasts. They include a vivid *Nativity* and *Baptism* in the south vault, the *Transfiguration* and *Entry into Jerusalem,* complete with playing children, in the west aisle, and *Doubting Thomas* and the *Pentecost* in the north vault, decorating the wall over the entrance.

The hillside with remains of Byzantine Mystrás, seen from the south

⛪ Moní Pantánassas
Dating to 1428, Pantánassas was the last church built at Mystrás. With its decorated apses and the brickwork of its arcaded belfry, it imitates Afentikó in the Vrontóchion as an eclectic architectural experiment. The highest frescoes, from 1430, are of most merit, particularly a vivid *Raising of Lazarus* in the north-east vault. Both the *Nativity* and the *Annunciation* in the southwest vault feature animals. The southeast aisle displays the *Descent into Hell*, in which Christ raises Adam and Eve from their coffins, opposite a lively *Entry into Jerusalem*.

⛪ Vrontóchion
A 13th century monastic complex built by Abbot Pachómios, the Vrontóchion was the cultural center of medieval Mystrás; in the 15th century, the Neo-Platonist philosopher Geórgios Gemistós Plethon (1355–1452) taught here. It has

two churches; the earliest, Agioi Theódoroi, dates from 1295 and has the largest dome at Mystrás, supported on eight arches. Few frescoes survive. The early 14th-century Afentikó (or Panagía Odigítria) is richly frescoed, with six domes. The galleries and two north-side chapels are shut, but in the west gallery dome a *Virgin Orans* (praying) and *Prophets* are visible; in the south vault, a crowded *Baptism* includes water monsters. Above the altar, apostles gesticulate toward the aura of the rising Christ in the *Ascension*. The best-preserved frescoes can be found in the north bay of the narthex.

⚜ Despots' Palace
The Despots' Palace consists of two wings now under reconstruction. The northeast wing was begun by the Franks; the northwest hall, erected after 1348 and a rare example of Byzantine civic

architecture, has the throne room of the rulers of the Cantacuzene and Palaiológos dynasties. The square was a venue for public events under the despots and a marketplace under the Ottomans.

The ruins of the Despots' Palace, viewed from the south

⛰ Kástro
Flanked by sheer ravines to the south and west, and crowning the summit of the upper town, the kástro is reached by a path leading from the upper entrance, which stands above the church of Agía Sofía. Built by Guillaume de Villehardouin in 1249, the kástro retains its original Frankish design, although it was greatly altered by the Byzantines and Turks. A double circuit of curtain walls encloses two baileys, and a walkway runs around most of the structure, affording panoramic views of the lower town.

It was here that the German writer Goethe, in Part Two of *Faust*, set the meeting of Faust and Helen of Troy, revived after 3,000 years.

Afendikó church, part of the Vrontóchion complex

Outer Máni

Έξω Μάνη

A HARSH, REMOTE REGION, bounded by mountains on the north, the rocky Máni was the last part of Greece to embrace Christianity, doing so in the 9th century with an enthusiasm borne out by dozens of surviving Byzantine chapels. Though well defended against invaders, the area has a history of internal feuding that led to the building of its many tower houses. A ravine at Oítylo divides Inner Máni, to the south *(see pp198–9)*, from the more fertile Outer, or Messenian, Máni, which boasts some of the finest country in the Mediterranean.

LOCATOR MAP

ANAVRYTI & PALAIOPANAGIA

Exochóri
Kardamýli
PIGADIA & Stoúpa
KALAMATA
Agios Nikólaos
Langáda

MOUNT TAYGETOS

OUTER MANI

GERAKI & MONEMVASIA

Gytheio

Oítylo
Néo Oítylo

Oítylo

Though administratively within the region of Lakonía, by tradition the village of Oítylo (pronounced "Ítilo") belongs to the Outer Máni. It affords superb panoramic views of Limeníou Bay and across a flanking ravine, traditionally the border betwen the Inner and Outer Máni, to Kelefá castle *(see p198)*. Its relatively good water supply fosters a lush setting around and below the village, with cypresses and a variety of orchard trees. Unlike most Mániot villages, Oítylo is not in economic decline. Its many fine houses include graceful 19th-century mansions. The village was capital of the Máni between the 16th and 18th centuries and was the area's most infamous slave-trading center; both Venetians and Turks were sold to each other here. A plaque in the square, written in French and Greek, commemorates the flight, in 1675, of 800 Oítylots of the Stefanopoúlou clan to Corsica. Seeking refuge from the Turks, the

Oítylots were granted passage by the Genoese and, once in Corsica, founded the villages of Paomia and Cargèse. Their presence there accounts for the theories of Napoleon's part-Mániot origins.

ENVIRONS: From the southwestern corner of Oítylo, a broad path descends west to **Moní tou Dekoúlou**, nestled in its own little oasis. The 18th-century church features an ornate *témblon* (wooden altar screen) and vivid original frescoes; though they have been preserved by the darkness, a flashlight is required to see them now. The monastery is only open in the evenings or by prior arrangement with the resident caretakers.

The village of **Néo Oítylo** stands 4 km (2 miles) south of the monastery. Quietly secluded, the village has a pebble beach with fine views.

THE MANIOT FEUDS

By the 15th century, a number of refugee Byzantine families had settled in the Máni, the most powerful forming a local aristocracy known as the Nyklians. Feuding between clans over the inadequate land was rife, though only Nyklians had the right to construct stone towers *(see p20)*, which attained four or five stories and came to dominate nearly every Mániot village.

Once commenced, blood feuds could last months, even years, with periodic truces to tend to the crops. Clansmen fired at each other from facing towers, raising them in order to be able to catapult rocks onto opponents' roofs. The hostilities ended only with the total destruction or submission of the losing clan. Historically, the most important clans were those of Mavromich(...) at Areópoli, Grigorákis at Gýtheio, and Troupákis at Kardamýli, whose members boasted of never having been completely subjugated by any foreign power. The Ottomans wisely refrained from ruling the Máni directly, but instead quietly encouraged the clans to feud in order to weaken potential rebellions, and appointed a Nyklian chieftain as *bey* (regional lord) to represent the sultan locally. Under the final *bey*, Pétros Mavromicháli, the clans finally united, instigating the Greek independence uprising on March 17, 1821 *(see pp40–41)*.

Pétros Mavromicháli

Oítylo viewed from the northwest, looking toward Kelefá castle

Agios Spyrídon south window, framed with marble reliefs

Kardamýli

Kardamýli was the lair of the Troupákis family, important rivals of the Mavromicháli clan. Nicknamed Moúrtzinos or "Bulldog" for their tenacity in battle, they claimed to be descended from the Palaiológon dynasty of Byzantine emperors. Kardamýli used to depend on olive oil *(see p283)*, but now tourism is the town's chief source of income.

Inland rises the ancient and medieval acropolis, represented by twin Mycenaean chamber tombs. Also on the site are Troupákis-built towers that stand alongside the 18th-century church of **Agios Spyrídon**. This building is made of Hellenistic masonry and graced by a pointed, four-story belfry; the south window and doorway are framed by intricate marble reliefs.

ENVIRONS: Two paths lead from Kardamýli, one upstream along the **Vyrós Gorge** where two monasteries shelter beneath the cliffs; the other to the villages of Gourniés and Exochóri. A short drive to the south, **Stoúpa** is popular for its two sandy bays; novelist Níkos Kazantzákis (1883–1957) lived here briefly and partly based his Zorba the Greek character on a foreman who worked nearby. The village of **Agios Nikólaos**, a short walk to the south, curls around Outer Máni's highly photogenic harbor. It has four tavernas, and the closest beach is at Agios Dimítrios, 3 km (2 miles) farther south.

Taÿgetos, seen through the Vyrós Gorge

Mount Taÿgetos

The distinctive pyramidal summit and knife-edged ridge of Mount Taÿgetos, standing at 2,404 m (7,887 ft), divides the regions of Messinía and Lakonía. Formed of limestone and densely clad in black pine and fir, the range is the watershed of the region and offers several days of wilderness trekking to experienced, well-equipped mountaineers.

Anavrytí and Palaiopanagiá, on the east, and Pigádia and Kardamýli on the west, are the usual trailhead villages. Various traverses can be made by using the Vyrós and Ríntomo gorges, which drain west from the main ridge; an unstaffed alpine refuge at Agía Varvára, above Palaiopanagiá, is the best starting point for those wanting to head straight for the summit.

The ridge of Mount Taÿgetos with an olive grove in the foreground

Inner Máni
Μέσα Μάνη

INNER, OR LAKONIAN, MANI is divided into two regions – the "Shadowed" western flank and the "Sunward" eastern shore. The former is famous for its numerous caves and churches, the latter for its villages perched dramatically on crags overlooking the sea. With its era of martial glory over *(see p194)*, Inner Máni is severely depopulated, its only future being as a vacation spot. Retired Athenians of Mániot descent have restored the famous towers *(see p20)* as hunting lodges for the brief autumn shoot of quail and turtledove.

VISITORS' CHECKLIST

Peloponnese. **Road map** C5.
🚌 *Gýtheio*. 🚢 *Areópoli*.
ℹ️ *Vasiléos Pávlou 21, Areópoli
(0733 22271).*
Museum of the Máni
Marathonísi Islet. [*0733
22676.* ◯ *daily.* 🎫
Pýrgos Diroú Caves & Museum
12 km (7 miles) S of Areópoli.
[*0733 52222.* ◯ *variable.*

LOCATOR MAP

Oítylo • Gýtheio
• Kelefá • Passavá
INNER MÁNI
Areópoli •
• Pýrgos Diroú
• Charoúda

• Vámvaka
Stavrí • Káto Gardenítsa
• Áno Mpoulárioi
Gerolimenas •

Vátheia •

CAPE TAÍNARO

Gýtheio
The lively town of Gýtheio is the gateway to the Máni peninsula and one of the most attractive coastal towns in the southern Peloponnese. It was once the naval base of ancient Sparta *(see p189)*, but the main ancient relic is a Roman theater to the north. The town was wealthy in Roman times, when it exported the purple mollusks used for coloring imperial togas. Until World War II, Gýtheio exported acorns used in leather tanning, gathered by women and children from nearby valleys.

The town's heart is Plateía Mavromicháli, with the dock extending to either side lined by tiled, 19th-century houses. The east-facing town enjoys sunrises over Cape Maléas and the Lakonian Gulf while snowy Mount Taÿgetos looms beyond a low ridge to the north.

In the bay, and linked to the waterfront by a causeway, lies the islet of Marathonísi, thought to be Homer's Kranaïs islet. It was here that Paris of Troy and Helen spent their first night together *(see p52)*. It is dominated by the Tzanetbey Grigorákis tower, a crenellated 18th-century fortress that now houses the **Museum of the Máni**. The subject of the exploration of the Máni in medieval times is covered on the ground floor, and the exhibits of the upper story place the tower houses in their social context.

ENVIRONS: Standing 12 km (7 miles) to the southwest, the **Castle of Passavá** was built in 1254 by the Frankish de Neuilly clan to guard a defile between Kelefá and Oítylo. Its name stems from *passe en avant*, the clan's motto, but the present building is an 18th-century Turkish construction. The Turks left the castle in 1780 after Tzanetbey Grigorákis avenged the murder of his uncle by massacring 1,000 Muslim villagers inside. Today's overgrown ruins are best approached from the southwest.

Areópoli
The Mavromicháli *(see p194)* stronghold of Tsímova was renamed Areópoli, "the city of Ares" (god of war), for its role in the War of Independence *(see p40)*; it was here that the Mániot uprising against the Turks was proclaimed by Pétros Mavromicháli. Now the main town of the Máni, its central old quarter features two 18th-century churches: **Taxiarchón** boasts the highest bell tower in the Máni, as well as zodiacal apse reliefs, while **Agios Ioánnis**, adorned with naïve frescoes, was the chapel of the Mavromichális.

ENVIRONS: With Passavá to the east, Ottoman **Kelefá Castle**, standing 10 km (6 miles) north of Areópoli, is the second castle guarding the Máni. It was built in 1670 to command the bays of Oítylo and Liméni and counter the impending Venetian invasion

19th-century houses lining the harbor of Gýtheio

◁ **Semiruined tower houses of Vátheia village, the architectural jewel of the Máni** *(see p38).* The bastions of the pentagonal curtain walls are preserved. The castle can be reached by paths from Areópoli and Oítylo *(see p194).*

Pýrgos Diroú Caves

The Pýrgos Diroú cave system is the largest and most colorful in Greece. During summer, crowds line up for the 30-minute boat ride along the underground stream that passes through Glyfáda cavern, reflecting the overhanging stalactites. A further 15-minute walk leads to the exit. An adjacent chamber, called Alepótrypa cave, is drier and, although currently shut, is equally spectacular with waterfalls and a lake; until an earthquake blocked the entrance, the cave was inhabited by Neolithic people, and a separate **museum** documents their life and death.

The Shadowed Coast

Between Pýrgos Diroú and Geroliménas lies the 17-km (11-mile) shore of the Shadowed Coast. Once one of the most densely populated regions of the Máni, it is famous for its numerous Byzantine churches built between the 10th and 14th centuries. The ruins of many Mániot tower houses can also be found.

Among the finest churches is 11th-century **Taxiarchón**, at Charoúda, with its interior covered by vivid 18th-century frescoes. Heading south, the road continues to **Agios Theódoros**, at Vámvaka, where the dome is supported by

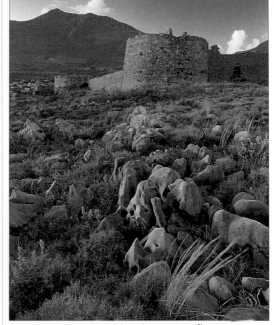
Corner turret of Ottoman Kelefá castle, near Areópoli

carved beams, and birds bearing grapes adorn its marble lintel.

Káto Gardenítsa boasts the 12th century **Agiá Soteíra**, with its frescoed iconostasis and domed narthex, while 12th-century **Episkopí**, near Stavrí, has a complete cycle of 18th-century frescoes.

Near Ano Mpouláríoi village, doorless **Agios Panteleímon** offers 10th-century frescoes (the earliest and the most primitive in the Máni), while in the village, the 11th-century **Agios Stratigós** bears a set of 12th and 13th-century frescoes – the *Acts of Christ* is the most distinguished.

Vátheia, 10 km (6 miles) east of Geroliménas, is one of the most dramatically located of the villages; overlooking the sea and Cape Taínaro, its bristling tower houses constitute a showpiece of local architectural history.

Tower houses of Vátheia village, viewed from the southeast

Koróni ㉖
Κορώνη

Peloponnese. **Road map** C5.
🏘 *1,400.* 🚌

O NE OF THE "eyes of Venice" (along with Methóni), Koróni surveys the shipping lanes between the Adriatic and Crete. It stands at the foot of a Venetian castle, begun in 1206, whose walls now shelter the huge **Timíou Prodrómou** convent. A Byzantine chapel and foundations of an Artemis temple stand by the gate of the convent whose cells and chapels command fine views.
The town, lying beneath the castle and divided by stepped streets, dates to 1830. It has changed little recently, and many houses retain elaborate wrought-iron balconies, horizontal-slat shutters, and tile "beaks" on the undulating roofs. A lively seafront is the sole concession to tourism.

Methóni ㉗
Μεθώνη

Peloponnese. **Road map** B5.
🏘 *1,300.* 🚌

M ETHÓNI, a key Venetian port, controlled the lucrative pilgrim trade to Palestine after 1209. With the sea on three sides, its rambling **castle** is defended on its landward side by a Venetian moat, bridged by the French in 1828. The structure combines Venetian, Ottoman, and even French military architecture. The remains within the walls include two ruined *hammam*s

(baths), a Venetian church, minaret bases, and the main street. Boúrtzi, an islet fortified by the Turks, stands beyond the Venetian sea-gate.

⚜ **Castle**
◻ *daily.*

Pýlos ㉘
Πύλος

Peloponnese. **Road map** C5.
🏘 *2,500.* 🚌

T HE TOWN OF PYLOS, originally known as Avaríno (later Navaríno), after the Avar tribes that invaded the area in the

BATTLE OF NAVARINO

An unexpected naval engagement that decided the War of Independence *(see pp40–41)*, the Battle of Navaríno took place on October 20, 1827. Victory here by the French, Russian, and English allies over the Ottoman fleet broke the Greek-Ottoman deadlock and resolved the problem of the Sultan's refusal of an armistice. The allied fleet of 27 ships, commanded by admirals Codrington, de Rigny, and Heyden, entered Navaríno Bay where Ibrahim Pasha's armada of 89 lay anchored. The outnumbered allies merely intended to intimidate Ibrahim into leaving the bay, but were fired upon, and a full-scale battle ensued. By nightfall three-quarters of the Ottoman fleet was sunk, with negligible allied casualties; Greek independence was now inevitable. The admirals are honored by an obelisk in their namesake square in Pýlos.

Scene from the dramatic *Battle of Navaríno*, **painted by Louis Ambroise Garneray (1783–1857)**

6th century, is French in design, like Methóni. Life is confined to Plateía Trión Navárchon and the seafront on either side.
To the west, the castle of **Niókastro**, Ottoman and Venetian in origin, was extensively repaired by the French after 1828; their barracks are now a gallery of antiquarian engravings by the artist René Puaux (1878–1938). An institute of underwater archaeology is situated in the former dungeons of the hexagonal keep. The roof gives views of the outer bailey, immense Navaríno Bay, and Sfaktiría island, site of a memorable Athenian victory over the Spartans.

The fortified islet of Boúrtzi, off the coast at Methóni, with its 16th-century octagonal tower

The arcaded former mosque, now Sotíros church, Pýlos

The perimeter walls are dilapidated, but it is possible to walk along the parapet, starting from the imposing west bastion overlooking the mouth of the bay, and finishing above the east gate. The domed and arcaded church of **Sotíros**, once a mosque, is the only medieval survival in the outer bailey.

♠ Niókastro
Town center. ☎ 0723 22897. ☐ Apr–Oct: daily; Nov–Mar: Tue–Sun. ● main public hols. 🎫 ♿ limited.

ENVIRONS: Boat tours visit a number of memorials on and around **Sfaktiría**, which commemorate sailors lost in the Battle of Navaríno, foreign philhellenes, and revolutionary heroes.

The north end of Navaríno Bay, 11 km (7 miles) north of Pýlos, has excellent beaches, especially **Voïdokoiliá** lagoon, where Telemachos, Odysseus's son, disembarked to seek news of his father from King Nestor. You can walk up the dunes to **Spiliá tou Néstora**, an impressively large cave, which may have been the inspiration for Homer's cave in which Nestor and Neleus kept their cows. A more strenuous path continues to Palaiókastro, the ancient acropolis and Franko-Venetian castle, built on Mycenaean foundations.

Nestor's Palace ❷⁹
Ανάκτορο του Νέστορα

16 km (10 miles) NE of Pýlos, Peloponnese. **Road map** B5. ☎ 0763 31437. ● Site & museum ☐ Tue–Sun. ● main public hols. 🎫 ♿ limited.

13th-century BC bathtub excavated from Nestor's Palace

DISCOVERED IN 1939, the 13th-century BC Palace of Mycenaean King Nestor was excavated by Carl Blegen from 1952. Hundreds of tablets in the ancient Linear B script were found, as well as a bathtub and olive oil jugs (the contents of which fueled the devastating fire of 1200 BC). Today, only waist-high walls and column bases under a protective roof suggest the typical Mycenaean plan of a two-story complex around a central hall. The **museum**, 3 km (2 miles) away in Chóra, has frescoes from the palace.

Ancient Messene ❸⁰
Αρχαία Μεσσήνη

34 km (21 miles) NW of Kalamáta, Peloponnese. **Road map** C5. ☎ 0724 51201. ● Site ☐ daily. **Museum** ☐ Tue–Sun. ● main public hols. 🎫 for museum.

ANCIENT MESSENE, now confusingly called Ithómi after the mountain overhead, is an underrated, intriguing site, still being excavated. City walls, 9 km (6 miles) long and dating from the 4th century BC, enclose a vast area that incorporates foundations of a Zeus temple and the acropolis on Mount Ithómi to the northeast. The massive double Arcadia Gate on the north side is flanked by square towers.

The archaeological zone includes the picturesque village of Mavrommáti, whose water is still supplied by the ancient Klepsýdra fountain at the heart of the site. Below the village, an odeion (theater), a *bouleuterion* (council hall), stoas, and a monumental stairway surround foundations of an Asklepios temple; just downhill from here lies a well-preserved stadium.

Between the village and the Arcadia Gate, a small museum contains sculpture and miniature bronzes from the site.

Remains of the Arcadia Gate, with its fallen lintel, Ancient Messene

CENTRAL AND WESTERN GREECE

EPIRUS · THESSALY · STEREA ELLADA

C ENTRAL AND WESTERN GREECE *encompass many of the lesser-known regions of mainland Greece and are, therefore, little touched by tourism. Though Epirus has produced a distinctive and largely autonomous culture, Stereá Elláda has always been of strategic importance, with the pass at Thermopylae and the Vale of Tempe providing invasion routes into the very heart of Greece.*

This region of Greece is dominated by the central plain of Thessaly (the former bed of an inland sea), and the sights of interest lie largely on the periphery. Isolated by the Píndos mountains, the Epirus region, to the west, has the strongest of regional identities, having played a minor role in ancient Greece and maintained a large degree of autonomy under the Turks. The regional capital, Ioánnina, is thus a fascinating mixture of Turkish architecture and the local traditions of silversmithing and wood-carving. To the east, the grand Katára Pass, guarded in Ottoman times by the town of Métsovo, cuts through the mountains, providing access to the Byzantine

Woman from Métsovo, northern Píndos

Metéora monasteries that soar on the summits of the area's steeply eroded peaks.

In Stereá Elláda, one of the country's most important ancient sights, the ruins of the Delphic Oracle, stands only a short drive away from the Monastery of Osios Loúkas, perhaps the finest of late Byzantine buildings, decorated with some of the period's greatest mosaics.

While the Gulf of Corinth has many popular resorts, the towns of Lamía, Arta, Tríkala, and Mesolóngi (where the British poet Lord Byron died) make few concessions to tourism and so offer a more accurate picture of life in Greece today: its markets, tavernas, church-going, and the evening *vólta.*

Megálo Pápigko, one of the many remote, once-isolated villages of Zagória in the Epirus region

◁ The Byzantine Monastery of Osios Loúkas, with the bell tower in the foreground

Exploring Central and Western Greece

STRETCHING FROM ATTICA in the south to Macedonia in the north, the vast expanse of Central and Western Greece has a little of everything, from excellent beaches to the venerable towns of Ioánnina and Métsovo with their craftsmen's guilds and Ottoman heritage. The Pílio offers the best combination of scenery and coastal resorts, while no one should miss the two prime attractions of Ancient Delphi, site of the oracle of Apollo, and the Byzantine splendor of the monasteries of Metéora. Walkers should head north where, in addition to the Víkos Gorge, the Píndos Mountains have several of Greece's highest peaks. The flora and fauna are both splendid here, especially in spring, but wildlife enthusiasts should not miss the wonderful wetlands around Mesolóngi and the beautiful Amvrakikós Gulf, near Arta.

KEY

	Divided highway
	Major road
	Scenic route
	River
☼	Viewpoint

Agiou Nikoláou, one of Metéora's soaring monasteries

SIGHTS AT A GLANCE

Ancient Delphi pp228–31 ⑲
Arta ⑩
Dodóni ⑥
Gulf of Corinth ⑳
Ioánnina ⑤
Kassópi ⑧
Lamía and Thermopylae ⑱
Mesolóngi ㉑ ·

Metéora pp216–17 ⑪
Métsovo ④
Monastery of Osios Loúkas pp222–3 ⑯
Mount Parnassus ⑰
Párga ⑦
Pílio pp218–20 ⑭
Píndos Mountains ①

Préveza ⑨
Thebes ⑮
Tríkala ⑫
Vale of Tempe ⑬
Zagória ②

Walks
Víkos Gorge ③

Doric columns of the Temple of Apollo, Delphi

LOCATOR MAP

GETTING AROUND

There are domestic airports at Préveza and Ioánnina, the former receiving European charter flights in summer. Internal flights are fairly inexpensive if traveling from another part of Greece, but within the region a car is by far the best way to travel. Central Greece's main roads are generally good, but twisting mountain routes can make trips longer than they seem on the map. The E55 is a good, fast road, as are the other major E roads that circle the region. Trains serve only a small part of the eastern side of the area, though bus connections are good between major towns, with services to smaller villages.

Terraced bar overlooking the west coast, Párga

SEE ALSO

- **Where to Stay** pp272–3

- **Where to Eat** pp293–4

0 kilometers   25

0 miles   25

Lake Drakolímni, behind the sheer cliffs of Astráka

Píndos Mountains ❶
Οροσειρά Πίνδου

Epirus. **Road map** B2. ✕ 🚌 *Ioánnina.*
🛈 *Napoléonta Zérva 2, Ioánnina
(0651 31456).*

THE PINDOS is a vast range
stretching from the Greek
border with Albania south
beyond Métsovo. It extends
east into Macedonia and west
toward the Ionian Sea, incorporating two national parks,
Greece's second longest

gorge, and its second highest
mountain, Oros Smólikas,
standing at 2,640 m (8,660 ft).
The Píndos National Park lies
just inside western Macedonia,
between Métsovo and Vovoúsa,
while the Víkos–Aóos National
Park is a boot-shaped area
encompassing the Víkos Gorge
(see p208) and the Aóos River.
The peaks are snow-covered
from October until May, when
the melting snows water the
ground, producing swathes
of lilac crocus, gentians,

grass-of-Parnassus, and many
species of orchid *(see p23)*.
The protection offered by the
parks provides the visitor
with an increased chance of
seeing roe deer, wild boar, and
the European wild cat, all of
which exist in small numbers.
Smólikas is accessible during
summertime for those who are
well equipped and prepared
for camping or staying in
mountain huts. Slightly easier
to reach from the fascinating
Zagorian villages by the Víkos
Gorge are Gamíla 2,500 m
(8,200 ft) and Astráka 2,440 m
(8,000 ft), while the two
mountain lakes both called
Drakolímni are each worth
the effort it takes to get to
them. One is below Gamíla,
near a sheer drop to the Aóos
River, and the other stands
beneath Smólikas.
Although there are good
walking guides and maps of
the area, with mountain huts
to stay in and accommodations
in some of the larger villages,
visitors should not venture into
the mountains unless they are
prepared for the terrain and
are experienced walkers. The
weather can change quickly,
and in many places you will be
a long way from any kind of
settlement – though this is
one of the main attractions
of the Píndos mountains.
They show the rugged side
of Greece, offering remote
valleys and routes where
few visitors venture.

WILDLIFE OF THE PINDOS MOUNTAINS

Visitors to the coastal lowlands are often scep-
tical when told that wolves and bears still
survive in Greece. Although their precise
number is uncertain and difficult to assess,
both European wolves and European
brown bears can be found. The Píndos
mountains, and particularly the northern
regions toward Albania, continue to
harbor the greatest numbers of these
endangered creatures. They are wary of
man, having been persecuted
by farmers and goatherds
down the centuries. As a
consequence of this, as well
as of their natural rarity,
visitors should consider
themselves very fortunate if
they see a bear. Wolves are
more conspicuous and can
often be heard howling at
dawn and dusk; they will
even respond to imitations
of their howls. They pose
no threat to visitors.

**The silver European
wolf, a rare native
of the region**

**One of the 80 European brown
bears of the northern Píndos**

Zagória ❷
Ζαγόρια

Epirus. **Road map** B2. 🚌

SOME OF EUROPE'S most spectacular scenery can be found only 25 km (15 miles) north of Ioánnina *(see p210)*, in the area known as Zagória. Though the soil is largely uncultivable, on the forested hillsides some 45 traditional Epirot villages still survive; many of them boast imposing *archontiká (see p21)* dating to prosperous 18th- and 19th-century Ottoman times when Zagória was granted autonomy.

Vlach shepherds *(see p209)* comprise most of the settled population, though the villages have also provided winter homes for the otherwise tent-dwelling Sarakatsans once their flocks have been taken down to the plains of Thessaly. Over the winter months, the shepherds turn to crafts, forming guilds of itinerant masons and woodcarvers who travel the Balkans in order to sell their trades.

A series of arched packhorse bridges are among the most memorable monuments to the skills of the local people and are unique features of the region. Two especially fine examples can be seen at either end of the village of **Kípoi**.

Vítsa village, by the Víkos Gorge

Southwestern Zagória is the busiest area, with a bus from Ioánnina to Monodéndri bringing in walkers and climbers. Some of the villages in the east of the region, such as **Vrysochóri**, were refuges for guerrillas during World War II and therefore burned by the Germans; they have recovered only slowly.

Near the almost-deserted village of **Vradéto**, a 15th-century mule track zig-zags its way up a steep rock face beyond which the path leads to a stunning view of the spectacular Víkos Gorge *(see p208)*. **Monodéndri**, opposite Vradéto, is the usual starting point for the gorge trail, though another path can be taken from **Vítsa**. Nearby are the two villages of **Megálo Pápigko** and **Mikró Pápigko**. They are 4 km (2 miles) apart and their names reflect their sizes, but even "big" Pápigko is no more than a scattering of houses around cobbled streets, with a choice of restaurants, and rooms available in renovated mansions.

Farther south, though still surrounded by mountains, is the relatively thriving village of **Tsepélovo**. It has a bus service to Ioánnina and a restored mansion that provides accomodations, as well as a number of pensions and tavernas. Its cobbled streets and slate-roofed houses provide a perfect portrait of a Zagorian village.

Packhorse bridge near the village of Kípoi

ZAGORIAN VILLAGES
Scattered across the limestone wilderness of the north Píndos, the villages of Zagória lie to the southwest of the Aóos River between Ioánnina and Kónitsa.

Kónitsa

Aóos

GAMILA ▲ 2,500 m 8,200 ft

Vrysochóri

Kleidoniá

Megálo Pápigko

ASTRAKA ▲ 2,440 m 8,000 ft

Mikró Pápigko

Vitsiko

Aristi

Víkos Gorge

Vodomátis

Z A G O R I A

Elafótopos

Vradéto

Tsepélovo

Kakaviá

Kalpáki

Monodéndri

Negádes

KEY
▬▬ Major road
▬▬ Minor road
═══ Road in poor condition
– – Scenic footpath

E90

Vitsa

Kípoi

Ioánnina

0 kilometers 2
0 miles 2

Víkos Gorge Walk ❸

To walk the length of the Víkos Gorge is to undertake what is arguably the greatest walk in Greece. Carved by the Voïdomátis River, the sheer, deeply eroded limestone walls rise to 914 m (3,000 ft). The gorge cuts through the Víkos-Aóos National Park, established in 1975. Cairns and waymarks define the route, which snakes through the boulder-strewn ravine bed and continues up through stands

Greek tortoise

of beech, chestnut, and maple to the higher ground. Several birds of prey, including the Egyptian vulture, are commonly seen circling in the thermals, and lizards and tortoises abound. Though the main route through the gorge begins at Monodéndri, a shorter 4-km (2-mile) walk can be made between the northern villages of Mikró Pápigko and Vítsiko.

Rock pinnacle ④
For the Pápigko villages, cross the Víkos here beneath a landmark pinnacle of rock. The path branches to the west for Vítsiko.

Agía Triáda ③
After three hours you pass the white shrine of Agía Triáda, standing opposite a well.

Megálo Pápigko ⑤
One of the area's protected traditional villages, stone-built Megálo Pápigko stands at 950 m (3,117 ft), beneath the cliffs of Pírgi.

Oxiá Viewpoint ②
From Monodéndri, a road leads to the Oxiá site, one of the area's finest viewpoints, along with Velóï opposite.

Monodéndri ①
With its magnificent views of the gorge, this village is the most popular start for the walk. The path is signposted from the church in the lower square.

0 kilometers _____ 5

0 miles _____ 2

KEY

- - - Walk route

=== Minor road

=== Road in poor condition

🏠 Monastery

☀ Viewpoint

🅿 Parking

Tips for Walkers

Starting point: *Monodéndri.*
Getting there: *40 km (25 miles) NW of Ioánnina, by car or bus.*
Length: *14 km (8 miles) to Megálo Pápigko.*
Difficulty: *Straightforward, but hiking boots required.*
Walking time: *6–7 hours.*

Métsovo ❹
Μέτσοβο

Epirus. **Road map** B2. 🚶 *3,500*. 🚌
🛈 *0656 41233*.

Shepherds' crooks, rugs, and silverware in a souvenir shop in Métsovo

Situated close by the Katára Pass (the route crossing the Píndos Mountains), Métsovo has a vitality unique among Greek mountain towns. It was originally a small village inhabited by Vlach shepherds, though it became one of the region's most important commercial centers after being granted tax privileges in return for guarding the pass during Ottoman times *(see pp38–9)*. Local merchant families invested their new wealth in the town and continue to do so today by providing endowments and grants to encourage industry among the local craftspeople.

One such family was the Tosítsas, and some idea of the size of their wealth can be gained by touring the rebuilt 18th-century **Archontikó Tosítsa**, preserved as a museum *(see pp20–21)*. Rising to three floors, the mansion contains an armory and washroom on the ground floor, with huge wood-paneled reception rooms and

bedrooms upstairs, carpeted with beautiful, locally woven *kilim* rugs. Intricate gold- and silverware are on display, as well as collections of Epirot costumes and embroidery. Would-be visitors must wait outside for the half-hourly guided tour.

Another of Métsovo's benefactors was the writer and politician Evángelou Avérof (1910–90), who founded the **Avérof Gallery**. The core of

Interior of the Archontikó Tosítsa, Métsovo

the gallery is Avérof's own collection of some 200 paintings and sculptures he acquired over the years, always with the ambition of opening a museum of modern Greek art in his home town. His collection has been expanded to show the work of several dozen Greek artists from the 19th and 20th centuries.

Ancient traditions have survived in the area, from the simple craft of carving shepherds' crooks (handed down since Métsovo first made its money through sheep farming in the rich pastures around) to embroidery, wine- and cheese-making. Some of the older men (and a few women) still wear traditional costumes; you can see them, dressed in black, sitting in the shelters and cafés around the town square. The shelters are needed during winter when the town, at 1,156 m (3,793 ft) becomes a popular ski resort. The rugs on sale in the souvenir shops also reflect this alpine character.

🏛 **Archontikó Tosítsa**
Off main thoroughfare. 📞 *0656 41084*. ⭕ *Mon–Wed, Fri–Sun*. 🌐
🏛 **Avérof Gallery**
Off central square. 📞 *0656 41210*. ⭕ *Mon, Wed–Sun*. 🌐

Environs: Fifteen minutes' walk south, signposted from the center of town, stands the small and charming 14th-century **Moní Agíou Nikoláou**. Now it is inhabited only by caretakers, who are more than happy to show visitors the church's vivid post-Byzantine frescoes, the monks' living quarters, and their own supplies of flowers, fruit, and vegetables.

VLACH SHEPHERDS

Believed to originate from farther north in the Balkan peninsula, the nomadic Vlach shepherds are today centered in the Píndos Mountains, particularly in and around Métsovo. Their language is a dialect of Romanian, and it is thought that they are descendents of Roman settlers who moved through Illyria into the northern Balkans. Traditionally, their way of life has been transhumant – spending summers in the mountains before moving down to the plains of Thessaly with their sheep for six months to avoid the worst of the winter snows. It is a hard way of life that is gradually disappearing, and the shepherds who remain can be found in villages to the north of Métsovo such as Avdélla, Vovoúsa, and Samarína – their traditional summer settlements. Their winter homes lie mainly around Kástoria *(see p240)*.

Zagorian Vlach shepherd

Ioánnina ●

Ιωάννινα

Aslan Pasha mosque, housing the Popular Art Museum

THE CAPITAL of the Epirus region, Ioánnina prospered during Ottoman times *(see pp38–9)*, when its famous craftsmen's guilds, including the silversmiths', were formed. The Turkish influence is most visible in the fortress area that extends on a small headland into Lake Pamvótis (it was once moated on its landward side). Though dating to the 13th century, the area was rebuilt in 1815 by Ali Pasha, the Turkish tyrant most closely associated with it. Inside the fortress precinct a villagelike peace reigns, though the bustle of the bazaar and the modern area is a reminder that this is still the region's busiest city.

Chalice made of Ioánninan silver

Ioánnina and the isle of Nisí, seen from the north

from Dodóni such as a bronze eagle from the 5th century BC and some statuettes of young children. Lead tablets inscribed with questions for the oracle can also be found.

◉ Folk Museum

Michaíl Angélou 42. ☎ 0651 20515. ○ Mon & Wed. ● main public hols. ♿
Opposite the Archaeological Museum is the mansion containing a collection of local crafts. In addition to silverwork and traditional costumes, there are woven textiles made by the nomadic, tent-dwelling Sarakatsans; these Epirot shepherds are the great rivals of the more numerous Vlach tribe *(see p209)*.

◉ Popular Art Museum

Aslan Pasha Mosque. ☎ 0651 26356. ○ daily. ● main public hols. ♿
Situated in the northern corner of the fortress, this small museum is housed within the Aslan Pasha mosque, built by Aslan Pasha in 1618. The interior of the mosque itself, which retains the original decoration on its dome, makes a visit worthwhile, and the weapons and costumes on display tell something of Ioánnina's recent past. Turkish furniture inlaid with mother-of-pearl can also be found alongside Jewish rugs and tapestries from the town's synagogues.

◉ Byzantine Museum

Inner Fortress. ☎ 0651 25989. ○ Tue–Sun. ● main public hols. ♿
This modern museum, situated in the inner fortress, contains a few items from local archaeological excavations, but the core is an imaginative display of icons from the 16th to the 19th centuries. In a separate building, once the treasury, a silverware annex displays items of the craft for which the town is renowned, alongside a reconstruction of a typical silversmith's workshop.

◉ Archaeological Museum

Plateía 25 Martíou 6. ☎ 0651 25490. ○ daily. ● main public hols. ♿
Set in a small park south of the fortress, the Archaeological Museum has a small collection of artifacts, including items

ALI PASHA

Ali Pasha was born in Albania in 1741 and, in 1788, was installed at Ioánnina by the Turks as Pasha of Epirus. Though a murderer, he was a great administrator who made the town one of the wealthiest in Greece. His aim was to gain independence from his overlords, and by 1820 he had an empire stretching from Albania to the Peloponnese. When news spread of his intention to create a Greco-Albanian state, Sultan Mahmud II of Turkey dispatched troops to put him to death. After a long siege within the fortress at Ioánnina, Ali Pasha agreed to meet the Turkish commander on the island of Nisí where, on January 24, 1822, he was hunted down, trapped, and killed.

Tapestry of Ali Pasha (center), Moní Agíou Panteleímona, Nisí

Nisí

15 minutes by boat NE from fortress.
Though its first inhabitants
were the monks who came
here in the early years of the
13th century, the single village
on the island of Nisí owes its
existence to 17th-century refugees from Mániot feuds *(see
p194)*. Its main building is
Moní Agíou Panteleïmona,
where the reconstructed room
in which Ali Pasha was shot
can be visited, the bullet holes
still visible in the floor. Other
rooms contain a few of his
possessions, some costumes,
and period prints.

Stalactites in the Pérama Caves

ENVIRONS: Greece's largest
cave network, the **Pérama
Caves**, can be found near
the village of Pérama, 4 km
(2.5 miles) north of Ioánnina.
Discovered in 1940 by a shepherd hiding from the Germans,
they were not fully explored
until 1942. Now there are
regular guided tours taking
visitors along the 1,700 m
(5,600 ft) of passages, where
multicolored lights pick out
the strange shapes of the
stalactites and stalagmites.

Pérama Caves

Pérama. 📞 0651 81521. ⏰ daily. 📷

The theater of Dodóni, one of the largest in Greece

Dodóni ❻

Δωδώνη

Epirus. **Road map** B3. 📞 0651 82287.
🚌 ⏰ daily. ⬤ main public hols.
📷 ♿

D ATING to at least 1000 BC,
the Oracle of Zeus at
Dodóni is the oldest in Greece
and was second in status
only to the one at Delphi *(see
pp228–9)*. The site is located
22 km (14 miles) southwest
of Ioánnina in a placid green
valley on the eastern slopes
of Mount Tómaros.
The oracle focused on a
sacred oak tree ringed with
tripods that held a number of
bronze cauldrons placed so
that they touched each other.
Prophecies were divined from
the sound these made, in
harmony with the rustling
of the oak leaves, when one
of the cauldrons was struck.
Petitioners would inscribe
their questions on lead tablets
for the priestess to read
to Zeus; some of
these have been
found on the
site and can
be seen in the
Archaeological
Museum in
Ioánnina. The
reputed power
of the oak tree
was such that
Jason, on his
quest for the
Golden Fleece *(see
p220)*, traveled across from
the Pílio to acquire one of its
branches to attach to his ship,
the Argo. By the 3rd century
BC a colonnaded courtyard
was built around the tree for

**Justinian, the last Roman
Emperor to live at Dodóni**

protection; it contained a small
temple of which only foundations remain. The tree was
uprooted in AD 393 on the
orders of the Roman Emperor
Theodosios (ruled 379–395)
in accordance with his policy
of stamping out pagan practices. He also believed that
buried treasure might be found
beneath the site.
The main feature of Dodóni
today is the theater which,
with its capacity for 17,000
spectators, is one of the largest in Greece. Its huge walls
rise to 21 m (69 ft) and are
supported by solid towers
where kestrels now nest. Used
by the ancient Greeks for drama
performances, the Romans
later converted it to an arena
for animal fights, bulls and
big cats would have been
kept in the two triangular pens
on either side of the stage.
The whole structure of the
theater was restored in the
early 1960s and is now used
for performances dur-
ing the summer.
Dodóni also in-
cludes the ruins
of a stadium,
acropolis, and
Byzantine
basilica – all
reminders of
the time when
this empty
valley was the
location of a
flourishing
market town.
Dodóni fell into ruin in the
6th century AD when the
Roman Emperor Justinian
decided to found the new
and more easily defendable
city of Ioánnina.

The tiered, horseshoe-shaped town of Párga, seen across Párga Bay

Párga 🐼
Πάργα

Epirus. **Road map** B3. 🏘 *2,000*. 🚌
🛈 *Alexandrou Pàga 18 (0684 31222)*.
�ⁿ *Tue*.

PARGA, the main beach resort of Epirus, is a busy vacation town whose charms are often overwhelmed by the number of summer visitors. The Venetian fortress dominating the west side of the harbor was built in 1624 on the site of an earlier building destroyed in 1537 during a brief period of Turkish rule. The Ottomans later returned under the command of Ali Pasha *(see p210)*, who bought the town from the British in 1819. After this, many of Párga's inhabitants left for Corfu, though it was regained by the Greeks in 1913.

There are two small beaches within walking distance from the center of town and a larger one, Váltos, a short stroll away through the olive groves to the southwest. Fish restaurants line Párga's waterfront, affording fine views southward across the harbor to a number of small islands.

ENVIRONS: 37 km (23 miles) south of Párga stands the **Necromanteion of Efyras** (Oracle of the Dead) – the mythological gateway to Hades. Steps descend to the vaults where, in the 4th century BC, drugs and mechanisms may have heightened the sensation of entering the Underworld for visitors who came to ask the advice of the dead.

Kassópi 🐼
Κασσώπη

Kamarína village, Epirus.
Road map B3. 🚌
🔲 *daily*.

THE KASSOPIANS were a tribe who lived in this region in the 4th century BC. The remains of their capital city stand on a hillside plateau overlooking the Ionian Sea, from where the shadowy island of Paxos is plainly visible. Kassópi is reached by a pleasant walk through pine groves from the village of Kamarína and, though the ruins are

Greek Orthodox priests in Párga

scarcely visible, a site plan illustrates the layout of the once-great city, now the home of birds and lizards.

Just to the southeast is **Moní Zalóngou**, with its monument to local women who threw themselves from the cliffs in 1806 rather than be captured by Albanian troops.

The remains of the city of Kassópi

Préveza 🐼
Πρέβεζα

Epirus. **Road map** B3. 🏘 *13,000*.
✈ 🚢 🚌 🛈 *Eleftheriou Venizélou (0682 27277)*. 🚢 *daily (fish)*.

OFTEN SEEN as a transit point, the charming town of Préveza repays a longer visit, particularly for the lively atmosphere among its waterfront cafés and tavernas. It is picturesquely situated on the northern shore of the narrow "Channel of Cleopatra," at the mouth of the Amvrakikós Gulf. It was here that the naval Battle of Actium was fought in 31 BC *(see p34)*.

Two ruined forts, on either side of the straits, recall the town's Venetian occupation in 1499, though in 1798 it passed, via the French, into the hands of Ali Pasha *(see p210)*.

ENVIRONS: Seven km (4 miles) north of Préveza stand the ruins of **Nikópoli** ("Victory City"), built by the Roman Emperor Octavian to celebrate his victory at Actium. The city was founded on the site where the emperor's army was camped, though as the ground was unstable it quickly fell into ruin. The remains are dominated by the city walls and the theater. A museum displays artifacts from the site, which is now overgrown.

 Nikópoli
☎ 0682 41336. **◯** Tue–Sun.
● main public hols.

Arta ⑩
Άρτα

Epirus. **Road map** B3. 🚶 33,000.
🚉 🚌 ℹ️ 0681 77010. 🎪 Mon –
Sat (veg).

THOUGH IT IS the second largest town in Epirus, after Ioánnina, Arta remains largely untouched by tourism and offers a chance to see a traditional Greek market town. It has a lively, bazaarlike market area, established by the Turks who occupied Arta from 1449 to 1881. The **fortress**, which now houses the Xenía Hotel, dates from the 13th century when the city was the capital of the despotate of Epirus. The despotate, which stretched from Thessaloníki to Corfu, was an independent Byzantine state set up after the fall of Constantinople in 1204 *(see p37)*. It lasted until the start of the Turkish occupation. Some

Timber-framed houses in the Ottoman quarter of Tríkala

of the town's many 13th- and 14th-century Byzantine churches can be found in the streets leading up to the fortress, the most striking being the **Panagía Parigorítissa**. Built between 1283 and 1296, it is a three-tier building crowned with towers and domes. **Agía Theódora**, on Pýrrou, contains the marble tomb of the wife of 13th-century Epirot ruler Michael II.

Approaching from the west, the main road into town crosses the Arachthos River by a 17th-century stone **bridge**. According to local folklore, the builder of the bridge, frustrated by each day's work being ruined by the river at night, was advised by a bird that the problem could be solved by putting his wife in the bridge's foundations. This he did, burying her alive, after which the bridge was successfully completed.

Metéora ⑪

See pp216–17.

Tríkala ⑫
Τρίκαλα

Thessaly. **Road map** C2. 🚶 68,000.
🚉 🚌 ℹ️ 0431 27401. 🎪 Mon – Sat.

TRIKALA WAS THE HOME of Asklepios, the god of healing, and today is the market center for the very fertile Plain of Thessaly. As such it is a thriving town with a number of remains from its Turkish past. One is the **market** near the main square, another the **Koursoúm Tzamí**, a graceful mosque built in 1550 on the south side of the Lithaíos River. Surrounding the fortress is the Ottoman quarter of Varoúsi, with a number of Byzantine churches *(see pp18–19)*. The **fortress** is also Byzantine, built on the site of the ancient acropolis, which has stood here since the 4th century BC. It is situated in beautiful grounds overlooking the river.

Vale of Tempe ⑬
Κοιλάδα των Τεμπών

Thessaly. **Road map** C2. 🚌

AS THE E75 approaches Macedonia, it follows the Pineíos River through the Vale of Tempe – the fertile valley where Apollo was said to have purified himself after slaying the serpent Python *(see p230)*. Near the **Wolf's Jaws** (the narrowest point of the gorge) is the **Spring of Daphne**, where a bridge leads to the chapel of **Agía Paraskeví**, carved out of the rock. The **Kástro Gónnou** at the northern end of the Vale was built by Philip II of Macedon, father of Alexander the Great *(see pp32–3)*, to control what has long been one of only a few routes between Central and Northern Greece.

The arched packhorse bridge of Arta, leading into town from the west

Metéora ⑪
Μετέωρα

Icon of Our Lord, Varlaám

Monastic cells

THE NATURAL sandstone towers of Metéora (or "soaring rocks") were first used as a religious retreat when, in AD 985, a hermit named Barnabas occupied a cave here. Others joined him, and in 1336 the monk Athanásios, from Mount Athos, founded the monastery of Megálo Metéoro on one of the thousand or so pinnacles. Twenty-three monasteries followed, though, due largely to their precarious location, many had fallen into ruin by the end of the 18th century. In the 1920s stairs were carved to make the remaining six monasteries more accessible, and today a religious revival has seen the return of many monks and nuns.

LOCATION OF MONASTERIES OF METEORA

Outer walls

Rousánou
Rousánou, perched precariously on the very tip of a narrow spire of rock, is the most spectacularly located of all the monasteries. Its church of the Metamórfosis (1545) is renowned for its harrowing frescoes, painted in 1560 by the iconographers of the Cretan school.

VARLAAM
Founded in 1518, the monastery of Varlaám is named after the first hermit to live on this rock in 1350. The *katholikón* was built in 1542 and contains some frescoes by the Theban iconographer Frágkos Katelávos.

Megálo Metéoro
Megálo Metéoro, or the Great Meteoro, was the first and, at 623 m (2,044ft), highest monastery to be founded. By the entrance is a cave in which Athanásios first lived. His body is buried in the main church.

◁ **Rousánou in the clouds, with its narrow footbridge in the foreground**

Katholikón
Dedicated to Agioi Pántes (All Saints), the church is adorned with frescoes, including one of Theofánis (right) and Nektários, its founders.

The refectory contains a small icon museum.

VISITORS' CHECKLIST

Thessaly. **Road map** B2.
Chagipétrou 10, Kalampáka (0432 22109).
Megálo Metéoro Mon & Wed–Sun.
Varlaám Mon–Thu, Sat & Sun.
Agiou Nikoláou Apr–Oct: daily.
Rousánou daily.
Agía Triáda daily.
Agios Stéfanos Tue–Sun.
all monasteries shut 1–3pm.
at all monasteries.
Agia Triáda & Agios Stéfanos.

Ascent Tower
Goods and people were pulled up by a winch mechanism made in 1536.

Net descending from tower

Entrance

THE BUILDING OF THE MONASTERIES

Though it is unknown how the first hermits reached the tops of these often vertical rock faces, it is likely that they hammered pegs into tiny gaps in the rock and hauled building materials to the summits. Another theory is that kites were flown over the tops, carrying strings attached to thicker ropes that were made into the first rope ladders.

Pílio ⓮
Πήλιο

Taxiárchis church fresco, Miliés

THE MYTHOLOGICAL HOME of the forest-loving centaurs, the Pílio peninsula, with its woods of chestnut, oak, and beech, is one of the most beautiful regions of the mainland. The mountain air is sweet with the scent of herbs that, in ancient times, were renowned for their healing powers. The area became populated in the 13th century by Greeks retreating from the Ottomans *(see pp38–9)*, under whom they were allowed only a measure of religious freedom. Most villages were built close to mountain monasteries, though the thick stone walls and narrow windows of a typical Pílio house indicate how uncertain this freedom was. The local culture is insular, and this is one of the few areas of Greece to have a strong local cuisine.

Makrynítsa
Cars are banned from the steep cobblestone streets of this traditional village (see p220).

Agía Kyriakí
Overlooked by the isolated hilltop village of Trikéri, this small fishing port lacks a beach and hotels but has a working boatyard and good, simple fish tavernas for those very few visitors who take the trouble to travel here.

Anakasiá, now little more than a suburb of Vólos, has a museum to the Greek painter Theófilos Chatzimichaïl.

Vólos is the capital of the region, straddling the only route into the peninsula. It has an excellent Archaeological Museum *(see p220).*

THEOFILOS CHATZIMICHAÏL

Born on Lésvos in 1873, Theófilos came to the Pílio in 1894 after reportedly killing a Turk in Smyrna. His favored medium was the mural, though he also painted ceramics and the sides of fishing boats, *kafeneío* counters, or horse carts when the mood struck him. He executed numerous mural commissions in the Pílio, notably at the Kontós mansion in Anakasiá.

Konstantine Palaiologos mural (1899) by Theófilos

Though unhappily isolated, and mocked by the locals for his strange habits (he dressed in the costumes of past heroes, including Alexander the Great), he had a passion for all things Greek. After Lésvos's unification with Greece in 1912, he returned home destitute and ill. His fortunes changed after meeting his future patron Stratís Eleftheriádis, who provided for the painter's needs until Theófilos's death in 1934.

KEY

▬▬	Major road
▬▬	Minor road
═══	Unpaved road
- - -	Ferry route
ℹ	Tourist information
☀	Viewpoint

Vyzítsa
Mansions have been converted to guesthouses in this small village with its cobblestone streets and large main square surrounded by old plane trees.

Agios Ioánnis
has one of the Pílio's most popular beaches.

VISITORS' CHECKLIST

Thessaly. **Road map** D3.
Vólos. Plateía Ríga Feraiou, Vólos (0421 24915).
Archaeological Museum, Athanasáki 1, Vólos. 0421 28563. Tue–Sun. main public hols.
Folk Museum, Miliés
0423 86602. Apr–Oct: Tue–Sun; Nov–Mar: Wed–Sun.
Theófilos Museum, Anakasiá
0421 49109. Tue–Sun. main public hols.

Tsagkaráda is a delightful mountain village on wooded slopes. In its central square is the largest and oldest (1,000 years) plane tree in Greece.

Miliés
This hill-village has a Folk Museum of local artifacts. Frescoes, such as this 18th century Archangel Michael, adorn the church, the Taxiárchis.

Argalastí
This is the main town of the southern Pílio, attractively set on the edge of a plateau. Though it has a busy market, its few tavernas and cafés retain a peaceful atmosphere.

Plataniá
With its fine beach and boats traveling back to Vólos and to Skíathos island, Plataniá is popular with Greek tourists. A number of fish tavernas provide excellent seafood.

Exploring the Pílio

TRAVELING BY CAR, a circular tour of the northern villages can be made in a day following the road southeast from Vólos to Afétes, via Tsagkaráda. The hills in this region rise to 1,650 m (5,415 ft) at the summit of Mount Pílio, and in addition to dense woodlands, the area produces a large number of apples, pears, peaches, and olives. While less dramatic, the southern Pílio is still hilly enough to ensure that many villages are at the end of single "dead end" roads, making travel here time-consuming.

Restored traditional mansions on the hillside of Makrynítsa

Vólos

Vólos is one of Greece's fastest-growing industrial centers, and, since it was devastated by earthquakes in the 1950s, it is difficult to imagine its mythological past. Once the site of ancient Iolkos, the home of Jason, who went in search of the Golden Fleece, Vólos's history is illustrated by what can be found in the excellent **Archaeological Museum**. The museum, situated in a flowered garden, contains an extensive collection of painted funerary stelae from the 3rd

Fisherman with his nets at the waterfront, Vólos

century BC, found at Dimitriás on the far side of the Gulf of Vólos. Important collections of Neolithic pottery from the nearby sites of Sésklo and Dimíni can also be found.

Northern Villages

From Vólos the road leads southeast, past Ano Lechóni, through the "Vólos Riviera," providing a circular route of the mountainous northern Pílio. From the popular inland resorts of **Miliés** and **Vyzítsa** (the latter preserved as a "traditional settlement" by the government), the road turns north past Tsagkaráda to **Agios Ioánnis**. This is the main resort of the east coast, and, though the village beach itself is often crowded, the beaches of Papá Neró and Pláka are particularly fine and are both within easy walking distance. Some of the Pílio's best restaurants can be found in nearby **Moúresi**.

Returning toward Vólos, take the turning to **Makrynítsa** – a traditional mountain village, widely regarded as the most important destination for any traveler in the area. Founded in the 13th century by refugees from the first sacking of Constantinople *(see p37)*, the village has several beautiful churches, the most impressive being Agios Ioánnis, and the Moní Theotókou. A number of traditional mansions also survive, some functioning as guest houses. Close to Agios Ioánnis, there is a café with an interior decorated with frescoes painted by the artist Theófilos *(see p218)*.

Anakasiá is the last village before Vólos. Though few people stop for long here, the delightful Theófilos Museum is well worth a visit.

JASON AND THE ARGONAUTS

According to legend, the Golden Fleece came from a winged ram sent by Hermes, the gods' messenger, to protect two children, Helle and Phrixos, from their evil stepmother. Though Helle drowned, Phrixos was reared in Kolchis, in present-day Georgia, where the ram was sacrificed and its fleece given to the king, Aiëtes. Years later, Jason, Phrixos's cousin, set sail from the kingdom of Iolkos (now Vólos) after his half-brother usurped the throne. Jason was in search of the Fleece, which made its wearer invincible. With a crew of 50, Jason came to Kolchis where King Aiëtes set several tasks before relinquishing the Fleece. After falling in love with the king's daughter, Medea, Jason achieved his tasks and the Argonauts carried the Fleece back to Iolkos in triumph.

Detail from *The Golden Fleece* (c.1905) by Herbert Draper (1864–1920)

Sarcophagus detail outside the
Thebes Archaeological Museum

Thebes ⓯
Θήβα

Stereá Elláda. **Road map** D4.
🏛 20,000. �909 🚌 🛈 Vourdoumpá
13 (0262 26033).

ALTHOUGH it was briefly
the most powerful city of
Greece, in the 4th century BC,
the Thebes of today is little
more than a quiet provincial
town. It played an important
role in the power struggles of
Classical Greece, until defeated
by Philip II of Macedonia.
Thebes' original acropolis has
been built over through the
years, but excavations have
unearthed Mycenaean walls
as well as jewelry, pottery,
and important tablets of Linear
B script that are now in the
Archaeological Museum.
One of the highlights of the
museum is the collection of
Mycenaean sarcophagi, similar
to those found on Crete. The
museum's courtyard and well-
tended garden stand alongside
a 13th-century Frankish tower,
all that remains of a castle
ruined in 1311 by the Catalans.

A bridge over the riverbed,
a short walk eastward from
the museum, marks the traditional site of the Fountain of
Oedipus, where the legendary
King Oedipus is said to have

THE LEGEND OF OEDIPUS

According to legend, Oedipus was the ill-fated son of Laius
and Iocasta, the king and queen of Thebes. Even before his
birth, the Delphic Oracle *(see p228)* had foretold that he
would kill his father and become his mother's husband. To
defy the prophecy, Laius abandoned Oedipus, but the child
was rescued and reared by the king and queen of Corinth
whom Oedipus believed to be his real
parents. Years later, when he heard
of the prophecy, Oedipus fled to
Thebes, killing a man on his
way, unaware that he was King
Laius. On reaching Thebes, he
found the city gates barred by
the Sphinx, which he van-
quished by solving one of its
riddles. The Thebans made him
their king, and he married the
widowed Iocasta. When the truth
about his past was revealed, Oedipus
blinded himself and spent his final
days as an outcast.

Oedipus and the Sphinx,
from a 5th-century BC cup

washed blood from his hands
after unwittingly killing his
father on his way to the city.

🏛 **Archaeological Museum**
Plateía Threpsiádou 1. 📞 0262
27913. ◯ Tue–Sun. 🌀 ♿

ENVIRONS: Lying 10 km (6
miles) north are the ruins of
Gla, a one-time stronghold of
the Mycenaeans. Even larger
than Mycenae *(see pp178–80)*,
its walls are 3 km (2 miles) long
and up to 5 m (16 ft) high,
surrounding a hill where the
ruins of a palace and the site
of the agora can be found.

Monastery of
Osios Loukás ⓰

See pp222–3.

Mount Parnassus ⓱
Όρος Παρνασσός

Stereá Elláda. **Road map** C3.
🚌 Delfoí. 🛈 Vasiléos & Pávlou
Freiderikis 44, Delfoí (0265 82900).

RISING to a height of 2,457 m
(8,061 ft), the limestone
mass of Mount Parnassus
dominates the eastern region
of Stereá Elláda. The lower
slopes are covered with
Cephalonian fir, and beneath
them, in summer, the wild-
flower meadows burst into
color. Vultures and golden
eagles are common, as are
wolves, which come down
from the Píndos Mountains
(see p206) in winter.

The village of **Aráchova** is
the best base for exploring
the area and is renowned for
its wine, cheese, and sheep-
skin rugs. There are many
mountain trails for summer
hikes, though a detailed
walking map is recommended.
Reaching the top of Liákoura,
the highest peak, involves a
long hike and camping overnight on the mountain.

From Aráchova, the ski center
at **Fterólakas** is only a 26-km
(16-mile) drive away. Open
from December to April, it
provides a chair lift to 1,900 m
(6,235 ft); from here another
lift leads up to the ski slopes.
In summer, Fterólakas
functions as an excursion
center for the area.

Fir-covered foothills beneath the ridge of Mount Parnassus

Monastery of Osios Loukás ⑯
Μονή Οσίου Λουκά

Madonna mosaic

DEDICATED to a local hermit, Holy Luke, Osios Loukás monastery was architecturally one of medieval Greece's most important buildings; built c.1011, it is an extension of an earlier church dating from AD 944. The octagonal style of the main church became a hallmark of late Byzantine church design *(see pp18–19)*, while the mosaics inside lifted Byzantine art into its final great period. During the days of the Ottoman Empire *(see pp38–9)*, Osios Loukás was the scene of a great deal of fighting, as the cannons in the courtyard testify. In 1821, it was here that Bishop Isaias declared his support for the Greek freedom fighters.

The Theotókos, built in the early 11th century, is a smaller church dedicated to the Mother of God; its name means "god-bearing."

The north transept contains medallion-shaped mosaics of saints.

The monastic cells are small, with arched roofs.

The exterior is a mixture of dressed Póros stone and red brick.

West portal

The narthex is the western entrance hall; it contains a number of mosaics of Christ's Passion.

The monastery seen from the west with the slopes of Mount Elikónas in the background

★ Washing of the Apostles' Feet
Based on a style dating to the 6th century, this 11th-century work is the finest of the narthex mosaics. Set on a gold background, it depicts Christ teaching his apostles humility.

STAR FEATURES

★ Washing of the Apostles' Feet

★ Crypt

Dome
The main dome is decorated with an imposing mural of Christ surrounded by saints and angels, painted in the 17th century to replace fallen mosaics.

The apse has a mosaic of the Virgin and Child, which predates a devastating earthquake in 1659.

The katholikón, or main church, dates to 1011 and is built in the octagonal style.

★ **Crypt**
This 10th-century shrine, from the original site, contains the sarcophagus of Holy Luke and such frescoes as this Descent from the Cross.

HOLY LUKE

Born near Delphi (see pp228–31) in 896, Osios Loukás ("Holy Luke") is known to have been a spiritual child who, in his early teens, left home to seek isolation in central Greece and developed a reputation as a healer. In around 940 he arrived at this spot on the western slopes of Mount Elikónas, with its glorious view of a peaceful valley of wheat fields and groves of almond and olive trees. Here he settled with some disciples, adding the gift of prophecy to his healing powers. He died in 953, by which time the first monastic cells and the site's first small church had been constructed.

The southwest chapel has early 11th-century frescoes.

The refectory was used as a workshop as well as for meals; it now contains a museum of Byzantine sculpture.

The waterfront houses of Galaxídi in the Gulf of Corinth

are the famous sulfur springs from which Thermopylae was given its name, which means "Hot Gates."

The present landscape has changed considerably from the narrow gorge of old; the coastline to the north has been extended by the silt brought down by the Spercheiós River, pushing the sea back over 5 km (3 miles).

🏛 **Lamía Museum**
Kástro. ▐ 0231 46106. ◯ Tue–Sun.
● main public hols. 📷 ⛬

Ancient Delphi ⑲

See pp228–31.

Gulf of Corinth ⑳
Κορινθιακός Κόλπος

Stereá Elláda. 🚍 to Náfpaktos.

THE NORTHERN COAST of the Gulf of Corinth contains several well-known resorts as well as many tiny coastal villages far removed from the usual tourist route. All are served by major roads that, like the resorts, offer fine views across the gulf to the mountains of the Peloponnese.

From Delphi the main road leads southward through the largest olive grove in Greece, passing **Itéa**, a busy industrial port. The church of Agios Nikólaos, 17 km (11 miles) west, stands prominently on a hill surrounded by the old stone buildings of **Galaxídi**. The history of the town is told in the Nautical Museum, and the 19th-century mansions on the waterfront are reminders of the great wealth brought by the town's shipbuilding industry. Though the industry cleared the region of trees, a reforestation plan begun earlier this century has successfully restored the area to its former beauty.

The next major town is **Náfpaktos**. Though perhaps less attractive than Galaxídi, it still possesses plenty of charm and character.

Lamía and Thermopylae ⑱
Λαμία καί Θερμοπύλαι

Stereá Elláda. **Road map** C3.
🏠 68,000. 🚍 ℹ Plateía Laoú 3 (0231 30065). 🚢 Sat.

SET IN THE VALLEY between two wooded hills, Lamía is typical of many medium-sized Greek towns; although it is little known, it has much to offer, with a lively Saturday market. A 14th-century Catalan **kástro**, built on the site of the town's ancient acropolis, provides excellent views over the roofs to the surrounding countryside.

Lamía is chiefly associated with the Lamian War (323–322 BC), when Athens tried to throw off Macedonian rule after the death of Alexander the Great (see pp32–3). This is recalled at the **Lamía Museum**, which also has displays of architectural remains from Delphi (see pp228–31).

A short drive east of Lamía, the Athens road crosses the **Pass of Thermopylae**. It was here, in 480 BC, that an army of some 7,000 soldiers, under the command of Leonidas I of Sparta, met an overwhelming force from Persia whose numbers Herodotus (see p56) cites as 2,641,610. Though Leonidas held the pass for a number of days, the Persians forced a path through and attacked the Greeks from the rear. Only two Greek soldiers survived the ordeal, after which all of central Greece, including Athens, fell to the Persians. The Persian land forces were eventually defeated by Athens and her allies at the Battle of Plataia in 479 BC (see p29).

An impressive bronze statue of King Leonidas, cast in 1955, stands at the roadside opposite the burial mound of the soldiers who died here. Just to the left of the mound

Statue of King Leonidas at the Pass of Thermopylae

A Venetian fortress stands above the town, its ramparts running down as far as the beach, almost enclosing the harbor. The Venetian name for the town was Lepanto. In 1571, the famous naval Battle of Lepanto (see p38), in which the Venetians, Spanish, and Genoese defeated the Ottomans, was fought here. A popular story to emerge from the battle purports that the Spanish author Miguel de Cervantes (1547–1616) lost an arm in the conflict, though in fact only his left hand was maimed.

At **Antírrio** the coast comes closest to the Peloponnese, and from here a regular car ferry sails across the stretch of water known as the "little Dardanelles" to Río, on the southern shore. There is little more to Antírrio than the ferry service, though beside the harbor, guarding the Gulf, stands the originally Frankish and Venetian Kástro Roúmelis. Another castle can be seen across the water on the Peloponnese.

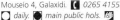

Nautical Museum
Mouseío 4, Galaxídi. 0265 41558. daily. main public hols.

Mesolóngi ㉑
Μεσολόγγι

Stereá Elláda. **Road map** B3.
12,000. Spyrídonos Trikoúpi 29 (0631 27220). Tue & Sat.

MEANING "amid the lagoons," Mesolóngi is a town perfectly located for fishing, though the industry is now in decline. Historically, the town is renowned for being a center of resistance to the Turks during the War of Independence (see pp40–41). After a leader, Aléxandros Mavrokordátos, made Mesolóngi his headquarters in 1821, the town became a rallying point, attracting, among others, the British poet Lord Byron (see p149), to fight for the cause of Greek independence. Byron arrived in January 1824 but died of a fever in April. His heart is buried beneath his statue, which stands in the Garden of Heroes.

Nearby, the Gate of the Exodus commemorates the 9,000 people whose revolt in 1826 eventually resulted in the Turkish surrender of the town in 1828.

Statue of Lord Byron at Mesolóngi

SALT PAN BIRDLIFE

With its importance for food preservation, the production of salt is a major enterprise in the Mediterranean, the most extensive areas in Greece being around Mesolóngi and the Gulf of Arta. Seawater is channeled into large artificial lakes, or salt pans, which, with their high concentrations of salt, attract a large amount of wildlife. Brine shrimp thrive, providing food for a wide variety of birds. Two of the most striking waders are the avocet and the great egret; also common is the black-winged stilt with its long red legs. The area is also home to Kentish plovers, stone curlews, and the short-toed lark.

Avocet

Great egret

The fortified harbor of Náfpaktos in the Gulf of Corinth

Ancient Delphi 🅑

Δελφοί

ACCORDING TO LEGEND, when Zeus released two eagles from opposite ends of the earth their paths crossed in the sky above Delphi, establishing the site as the center of the world. Renowned as a dwelling place of Apollo, from the end of the 8th century BC individuals from all over the ancient world visited Delphi to consult the god on what course of action to take, both in public and private life. With the political rise of Delphi in the 6th century BC and the reorganization of the Pythian Games *(see p230)*, the sanctuary entered a golden age that lasted until the Romans came in 191 BC. The oracle was abolished in 393 with the Christianization of the Byzantine Empire under Theodosius.

Siphnian Treasury caryatid

LOCATOR MAP

The Athenian Treasury was built after the Battle of Marathon *(see p145)* and reconstructed in 1906.

To museum *(see p231)*

Bouleuterion (Delphic Council House)

Siphnian Treasury

SACRED WAY

THE ORACLE OF DELPHI

The Delphic Oracle was the means through which worshipers could hear the words of the god Apollo, spoken through a priestess, or *Pythia*, over the age of 50. Questioners paid a levy called a *pelanos* and sacrificed an animal on the altar. The question was then put to the *Pythia* by a male priest. The *Pythia* would answer in a trance, perhaps induced by vapors from a crack in the ground over which she sat on a tripod. Her incantations were interpreted by the priest, though the answers were often ambiguous. King Croesus of Lydia (560–546 BC) came to ask if he should make war against Cyrus the Great of Persia and was told that if he crossed a river then he would destroy a great empire. In marching on Cyrus his troops crossed the River Halys and he destroyed an empire, though it turned out to be his own.

The main entrance was once a market place (agora) where religious objects could be bought.

The Rock of the Sibyl marks the place where, according to legend, Delphi's first prophetess pronounced her oracles.

★ **Sacred Way**
Leading to the Temple of Apollo, this path was lined with up to 3,000 statues and treasuries, built by city-states to house their peoples' offerings.

◁ **Dramatic view over the theater at Delphi**

THE SANCTUARY OF APOLLO

Also known as the Sacred Precinct, this is at the heart of a complex that also included a stadium and a sacred spring *(see pp230–31)*. It is entered through an agora from which the Sacred Way winds through the ruins of memorials and treasuries.

To the stadium
(see p230)

The theater, built 2,500 years ago, seats 5,000 people. It rivals Epidaurus *(see pp184–5)* as one of the finest theaters in Greece.

★ **Temple of Apollo**
A temple has stood on this site since the 6th century BC, but the remains visible today date from the 4th century BC. Some reconstruction work has been done since French archaeologists uncovered the foundations in 1892, to give an impression of its original grandeur.

A column once supported a statue of Prusias, King of Bithynia.

RECONSTRUCTION OF DELPHI IN 200 BC

Bouleuterion

Theater

Archaic Treasuries

Athenian Treasury

Sacred Way

Siphnian Treasury

Meeting Hall of the Knidians

Temple of Apollo

Stoa of Attalos

Stoa of the Athenians

Altar of the Chians

Sikyonian Treasury

Magistrates' Hall

Columns of the Messenians

STAR SIGHTS

★ **Temple of Apollo**

★ **Sacred Way**

Exploring Delphi

THE FIRST EXCAVATIONS at Delphi began in 1892, uncovering a much larger area than is apparent now. Though it is most famous for the Sanctuary of Apollo, Delphi also had a sanctuary dedicated to the goddess Athena, whose temple, along with a structure known as a *tholos*, can be seen in a second enclosure to the south. North of the theater is the stadium where the Pythian Games were held. These, after the Olympian Games *(see p173)*, were the most important pan-Hellenic cultural, religious, and athletic gathering of peoples who were otherwise divided into mostly rival city-states, and provided an opportunity to strengthen the ethnic bonds of all Greeks.

Caryatid from the Siphnian Treasury

The Stadium, viewed from the remains of the entrance archway

⋔ Marmaria Precinct
Southeast of the Temple of Apollo, a path leads to the Marmaria Precinct, or marble quarry, where the Sanctuary of Athena Pronaia can be found. At the sanctuary's entrance stand the ruins of a 4th-century BC temple dedicated to Athena. At the far end of the sanctuary are the remains of an earlier temple to the goddess, which was built around 510 BC. Between the two temples stands the Marmaria's most remarkable, and most photographed, monument: the circular *tholos*. The purpose of this structure is still unknown. The rotunda dates from the start of the 4th century BC and was originally surrounded by 20 columns. Three of these columns were reerected in 1938. They stand to provide some hint of the building's former beauty.

⋔ Stadium
This is one of the very best-preserved stadia in the country. Almost 200 m (656 ft) long and partly hewn out of the rocks above the main sanctuary, it held 7,000 spectators who gathered for the field and track events every four years during the Pythian Games. The games grew out of a musical festival, held in the theater every eight years, to celebrate Apollo's mythical slaying of the serpent Python *(see p228)*. Though poetry and musical recitals remained central to the occasion, from 582 BC athletic events in the stadium were added, and the festival became known as the Pythian Games. All prizes in these tournaments were purely honorary; each winner was awarded the traditional laurel wreath and the right to have his statue in the sanctuary.

Made entirely of limestone from Mount Parnassus, the present structure dates from Roman times, and most of the seating is still intact. The best-preserved seats are the backed benches on the north side, made for the presidents of the games and honored guests.

⋔ Castalian Spring
Before entering the Sacred Precinct, it is believed that everyone visiting Delphi for religious purposes, including

The *tholos* beside the Sanctuary of Athena Pronaia, Marmaria Precinct

athletes, were required to purify themselves in the clear but icy waters of the Castalian spring – this process principally involved the washing of the hair. The oracle *Pythia* *(see p228)* would also wash here before making her pronouncements. The visible remains of the fountain date either from the late Hellenistic or the early Roman period. A number of niches in the surrounding rock once held the votive offerings left for the nymph Castalia, to whom the spring was dedicated.

It is said that the British romantic poet Lord Byron *(see p149)* once plunged into the spring, inspired by the belief that the waters would enhance the poetic spirit.

The niches of the Castalian Spring

⋔ Gymnasium

Water from the Castalian Spring ran down to this area to provide cold baths (until the Romans added hot baths in the 2nd century AD) for athletes training for the Pythian Games. The original cold baths, which can be seen in a square courtyard, are some 9 m (30 ft) in diameter. East of the baths lies the Palaestra, or training area, surrounded by the remains of what once were changing rooms and training quarters. As well as an outdoor running track, a covered track 180 m (591 ft) in length provided a venue for the games in bad weather. The gymnasium was also used for intellectual pursuits – Delphi's poets and philosophers taught here – and was built on many levels due to the sloping terrain.

🏛 Delphi Museum

The museum at Delphi contains a collection of sculptures and architectural remains of an importance second only to those of the Athenian Acropolis *(see pp94–101)*. Just inside the entrance stands the Omphalos, or navel stone. This is a Hellenistic or Roman copy of the stone that was believed to have marked the place above which Zeus's eagles met, establishing the sanctuary of Delphi as the center of the world *(see p228)*.

There are 13 rooms of exhibits, all on the ground floor. In one of the rooms there is a scale model that reconstructs the Sanctuary of Apollo in a triumph of limestone whites, blue marble, gold, and terra-cotta. Surrounded by friezes and statues, the extent of Delphi's size and its former beauty is represented vividly.

Votive chapels, or treasuries, lined the Sacred Way *(see p228)* and contained offerings of thanks, in the form of money or works of art, from towns grateful for good fortune following a favorable prophecy from the oracle. The Theban Treasury, for example, was established after the victory of Thebes at the Battle of Leuktra in 371 BC. There are two rooms

The bronze
Charioteer

dedicated to the surviving sculpture from the Siphnian and Athenian Treasuries, the wealth of the former illustrated by an outstanding frieze depicting Homeric heroes waging war on the giants.

The colossal Naxian Sphinx was presented by the wealthy citizens of Naxos in 560 BC; it stands 2.3 m (7.5 ft) high, and once had its place atop a column reaching over 10 m (33 ft) in height.

The most famous of the museum's exhibits is a life-size bronze statue, the *Charioteer*. The statue was commissioned by a Sicilian tyrant named Polyzalos to commemorate a chariot victory in the Pythian Games in 478 BC. Another notable exhibit is the sculpture of *Three Dancing Girls* grouped around a column. The column is believed to have supported a tripod of the kind sat on by the *Pythia* as she went into her oracular trances. The girls are thought to be celebrating the feast of the god Dionysos *(see p52)*, who also resided in the sanctuary. His presence was honored in the winter months, when Apollo was resting or away elsewhere.

Detail from the frieze of the Siphnian Treasury on display in the museum

NORTHERN GREECE

MACEDONIA · THRACE

MACEDONIA IS GREECE'S *largest prefecture and contains the country's second city, Thessaloníki. It is the homeland of Alexander the Great, whose conquests gave rise to Hellenistic culture. In contrast, Thrace has been largely influenced by Turkish culture, but, like Macedonia, it is an area of comparatively unexplored natural beauty, with many mountain ranges and rivers.*

The name Macedonia derives from the Makednoi, one of the tribes who first inhabited the region in the late 4th century BC. The legacy of Macedonian culture is evident in the many ancient sites, including Vergína, the location of Philip's tomb; Pélla, the birthplace of Alexander; and Díon, Philip's city in the foothills of Mount Olympos. During the reign of the Roman emperor Galerius in the 3rd century AD, many fine monuments were built, including the landmark arch in Thessaloníki. The Byzantine era also left an outstanding legacy of architecture, seen in the many churches that abound throughout Northern Greece. Turkish influences remain strong, particularly

Head of Serapis in the Thessaloníki Archaeological Museum

in Thrace, where eastern-style bazaars and minarets can still be seen today. Macedonia and Thrace have a cooler, damper climate than much of Greece and hence a flourishing flora. Bordering Central Greece is the country's highest mountain, Olympos, and in the northwest lie the Préspa Lakes, part of a wildlife preserve. Local produce includes tobacco from Thrace and wine from Náousa.

In contrast to the busy beaches on its western side, the Chalkidikí peninsula in Macedonia has the holy Mount Athos to the east. Athos is said to have been visited by the Virgin Mary, who declared it sacred and forbade any other female, animal or human, ever to set foot on it.

Villagers at a taverna in the Néstos Valley

◁ **Moní Grigoríou on the holy peninsula of Mount Athos**

Exploring Northern Greece

NORTHERN GREECE OFFERS varied pleasures.
The bustle of modern Thessaloníki can be
combined with a beach holiday in Chalkidikí,
or with an exploration of some of the ancient
Macedonian sites. Lovers of natural history will
appreciate the National Park around the Préspa
Lakes on the border with Albania, and the
Dadiá Forest and Evros River Delta to the east
near Turkey. Walkers will want to explore the
paths of Mount Olympos. Kastoriá and Kavála,
two relatively little-known Greek towns, both
reward a lengthy visit as well as making
excellent bases for traveling farther afield.
Kavála offers access to the fascinating but
little-visited region of Thrace. This region's
three main towns – Xánthi, Komotiní, and
Alexandroúpoli – all offer the attractive
combination of Greek and Turkish influence.
Alexandroúpoli is also ideal as a
family resort with its beaches
and waterfront cafés.

A typical stall at the fruit and vegetable
market in Xánthi, selling local produce

Mikrolímni, one of the beautiful Préspa Lakes

SIGHTS AT A GLANCE

GETTING AROUND

Thessaloníki's airport serves both
international and domestic routes.
Airports at Kastoriá, Kozáni, and
Alexandroúpoli are for domestic
flights only. Ferry connections link
Thessaloníki with the Sporades, and
Kavála and Alexandroúpoli with the
northern Aegean islands. Fast trains
travel south from Thessaloníki to
Athens, and east into Thrace and
beyond to Istanbul. The main E75
highway runs south to Athens from
Thessaloníki and east into Thrace.
Buses go from Thessaloníki to
Alexandroúpoli and Kastoriá.

LOCATOR MAP

0 kilometers 50

0 miles 20

NESTOS VALLEY 16   17 **XÁNTHI**   19 **KOMOTINÍ**   22 **DÁDIA FOREST**

PHILIPPI

KAVÁLA 15   **AVDIRA** 18   *Lake Vistonída*   *Istanbul*

MARONEIA 20

ALEXANDROÚPOLI 21

STHONIA

14 **MOUNT ATHOS**

SEE ALSO

• *Where to Stay* pp273–5

• *Where to Eat* pp294–5

KEY

▬ Divided highway

▬ Major road

▬ Paved road

▬ Scenic route

▬ River

☀ Viewpoint

The harbor of Kavála, in eastern Macedonia

Beautiful landscape of the Préspa Lakes

Préspa Lakes ❶
Εθνικός Δρυμός Πρεσπών

Macedonia. **Road map** B1.
🚍 to Flórina. ⓘ Agios Germanós
(0385 51452); Psarádes (0385
44015).

THIS IS THE ONLY national
park in Greece that is
made up largely of water. It
is one of the mainland's most
beautiful and unspoiled places
and was little visited until recently because of its rather
inaccessible location. The
border with Albania runs
through the southwest corner
of the Megáli Préspa lake,
joining the border of the
Republic of Macedonia,
formerly part of Yugoslavia.
The Greek area of the lake,
together with the smaller
Mikrí Préspa lake and surrounding countryside, make

up the 257 sq km (100 sq
miles) of national park,
established in 1974. The area
is so important for wildlife
that Mikrí Préspa and the
reed beds that fringe it form
a park within a park, a core
of some 49 sq km (19 sq
miles) regarded as a com-
plete protection area. The
boundary of the core area is
clearly indicated by signs.
    Over 1,300 species of plant
can be found here, including
the endemic *Centaurea
prespana*, which has small
daisylike flowers. There are
over 40 species of mammal,
such as bears, wolves, otters,
roe deer, wild boar, and wild
cats. The area is also one of
the last remaining breeding
refuges in Europe for the
Dalmatian pelican, whose
numbers are down to less
than 1,000 pairs worldwide,
with about 150 of those
nesting in the Préspa Lakes.

Wetland Wildlife

IN CONTRAST TO THE DRY AND STONY terrain found
in much of Greece, the north has some
outstanding wetlands with a range of different
habitats. Reed-fringed lake shores hold large
colonies of breeding birds and amphibians,
while the open water is home to numerous
fish and aquatic insects. The marshes are rich
in flowers and full of songbirds; the man-
made habitats such as salt pans and lagoons
offer sanctuary to nesting waders.

Lake Korónia *is easy to view from nearby
villages, most of which have their own
colonies of white storks. In spring, terrapins
and frogs gather in the shallow
margins of the lake.*

Kentish plovers nest on
the margins of wetlands,
such as the Préspa Lakes.

Macedonia

Thessaloníki

Kastoriá

The Préspa Lakes *support
colonies of rare Dalmatian
pelicans. When nesting they
need the peace and quiet
this protected area provides.*

The Axiós Delta is home
to dragonflies and, on the
shores, a wealth of spring
flowers and bee orchids.

Whipsnakes are common in
northern Greece, particularly
around Lake Korónia.

Other birds more frequently seen include herons, cormorants, egrets, storks, golden eagles, and mergansers.

Scattered around the lakes are several small villages. One of these, on the shore of Megáli Préspa, is **Psarádes**, a pretty, traditional village where fishermen provide a boat service on the lake.

Psarádes village on the banks of Megáli Préspa

From the boat you can see hermitages, icons painted on the rocks by the shore, and two churches: the 15th-century **Panagía i Eleoúsa** and the 13th-century **Metamórfosi**. To the east of Mikrí Préspa is **Mikrolímni**. The village has wet meadows to the north that are rich in birdlife. Southwest of Mikrolímni a path leads to the Ellinikí Etaireía Biological Station, used as a base by research scientists who want to stay in the area while studying.

In summer, the beaches of fine, pale sand that stretch alongside Megáli Préspa can be enjoyed along with a dip in the blue, but rather cold, waters of the lake.

Fresco from Metamórfosi church

ENVIRONS: Northeast of the park lies the village of **Agios Germanós**, which has an 11th-century Byzantine church and a number of pretty, traditional houses, built in the local architectural style. The village is also home to the **Préspa Information Center**, which has a permanent exhibition explaining the ecological importance of the Préspa National Park. Guides are available to show visitors around the park, but this must be arranged in advance with the center.

Just out of the village, a road leads up to the summits of Kaló Neró, at 2,160 m (7,090 ft) and Mazi, at 2,060 m (6,760 ft), which give superb views of the lakes below.

Glossy ibises have one of their last remaining European strongholds in the wetlands of northern Greece Seen in good light, their feathers have a metallic sheen.

Purple herons nest in the reedbeds of the Evros Delta.

Pórto Lágos's lagoons, pools, and marshes are a haven for ruddy shelducks.

The Evros Delta lies close to the border with Turkey, and access to many of the best areas can be difficult. Numerous water birds, including little egrets, nest and feed in easily viewed locations.

Xánthi

Kavála

Thrace

Alexandroúpoli

The Néstos Delta is one of the finest wetlands in Greece. Many species of birds inhabit the extensive reedbanks and clumps of trees, in particular large breeding colonies of herons and egrets.

KEY

▢	Préspa Lakes
▢	Axiós Delta
▢	Lake Korónia
▢	Néstos Delta
▢	Pórto Lágos
▢	Evros Delta
—	International border

0 kilometers   50

0 miles   50

Fishing on the Préspa Lakes in the early morning ▷

Kastoriá ❷
Καστοριά

Macedonia. **Road map** B2. ☗ *17,000*.
☒ *10 km (6 miles) S of Kastoriá*. ▦
🛈 *0467 22312*. ▣ *Wed.*

KASTORIA IS THE GREEK word for beavers. These animals used to live in Lake Kastoriá (also known as Lake Orestiás) by which the town stands, one of the loveliest settings in Greece. Evidence of a prehistoric settlement was unearthed here in 1940. In 200 BC the Romans captured the town, then known as Keletron. The beavers first brought the furriers here in the 17th century, and, despite the fact that the animals were locally extinct in the area by the 19th century, trading continued. By then the furriers were also importing unwanted fur scraps, including mink castoffs, and making desirable garments out of them. The fur trade exists today, with the craftsmen still making the fur coats that can be bought in shops in Thessaloníki and Athens.

The town prospered as a result of the fur trade, as its several remaining 17th- and 18th- century mansions testify *(see p20)*. Most of these are found in the southeast quarter of the town. The elegant Skoutári and Nátzi mansions have interior courtyards and three floors. The ground floor in each case is built of stone; the upper two are made of wood. They have fine timbered rooms fitted with cupboards, hearths, and raised platforms. The lower stone floor is used for storage, and the living quarters are in the wooden upper floor, which juts out over the street.

The town's **Folk Museum** is housed in the Aïvázi mansion. Built in the 15th century, it was lived in until as recently as 1972. It now has an eloquent display of the lifestyle of the wealthy fur traders. There is typically elaborate

The Skoutári mansion in Kastoriá, built in the 18th century

woodwork in the salon on the upper floor. The kitchens beneath and the wine cellar have also been restored.

Another notable feature of the town is its many Byzantine churches. Fifty-four survive, and most are listed as ancient monuments, including the 11th-century **Panagiá Koumbelídiki**, situated towards the south end of Mitropóleos. The church is named after its unusually tall dome (or *koumbes*, in Turkish). Some churches are tiny and hidden away in Kastoria's labyrinth of streets, as they were originally private chapels. Many are closed to the public, with some of their icons removed, most of which are now

Apse and cupola of Panagiá Koumbelídiki

on display in the **Byzantine Museum**, which is also confusingly referred to as the Archaeological Museum. The collection is small, with the

exhibit labels only in Greek, but there are some exquisite pieces on display, including some fine icons.

🛈 **Folk Museum**
Kapetán Lázou. ☎ *0467 28603*.
▢ *daily*. 🎨 ● *main public hols*.
🛈 **Byzantine Museum**
Plateía Dexamenís. ☎ *0467 26781*.
▢ *Tue–Sun*. ● *main public hols*.

Siátista ❸
Σιάτιστα

Macedonia. **Road map** B2. ☗ *5,000*.
🛈 *Plateía Tsistopoúlou (0465 21280)*.

SIATISTA WAS FOUNDED in the 1430s, after the second Turkish invasion of Thessaloníki. Like Kastoriá, the town flourished as a result of the fur trade despite the lack of local fur. Sable and martin remnants were brought in, mainly from Russia, made up into garments in Siátista, and then traded or sold in Western Europe.

The wealth that this created in the 18th century went into the building of many fine mansion houses *(see p20)*, very similar to those in Kastoriá. The Ottoman influence in their decoration is strong. The **Nerantzopoúlou** mansion is one of several in the town that can be visited. Keys and directions to the other mansions, including the **Manoúsi** and **Poulkídou**, can also be obtained here.

🏛 **Nerantzopoúlou Mansion**
Plateía Chorí. ▢ *Tue–Sun*.
● *main public hols*.

View across Siátista, in the Mount Askion range, western Macedonia

The impressive peaks of the Mount Olympos range rising above the village of Litóchoro

Mount Olympos ❹
Όλυμπος

17 km (10 miles) W of Litóchoro,
Macedonia. **Road map** C2.
🚌 Litóchoro. 🛈 EOS: Evángelou
Karavákou 20, Litóchoro (0352 81944).

THE NAME Mount Olympos
refers to the whole range
of mountains, 20 km (12 miles)
across. The highest
peak in the range,
at 2,917 m (9,570
ft), is Mýtikas. The
whole area consti-
tutes the Olympos
National Park.

An estimated
1,700 plant species
are to be found
here, many of them
endemic to the park.
Chamois, boars, and roe deer
also live within this area.

The base for walkers is the
village of **Litóchoro**, a lively
place with a youth hostel and
several hotels and tavernas.
Walking maps are available
here, and a marked trail leads
up into the national park.
Mýtikas can be reached in a
demanding walk of at least
six hours. It is imperative to
camp out overnight or stay
in one of the two mountain
shelters, rather than attempt
to get up and down in a day.

ENVIRONS: About 10 km
(6 miles) north of Litóchoro
is the village of Díon, which
has an excellent museum
showing finds from **Ancient
Díon**. This site is east of the
modern village and splendidly
set between the coast and the
Olympian peaks, its very name
deriving from *dios*, or "of
Zeus." To the Macedonians
it was a holy city, and in the
4th century BC some 15,000
people lived here. The flat
plains were used as a military
camp and rallying point by
King Philip II of Macedon *(see
pp32–3)*. Although
Díon was primarily
a military camp,
rather than a civil-
ian city, there was
a temple to Zeus,
a theater, and a sta-
dium at the site.
Later, the Romans
built a city here.
The ruins visible
today date mainly
from that era and include fine
mosaics from the 2nd century
AD and some well-preserved
Roman baths. The remains

Roman mosaic from
Ancient Díon

also include a theater and the
remnants of a sanctuary dedicated to the Egyptian goddess
Isis. She was worshiped by
the Romans as a foreign deity,
along with many others that
were similarly "adopted" into
the pantheon.

The bright and modern
Díon Museum in the village
shows films of the excavations in several languages,
and it is worth seeing before
visiting the site. Also on display are toys, kitchen utensils,
and jewelry, all finds from the
sanctuary of Isis. Together
they give a vivid picture of
life in Ancient Díon.

🏛 **Ancient Díon**
E of Díon. ⬜ daily. ⬤ main
public hols. 🎦 except Sun.
🏛 **Díon Museum**
Díon. 📞 0351 53206. ⬜ daily.
⬤ main public hols.
🎦 except Sun.

THE HOME OF ZEUS

Zeus, chief and most powerful
of the ancient Greek gods, lived
on Mount Olympos along with
the other immortals and was
thought to be responsible for the
destinies of men. He was also god
of weather and thunderstorms.
Many of the myths tell of Zeus's
amorous liaisons and his numerous
children, some of whom were
gods or goddesses and some
heroes *(see pp52–3)*. He was
worshiped at Olympia and
at Dodóni in Epirus, site of
the oldest oracle in Greece.

Vergína ❺
Βεργίνα

12 km (7 miles) SE of Véroia,
Macedonia. **Road map** C2. 🚌 🚹 *at
archaeological site (0331 92394).*

**Terracotta head of a young man,
from the Museum at Véroia**

OUTSIDE THE VILLAGE of Vergína, during excavations in 1977, archaeologist Professor Manólis Andrónikos found an entrance to a tomb. The bones inside included a skull with one eye socket damaged, evidence that the tomb belonged to King Philip II of Macedon, who died from such a wound. The bones were discovered in a stunning gold funerary box, embellished with the symbol of the Macedonian Sun. The discovery confirmed that this area was the site of Aigai, the first capital of Macedonia. The finds from this tomb, as well as several other **Royal Tombs** nearby, included many more gold objects as well as other items. They are displayed in Thessaloníki's Archaeological Museum *(see pp246–7)* and are considered the most important in Greece since Schliemann's discoveries at Mycenae *(see pp178–80)*.

A short walk farther along the road from Philip's tomb are some earlier discoveries, which are known as the **Macedonian Tombs**. Inside, although it is quite dark, solid marble doors can be seen, as well as a marble throne.

The **Palace of Palatitsia** stands beyond on a mound. It is thought to have been first occupied in about 1000 BC, though the building itself dates from the 3rd century BC. Today only low foundations remain, along with the ruins of a theater 100 m (330 ft) below, thought to be the site of Philip II's assassination.

🏛 **Royal Tombs,
Macedonian Tombs, Palace
of Palatitsia**
📞 *0331 92347.* 🕐 *Jan–May: Tue–
Sun; Jun–Dec: daily.* ⬤ *main public
hols.* 🏷

THE MACEDONIAN ROYAL FAMILY

The gold burial casket found at Vergína is emblazoned with the Macedonian Sun, the symbol of the king. Philip II was from a long line of Macedonian kings that began in about 640 BC with Perdiccas I. Philip was the first ruler to unite the whole of Greece as it existed at that time. Also incorrectly known as the Macedonian Star, the Sun is often seen on flags within the region. Much of Greece's pride in the symbol lies in the fact that Alexander the Great used it throughout his empire *(see pp32–3)*. He was just 20 when his father was assassinated at Palatitsia in 336 BC. He inherited his father's already large empire and also his ambition to conquer the Persians. In 334 BC Alexander crossed the Dardanelles with 40,000 men and defeated the Persians in three battles, advancing as far as the Indus Valley before he died at the age of 33. With his death the Macedonian empire divided.

The Macedonian Sun

Véroia ❻
Βέροια

Macedonia. **Road map** C2.
🚶 *48,000.* 🚌 🚉 🚹 *Mitropóleos
47 (0331 26383).* 🛒 *Tue.*

THE LARGEST TOWN in the region, Véroia is interesting mainly for its 50 or so barnlike churches, which have survived from the 17th and 18th centuries.

The town's **Archaeological Museum** has a selection of interesting exhibits, discovered locally, and the bazaar area bustles on market days, as Véroia is the center of the local peach-growing industry.

🏛 **Archaeological Museum**
Anoixiós 47. 📞 *0331 24972.*
🕐 *Tue–Sun.* ⬤ *main public hols.* 🏷

**Chília Déndra park at Náousa,
near Lefkádia**

Lefkádia ❼
Λευκάδια

Macedonia. **Road map** C2.
📞 *0332 41121.* 🚌 🕐 *Tue–Sun.*
⬤ *main public hols.*

THE FOUR MACEDONIAN Tombs of Lefkádia are set in a quiet agricultural area. The caretaker is usually at one of the two tombs that are signposted. The first of these is the **Tomb of the Judges**, or Great Tomb. This is the largest tomb yet discovered in Macedonia, with a chamber 9 m (30 ft) square. Its frescoed façade portrays Aiakos and Rhadamanthys, the Judges of Hades. Beyond is the **Anthemíon Tomb**, or Tomb

Pebble mosaic of the Lion Hunt from the House of the Lion Hunt at Ancient Pélla

of the Flowers, with well-preserved flower paintings on the roof. The key to the **Tomb of Lyson and Kallikles** is sometimes available from the caretaker. The entrance is through a metal grate in the roof. The fourth tomb, the **Tomb of Kinch**, is named not after its onetime inhabitant but after its Danish discoverer, and is not open to visitors.

ENVIRONS: Renowned for the large park of Agios Nikólaos, also known as Chília Déndra (1,000 trees), **Náousa** is the home of the Boutari wine-making family. It is situated on the edge of the hills above the plain that extends east to Thessaloníki. Like Edessa, Náousa has waters flowing through it. Riverside tavernas in the park offer fresh trout as well as the good local wine.

Edessa ❽
Εδεσσα

Macedonia. **Road map** C1.
🏛 16,000. 🚍 🚉 🛈 Plateia Egon 1 (0381 23245). 🔄 Thu.

E DESSA IS THE CAPITAL of the modern Pélla region and a popular summer resort. It is renowned for its waterfalls, which plunge down a ravine from the town to the valley floor below. The largest fall is the **Káranos**, at 24 m (79 ft), which has a cave behind it. The surrounding gardens and park are pleasant, with cafés and restaurants.

Ancient Pélla ❾
Πέλλα

88 km (55 miles) NW of Thessaloniki, Macedonia. **Road map** C1. 🚍
🎫 0382 31278. ⬜ daily.
⬤ main public hols. 🈺 ♿

T HIS SMALL SITE, which straddles the main road, was once the flourishing capital of Macedonia. The court was moved here from

Káranos waterfall at Edessa

Aigai (near modern Vergína) in 410 BC by King Archelaos, who ruled from 413 to 399 BC. It is here that Alexander the Great was born in 356 BC and later tutored by the philosopher Aristotle. Some sense of the existence of a city can be gained from a plan of the site, which shows where the main street and shops were located. The palace is believed to have been north of the main site, but is still being excavated.

At the site, and in the museum, are some of the best-preserved and most beautiful pebble mosaics in Greece. The stones are uncut and have been carefully picked not only for their size, but also for their warm, subtle coloring. Dating from about 300 BC, the mosaics include vivid hunting scenes. One of the most famous is of Dionysos riding a panther; this is protected from the weather in the now-covered House of the Lion Hunt. This was built at the end of the 4th century BC and originally consisted of 12 rooms around three open court-yards, the whole structure being 90 m (295 ft) long by 50 m (164 ft) wide.

Thessaloníki ⑩
Θεσσαλονίκη

Lion from the Archaeological Museum

THESSALONÍKI, ALSO KNOWN AS Salonica, is Greece's second city, founded by King Kassandros in 315 BC. The Romans made it capital of their province of Macedonia Prima in 146 BC, and in AD 395 it became part of the Byzantine Empire. In 1430 it was captured by the Turks who held it until 1912. Today Thessaloníki is a bustling cosmopolitan city. It has a flourishing cultural life and is a major religious center, with an array of splendid churches *(see p248)*, such as Agía Sofía and Agios Dimítrios, which is the largest church in Greece.

Cafés and fountains in the park near Plateía Chánth

Exploring Thessaloníki

Greece's second city is the country's busiest port, which adds to the bustle and the wealth of this fascinating metropolis. Situated on the Thermaic Gulf, it has an attractive waterfront promenade, known as the *paralía*, and a tree-filled park. It also boasts a large number of beautiful Byzantine churches *(see p248)*. In recent years Thessaloníki has developed its international exhibition facilities and become a major trade fair center. The city has many museums, including the Archaeological Museum *(see pp246–7)*.

The **Modiano** (also known as the Bezesténi), the old Turkish bazaar, still thrives at the northern end of Aristotélous. It was renowned as

Furniture shop in the back streets

the finest in the Balkans in the 16th century, and a stroll around shows its Eastern influences, including mosques and bathhouses. The best eating places are also in this area, with large numbers of tavernas and *ouzerí* bars. At the south end of Aristotélous is **Plateía Aristotélous**, a large square overlooking the *paralía*, which is full of coffee bars.

↟ Arch of Galerius
Egnatía.
The principal architectural legacy of Roman rule is found at the eastern end of the long main street, Egnatía, which was itself a Roman construction, known as Via Egnatia. Here stands the Arch of Galerius, built in AD 303 by Galerius (then Caesar of the East), to celebrate his victory over the Persians in AD 297. Its carvings show scenes from the battle. There was once

Section of carving from the Arch of Galerius

a double arch here, with a palace to the south. Some of its remains can be seen in Plateía Navarínou.

⊞ White Tower
On the waterfront. ☎ 031 267832. ☐ daily. 🏛
Probably Thessaloníki's most famous sight is the White Tower on the *paralía*. It was once part of the 8 km (5 miles) of city walls, built by the Turks in 1430 *(see p36)*. Today it contains a collection of Byzantine icons and historical displays on several floors of small circular rooms. The original stone steps climb around the rooms up to a roof with lovely views of the *paralía*.

⊞ Rotónda
Filippou.
Standing north of the Arch of Galerius is the Rotónda. It is thought that this impressive building was constructed as a Mausoleum for Galerius, emperor of Macedonia Prima AD 305–311. Today it is closed, but it has been used both as a church – it is also known as Agios Geórgios – and as a mosque. The minaret alongside it is now the only one in Thessaloníki.

▣ Museum of Byzantine Culture
Leofórou Stratoú 2. ☎ 031 868570. ☐ daily. ● main public hols. 🏛 &
Situated behind the Archaeological Museum *(see pp246–7)*, this small, modern museum was opened in 1995. The museum houses Byzantine icons that date from the 15th to the 19th centuries, and also some fine jewelry. All of the exhibits are beautifully displayed and lit, and there are plans underway to expand the museum's collection.

White Tower on the shore

🏛 Museum of the Macedonian Struggle

Proxénou Koromilá 23. **[** *031 229778.* **◯** *Mon–Fri, Sun.* **●** *main public hols.*

This is situated in a late 19th-century mansion that originally housed the Greek Consulate when Thessaloníki

was under Turkish rule. Photographs, newspapers, weapons, documents, and personal items tell the story well. Vivid tableaux depict the fight and its effect on ordinary people. In one, a Turk with a rifle bursts into a schoolroom while a Greek bandit hides beneath the floorboards. The bandit was Pávlos Melás, a freedom fighter, who is commemorated widely in Greece. Elsewhere in the museum, his gun and dagger are on display.

🏛 Folklife and Ethnological Museum

Vasilíssis Olgas 68. **[** *031 830591.* **◯** *Mon–Wed, Fri–Sun.* **●** *main public hols.*

Currently closed until summer 1997 for refurbishment, this museum is also housed in a 19th-century mansion, a

VISITORS' CHECKLIST

Macedonia. **Road map** C2.
🏠 *1,000,000.* ✈ *25 km (15 miles) SE of Thessaloníki.* ⛴ *off Koundouriótou.* 🚉 *Monastiríou.* 🚌 *Plateía Dikastiríou (local buses) 28 Octovríou (long distance).* ℹ *Plateía Aristotélous 8 (031 271888).* 🎭 *Thessaloníki Cultural Festival (cinema): Oct.*

20-minute walk from the Archaeological Museum directly along Vasilíssos Olgas. There are displays of folk costumes and detailed small models showing rural activities such as bread-making, plowing, winnowing, threshing, and children playing. The life of the nomadic Sarakatsan shepherds is well documented, and a vivid display shows events at the annual fire-walking ceremony in Lagkádas, a village 20 km (12 miles) northeast of Thessaloníki. The museum also has an extensive archive of period photography showing life in Thessaloníki during the early 20th century.

THESSALONIKI TOWN CENTER

Agía Sofía ③
Archaeological Museum ⑦
Arch of Galerius ②
Museum of the Macedonian Struggle ⑤
Plateía Aristotélous ④
Rotónda ①

White Tower and Paralía ⑥

Kástro
Agios Nikólaos Ortanos
Agia Aikaterini
Acheiropoíitos

Agios Dimitrios
Modiano

Agioi Apostóloi

Railroad station
Port
ATHENS

Museum of Byzantine Culture

PLATEIA CHANTH

Folklife and Ethnological Museum
Airport

KEY

ℹ Tourist information

✝ Church

Thessaloníki Archaeological Museum
Αρχαιολογικό Μουσείο Θεσσαλονίκης

THIS MODERN MUSEUM, opened in 1963, contains a host of treasures. It concentrates on the finds made within the city and at the many sites in Macedonia. The displays progress chronologically, giving a clear picture of the area's history. A new wing, opened in 1980, contains the treasures found at the Royal Tombs at Vergína, including crowns and armor belonging to Philip II of Macedon, the father of Alexander the Great. From the burial ground at Síndos, northwest of the city, exhibits include armor and children's toys.

Glass Vase
During the Roman period, the art of coloring glass came into use, as in this pink vase. Craftsmen experimented with shapes and colors, and a wide variety of glass items have been recovered from Roman tombs in Thessaloníki.

Faience Vase
Found in a 2nd-century BC grave in Thessaloníki, this ornate vase is from Ptolemaic Egypt and is the only such faience vase in Greece. Depicted on the bas-relief, among other subjects, is a detail of the goddess Artemis in a forest.

GALLERY GUIDE
An outer circle of rooms surrounds a block of inner rooms that houses the finds from Síndos. The outer rooms progress from Neolithic, through Classical, to Roman and Hellenistic artifacts and mosaics. An annex contains items from Vergína, and in a room below them are prehistoric exhibits.

Main entrance

★ Floor Mosaics from a Thessaloníki House
These detailed mosaics depicting marine-world mythology are Roman. This mosaic shows a nereid (sea nymph) and a dolphin.

Outdoor courtyard with Roman floor mosaic

Marble Sarcophagus
This 2nd- or 3rd-century BC sarcophagus originates from Attica. The relief depicts Dionysiac themes of satyrs, maenads (frenzied women), Eros figures, and children gathering grapes.

Statue of Harpokrates

The marble statue of Harpokrates, the son of Isis and Osiris, was found in Thessaloníki at the site of a sanctuary devoted to Serapis and other Egyptian gods. It has been dated to the end of the 2nd century BC.

VISITORS' CHECKLIST

Manóli Andrónikos & Leof Stratoú. 031 830538. 3. 8am–5pm Tue–Fri, 11am–5pm Mon, 8:30am–3pm Sat & Sun. Jan 1, Mar 25, Good Fri am, Easter Sun, May 1, Dec 25, 26.

Head of Serapis

This fine marble head was discovered in the same sanctuary as the statue of Harpokrates and dates from the 2nd century BC. Originally an Egyptian deity, Serapis was adopted by the Romans as a foreign cult.

★ Gold Burial Caskets from Vergína

These gold caskets form the focal point of the collection of Macedonian gold. This one, emblazoned with the Macedonian Sun (see p242), held the bones of King Philip II, which are also on display.

Annex containing gold finds from Vergína

KEY TO FLOOR PLAN

- Prehistoric collection
- 2,300 years of Thessaloníki
- Finds from Síndos
- Finds from Vergína
- Roman collection
- Hellenistic collection
- Temporary exhibition space
- Nonexhibition space

STAR EXHIBITS

★ Gold Burial Caskets from Vergína

★ Floor Mosaics from a Thessaloníki House

★ Dervéni Krater

★ Dervéni Krater

Dating from 330 BC, this bronze wine-mixing bowl stands 1 m (3 ft) high. The detailed figures of maenads are exquisite; one is shown dancing with a satyr. The volutes at the top are decorated with the head of Herakles.

Exploring Thessaloníki's Churches

THESSALONIKI HAS THE RICHEST COLLECTION of Byzantine churches in Greece. Of the hundreds of 5th-century basilicas that once stood across the country, only two remain. Both of these, Agios Dimítrios and Acheiropoíitos, are in Thessaloníki. The 8th-century Agía Sofía is a very significant Byzantine building, both for its mosaics and its role in influencing future architectural development. Three different 14th-century churches – Agios Nikólaos Orfanós, Agioi Apostóloi and Agía Aikateríni – give an insight into what was a period of architectural innovation.

Agía Sofía church

The mosaic of Ezekiel's vision in Osios Davíd

⛪ Agios Dimítrios

Agíou Dimitríou. ○ Tue–Sat. &

This is the largest church in Greece, though it has been very substantially rebuilt over the years. The oldest surviving part is the crypt, below the altar, in which Dimítrios, the patron saint of Thessaloníki, was imprisoned, tortured, and buried by Roman soldiers in AD 305. He was born in the city 20 years earlier, joined the Roman army, and became an early convert to Christianity. The emperor Galerius was a renowned persecutor of Christians and ordered Dimítrios be put to death when he would not renounce his beliefs.

The first church on the site was built in about 313. It was rebuilt in 629–34 after destruction by fire, then completely restored in the 13th century. It was finally faithfully restored in 1926–48.

⛪ Osios Davíd

Kástro. ○ daily.

This delightful small chapel was founded some time in the late 5th century. Behind the altar is an original vivid

mosaic of the *Vision of Ezekiel*, rare in that it depicts Christ without a beard. It is one of the finest mosaics in the city and owes its freshness to having been concealed beneath plaster and only discovered in 1921. Other mosaics date from the 12th century and include a fine *Baptism* and *Nativity*. Although the church is usually locked, there is a caretaker who greets visitors and will unbolt the doors.

⛪ Agía Sofía

Plateía Agías Sofías. ○ daily.

The church of Agía Sofía resembles the mosque of the same name in Istanbul. It was built in the mid-8th century. In 1585 it became a mosque, but was reconsecrated as a church in 1912 and survived

the fire of 1917. It contains many mosaics and frescoes dating back to the 9th and 10th centuries, including a fine *Ascension* scene in the 30-m (100-ft) high dome, which is 10 m (33 ft) in diameter. The entrance formerly had a portico, which was obliterated during an Italian air raid in 1941. The imposing nature of the building is emphasized by its location in a partially sunken garden.

⛪ Agios Nikólaos Orfanós

Kástro. ○ Tue–Sun. &

This small church probably dates from the early 14th century. Situated in the old part of the city, known as Kástro, its interior houses a rich profusion of frescoes. It was originally a monastery, part of the smallholding belonging to the larger Moní Vlattádon, a short distance from Agios Nikólaos Orfanós. Moní Vlattádon also still has the frescoes that were painted when it was built in the 14th century. Agios Nikólaos Orfanós is distinctive for its mixture of Byzantine building styles and stands in a partly overgrown garden. If locked, ask locally for the key-holder.

Agios Dimítrios, the largest church in Greece

The stretch of sandy beach at Kallithéa on Kassándra

Northern Chalkidikí ⓫
Βορεία Χαλκιδική

Macedonia. **Road map** D2. 🚌 *to Polýgyros.*

THE NORTH OF CHALKIDIKI is a quiet and delightful hilly region, often overlooked by those whose main interests are the beaches to the south. A glimpse of the hidden interior is given when visiting the **Petrálona Caves**, situated on the edge of Mount Katsíka, 55 km (34 miles) southeast of Thessaloníki. It was in these red-rock caverns in 1960, the year after the caves were discovered by local villagers, that a skull was found. It was believed to be that of a young woman, aged about 25 when she died. A complete skeleton was subsequently discovered, and these are the oldest bones yet to be found in Greece, dating back at least 250,000 years, and possibly even 700,000. Amid the stalactites and stalagmites, reconstructions of the cave dwellers have been arranged in the caves, along with the bones, teeth, and tools that were also found here.

In the northeast of the area is the small village of **Stágeira**, the birthplace of Aristotle (384–322 BC). On a hilltop, just outside the village, is a huge white marble statue of the philosopher, and there are sweeping views of the surrounding countryside.

Statue of Aristotle, Stágeira

♙ Petrálona Caves
Mount Katsíka, 55 km (34 miles) SE of Thessaloníki. ◯ *daily.* ● *main public hols.* 🖼

Kassándra ⓬
Κασσάνδρα

Southern Chalkidikí, Macedonia. **Road map** D2. 🚌 *to Kassándreia.*

MUCH OF THIS area's population was killed in the War of Independence in 1821, and the numbers never really recovered. Little was left on the promontory of Kassándra other than a few fishing villages. However, over the last 30 years, many resorts have sprung up in this area.

Néa Poteídaia marks the start of Kassándra proper and straddles the narrow neck of the peninsula, with a good sandy beach, a marina, and an attractive town square. On the west coast, **Sáni** has excellent beaches and a luxury resort complex. There are quiet bays around the village of **Possídi**, on a promontory halfway down the west coast. On the east coast, **Néa Fókaia** still functions as a fishing village in spite of the steady invasion of tourism, whereas **Kallithéa**, to the south, is the largest resort on Kassándra.

Sithonía ⓭
Σιθωνία

Southern Chalkidikí, Macedonia. **Road map** D2. 🚌 *to Agios Nikólaos.*

WHILE THE PENINSULA of Sithonía is only marginally larger than Kassándra, it has fewer resorts and a thickly wooded interior. The peninsula begins at **Metamórfosi**, which has a sandy beach shaded by pine trees. **Vourvouroú** is one of the first villages you come to on the north side. A collection of villas spread along the coast, it has a few hotels and a selection of eating places.

To the south of this area is a long undeveloped stretch of coast, with several unspoiled beaches, until you reach the large resort of **Sárti**. At the tip of Sithonía is **Kalamítsi**, little more than a sandy beach and a few bars, while **Pórto Koufós** at the end of the west coast is still a pleasant fishing village set on a bay amid wooded hills. The **Pórto Karrás** resort complex, halfway down the west coast, was set up by the Karrás wine family. It has three hotels, a marina, a shopping center, water sports, horseback-riding, a golf course, and tennis.

Boats docked at Pórto Koufós on Sithonía

Mount Athos ⑭
Αγιον Ορος

Mount Athos monk

To the greeks, this is the Holy Mountain, which at 2,030 m (6,660 ft) is the highest point of Chalkidikí's most easterly peninsula. Unique in Greece, Athos is an autonomous republic ruled by the 1,700 monks who live in its 20 monasteries. Only adult males may visit the peninsula, but it is possible to see many of the monasteries from a boat trip along the coast. Together, they include some fine examples of Byzantine architecture and provide an insight into monastic life.

THE MONASTERIES OF ATHOS

- - - Ferry route

MOUNT ATHOS FROM THE WEST

This illustration shows the view from a boat traveling along the west of Athos. The most northerly monastery is Zográfou and the most southerly is Agíou Pávlou. The eastern monasteries are covered on p254.

Ouranoúpoli
The main town on Athos is where boat trips around the peninsula start.

Zográfou was founded around AD 971, but the present buildings are 18th- and 19th-century.

Xiropotámou was founded in the 10th century, but the present buildings date from the 18th century.

To Ouranoúpoli ←

Kastamonítou was founded in the 11th century by a hermit from Asia Minor.

Xenofóntos was founded in the late 10th century. A second chapel was built in 1837, incorporating some 14th-century mosaic panels.

0 kilometers   15

0 miles   10

Docheiaríou
This 10th-century monastery houses a fragment of the True Cross and an icon of the Virgin with healing powers.

Agíou Panteleímonos
Also known as Rousikón (of the Russians), this 12th-century monastery's imposing walls hide many colorful onion-domed churches, evidence of the Russian Orthodox influence on Athos.

◁ The monastery of Agíou Panteleímonos, Mount Athos

Agíou Pávlou
*This monastery houses 90
monks, many from Zákynthos
and Kefalloniá, and has some
13,000 books and manu-
scripts in its library.*

Símonos Pétras was named
after Saint Simon who founded
the monastery in the 14th century
AD after seeing a strange light
burning on this remote and
rocky ridge one Christmas night.

Agíou Dionysíou is
perched 80 m (260 ft)
above the sea. Its
walls conceal the
16th-century church
of Agios Ioánnis
Prodrómou.

**Mount
Athos**

Néa Skíti
belongs to
Agíou
Pávlou.

Dáfni is Athos's port and has
a population of 16. A bus
goes from here to the capital,
Karyés, 15 minutes away.

Grigoríou
*Founded in the 14th century,
this monastery was totally
rebuilt after a disastrous fire
in 1761 that destroyed all
but a few holy relics. About
40 monks live here today.*

VISITING MOUNT ATHOS

Foreign visitors first need a letter
of recommendation from the
Greek consul in their country
for which a small charge will be
made. The Ministry of Foreign
Affairs in Athens, or the Ministry
of Macedonia and Thrace in
Thessaloníki, will then issue a
permit to visit Athos. Only ten
such permits are issued each
day in each city, so the start
date of your visit is unpredictable and may be days or weeks
ahead. Permits allow a stay of
four nights, which may be extended by two nights.
Accommodations and meals are provided, with no payment
expected, although donations in the chapels will be appreciated. Visitors may be allowed into the services, and meals
are generally taken in communal refectories with the monks.

Vatopedíou refectory

Exploring Mount Athos

Not all of the 20 monasteries on Athos can be seen from the popular boat trips from Ouranoúpoli, although some boats do go around the whole peninsula. A few are hidden in the mountains, and others cling to the eastern coast of the peninsula. In addition to the Greek Orthodox monasteries on Mount Athos, there is one Russian (Agíou Panteleímonos), one Bulgarian (Zográfou), and one Serbian (Chelandaríou). Remote hermitages and monastic villages in the hills of the peninsula are preferred by some monks, as a quieter alternative to the relatively busy monastery life.

The East Coast Monasteries
The first monastery to be founded on Athos was the **Megístis Lávras** (Great Lavra). It is situated at the southeastern end of the peninsula, on a rocky outcrop *(see pp36–7)*. It was founded in AD 963 by Athanásios the Athonite and is the only one of the monasteries never to have suffered from fire. It also has the largest font of all the monasteries, which is outside, shaded by a cypress tree said to have been planted over 1,000 years ago by Athanásios himself.

Painting in Megístis Lávras

Halfway along the eastern coast stand the monasteries of Ivíron and Stavronikíta. **Ivíron** was founded in the late 10th century by monks from Iberia (modern Georgia), hence its name. Its church was built in the early 11th century and restored in 1513. The monastery's main courtyard contains another 16 chapels, one housing a miraculous icon of the Virgin Mary.

Stavronikíta, to the north, stands on top of a rocky headland. It was first mentioned in a document dated AD 1012.

Vatopédiou, one of the largest monasteries on Athos, is sited on a small promontory at the northern end of the east coast. It was founded in the latter half of the 10th century, and a notable feature is its *katholikón*, or main church, also built in the 10th century. It contains icons dating from the 14th century, though they have been retouched over the years. A wealthy monastery, it is among the best preserved on Mount Athos.

ORTHODOX LIFE ON MOUNT ATHOS

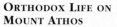

Monks growing their own fruits and vegetables

Under the Byzantine time system operating on Athos, midnight is at dawn, and morning services begin about an hour before – around 3 or 4am, Greek time. A monk walks around striking a small wooden *símandro* (a carved plank) with a mallet to wake the other monks and call them to prayer. The monks eat two meals a day, which consist mostly of food they grow themselves. There are 159 fasting days in the year, when only one meal is allowed that must contain no fish, eggs, cheese, milk, oil, or wine. Meals are eaten after the morning and evening services, and the time in between is spent working, resting, and praying.

The Megístis Lávras monastery, with its red *katholikón* in the center

Kavála ⑮
Καβάλα

Macedonia. **Road map** D1. 🏛
56,000. ✈ 35 km (22 miles) SE of
Kavála. 🚌 🚆 ℹ Dragoúmi (051
222425). 🛒 daily.

Kavala's history goes back
to the 6th century BC,
when it was founded by
islanders from Páros. It became
part of the Roman Empire in
168 BC, and is where St. Paul
first set foot on European soil
in AD 50 or 51 on his way to
Philippi. The biggest impact,
however, was the Turkish
occupation from 1371 to 1912.
It was the Turks who built the
16th-century aqueduct here.
Mehmet Ali (1769–1849), the
Pasha of Egypt, was born in
Kavála. His **birthplace**, a well-
preserved house, set in gardens and marked by a bronze
statue of Ali on horseback, is
open to visitors.
Kavála is a busy
city, with an indus-
trial port that also
has a ferry service
to the northeast
Aegean islands.
Life centers around
the harbor be
low the castle,
which is flood-
lit at night. At
its eastern end
there is a busy
fish, fruit, and vegetable market.
To the west is the **Archaeological Museum**, which has
finds from Avdíra *(see p256)*,
including a dolphin mosaic
and a painted sarcophagus.
There are also some delicate
3rd-century BC gold laurel
wreaths found at Amphipolis,
west of Kavála, and clay masks
and a 4th-century BC bust of
an unknown goddess.
The **Municipal Museum** is
housed in a late 19th-century
Neo-Classical building to the
west of the town hall. It has
a collection of costumes and
household items, and a good
display of work by local
artists, in particular Thasiot
sculptor Polýgnotos Vágis
(1894–1965).

**Sculpture by
Polýgnotos Vágis**

🏛 **Mehmet Ali's Birthplace**
Theodórou Poulídou 63. ℂ 051
220061. ◯ Apr–Oct: daily; Oct–Mar:
Sat & Sun. ● main public hols.

The town and harbor of Kavála

🏛 **Archaeological Museum**
Erythroú Stavroú 17. ℂ 051 222335.
◯ Tue–Sun. ● main public hols.
📷 ♿

🏛 **Municipal Museum**
Filíppou 4. ℂ 051 222706.
◯ Mon–Sat. ● main public hols.

Néstos Valley ⑯
Κοιλάδα του Νέστου

Macedonia/Thrace border. **Road
map** D1. 🚆 🚌 Xánthi (liable to be
cancelled Nov–Apr).

The nestos river rises high
in the Rodópi mountains
in Bulgaria, and its meandering
course down to the Aegean
near the island of Thásos
marks the boundary between
Macedonia and Thrace. On its
way it threads through remote
and inaccessible gorges, fed
by other rivers and streams,
until it passes under the
scenic mountain road that
links Xánthi in
Thrace with the
town of Dráma
in Macedonia.
This road, some-
times closed by
snowdrifts in
winter, makes
for a spectacular
scenic drive
through the
wooded gorge,
past the valley's
heavy beech
forests and
scattering of
small villages.
Stavroúpoli is
the largest of
these villages
and has a good
café in its quiet
village square.

Xánthi ⑰
Ξάνθη

Thrace. **Road map** E1. 🏛 25,000.
🚆 🚌 🛒 Sat.

Founded in the 11th century,
it was not until the 1800s
that Xánthi flourished with the
development of the tobacco
industry. Displays on tobacco
are included in the **Folk
Museum**, which is housed
in two old mansions. The
museum's collection includes
embroidery, jewelry, and
costumes. Xánthi's main
square has cafés and fountains and east of the square
is the bazaar. This is over-
flowing on Saturdays when
Greeks, Turks, Pomaks, and
gypsies all visit the busiest
market in the area.

🏛 **Folk Museum**
Antíka 7. ℂ 0541 25421. ◯ daily.
● main public hols. 📷

The lush landscape of the Néstos Valley

The monastery of Agios Nikólaos on the banks of Lake Vistonída

Avdira
Άβδηρα

6 km (4 miles) S of modern Avdira,
Thrace. **Road map** E1. ▣
◯ daily. ● main public hols.

THE ANCIENT CITY of Avdira
was founded in the mid-
7th century BC by refugees
from Klazomenai in Asia
Minor. The site is quite dispersed and overgrown. Most
of what can be seen today
dates from the Roman period.
Some Archaic and Classical
ruins are also evident, including the acropolis. The remains
of its walls stand on a small
headland, and ancient graves
have been discovered and
excavated just outside the
walls. Part of the original city
wall can also be seen.

ENVIRONS: Along the road
from Avdira to Maróneia is
Lake Vistonída, a haven for
wildlife. At one end is Pórto
Lagós *(see pp236–7)*, an old
harbor with the white monastery of Agios Nikólaos.

Komotiní ⑲
Κομοτηνή

Thrace. **Road map** E1. ▨ 38,000.
▣ ▤ ▤ Tue.

ONLY 25 km (16 miles)
from the Bulgarian
border to the north, and less
than 100 km (62 miles) from
Turkey to the east, Komotiní
is a fascinating mix of Greek
and Turkish influence. First
founded in the late 4th
century AD, it was taken by

the Turks in 1363 and re-
mained part of the Ottoman
Empire until the final settling
of boundaries in 1920. Over
500 years of Turkish rule is
clearly evident around the
town, one of the few
places in Greece to
have minarets and 14
mosques that are still
in use. It boasts a
thriving market
with fish, cattle, and
tobacco for sale.
There is also a good
selection of fresh
produce grown in
fertile land. The
numerous old
wooden shops sell everything
from bric-a-brac to genuine,
valuable antiques.

A feel of the town's recent
past is given in the well cared
for **Museum of Folk Life
and History**. Its few rooms,

**Finial from a
gravestone,
Archaeological
Museum, Komotiní**

The domed roof and tall minaret
of a Turkish mosque, Komotiní

in an 18th-century mansion,
are crammed with costumes,
local copperware, and
domestic items. There is also
a particularly good collection
of embroidery, including
examples of a type
known as Tsévres, used
in Thracian wedding
ceremonies. The town's
**Archaeological
Museum** displays
the best of the finds
from the sites at
ancient Avdira and
Maróneia, including
gold jewelry found in
4th-century BC
graves at Avdira. A
4th-century BC clay mask of
Dionysos is on display, found
at the god's sanctuary at
Maróneia. The museum also
has an extensive coin collection, painted sarcophagi,
votive reliefs, and maps.

🏛 **Museum of Folk Life
and History**
Agios Geórgios. ◯ Mon–Sat.
● main public hols. ▨ ☒ limited.
🏛 **Archaeological Musuem**
Symeonidi. █ 0531 22411.
◯ Tue–Sun. ● main public hols. ▨

Maróneia ⑳
Μαρώνεια

5 km (3 miles) SE of modern Maróneia,
Thrace. **Road map** E1. ▤ to modern
Maróneia. ◯ daily. ● main public
hols. ▨ ☒

THE ROAD to ancient
Maróneia leads through
tobacco and cotton fields,
past woodlands and small
rural communities. A signpost

to the harbor of Agios Charálampos shows the way down a track to the remains of the site that are in a scenic position overlooking the sea. The city flourished from the 8th century BC until AD 1400. Olive groves now cover the area, which sits between Mount Ismaros and the sea, but a small theater has been discovered and renovated. Farther down the track are the remnants of a sanctuary, thought to have been dedicated to Dionysos, whose son, Maron, is credited with founding Maróneia.

Beyond the city of ancient Maróneia is the small but developing harbor of **Agios Charálampos**, surrounded by red cliffs, topped by a large hotel, a taverna, and a scattering of houses.

ENVIRONS: Medieval **Maróneia** is a tiny but attractive place, mainly a farming community but with some larger mansions that provide evidence of a more prosperous past.

Alexandroúpoli ㉑
Αλεξανδρούπολη

Thrace. **Road map** E1. 🏛 *36,000.*
✈ 🚢 🚊 🚌 *Tue.* 🛈 🛈 *Mákris (0551 228735).*

A LEXANDROÚPOLI lacks the cultural mix of other large Thracian towns. It was only built up in 1878, under the Turkish name of Dedeagaç (meaning "Tree of the Holy Man"), derived from a group of whirling dervishes who

The landmark lighthouse in Alexandroúpoli

settled here in the 15th century. Prior to that, it was a fishing village. It was renamed in 1919 after the Greek king at the time, Aléxandros.

Today the town is a thriving resort with a port, its own domestic airport, and train connections east to Istanbul, north into Bulgaria and west to Thessaloniki.

In the evening the promenade by the long stretch of beach is thronged with people, both visitors and locals. The lighthouse, built in 1800, is situated along the seafront. It is the town's most famous feature and is lit up at night.

Inland from the promenade is a warren of narrow streets with junk shops, grocers, cobblers, goldsmiths, and fish restaurants. The best eating

places are around tiny Plateía Polytechneíou. North from the square, beyond the main road, is the modern cathedral of Agios Nikólaos, notable for the **Ecclesiastical Art Museum** contained in its grounds. This fine collection of icons and other religious items is unfortunately seldom open, but those with a particular interest in seeing it may ask for access at the cathedral.

🛉 **Ecclesiastical Art Museum**
Palaiológou. ⭕ *variable.* ⬤ *main public hols.*

Dadiá Forest ㉒
Δάσος Δαδιάς

27km (17 miles) NW of Féres, Thrace.
Road map F1. 🚆 🚌 *Féres.*
🛈 *1 km (0.5 miles) N of Dadiá village (0554 32209).*

N ORTH OF THE SMALL town of Féres in the Evros valley is the lovely Dadiá pine forest. Covering a series of hills known as the Evros mountains, it is considered to be one of the best places in Europe for observing rare birds. Of special interest is the presence of birds of prey, an indication of the remote location of the forest. There are 39 known species of birds of prey in Europe, 26 of which live and nest in this region.

Rare black vulture

There is an information center in the heart of the forest, and observation huts have been placed near feeding stations, built to help preserve the rarer species that nest here. This is one of the black vulture's last refuges in eastern Europe. The forest is home to a huge number of protected and endangered species, including imperial eagles, golden eagles, griffon vultures, sparrowhawks, and peregrines. Midmorning is the best time to watch the different birds as they fly on the first thermals of the day.

Old mansion in modern Maróneia

TRAVELERS' NEEDS

WHERE TO STAY 260-275
WHERE TO EAT 276-295

WHERE TO STAY

Doorman at the Grande Bretagne hotel, Athens

ACCOMMODATIONS IN GREECE are best described as functional in most cases, and only occasionally inspired. However, it is nearly always abundant in a country so heavily dependent on the tourist industry and, as a consequence, is a bargain compared with most other European destinations. Despite inroads of commercialization in the busier resorts, hospitality off the beaten track can still be warm and heartfelt. Various types of accommodations are described over the next four pages. Information is included for the network of campsites and the more limited facilities for hosteling and alpine refuge stays. The listings section *(see pp264–75)* includes over 150 places to stay, ranging from informal *domátia* (rooms) to luxurious hotels and accommodations in restored buildings.

Malvásia Hotel *(see p270)* at Monemvasía, restored by the EOT during the 1970s

HOTELS

MOST GREEK HOTELS are of standard Mediterranean concrete architecture, though in coastal resorts height limits restrict towering structures. Many surviving hotels date from the 1967–74 Junta era, when massive investment in "modern" tourism was encouraged. A very few Neo-Classical, or older, hotels remain, now benefiting from government preservation orders. Hotels built since the 1980s are generally designed with more imagination and sensitivity to the environment. The more expensive hotels will have a correspondingly higher level of service, offered by trained personnel.

CHAIN HOTELS

GREECE, with its tradition of family business ownership, has not taken to the idea of chain hotels. Among the few that operate on the mainland, the oldest is the formerly state-run Xenía chain, founded during the 1950s. Most of their hotels, with well-worn facilities and indifferent service, are worth avoiding, though some, such as those at Arta or Andrítsaina, are the best, or only, hotels available. Newer chains, such as **Chandrís** and **Divani**, are a better bet. They both offer accommodations in the Athens area, and Divani also has hotels in central Greece.

RESTORED SETTLEMENTS AND BUILDINGS

DURING THE 1970s, the EOT (Greek Tourist Office) began sponsoring the restoration of derelict buildings in vernacular style, located in isolated parts of the country. The completed units usually offer a good bargain and an exceptionally atmospheric environment, though preservation considerations often mean that bathrooms are shared rather than in-room. Such properties are found at Areópoli and Vátheia

in the Máni, at Makrinítsa on the Pílio, at Megálo Pápigko in Epirus, and at Monemvasía. Some, such as the complex at Megálo Pápigko, have recently been privatized, with variable effects on efficiency.

In recent years, private entrepreneurs have seized the initiative in such renovation projects, installing small and medium-sized hotels in centuries-old buildings. Particularly successful ventures can be found at Stemnítsa, Galaxídi, Náfplio, and in several villages of the Zagória region and the Pílio.

DOMATIA

A LARGE PROPORTION of Greek accommodations are in *domátia*, or rented rooms. In the past, these often used to be in the home of the managing family, but nowadays they are far more likely to be within a separate, modern, custom-built structure. They tend to be a good value compared with hotels of a similar standard. Increasingly they have in-room bathrooms, are well appointed with neutral pine furniture, and often have a

Front exterior of the King Othon Hotel, Náfplio *(see p270)*

◁ **Waterside café at Koróni in the Peloponnese**

Lobby at Hotel Grande Bretagne, Athens *(see p267)*

kitchen for the use of guests. There is usually no communal area, however, and hot water is provided either by an electric immersion heater or by a solar heating device.

GRADING

THE EOT grades Greece's hotels and *domátia*. Hotel categories range from E-class up to A-class, plus deluxe. *Domátia* range from C-class to A-class. There is supposed to be a direct correlation between amenities and the classification, but there are many local deviations usually the result of a dispute with local authorities.

E-class hotels, with the most basic facilities and narrow profit margins, are almost extinct. D-class still survive, and these should have at least some rooms *en suite*. In a C-class hotel, all rooms must have *en suite* baths, and the hotel must have some sort of common area, if only a small combination bar and breakfast area where a basic continental breakfast can be served.

B-class hotels have extra amenities such as a full-service restaurant, a more substantial breakfast, and at least one sports facility, such as a pool or tennis court. A-class hotels are usually at seafront locations, and offer all conceivable diversions, as well as aids for the business traveler, such as conference halls and telecommunications facilities. Deluxe category hotels are effectively self-contained resort complexes. C-class *domátia*, with baths

down the hall and "jail-like" decor, are on the way out, now supplanted by modern B-class blocks that guarantee bathrooms *en suite* and often have the benefit of a shared kitchen for the use of visitors. A-class *domátia* are nearly synonymous with apartments. The furnishings are superior, and there is generally land-scaping outside the building. A well equipped kitchen is fitted into each unit.

A sign for rooms to rent

PRICES

THE PRICE of hotel rooms and *domátia* should correspond to their official category, though this is variable, depending on high or low season and their location. For 4,000 Dr or under, it is possible to find a C-class *domátio* for two without *en suite* bathroom, or an E/D-class hotel; 6,000 Dr should cover a B-class double *domátio*, while A-class

domátia and C-class hotels charge between 7,000 and 9,000 Dr. B-class hotels ask 9,000 to 13,000 Dr per double room, while A-class hotels typically cost 13,000 to 17,000 Dr. Deluxe resorts are exempt from the EOT price control plan and can easily run in excess of 22,000 Dr per night.

All of these rate approximations are for high season, including sales and municipal taxes; prices can drop by as much as 50 percent in early spring or late autumn. Hotel rates include breakfast. Stays of less than 3 nights can be heavily penalized by surcharges in tourist season. In mainland skiing resorts there is often a vast difference between weekend and mid-week rates.

OPENING SEASONS

MAINLAND HOTELS stay open year-round, except those at seafront resorts, which operate only from May to October. Hotels in skiing areas, conversely, may open only during the winter period.

BOOKING

THE MOST COMMON and cost-effective way of booking accommodation is through a package travel agency. If you contact a hotel direct, do so by fax so that the transaction is recorded in writing. You may need to provide a credit card number or send travelers' checks equivalent to the value of the first night's stay.

The pool at the Aphrodite Astir Palace Hotel *(see p268)*

Monastery on Mount Athos *(see p252)*, **Northern Greece**

YOUTH HOSTELS

THE GREEK MAINLAND has eight IYHA-recognized youth hostels *(xenón neótitos)*. They are found in Athens, Náfplio, Mycenae, Olympia, Pátra, Delphi, Thessaloníki, and Litóchoro. In addition, there are a handful of un-official hostels, which can be just as good, if not better.

Greek hostels are not nearly as regimented as their northern European equivalents. Even without an IYHF (International Youth Hostel Federation) card you can usually stay if a vacancy is available, upon payment of a small sup-plementary charge. However, the cost of a dormitory bunk is such that, if traveling as two, you will generally find that a less expensive *domátio* is better value.

ALPINE REFUGES

MOUNTAINS OF THE Greek mainland are dotted with over 40 alpine refuges *(katafýgia)*. Very few are continuously staffed – two on Mount Olympos *(see p241)* and one on Mount Gamíla, in the Píndos range, being notable exceptions – so you must contact the relevant branch of the **EOS** (Greek Alpine Club) to rent keys. This is expensive and not worthwhile unless you muster a large group.

Some of the mountain huts make wonderful base camps, fully equipped with kitchens, bed linen, and well-designed common areas; others are little more than shacks originally built for shepherds or fire-control personnel. Another complication is that, as many were built at a time when approaches to the mountain ranges were quite different, today they are often located well away from the preferred hiking routes.

RURAL TOURISM

CONCEIVED DURING the 1980s to give women in the Greek provinces a measure of financial independence, rural tourism allows foreigners to stay on a bed-and-breakfast basis in a village house, but also provides the opportunity to participate, if desired, in the daily life of a farming community. There are four such programs: Agios Germanós (Préspa Lakes), Ampelákia (Thessaly), Maróneia (Thrace), and

Aráchova in central Greece. They are all managed by a **Women's Rural Tourism Cooperative**, and also usually run a bargain restaurant in the center of the village, featuring regional cuisine.

MONASTERIES

THE LESS VISITED monasteries and convents in Greece operate *xenónes*, or hostels, intended primarily for Greek Orthodox pilgrims on weekend visits. Pilgrims will always have priority, but it is often possible to find a vacancy at short notice.

Accommodation is of the spartan dormitory variety, with a frugal evening meal and morning coffee also provided; it is customary to leave a donation in the *katholikón* (main church).

The monasteries on Mount Athos are the most accustomed to non-Orthodox visitors, though these are open to men only. Visits – especially in tourist season – need to be carefully planned, as the procedure for reserving space and obtaining an entry permit to this semi-autonomous monastic republic is suitably Byzantine *(see p253)*.

CAMPING

THE GREEK MAINLAND has nearly 150 campsites that are officially recognized. Most of them are in attractive beachfront settings, and usually cater to RVs as well. A small minority are owned and managed by the EOT, or by the local municipality; most are privately run. All but the most primi-tive sites have hot showers heated by solar power, shady landscaping, and a snack bar or café. Power hookups are generally available for an extra fee.

The most luxurious campsites are miniature vacation villages, with swimming pool, tennis courts, laundry rooms, banking and postal facilities, and bunga-lows for the tentless.

Mountain refuge, Kóziakas mountain, Tríkala

Established sites usually have the advantage of mature shady trees. The ground is often sun-baked and very hard, so short pegs that can be banged in with a mallet are best. For a regularly updated booklet covering campsites and their amenities, contact the **Greek Camping Association**.

DISABLED TRAVELERS

FACILITIES FOR disabled travelers are far less elaborate in Greece than in Western Europe. **Access-Able Travel Source** maintains a web site (*http://www.access-able.com*) that provides general information on travel for the disabled, as

well as links to many other Internet sites. In Greece, **Hermes** can be contacted for advice. In the hotel listings of this guide we have indicated which establishments have facilities, such as elevators, for the disabled.

Greek information sources for disabled travelers tend to be rudimentary; the EOT only publishes a questionnaire, which can be sent to specific accommodation establishments to assess the suitability of their facilities.

FURTHER INFORMATION

AN INVALUABLE BOOKLET is published yearly by the EOT. It is called *Guide to Hotels*, and a current copy can be obtained from any EOT office. The booklet covers all officially registered hotels, indicating prices, facilities, and their operating season. The guide does not, however, offer information on *domátia* or villas. The EOT also periodically

Nikos Saxónis *(see p273)* at Mégalo Pápigko

Camping in one of the valleys of the Píndos mountain range

publishes an informative leaflet entitled *Rural Tourism*. Two other hotel manuals, issued by private organizations, are *Greek Travel Pages* (GTP) and *Tourist Guide of Greece*. Although they are not as complete or authoritative as the EOT guides, they do have the advantage of being published more frequently. The GTP appears monthly, but offers only skeletal information unless the hotel concerned has purchased advertising space; this is equally true of the quarterly publication *Tourist Guide of Greece*.

DIRECTORY

CHAIN HOTELS

Chandrís Hotels
Syngroú 385,
17564 Paleó Fáliron,
Athens.
(01 941 4825.

Club Mediterranée Hellas SA
Omírou 8, 10564 Athens.
(01 325 4110.

Divani Hotels
Parthenónos 19/23,
11742 Athens.
(01 922 9650.

Stathópoulos Hotels
Filellínon 4,
10557 Athens.
(01 323 5606.

Xenotel Hotels
Akadeimías 35,
10672 Athens.
(01 323 5606.

HOSTELS

American Youth Hostels
733 15th St. NW, Ste 840
Washington, DC 20005.
((202) 783-6161.

YHA (Greece)
Dragatsaníou 4,
10559 Athens.
(01 323 4107.

ALPINE REFUGES

EOHO (Ellinikí Omospondía Chionodromías kai Oreivasías)
(Hellenic Federation of Mountaineering Clubs)
Milióni 5, 10673 Athens.
(01 364 5904.

EOS (Ellinikós Oreivatikós Sýndesmos) (Greek Alpine Club)
Plateía Kentríki 16,
13671 Acharnés, Attica.
(01 246 1528.

SEO (Sýllogos tón Ellínon Oreivatón)
(Association of Greek Climbers) Plateía Aristotélous 5, Thessaloníki.
(0312 24710.

WOMEN'S RURAL TOURISM COOPERATIVES

Agios Germanós
(0385 51470.

Ampelákia
(0495 31495.

Aráchova
(0267 31519.

Maróneia
(0533 41258.

CAMPING

Greek Camping Association
Sólonos 76, 10680 Athens.
(01 362 1560.

DISABLED TRAVELERS

Hermes
Patriárchou Grigoríou toú Pémptou 13,
16542 Argyroúpoli, Attica.
(01 996 1887.

SATH
347 Fifth Ave.
New York, NY 10016.
((212) 447-7284.

FURTHER INFORMATION

Greek Travel Pages
Psýlla 6, corner Filellínon,
10557 Athens.
(01 324 7511.

Tourist Guide of Greece
Patissíon 137,
11251 Athens.
(01 864 1688.

Choosing a Hotel

THESE HOTELS have been selected across a wide price range for their good value, facilities, and location; they are listed by region, starting with Athens. Use the color-coded thumb tabs, which indicate the areas covered on each page, to guide you to the relevant section of the chart. For Athens map references see pages *128–35*; for road map references see the inside back cover.

	NUMBER OF ROOMS	RESTAURANT	GARDEN OR TERRACE	SWIMMING POOL	AIR-CONDITIONING

ATHENS

AMPELOKIPOI: *Androméda*　　　　　　　　Ⓓ Ⓓ Ⓓ Ⓓ
Timoléontos 22, 11521. **Map 6 F4.** 〖 *01 643 7302.* FAX *01 646 6361.*
A deluxe hotel with immaculate attention to detail in all the rooms and a
reception area featuring work by contemporary designers. ⊟ P & ⊠

| 30 | ● | | | ■ |

AREOS: *Park*　　　　　　　　　　　　　Ⓓ Ⓓ Ⓓ Ⓓ
Leofóros Alexándras 10, 10682. **Map 3 A1.** 〖 *01 883 2712.* FAX *01 823 8420.*
Situated opposite the relaxing Areos Park, this hotel has spacious rooms.
There is also a good rooftop bar and a 24-hour coffee shop. ⊟ P & ⊠

| 146 | ● | ■ | ● | ■ |

EXARCHEIA: *Exarcheíon*　　　　　　　　　　　Ⓓ Ⓓ
Themistokléous 55, 10683. **Map 2 F3.** 〖 *01 380 5611.* FAX *01 380 3296.*
This hotel is close to the late-night action of Plateía Exarcheíon. The
rooms are basic, and there is a good sidewalk café. ⊟ & ⊠

| 54 | | | | |

EXARCHEIA: *Museum*　　　　　　　　　　　Ⓓ Ⓓ
Mpoumpoulínas 16, 10682. **Map 2 F2.** 〖 *01 380 5611.* FAX *01 380 0507.*
The modern façade of this building hides a genteel interior. Situated
opposite the National Archaeological Museum, it is frequented by
academics. The rooms are clean and quiet. ⊟ P & ⊠

| 58 | | | | |

ILISIA: *Hilton*　　　　　　　　　　　Ⓓ Ⓓ Ⓓ Ⓓ Ⓓ
Leofóros Vasilíssis Sofías 46, 11528. **Map 4 D5.** 〖 *01 725 0201.* FAX *01 725 3110.*
Athens' best-known modern hotel. All the rooms have large balconies,
providing stunning views across the city. ⊟ P & ⊠

| 453 | ● | ■ | ● | ■ |

ILISIA: *Holiday Inn*　　　　　　　　　Ⓓ Ⓓ Ⓓ Ⓓ
Michalakopoúlou 50, 11528. **Map 8 E1.** 〖 *01 724 8322.* FAX *01 724 8187.*
This efficiently run hotel is popular with business travelers. It has large
rooms, good restaurants, and a rooftop swimming pool. ⊟ P & ⊠

| 191 | ● | ■ | ● | ■ |

KAISARIANI: *Divani Caravel*　　　　　　　Ⓓ Ⓓ Ⓓ Ⓓ Ⓓ
Leofóros Vasiléos Alexándrou 2, 16121. **Map 8 D1.** 〖 *01 725 3725.* FAX *01 723 6683.*
A popular hotel for conferences, the Caravel has spacious rooms and several
eating and drinking areas, including the Lord Byron piano bar. ⊟ P & ⊠

| 470 | ● | ■ | ● | ■ |

KOLONAKI: *Athenian Inn*　　　　　　　Ⓓ Ⓓ Ⓓ Ⓓ
Cháritos 22, 10675. **Map 3 B5.** 〖 *01 723 9552.* FAX *01 724 2268.*
This hotel offers clean, basic rooms and friendly management. Situated in the
heart of Kolonáki among a choice of shops, restaurants, and cafés. ⊟ ⊠

| 25 | | | | ■ |

KOLONAKI: *St George Lykavittós*　　　　Ⓓ Ⓓ Ⓓ Ⓓ Ⓓ
Kleoménous 2, 10675. **Map 3 B4.** 〖 *01 729 0711.* FAX *01 729 0439.*
Situated beneath Lykavittós Hill, this small, luxury hotel offers large rooms
with a good views. The rooftop restaurant is excellent. ⊟ P & ⊠

| 167 | ● | | ● | ■ |

KOUKAKI: *Marble House*　　　　　　　　　　Ⓓ Ⓓ
Zínni Anastasíou 35, 11741. **Map 5 C4.** 〖 *01 923 4058.*
At the end of a quiet cul de sac, this is a firm favorite among mid-range
pensions for its cleanliness and helpful management. Most rooms are
en suite and many have vine-covered balconies. ⊟

| 16 | | ■ | | |

KOUKAKI: *Fíllipos*　　　　　　　　　Ⓓ Ⓓ Ⓓ Ⓓ
Mitsaíon 3, 11742. **Map 6 D3.** 〖 *01 922 3611.* FAX *01 922 3615.*
Sister property to the Iródeion, this modern hotel offers basic but clean
accommodation. Some rooms have balconies. ⊟ & ⊠

| 48 | | | | ■ |

MAKRYGIANNI: *Ira*　　　　　　　　　Ⓓ Ⓓ Ⓓ Ⓓ
Falírou 9, 11742. **Map 6 D4.** 〖 *01 923 5618.* FAX *01 924 7344.*
The rooms and public areas in this modern hotel are spotless. The hotel
also has a coffee shop and a rooftop terrace. ⊟ P & ⊠

| 49 | | ■ | | ■ |

Price categories are for a standard double room for one night in peak season, including tax, service charges, and breakfast:
- ⓓ under 8,000 Dr
- ⓓⓓ 8–12,000 Dr
- ⓓⓓⓓ 12–16,000 Dr
- ⓓⓓⓓⓓ 16–21,000 Dr
- ⓓⓓⓓⓓⓓ over 21,000 Dr.

RESTAURANT
Restaurant within the hotel sometimes reserved for residents only.

GARDEN OR TERRACE
Hotel with garden, courtyard, or terrace, often providing tables for outside eating.

SWIMMING POOL
Hotel swimming pools are usually quite small and are outdoors unless otherwise stated.

AIR-CONDITIONING
Hotel with air-conditioning in all the rooms.

		NUMBER OF ROOMS	RESTAURANT	GARDEN OR TERRACE	SWIMMING POOL	AIR-CONDITIONING
MAKRYGIANNI: *Athens Gate* — ⓓⓓⓓⓓ	Leofóros A Syngroú 10, 11742. **Map 6 E3.** ☎ 01 923 8302. FAX 01 923 7493. This centrally located modern hotel offers comfortable rooms and a rooftop garden with views of the Acropolis and Hadrian's Arch.	100	●	■		■
MAKRIGIANNI: *Divani Palace Acropolis* — ⓓⓓⓓⓓ	Parthenónos 19–25, 11742. **Map 6 D3.** ☎ 01 922 2945. FAX 01 921 4993. Beautifully upgraded to deluxe standard, this hotel is just a short stroll from the Acropolis. An original section of the Themistoklean Long Walls is displayed in the hotel lobby.	251	●	■	●	■
MAKRYGIANNI: *Iródeion* — ⓓⓓⓓⓓ	Rovértou Gkálli 4, 11742. **Map 5 C3.** ☎ 01 923 6832. FAX 01 923 5851. This hotel has large modern rooms, a patio shaded by pistachio trees, and a roof terrace with views of the Acropolis.	90	●	■		■
MAKRYGIANNI: *Royal Olympic* — ⓓⓓⓓⓓ	Athanasíou Diákou 28–32, 11743. **Map 6 E3.** ☎ 01 922 6411. FAX 01 923 3317. The Royal Olympic has wonderful large rooms, all with superb views of the Temple of Olympian Zeus. Good grill restaurant.	304	●	■	●	■
MONASTIRAKI: *Témpoi* — ⓓ	Aiólou 29, 10551. **Map 2 D5.** ☎ 01 321 3175. FAX 01 325 4179. Overlooking the flower market and Agía Eiríni church, this hotel is ideal for those who want to explore Athinás market's food and stalls.	24		■		
MONASTIRAKI: *Attalos* — ⓓⓓ	Athinás 29, 19554. **Map 2 D5.** ☎ 01 321 2801. FAX 01 324 3124. Ideally situated for shopping, near Monastiráki and Athinás, the Attalos offers adequate rooms, some with balconies. The hotel also has a roof garden with good views of the Acropolis.	80		■		■
NEOS KOSMOS: *Christína* — ⓓⓓⓓ	Petmezá 15, 11743. **Map 6 D4.** ☎ 01 921 5353. FAX 01 921 5569. This is a fairly standard businessman's hotel just a short walk from the Acropolis. The rooms are clean and homey.	93	●			■
NEOS KOSMOS: *Athenaeum Inter-Continental* — ⓓⓓⓓⓓ	Leofóros Andrea Syngroú 89–93, 11745. **Map 6 E4.** ☎ 01 902 3666. FAX 01 924 3000. Decorated throughout by modern Greek artists, this luxurious hotel offers a choice of fine restaurants, bars and shops. Facilities also include a fully equipped gymnasium.	520	●		●	■
NEOS KOSMOS: *Ledra Marriot* — ⓓⓓⓓⓓⓓ	Leofóros Andrea Syngroú 115, 11745. **Map 6 D4.** ☎ 01 934 7711. FAX 01 935 8603. As well as all the amenities expected from a luxury hotel, the Marriot's rooms are large and spacious, and the hotel boasts superb restaurants, particularly the trendy Polynesian Kona Kai.	259	●		●	■
OMONOIA: *La Mirage* — ⓓⓓⓓ	Maríchas Kotopoúli 3, 10431. **Map 2 D3.** ☎ 01 523 4755. FAX 01 523 3992. A favorite for those who want to be close to the 24-hour hustle and bustle of Plateía Omonoías. All rooms are double-glazed.	208	●			■
OMONOIA: *Dorian Inn* — ⓓⓓⓓⓓ	Peiraiós 15–19, 10552. **Map 2 D3.** ☎ 01 523 9782. FAX 01 522 6196. Situated in the heart of the city center, the roof garden of this stylish hotel offers spectacular views of Athens and the Acropolis.	146	●	■	●	■
OMONOIA: *King Minos* — ⓓⓓⓓⓓ	Peiraiós 1, 10552. **Map 2 D3.** ☎ 01 523 1111. FAX 01 523 1361. The hotel's large and comfortable public lounge areas, including restaurant and bar, are good for relaxing. All rooms are quiet.	194	●	■		■

For key to symbols see back flap

Price categories are for a standard double room for one night in peak season, including tax, service charges, and breakfast:
Dr under 8,000 Dr
DrDr 8–12,000 Dr
DrDrDr 12–16,000 Dr
DrDrDrDr 16–21,000 Dr
DrDrDrDrDr over 21,000 Dr.

RESTAURANT
Restaurant within the hotel sometimes reserved for residents only.

GARDEN OR TERRACE
Hotel with garden, courtyard, or terrace, often providing tables for outside eating.

SWIMMING POOL
Hotel swimming pools are usually quite small and are outdoors unless otherwise stated.

AIR-CONDITIONING
Hotel with air-conditioning in all the rooms.

	Price	NUMBER OF ROOMS	RESTAURANT	GARDEN OR TERRACE	SWIMMING POOL	AIR-CONDITIONING
OMONOIA: *Titánia* Panepistimíou 52, 10678. **Map 2 E4.** 01 330 0111. FAX 01 330 0700. The entrance to this well-appointed hotel is through a shopping arcade close to Plateía Omonoías. Rooms are well equipped and the rooftop terrace bar and ground-floor café are always busy. 🖼 P 🚻 📧	DrDrDrDr	396	●	▪		▪
ORTHON: *Stanley* Odysséos 1, Plateía Kairaskáki, 10437. **Map 1 B3.** 01 524 1611. FAX 01 524 4611. The Stanley hotel has large fully-equipped rooms with balconies. Facilities include a rooftop garden and pool as well as a restaurant and bar that are always busy. 🖼 P 🚻 📧	DrDrDrDrDr	400	●	▪	●	▪
PLAKA: *John's Place* Patróou 5, 10557. **Map 6 E1.** 01 322 9719. One of the better bargain backpacking hotels. The rooms are small but very clean, and bathrooms are shared.	Dr	15				
PLAKA: *Koúros* Kódrou 11, 10557. **Map 6 E2.** 01 322 7431. Situated in the heart of Pláka, this inexpensive and cheerful small pension is housed in a converted Neo-Classical mansion house. Rooms are basic but clean, and all have balconies.	Dr	10				
PLAKA: *Faídra* Chairofóntos 16, 10558. **Map 6 E2.** 01 323 8461. The hotel's location next to the Lysikrates monument more than makes up for the slightly tacky quality of its rooms and public areas.	DrDr	27				
PLAKA: *Acropolis House Pension* Kódrou 6–8, 10557. **Map 6 E1.** 01 322 2344. FAX 01 323 3143. Housed in a converted 19th-century building, the rooms in this pension are large and airy. All rooms have private balconies. 🖼 📧	DrDrDr	19				▪
PLAKA: *Adonis* Kódrou 3, 10557. **Map 6 E2.** 01 324 9737. FAX 01 323 1602. The Adónis is a modern, resonably priced hotel offering decent, basic accommodations and panoramic views across Athens from its roof garden. All the rooms have balconies. 🖼 P 🚻	DrDrDr	26		▪		
PLAKA: *Adrian* Adrianoú 74, 10556. **Map 6 E2.** 01 322 1553. FAX 01 325 0461. Situated in central Pláka, this hotel has simple, comfortable rooms as well as a quiet terrace to escape the bustle of the city. 🖼 🚻 📧	DrDrDr	22		▪		▪
PLAKA: *Aphrodite* Apóllonos 21, 10557. **Map 6 E1.** 01 323 4357. FAX 01 322 5244. This hotel is well located and offers clean, good-value rooms, some of which have wonderful views of the Acropolis. 🖼 P 🚻 📧	DrDrDr	84	●	▪		▪
PLAKA: *Ermís* Apóllonos 19, 10557. **Map 6 E1.** 01 323 5514. FAX 01 323 2073. Despite a rather drab lobby, the rooms of this hotel are large, some having balconies overlooking a playground. 🖼 🚻 📧	DrDrDr	45				▪
PLAKA: *Neféli* Angelikís Chatzimicháli 2, 10558. **Map 6 E1.** 01 322 8044. A modern hotel, hidden away in a peaceful backwater in Pláka. The rooms are clean and of a good, basic standard. 🖼 🚻 📧	DrDrDr	18				▪
PLAKA: *Omiros* Apóllonos 15, 10557. **Map 6 E1.** 01 323 5486. FAX 01 322 8059. A lovely roof garden distinguishes this otherwise basic hotel, which is located in a quiet area of Pláka. 🖼 🚻 📧	DrDrDr	37		▪		▪

Pláka: *Byron* ⒹⒹⒹⒹ 20
Výronos 19, 10558. **Map** 6 E2. **(** *01 323 0327.* **FAX** *01 322 0276.*
Situated on the southern fringe of Pláka, this small and basic hotel
is close to the Acropolis. Some rooms have balconies. 🛏 ♿

Pláka: *Myrtó* ⒹⒹⒹ 12
Níkis 40, 10558. **Map** 6 F1. **(** *01 322 7237.*
Close to the central areas of Plateía Syntágmatos and Pláka, this
small hotel is ideal for short stays in Athens. 🛏 ♿

Pláka: *Electra Palace* ⒹⒹⒹⒹⒹ 106
Navárchou Nikodímou 18, 10559. **Map** 6 E1. **(** *01 324 1401.* **FAX** *01 324 1875.*
A popular hotel with a roof garden and swimming pool, the Electra
Palace has good views and rooms with balconies. 🛏 P ♿ 🖥

Stathmos Larissis: *Novotel Athens* ⒹⒹⒹⒹ 195
Michaíl Vóda 4–6, 10439. **Map** 1 D1. **(** *01 825 0422.* **FAX** *01 883 7816.*
Run by the French group Novotel, this stylish, centrally located
hotel has modern well-equipped rooms and a stunning rooftop
garden and swimming pool. 🛏 P ♿ 🖥

Stathmos Larissis: *Oscar* ⒹⒹⒹⒹ 164
Filadelfeías 25, 10439. **Map** 1 C1. **(** *01 883 4215.* **FAX** *01 821 6368.*
Close to Laríssis railroad station, this excellent modern hotel has large
rooms, a rooftop pool, and a good restaurant. 🛏 P 🖥

Strefi Hill: *Oríon* ⒹⒹ 38
Anexartisías 5 & E Mpenáki 105, 11473. **Map** 3 A2. **(** *01 382 7362.* **FAX** *01 380 5193.*
Beside Stréfi Hill, just above the bustling Exárcheia area, this quiet hotel
is popular with students looking for short-term accommodations.

Syntagma: *Imperial* ⒹⒹ 25
Mitropóleos 40, 10563. **Map** 6 D1. **(** *01 322 7617.*
Friendly staff greet you at this five-story hotel enjoying views of Athens'
Mitrópoli (cathedral). Rooms are large and clean. 🛏 ♿ 🖥

Syntagma: *Aretoúsa* ⒹⒹⒹⒹ 87
Mitropóleos 6–8 & Níkis 12, 10563. **Map** 6 F1. **(** *01 322 9431.* **FAX** *01 322 9439.*
Decent value characterizes this centrally located hotel. The rooms are
modern, and there is a roof garden as well as a lively bar. 🛏 ♿ 🖥

Syntagma: *Astor* ⒹⒹⒹⒹ 130
Karageórgi Servías 16, 10562. **Map** 6 F1. **(** *01 325 5555.* **FAX** *01 325 5115.*
The popular all-year-round rooftop restaurant of this hotel boasts
stunning views of Athens. The double rooms from the sixth floor
upward share this impressive view of the city. 🛏 ♿ 🖥

Syntagma: *Amalía* ⒹⒹⒹⒹⒹ 98
Leofóros Vasilíssis Amalías 10, 10557. **Map** 6 F1. **(** *01 323 7301.* **FAX** *01 323 8792.*
Although the rooms are fairly small, all the bathrooms are marble.
The hotel is centrally located and has good views of both the
Parliament building and the National Gardens. 🛏 ♿ 🖥

Syntagma: *Electra* ⒹⒹⒹⒹ 110
Ermoú 5, 10557. **Map** 6 F1. **(** *01 322 3223.* **FAX** *01 322 0310.*
This centrally located hotel is ideally situated for shopping expeditions
to Monastiráki. All the rooms are clean and pleasant. 🛏 ♿ 🖥

Syntagma: *Esperia Palace* ⒹⒹⒹⒹ 184
Stadíou 22, 10564. **Map** 2 E4. **(** *01 323 8001.* **FAX** *01 323 8100.*
A smart city hotel with marble lobbies and tastefully decorated rooms.
Its restaurant and bar are popular with Athenians. 🛏 ♿ 🖥

Syntagma: *Grande Bretagne* ⒹⒹⒹⒹ 450
Plateía Syntágmatos, 10563. **Map** 6 F1. **(** *01 323 0251.* **FAX** *01 322 8034.*
This luxurious hotel was built in 1852 and is the landmark of Plateía
Syntágmatos, the most desirable hotel location in Athens. The lobby
and rooms are beautiful, and the service is excellent. 🛏 ♿ 🖥

Syntagma: *NJV Meridien* ⒹⒹⒹⒹ 177
Vasiléos Georgíou, 10564. **Map** 6 F1. **(** *01 325 5301.* **FAX** *01 323 5856.*
This grand hotel offers luxurious blue and white rooms, all of which
are sound-proofed. There are good facilities, and its Explorers' Lounge
and Marco Polo restaurant are always busy. 🛏 P ♿ 🖥

For key to symbols see back flap

Price categories are for a standard double room for one night in peak season, including tax, service charges, and breakfast:
- ⒹⓇ under 8,000 Dr
- ⒹⒹ 8–12,000 Dr
- ⒹⒹⒹ 12–16,000 Dr
- ⒹⒹⒹⒹ 16–21,000 Dr
- ⒹⒹⒹⒹⒹ over 21,000 Dr.

RESTAURANT
Restaurant within the hotel sometimes reserved for residents only.

GARDEN OR TERRACE
Hotel with garden, courtyard, or terrace, often providing tables for outside eating.

SWIMMING POOL
Hotel swimming pools are usually quite small and are outdoors unless otherwise stated.

AIR-CONDITIONING
Hotel with air-conditioning in all the rooms.

AROUND ATHENS

	NUMBER OF ROOMS	RESTAURANT	GARDEN OR TERRACE	SWIMMING POOL	AIR-CONDITIONING
ANAVYSOS: *Xenía Ilios* — ⒹⒹⒹⒹ 3 km (2 miles) N of Anávysos, 19013. **Road map** D4. 0291 37024. FAX 0291 36998. On a hillside overlooking the ocean, this hotel has adequate rooms and is next to a beach. It is a training school for hotel staff in winter, and students work here in the summer. ● *Oct–May.*	103	●			▪
GLYFADA: *John's* — ⒹⒹⒹⒹ Pandóras & Lazaráki 3, 16674. **Road map** D4. 01 894 6837. FAX 01 898 0210. Situated in Glyfáda, 2 km (1 mile) north of Vouliágmeni, John's is ideally located near the airport and the town's chic shops. Rooms are well equipped, and there is a wonderful palm-shaded pool in the grounds.	68	●	▪	●	▪
KIFISIA: *Semíramis* — ⒹⒹⒹ Chariláou Trikoúpi 48, 14562. **Road map** D4. 01 808 8101. FAX 01 808 8106. This old-style Neo-Classical mansion is a long-standing favorite of the Athenian aristocracy. The service here is impeccable, and the rooms clean and stylishly furnished.	42	●	▪		▪
KIFISIA: *Pentelikón* — ⒹⒹⒹⒹ Deligiánni 66, 14562. **Road map** D4. 01 808 0311. FAX 01 801 0314. Set within landscaped gardens, this Neo-Classical deluxe hotel offers beautiful, spacious rooms and discreet service.	44	●	▪	●	▪
MARATHONAS: *Golden Coast* — ⒹⒹⒹⒹ Marathónas beach, 19005. **Road map** D4. 0294 57100. FAX 0294 57300. This luxury hotel is situated near the ancient site of Marathon. Amenities include a night club, restaurants, four swimming pools (one for children), and other sports facilities and shops.	541	●	▪	●	▪
MOUNT PARNITHA: *Casino Mont Parnes* — ⒹⒹⒹ 4 km (2 miles) N of Acharnaí, 13571. **Road map** D4. 01 246 9111. FAX 01 246 0768. Overlooking the plain of Attica, this hotel is known primarily for its casino. Whether you gamble or not, the fresh air and pine trees around the hotel are a wonderful relief from the Athens summer heat.	108	●	▪	●	▪
PIRAEUS: *Cava D'Oro* — ⒹⒹⒹⒹ Vasiléos Pávlou 19, 18533. **Road map** D4. 01 412 2210. FAX 01 412 2210. Overlooking Mikrolímano harbor, this smart hotel boasts a popular disco and bar. The rooms are cool and airy.	74	●			
PIRAEUS: *Kastélla* — ⒹⒹⒹⒹ Vasiléos Pávlou 75, 18533. **Road map** D4. 01 411 4735 FAX 01 417 5716. Situated in the stylish area of Kastélla, the modern rooms in this hotel have views of the yacht marina below.	32	●	▪		▪
PIRAEUS: *Park* — ⒹⒹⒹⒹ Kolokotróni 103, 18535. **Road map** D4. 01 452 4611. FAX 01 452 4615. The central location of the Park hotel makes it ideal for exploring Piraeus. There is a breakfast terrace, and the rooms are large.	80		▪		▪
SOUNIO: *Agaíon* — ⒹⒹⒹ Waterfront, 19500. **Road map** D4. 0292 39200. FAX 0292 39234. Overlooking a picturesque bay, this long-running hotel provides easy access to the Temple of Poseidon. All rooms have balconies, and a wonderful sunset can be enjoyed from the large restaurant.	45	●	▪		▪
VOULIAGMENI: *Aphrodite Astir Palace* — ⒹⒹⒹⒹ Apóllonos 40, 16671. **Road map** D4. 01 896 0211. FAX 01 896 2582. A luxury hotel in a resort development, 23 km (37 miles) south of Athens, by the sea. The plushest place to stay for combining the sites of Athens with the pleasures of the beach. ● *Oct–Apr.*	570	●	▪	●	▪

THE PELOPONNESE

ANCIENT CORINTH: *Shadow*   (D)   12
On access road to village, 20007. **Road map** C4. 📞 *0741 31481.*
The rear rooms of this simple family hotel overlook Acrocorinth and the
lush Kórinthos plain. The affiliated restaurant has live music. 🛏 🅿 🗒

AREOPOLI: *Pyrgos Kapetanákou*   (D)(D)   6
Off Plateía Areopóleos, 23062. **Road map** C5. 📞 *0733 51233.* **FAX** *0733 51401.*
This hotel is housed in a three-story tower dating from 1865. The rooms
vary sharply in price and range from a lone single to a family quintuple
loft. There are mature gardens and a lovely breakfast salon. 🅿

AREOPOLI: *Xenónas Lontas*   (D)(D)(D)   4
Off Plateía Taxiarchón, 23062. **Road map** C5. 📞 *0733 51360.* **FAX** *0733 51012.*
This recently restored tower house hotel has *en suite* rooms with good,
arty decor. It is, however, slightly overpriced. 🛏 🅿

CHLEMOUTSI: *Chryssí Avgí*   (D)   10
Loutropóleos 9, 27050. **Road map** B4. 📞 *0623 95224.*
Conveniently situated near the center of the village, this hotel has
spacious rooms, the rear six with magnificent views north looking
over the countryside and east to the castle. ⬤ *Nov–Apr.* 🛏 🅿

DIAKOFTO: *Chris-Paul*   (D)(D)(D)   25
Next to railroad station, 25003. **Road map** C4. 📞 *0691 41715.* **FAX** *0691 42128.*
Still close to the town center, this modern hotel is set in a peaceful
location hidden by trees. All the rooms have private balconies with fine
views, and a cozy fireplace greets guests in winter. 🛏 🅿 ♿

DIMITSÁNA: *Dimitsána*   (D)(D)   27
Off Dimitsána–Stemnítsa road, 22100. **Road map** C4. 📞 *0795 31518.*
This recently modernized hotel is not extraordinary architecturally but is
situated in a lush and leafy setting overlooking the Loúsios Gorge. Most
of the rooms have balconies. 🛏 🅿 🗒

FOINIKOUNTA: *Pórto Finíssia*   (D)(D)   27
Foinikoúnta beach, 24006. **Road map** C5. 📞 *0723 71457.* **FAX** *0723 71458.*
Situated in a quiet resort, 14 km (9 miles) southeast of Methóni, the
Foinikoúnta offers clean, well-equipped rooms, most of which overlook a
beach. All rooms have balconies and telephones. ⬤ *Nov–Apr.* 🛏 🅿 ♿ 🗒

GYTHEIO: *Aktaíon*   (D)(D)   22
Vasiléos Pávlou 39, 23200. **Road map** C5. 📞 *0733 23500.* **FAX** *0733 22294.*
Housed in a Neo-Classical building on the dockside, the Aktaíon offers
clean rooms and balconies with ocean views. 🛏

KALAMATA: *Floísvos*   (D)(D)   41
Navarínou 135, 24100. **Road map** C5. 📞 *0721 82282.* **FAX** *0721 82177.*
Situated on the beachfront, this moderately priced, comfortable hotel
allows you to take full advantage of Kalamáta's ocean setting. 🛏 ♿

KALAVRYTA: *María*   (D)(D)(D)   18
Syngroú 10, 25001. **Road map** C4. 📞 *0692 22296.* **FAX** *0692 22686.*
Well-decorated rooms are available at this small, quiet hotel overlooking
a pedestrian street at the western edge of the town. 🛏 🅿

KALOGRIA: *Kalogriá Beach*   (D)   220
Kalogriá beach, 27052. **Road map** B4. 📞 *0693 31380.* **FAX** *0693 31381.*
This hotel comprises a main building and individual bungalows. All the
rooms have verandas with views of the sea or nearby forest. A frequent
bus service runs from Pátra to the hotel. ⬤ *Nov–Mar.* 🛏 🅿 🗒

KARDAMYLI: *Kardamýli Beach*   (D)(D)(D)   30
Kardamýli beach, 24022. **Road map** C5. 📞 *0721 73180.* **FAX** *0721 73184.*
Situated in Kardamýli, 34 km (21 miles) south of Kalamáta, this modern,
friendly hotel sits at the foot of the Taÿgettos range and has excellent
views of the sea and the mountains. 🛏 🅿 ♿ 🗒

KORINTHOS: *Efira*   (D)(D)   45
Ethnikís Andístasis 52, 20100. **Road map** C4. 📞 *0741 22434.* **FAX** *0741 24514.*
Situated in Kórinthos, 6 km (4 miles) northeast of ancient Corinth, the Efira
is one of only a few hotels in the town from which to choose. Affordable
accommodations are offered, and the rooms are basic but clean. 🛏 ♿

For key to symbols see back flap

Price categories are for a standard double room for one night in peak season, including tax, service charges, and breakfast:
Dr under 8,000 Dr
DrDr 8–12,000 Dr
DrDrDr 12–16,000 Dr
DrDrDrDr 16–21,000 Dr
DrDrDrDrDr over 21,000 Dr.

RESTAURANT
Restaurant within the hotel sometimes reserved for residents only.
GARDEN OR TERRACE
Hotel with garden, courtyard, or terrace, often providing tables for outside eating.
SWIMMING POOL
Hotel swimming pools are usually quite small and are outdoors unless otherwise stated.
AIR-CONDITIONING
Hotel with air-conditioning in all the rooms.

	Price	NUMBER OF ROOMS	RESTAURANT	GARDEN OR TERRACE	SWIMMING POOL	AIR-CONDITIONING
KORONI: *Auberge de la Plage* Zánga beach, 24004. **Road map** C5. ☎ 0725 22401. FAX 0725 22508. This hotel is remarkable for its spectacular setting overlooking the castle of Koróni as well as one of the best beaches in the Peloponnese. All of the rooms have balconies with good views. ● *Nov–Mar.*	DrDr	49	●	▪		▪
KYLLINI: *Robinson Club Kyllíni Beach* Kyllíni beach, 27050. **Road map** B4. ☎ 0623 95205. FAX 0623 95206. This large-scale complex is set in beautiful grounds next to a sandy beach. Organized sports for adults and children are offered, as well as health facilities, such as massage treatments. ● *Nov–Mar.*	DrDrDrDrDr	304	●	▪	●	
METHONI: *Odysséas* Platíea Syngroú, 24006. **Road map** B5. ☎ 0723 31600. FAX 0723 31646. This traditional style hotel, with terra-cotta roof tiling and white walls overlooks the castle of Methóni. The hotel has a television room and a large garden area. All rooms have balconies. ● *Nov–Mar.*	DrDrDrDr	9	●			▪
MONEMVASIA: *Malvásia* Kástro, 23070. **Road map** C5. ☎ 0732 61323. FAX 0732 61722. This restoration complex is scattered about the old town on three different sites that vary in price. Each room, furnished in wood, marble, and bright textiles, has its own individual charm.	DrDrDr	28				
MYCENAE: *Belle Hélène* Chrístou loúda, 21200. **Road map** C4. ☎ 0751 76225. FAX 0751 76179. Dating from 1862, this simple but atmospheric building housed the archaeologist Schleimann during his excavations here. The ground floor restaurant features an impressive guest register. ● *Jan–Feb.*	DrDr	8	●			
NAFPLIO: *King Othon* Farmakopoúlon 3, 21100. **Road map** C4. ☎ 0752 27585. Housed in a Neo-Classical building, the King Othon has high ceilings and windows that contribute to its atmosphere. ● *Nov–Mar.*	Dr	12				
NAFPLIO: *Byron* Plátonos 2, 21100. **Road map** C4. ☎ 0752 22352. FAX 0752 26338. A beautifully restored hotel situated near the top of the old town. Some of the upper-floor rooms have views of the ocean. ● *Nov.*	DrDr	18		▪		▪
NAFPLIO: *Epídavros* Kokkínou 2, 21100. **Road map** C4. ☎ 0752 27541. FAX 0752 27541. Every room of this tastefully renovated hotel is different, though all of them have pine floors and coffered ceilings. Some rooms have balconies. There are eight additional rooms available in an affiliated pension nearby.	DrDrDr	25		▪		
NEOS MYSTRAS: *Byzántion* Main square, 23100. **Road map** C5. ☎ 0731 83309. FAX 0731 20019. Situated in Néos Mystrás, 1 km (0.5 miles) east of Byzantine Mystrás, this recently restored hotel has individually decorated rooms with vaulted ceilings and wooden furniture. Prices vary depending on the view. ● *Nov–Feb.*	DrDr	22	●			
OLYMPIA: *Pelops* Varelá 2, 27065. **Road map** B4. ☎ 0624 22543. FAX 0624 22213. Situated in Olympía, 500 m (1,600 ft) east of ancient Olympia, this hotel is run by an Australian-Greek team. The family atmosphere and vine-covered bar area make for a pleasant stay. ● *mid-Nov–mid-Feb.*	DrDr	25	●	▪	●	
OLYMPIA: *Europa* Droúva 1, 27065. **Road map** B4. ☎ 0624 22650. FAX 0624 23166. A member of the Best Western chain, this modern hotel enjoys a superb hillside site in Olympía, 500 m (1,600 ft) east of ancient Olympia. Facilities include a tennis court and riding stable.	DrDrDrDr	42	●	▪	●	▪

PATRA: *Ránnia* ⑩⑩ 30
Plateía Kolokotróni, 26221. **Road map** C4. **[** 061 220114. **FAX** 061 220435.
This is a reasonably priced hotel in a quiet location. The rooms have wooden furniture and balconies, and some overlook a lovely square.

PORTOCHELI: *Ververóda* ⑩⑩ 246
Sea front, 21300. **Road map** C4. **[** 0754 51345. **FAX** 0754 51345.
A ten-minute walk from the town, this hotel overlooks a picturesque bay and consists of a complex of traditionally styled villas and bungalows. 🚗 **P**

PYLOS: *Káralis Beach* ⑩⑩⑩ 35
Kolokápas 26, 24001. **Road map** C5. **[** 0723 23021. **FAX** 0723 22970.
Set at the foot of the castle, this hotel is in a wonderful pine grove overlooking the ocean. Some rooms have sea views. ● *Nov–Mar.* 🚗 **P** 🔋 🖥

SPARTI: *Maniátis* ⑩⑩ 80
Palaiológou 72, 23100. **Road map** C5. **[** 0731 22665. **FAX** 0731 29994.
Situated in the center of Spárti, this modern, efficiently run hotel lacks atmosphere, but is an excellent value for the money. 🚗 🔋 🖥

SPARTI: *Spárta Inn* ⑩⑩⑩ 147
Thermopylón 109, 23100. **Road map** C5. **[** 0731 25021. **FAX** 0731 24855.
One of the more stylish hotels in this area, the Spárta Inn is situated in a tranquil spot and has a roof garden. 🚗 🔋 🖥

STEMNITSA: *Trikolóneio* ⑩ 20
Off main square, 22024. **Road map** C4. **[** 0795 81297
Situated in Stemnitsa, 8 km (5 miles) south of Dimitsána, the traditional-style Trikolóneio is housed in two 19th-century mansions with an annex. There is an excellent restaurant attached. 🚗 **P**

VATHEIA: *EOT Traditional Settlement* ⑩⑩⑩ 8
Main square, 23071. **Road map** C5. **[** 0733 55244. **FAX** 0733 55292.
Situated in Vatheía, 8 km (5 miles) southeast of Geroliménas, this hotel is one of several 18th- and 19th century tower houses converted into six studio units. All units have balconies and a garden. ● *Oct–Mar.* 🚗

ZACHLOROU: *Romántzo* ⑩⑩ 10
Next to railway station, 25001. **Road map** C4. **[** 0692 22758.
Situated in Zachloroú, 14 km (9 miles) west of Diakoftó, this is a rambling structure with verandas overlooking the Vouraikós river. 🚗

CENTRAL AND WESTERN GREECE

AGIOS IOANNIS: *Eftychía* ⑩⑩⑩ 17
Main road into village, 37012. **Road map** C3. **[** 0426 31150.
Situated in Agios Ioánnis, 25 km (16 miles) north of Miliés, the Eftychía, with stone roof-tiles and a whitewashed exterior, is a typical Pílio style hotel. There are ocean views but no rooms with balconies. ● *Sep–May.* 🚗 **P**

ARACHOVA: *Apollon Inn* ⑩⑩⑩ 20
Delfón 20, 32004. **Road map** C3. **[** 0267 31057.
This excellent family-run hotel in Aráchova, 11 km (8 miles) east of ancient Delphi has a friendly atmosphere. There are no *en suite* rooms. 🚗 **P** 🖥

DELFOI: *Ermís* ⑩⑩⑩ 40
Freiderikís 27, 33054. **Road map** C3. **[** 0265 82318. **FAX** 0265 82639.
The Olympic is situated in Delfoí, 600 m (1,900 ft) east of ancient Delphi. Rooms have good views of olive groves to the Gulf of Corinth. 🚗 🔋 🖥

DELFOI: *Olympic* ⑩⑩⑩ 20
Freiderikís 53B, 33054. **Road map** C3. **[** 0265 82163. **FAX** 0265 82639.
Situated in Delfoí, 600 m (1,900 ft) east of ancient Delphi, this luxurious hotel offers *en suite* rooms with fine views over an olive-filled valley. 🚗 🖥

DELFOI: *Varanos* ⑩⑩⑩ 10
Vasiléos Pávlou & Freiderikís 25, 33054. **Road map** C3. **[** 0265 82345.
Set in a Neo-Classical-style building in Delfoí, 600 m (1,900 ft) east of ancient Delphi, this hotel has spacious rooms and large balconies. 🚗 🖥

DELFOI: *Xenía* ⑩⑩⑩⑩⑩ 45
Apóllonos 69, 33054. **Road map** C3. **[** 0265 82151. **FAX** 0265 82644.
Situated in Delfoí, 600 m (1,900 ft) east of ancient Delphi, the rooms of this chain hotel are spacious; all have private balconies. 🚗 **P** 🔋 🖥

For key to symbols see back flap

Price categories are for a standard double room for one night in peak season, including tax, service charges, and breakfast:
- Dr under 8,000 Dr
- DrDr 8–12,000 Dr
- DrDrDr 12–16,000 Dr
- DrDrDrDr 16–21,000 Dr
- DrDrDrDrDr over 21,000 Dr.

RESTAURANT
Restaurant within the hotel sometimes reserved for residents only.

GARDEN OR TERRACE
Hotel with garden, courtyard, or terrace, often providing tables for outside eating.

SWIMMING POOL
Hotel swimming pools are usually quite small and are outdoors unless otherwise stated.

AIR-CONDITIONING
Hotel with air-conditioning in all the rooms.

	NUMBER OF ROOMS	RESTAURANT	GARDEN OR TERRACE	SWIMMING POOL	AIR-CONDITIONING
GALAXIDI: *Ganiméde* DrDrDr Níkou Gourgourí 20, 33052. **Road map** C3. 0265 41328. FAX 0265 42160. This atmospheric, Italian-run hotel has rooms overlooking a beautiful garden. Homemade jam is offered at breakfast. ● *Nov–20 Dec.*	8		■		■
IGOUMENITSA: *Savoy* DrDrDrDr Voreíou Ipeírou 3, 46100. **Road map** B2. 0665 23957. FAX 0665 23781. Accommodations here consist of 12 traditional-style, furnished apartments. Units have wooden interiors and shutters and are equipped with a television. The children's playground makes it an ideal choice for families.	12				
IOANNINA: *Olympic* DrDrDr Melanídi 2, 45332. **Road map** B2. 0651 25888. FAX 0651 22041. A long-established, friendly hotel near the town center offers some of the best reasonably priced accommodations in Ioánnina.	55	●			■
IOANNINA: *Xenía* DrDrDrDr Leofóros Dodónis 33, 45221. **Road map** B2. 0651 47301. FAX 065147189. Situated on the pleasant, tree-lined avenue of Dodónis, this modern hotel offers comfortable, well-equipped rooms. The hotel is surrounded by gardens, and there is a conference room available.	60	●	■		
KALAMPAKA: *Rex* DrDr Kastrakíou 11A, 42200. **Road map** B2. 0432 22042. FAX 0432 22372. A simpler and less expensive hotel than many near Metéora. The Rex is in a peaceful location, with big well-furnished rooms.	34	●			
KALAMPAKA: *Antoniádi* DrDrDr Trikálon 148, 42200. **Road map** B2. 0432 24387. FAX 0432 24319. A new, but homey, small hotel lacks views of Metéora but has a very friendly atmosphere and a first-class restaurant.	59	●	■	●	■
KALAMPAKA: *Diváni* DrDrDrDr At entrance to village, 42200. **Road map** B2. 0432 23330. FAX 0432 23638. This chic hotel in the Divani chain has close-up views of the Metéora rocks. All rooms have balconies, and there is an open-air bar.	164	●	■	●	■
MAKRINITSA: *Archontikó Moueslí* DrDrDr Pílio, 37011. **Road map** D3. 0421 90151. FAX 0421 99140. This restored traditional Pílio mansion in Makrinítsa, 14 km (9 miles) north of Vólos, has a tree-shaded patio and is an ideal place to relax.	8		■		
MAKRINITSA: *Archontikó Xiradáki* DrDrDrDr Near main square, 37011. **Road map** D3. 0421 99250. FAX 0421 99140. Situated in a peaceful part of Makrinítsa, 14 km (9 miles) north of Vólos, this 19th-century building has spacious verandas with good views.	12		■		
MEGALO PAPIGKO: *Níkos Saxónis* DrDrDrDr Off main square, 44016. **Road map** D3. 0653 41615. Situated in Megálo Pápigko, 40 km (25 miles) south of Kónitsa, this stylish hotel is made up of a cluster of tastefully restored 18th-century buildings. Rooms have original fireplaces, and there is a delightful rose garden.	8		■		
METSOVO: *Egnatía* DrDr Tosítsa 19, 44200. **Road map** B2. 0656 41900. FAX 0656 41485. A mountain hotel with stone and woodwork decor. All the rooms are *en suite*, and many have private balconies commanding fine views out across the Píndos mountains.	37	●			
METSOVO: *Apóllon* DrDrDr Main square, 44200. **Road map** B2. 0656 41844. FAX 0656 42110. Situated in the heart of the town, the Apóllon is a chalet-style hotel with a wooden exterior and cozy wooden interior.	40	●	■		

METSOVO: *Victória* ⒹⒹⒹⒹ | 37
Near Agios Geoórgios Park, 44200. **Road map** B2. **(** *0656 41777.* **FAX** *0656 41454.*
Situated near the village center, this traditional-style hotel offers rooms
with good views of the Píndos mountains.

MIKRO PAPIGKO: *Días* ⒹⒹ | 10
Xenónas Días, 47016. **Road map** D3. **(** *0653 41257.*
This traditional-style hotel in Mikró Pápigko, 38 km (24 miles) south of
Kónitsa, has been modernized. It is within easy reach of the Víkos Gorge,
and it overlooks the famous limestone rock towers of the village.

MPOURAZANI: *Mpourazáni* ⒹⒹⒹⒹ | 20
SE of Melissópetra, 44100. **Road map** C3. **(** *0655 61283.* **FAX** *0655 61321.*
Set in a wonderful wildlife park, 3 km (2 miles) southeast of the village of
Melissópetra and 12 km (7 miles) west of Kónitsa, this hotel and wildlife
research center has rooms with balconies and mountain views.

NAFPAKTOS: *Náfpaktos* ⒹⒹⒹ | 50
Korydalloú 4, 30300. **Road map** C3. **(** *0634 29551.* **FAX** *0634 29553*
Well-situated near the harbor, this hotel has a whitewashed interior and
marble floors. All rooms have balconies, some with ocean views.

PARGA: *Parádeisos* ⒹⒹ | 18
Plateía Agíou Nikoláou, 48060. **Road map** B3. **(** *0684 31229.* **FAX** *0684 31266.*
Close to the town center, this Neo-Classical building is situated on a
beautiful square and has a very friendly atmosphere.

PREVEZA: *Mínos* ⒹⒹ | 23
21 Oktovríou, 48100. **Road map** B3. **(** *0682 28424.* **FAX** *0682 24644.*
One of the best of Préveza's limited choice of hotels, the Mínos has a
friendly family atmosphere, with clean and comfortable *en suite* rooms.

TRIKALA: *Achílleion* ⒹⒹⒹⒹ | 60
Asklipeioú 2, 42100. **Road map** C2. **(** *0431 28291.* **FAX** *0431 74858.*
A modern hotel, right by the main square in the town center. Rooms are
en suite with balconies that look out onto the old town.

VOLOS: *Fílippos* ⒹⒹⒹ | 39
Sólonos 9, 39001. **Road map** C3. **(** *0421 37607.* **FAX** *0421 39550.*
A new and simple hotel, set one block back from the waterfront, on the
edge of the main square. The upper rooms all have sea views.

VOLOS: *Park* ⒹⒹⒹⒹ | 119
Deligiórgi 2, 38221. **Road map** C3. **(** *0421 36511.* **FAX** *0421 28645.*
This is one of the best hotels in Vólos. The rooms are modern, stylishly
decorated, and have balconies that overlook the sea or park.

VYZITSA: *Vergos Mansion* ⒹⒹ | 7
Off main square, 37010. **Road map** D3. **(** *0423 86293.*
Situated in Vyzítsa, 2 km (1 mile) north of Miliés, this hotel is housed in a
traditional mansion. The terrace overlooks Pagasitikós bay.

NORTHERN GREECE

ALEXANDROUPOLI: *Alkyón* ⒹⒹ | 30
Moudaníon 1, 68100. **Road map** E1. **(** *0551 27465.* **FAX** *0551 27465.*
A modern but traditional-style whitewashed hotel with rustic furnishings
and a friendly atmosphere. The rooms have good sea views.

ALEXANDROUPOLI: *Egnatía* ⒹⒹⒹⒹ | 96
Leofóros Makrís, 68100. **Road map** E1. **(** *0551 37630.* **FAX** *0551 37634.*
Peacefully located in its own grounds, at the western edge of the seafront, the Egnatía is only a short walk from the town center. The rooms
are simply decorated but pleasant and functional.

FANARI: *Fanári* ⒹⒹ | 32
Next to campsite, 67063. **Road map** E1. **(** *0535 31300.* **FAX** *0535 31388.*
All rooms in this clean, modern hotel boast good ocean views. The
Fanári also has its own bar and pastry shop.

FANARI: *Vósporos* ⒹⒹ | 20
2 km (1 mile) SE of Fanári, 67063. **Road map** E1. **(** *0535 31216.*
This modern hotel has pleasant, good-sized rooms, all with balconies
overlooking the sea. Beaches are a short walk away. ● *Nov.*

For key to symbols see back flap

Price categories are for a standard double room for one night in peak season, including tax, service charges, and breakfast:
Dr under 8,000 Dr
Dr Dr 8–12,000 Dr
Dr Dr Dr 12–16,000 Dr
Dr Dr Dr Dr 16–21,000 Dr
Dr Dr Dr Dr Dr over 21,000 Dr.

RESTAURANT
Restaurant within the hotel sometimes reserved for residents only.

GARDEN OR TERRACE
Hotel with garden, courtyard, or terrace, often providing tables for outside eating.

SWIMMING POOL
Hotel swimming pools are usually quite small and are outdoors unless otherwise stated.

AIR-CONDITIONING
Hotel with air-conditioning in all the rooms.

	NUMBER OF ROOMS	RESTAURANT	GARDEN OR TERRACE	SWIMMING POOL	AIR-CONDITIONING
FLORINA: *Língos* Dr Dr Dr Dr Tagmatárchou Naoúm 3, 53100. **Road map** B1. 0385 28322. FAX 0385 29643. This modern hotel, situated close to all amenities, offers an Italian-style roof garden and rooms with mountain views.	40	●	■		
GERAKINI: *Gerakíni Beach Hotel* Dr Dr Dr Dr Gerakíni beach, 36100. **Road map** D2. 0371 52302. FAX 0371 52118. A modern complex in Gerakíni, 17 km (11 miles) south of Néa Moudaniá, comprising a hotel and bungalows. Rooms are spacious, with balconies overlooking the sea. ● Nov–Apr.	503	●	■	●	
KASTORIA: *Oréstion* Dr Dr Dr Plateía Daváki 1, 52100. **Road map** B2. 0467 22257. FAX 0467 22257. Small, reasonably priced hotel situated below the old town of Kastoriá. All rooms are *en suite* and well maintained.	20				
KASTORIA: *Tsámis* Dr Dr Dr Koromilá 3, Dispílio, 52100. **Road map** B2. 0467 85334. FAX 0467 85777. Quietly situated on the far side of the lake from the town center, this modern but traditional-style hotel has its own gymnasium and bar. Acivities on the lake make the Tsámis an ideal choice for water-sports enthusiasts.	78	●	■		
KAVALA: *Lucy* Dr Dr Kalamítsa beach, 65404. **Road map** D1. 051 242830. FAX 051 242501. Set on the best beach outside Kavála, this comfortable hotel is suitable for those wanting to avoid the bustle of the town.	210	●	■	●	■
KAVALA: *Neféli* Dr Dr Dr Erythroú Stavroú 50, 65403. **Road map** D1. 051 227441. FAX 051 227440. A modern and comfortable hotel in the center of Kavála, overlooking the sea. The roof garden has beautiful views of the old town.	94	●	■		
KAVALA: *Galaxy* Dr Dr Dr Dr Venizélou 27, 65302. **Road map** D1. 051 224811. FAX 051 226754. Situated in the heart of the town center, this large modern hotel is close to archaeological sites of interest and beaches.	150	●	■		■
KOMOTINI: *Rodópi* Dr Dr Dr Ethnárchi Makaríou 3, 69100. **Road map** E1. 0531 35988. FAX 0531 35991. The Rodópi is housed in a traditional wooden building with spacious rooms and balconies overlooking Mount Rodópi.	20	●	■		
KOMOTINI: *Anatólia* Dr Dr Dr Dr Anchyálou 53, 69100. **Road map** E1. 0531 36242. FAX 0531 23170. This friendly, family-run hotel is set in a peaceful location not far from the main park. Rooms are basic but clean.	56	●			■
KRYOPIGI: *Forest Park* Dr Dr Dr Dr Kripopigí beach, 63077. **Road map** D2. 0374 23771. FAX 0374 23772. Situated in Kryopigí, 25 km (16 miles) northeast of Néa Moudaniá, this hotel is surrounded on three sides by the beautiful Kassándra pinewoods. Rooms have modern facilities and spacious verandas. ● Nov–Apr.	50	●	■	■	■
LITOCHORO: *Mirtó* Dr Dr Agios Nikólaos 5, 60200. **Road map** C2. 0352 81398. FAX 0352 82298. Situated in Litóchoro, 21 km (13 miles) south of Katerína, this hotel has large, *en suite* rooms and a friendly atmosphere. ● 20 Sep–10 Oct.	32	●	■		
NEOS MARMARAS: *Sithonía Beach Hotel* Dr Dr Dr Dr Dr 3 km (2 miles) E of village, 63081. **Road map** D2. 0375 /1221. FAX 0375 72130. Situated in Néos Marmarás, 52 km (30 miles) southeast of Néa Moudaniá, this modern hotel lies in a bay at the foot of the Melítonas mountains. All rooms have verandas with magnificent views of the Aegean.	442	●	■	●	■

NYMFAIA: *La Moára* ⓓⓓⓓⓓ 8
At entrance to village, 53078. **Road map** E1. 【 *031 287626.* FAX *031 287401.*
This traditional old building offers spacious accommodations on beautiful
grounds. Facilities include billiards, a library, and a wine bar, and the hotel
provides easy access to the Vítsi mountain ski resort. ● *Jul.* 🔒 **P** 🗐

OURANOUPOLI: *Skítes* ⓓⓓⓓⓓ 15
Road to Mount Athos, 63075. **Road map** D2. 【 *0377 71140.* FAX *0377 71322.*
A family-run hotel set in a peaceful spot, surrounded by pinewoods, with
whitewashed bungalows that are decorated in a rustic style. The veranda
restaurant has spectacular views of the sea. ● *Nov–Apr.* 🔒 **P** 🔶 🗐

PRESPA LAKES: *Pelekáni* ⓓ 10
Main road, Agios Germanós village, 53077. **Road map** B1. 【 *0386 51442.*
Situated in the picturesque village of Agios Germanós, this simple hotel
overlooks the Préspa Lakes. Rooms are well kept. 🔒 **P**

THESSALONIKI: *Vergína* ⓓⓓⓓ 133
Monastiríou 19, 54627. **Road map** C2. 【 *031 516021.* FAX *031 529308.*
One of the better hotels near the train and bus stations, this is a large and
efficiently run establishment with spacious rooms. 🔒 🗐

THESSALONIKI: *Victoria* ⓓⓓⓓ 68
Langadá 13, 54629. **Road map** C2. 【 *031 522422.* FAX *031 512892.*
A Neo-Classical-style hotel within walking distance of the central square
and port, and close to the bazaar. The rooms have balconies. 🔒 **P** 🔶 🗐

THESSALONIKI: *Electra Palace* ⓓⓓⓓⓓ 135
Plateía Aristotélous 9, 54624. **Road map** C2. 【 *031 232221.* FAX *031 235947.*
An upscale central hotel, ideally situated just off the waterfront, with a
style that mixes the modern and the traditional. All rooms are fully
equipped with a telephone, television, and minibar. 🔶 🗐

THESSALONIKI: *Macedonia Palace* ⓓⓓⓓⓓ 288
Megálou Alexándrou 2, 54640. **Road map** C2. 【 *031 861400.* FAX *031 868942.*
A chic hotel within walking distance of the city center. It has an unrivaled
seafront setting and a cool, modern marbled interior. 🔒 🔶 🗐

THESSALONIKI: *Olympía* ⓓⓓⓓⓓ 110
Olýmpou 65, 54631. **Road map** C2. 【 *031 235421.* FAX *031 276133.*
This is a well-kept hotel with good facilities. It is situated in the quieter
back streets but is just a short stroll from the city center. 🔒 **P** 🔶 🗐

THESSALONIKI: *Panórama* ⓓⓓⓓⓓ 50
Analípseos 26, Panórama, 55236. **Road map** C2. 【 *031 344871.* FAX *031 341229.*
Situated in the eastern hilltop suburb of Panórama, this comfortable hotel
has a wonderful view of the city. Car or taxi is needed to reach the city
center, but the superior rooms compensate. 🔒

THESSALONIKI: *Park* ⓓⓓⓓⓓ 56
Iónos Dragoúmi 81, 54630. **Road map** C2. 【 *031 524121.* FAX *031 524193.*
located in a modern block close to the city center, the hotel offers simply
but comfortably furnished *en suite* rooms with balconies. 🔒 🔶 🗐

THESSALONIKI: *Queen Olga* ⓓⓓⓓⓓ 148
Vasilíssis Olgas 44, 54641. **Road map** C2. 【 *031 824621.* FAX *031 830550.*
A modern and comfortable hotel, the Queen Olga is close to the city
center and has some rooms that overlook the sea. 🔒

XANTHI: *Síssy* ⓓⓓ 27
Lefkíppou 14, 67100. **Road map** E1. 【 *0541 22996.* FAX *0541 73002.*
This spacious hotel offers stylish, clean rooms, most with balconies. It is
well situated near shops and restaurants and has views over Xánthi. 🔒 **P**

XANTHI: *Néstos* ⓓⓓⓓ 74
On Xánthi–Kavála road, 67100. **Road map** E1. 【 *0541 27531.* FAX *0541 27535.*
A large and modern, businesslike hotel with good facilities. It is located
outside the town center and near the railroad station. 🔒 **P** 🔶 🗐

XANTHI: *Xenía* ⓓⓓⓓ 24
Vasilíssis Sofías 9, 67100. **Road map** E1. 【 *0541 24135.* FAX *0541 27260.*
Though the Xenía is a modern hotel, the wooden interior gives it a
traditional feel. The hotel is set in a picuresque spot next to a river and
green lawns. Rooms have balconies, some with mountain views. 🔒 **P**

For key to symbols see back flap

WHERE TO EAT

To DINE OUT IN GREECE is to experience the democratic tradition at work. Rich and poor, young and old, all enjoy their favorite local restaurant, taverna, or café. Greeks consider the best places to be where the food is fresh, plentiful, and well cooked, not necessarily where the setting or the cuisine is the fanciest. Visitors, too, have come to appreciate the simplicity and health of the traditional Greek kitchen – olive oil, yogurt, vegetables, a little meat and some wine, always shared with friends. The traditional three-hour lunch and siesta – still the daily rhythm of the countryside – is now only a fading memory for most city Greeks, who have adapted to a more Western European routine. But the combination of traditional cooking and outside influences has produced a vast range of eating places in Greece, with somewhere to suit almost everyone.

A local cheese from Métsovo

The Neon restaurant in the center of Athens *(see p288)*

TYPES OF RESTAURANT

Often DIFFICULT for a visitor to find, the traditional Greek restaurant *(estiatórion)* is one of the world's most enjoyable places to eat. Friendly, noisy, and sometimes in lovely surroundings, there you will invariably find good local dishes and wines. It is a common practice in Greece for the whole family to dine together; they visit the kitchen to choose their dishes and take plenty of time to enjoy the meal.

Traditional restaurants range from the very expensive in Athens and the wealthier suburbs to the magnificently inexpensive, the best of which is called a *mageirió*. Here, there is no menu and

little choice of either food or wine. However, you will be given very fresh food, cooked in the style of the owner's home village, with drinkable, and sometimes good, barreled wine from the same area. The cheapest kind of *mageirió* is known as a *koutoúki* and is usually found in student areas and working neighborhoods of the larger towns and cities.

Many traditional restaurants specialize in either a regional cuisine, a method of cooking, or a certain type of food. In Thessaloníki and the suburbs of Athens, where Greeks from Asia Minor have settled, you can still find a *kapnistarió*, serving smoked foods – pork chops, sausages, and fish – and charcoal-grilled dishes. A *patsadzídiko*, most often found in the towns of northern Greece, serves tripe dishes.

The menu *(see pp280–81)* in a traditional restaurant tends to be short, consisting of

A sign for a taverna in Párga

a dozen *mezédes* (appetizers), about eight main dishes, four or five vegetable dishes and salads, with a dessert of fresh fruit or something sweet, and a selection of local and national wines.

Many hotels have restaurants open to nonresidents. Smaller country hotels occasionally have excellent kitchens and serve good local wines, so check on any that are close to where you are staying.

In the last few years a new breed of young Greek chefs has emerged in *kultúra* restaurants, developing a style of cooking that encompasses Greece's magnificent raw materials, flavors, and colors. These dishes are served with the exciting new Greek wines.

The Ostria restaurant *(see p293)* at Agios Ioánnis, on the Pílio peninsula

Waiter outside a restaurant in Pláka, Athens

TAVERNAS

ONE OF THE GREAT pleasures for the traveler in Greece is the tradition of the taverna, a place to eat and drink, even if you simply snack on *mezédes* (Greeks rarely drink without eating). Traditional tavernas are open from mid-evening and stay open late; occasionally they are open for lunch as well. Menus are short and seasonal – perhaps six or eight *mezédes* and four main courses consisting of casseroles and dishes cooked *tis óras* (to order), along with the usual accompaniments of vegetables, salads, fruit, and wine.

Like traditional restaurants, some tavernas specialize in the foods and wines of the owner's home region, some in a particular cooking style, and others in certain foods.

A *psarotavérna* is the place to find good fish dishes but, because fish is expensive, these tavernas often resemble restaurants and are patronized mainly by wealthy Greeks and tourists. In small fishing villages it is quite different, and you may find the rickety tables of a *psarotavérna* literally on the beach. Close to the lapping waves the owner may serve fish that he himself caught that morning.

For delicious grills try a *psistariá*, a taverna that specializes in spit-roasts and charcoal grilling *(sta kárvouna)*. In countryside *psistariés* lamb, kid, pork, chicken, game,

offal, lambs' heads, and even testicles are chargrilled, and whole lamb is roasted on the spit. At the harborside, fish and shellfish are grilled and served with fresh lemon juice and olive oil. Country, family-run tavernas and cafés will invariably provide simple meals such as omelettes and salads throughout the day, but many of these places close quite early in the evening. After your meal in the taverna, follow the Greeks and enjoy a visit to the local *zacharoplasteío (see p278)* for sweets and pastries.

CAFES AND BARS

CAFES, KNOWN AS *kafeneía*, are the pulse of Greek life, and even the tiniest hamlet has a place to drink coffee or wine. Equally important is the function it performs as the center of communication – mail is collected here, telephone calls made, and newspapers read, dissected, and discussed. *Kafeneía* serve Greek coffee, sometimes *frappé* (instant coffee served cold, in a tall glass), soft drinks, beer, ouzo, and wine. Most also serve some kind of snack to order. All open early and remain open until late at night.

Bottle of ouzo

As the social hub of their communities, country *kafeneía*, as well as many in the city, open seven days a week.

A *galaktopoleío*, or "milk shop," has a seating area where you can enjoy fine yogurt and honey; those around Plateía Omonoías in Athens remain open for most of the night.

An *oinopoleío* (wine shop with a café-bar attached) is the place to try local wines from the cask, and you may find a few bottled wines as well. The owner is invariably from a wine village or family and will often cook some simple regional specialties to accompany the wine.

In a *mezedopoleío*, or *mezés* shop, the owner will not only serve the local wine and the *mezédes* that go with it, but also ouzo and the infamous liquor raki, both distilled from the remnants of the grape harvest. Their accompanying *mezédes* are less salty than those served with wine.

No vacation in Greece is complete without a visit to an *ouzerí*. Some of the best of these are to be found in Thessaloníki and in Athens' central arcades. You can order a dozen or more little plates of savory meats, fish, and vegetables and try the many varieties of ouzo that are served in small jugs. A jug or glass of water accompanies the ouzo to wash it down. These are traditionally inexpensive, noisy, and fun places to eat and drink.

The O Vláchos taverna *(see p290)* at Mount Párnitha, north of Athens

Waitress at To Geráni restaurant in Pláka, Athens (see p288)

FAST FOOD AND SNACKS

Visitors can be forgiven for thinking Greeks never stop eating, for there seem to be snack bars on every street and vendors selling sweets, nuts, rolls, and seasonal corn and chestnuts at every turn.

Although American-style fast food outlets dominate city streets, traditional Greek eateries offer intriguing alternatives. The extremely cheap *souvlatzídiko* offers chunks of meat, fish or vegetables roasted on a skewer and served with bread, while an *ovelistírio* serves *gýros* – meat from a revolving spit in a pita bread pocket. The food is sold *sto chéri* (in the hand).

Many bakeries serve savory pies and a variety of tasty bread rolls, and in busy city neighborhoods you can always find a *kafeneío* serving substantial snacks and salads. Street vendors sell *koulourákia* (rolls), small pies, corn on the cob, roast chestnuts, nut brittle, and candies. Snacks are often local specialties: tiny open pizzas in Thessaloníki; pies of wild greens or cheese *(see p284)* in Métsovo, and small, flavorful sausages in Ioánnina.

If you have a sweet tooth you will love the *zacharoplasteío* (literally, "shop of the sugar sculptor"). The baker there makes traditional sweet breads *(see p282)*, tiny sweet pastries, and a whole variety of fragrant honey cakes.

BREAKFAST

For greeks, this is the least important meal of the day. In traditional homes and cafés a small cup of Greek coffee accompanies *paximádia* (slices of rusklike bread) or *koulourákia* (firm, sesame-covered or slightly sweet rolls in rings or s-shapes), or pound cakes with homemade jam. Elsewhere, and in many city *kafeneía*, this has been replaced by a large cup of brewed coffee and French-style croissants or delicious brioche-style rolls, also called *koulourákia*. In the summer, some *kafeneía* will still serve fresh figs, thick yogurt, pungent honey, and slightly sweet currant bread.

RESERVATIONS

The more expensive the restaurant, the more advisable it is to make a reservation, and it is always worth doing so on weekends. In country areas, and in the suburbs, it is the practice to visit the restaurant or taverna earlier in the day, or the day before, and check on the dishes to be served. The proprietor will take your order and reserve any special dish that you request.

Serving gýros on an Athens street

WINE

Restaurateurs in Greece are only now learning to serve bottled wines. If the wine list contains the better bottles, such as Ktíma

Merkoúri, Seméli, or Strofiliá, the proprietor probably knows how to store and serve the wine, and it will be safe to order a more expensive bottle. For a good-value bottle there are the nationally known Kourtáki or Boutári wines *(see p285)*.

Traditional restaurants and tavernas may stock only carafe wine, which is served straight from the barrel and is always inexpensive. Carafe wines are often of the region and, among Greek wines, the rosé in particular is noted for having an unusual but pleasing flavor.

HOW TO PAY

Greece is still largely a cash society. If you need to pay by credit card, check first that the restaurant takes credit cards, and if so, that they take the card you intend to use – many proprietors accept some but not others. *Kafeneía* almost never take credit cards, and cafés rarely, but many will be happy to take travelers' checks. In rural areas, country tavernas, restaurants, and *kafeneía* will accept only cash. The listings in this guide indicate whether or not credit cards are accepted at each establishment.

SERVICE AND TIPPING

Greeks take plenty of time when they eat out and expect a high level of attention. This means a great deal of running around on the part of

Patrons outside Thanássis kebab restaurant, Athens (see p287)

Interior patio of Ouzerí Aristotélous in Thessaloníki *(see p295)*

the waiter, but in return they receive generous tips – as much as 20 percent if the service is good, though more often a tip is 10–15 percent. Prices in traditional establishments do not usually include service, but they do include a cover charge for bread and place settings.

Western-style restaurants and tourist tavernas sometimes add a service charge to the bill; their prices can be much higher because of trimmings, such as telephones and air-conditioning.

**Bread ring
seller, Athens**

the bars. In formal restaurants children are expected to be well behaved, but in summer, when Greeks enjoy eating outside, it is perfectly acceptable for children to play and enjoy themselves too. Facilities such as high chairs are unknown except in the most considerate hotel dining rooms, but more casual restaurants and tavernas are fine for dining with children of any age.

DRESS CODE

THE GREEKS dress quite formally when dining out. Visitors should wear whatever is comfortable, but skimpy tops and shorts and active sportswear are not acceptable, except near the beach, although it is unlikely that tourist establishments would turn business away. Some of the most expensive city restaurants, especially those attached to hotels, request formal dress; the listings indicate which places fall into this category.

In summer, if you intend to dine outside, take a jacket or sweater for the evening.

CHILDREN

GREEK CHILDREN become restaurant and taverna habitués at a very early age – it is an essential part of their education. Consequently, children are welcome everywhere in Greece except in

SMOKING

SMOKING is commonplace in Greece and, with the exception of the most expensive dining rooms, you will have difficulty finding anywhere that maintains a no smoking policy. However, most restaurants are airy, and for at least half the year it is generally possible to enjoy your meal outside in the open air.

Fresh squid at a restaurant in Geroliménas, on the Máni peninsula *(see p199)*

WHEELCHAIR ACCESS

IN COUNTRY AREAS, where room is plentiful, there are few problems for wheelchair users. In city restaurants, however, it is a different matter, and access is often restricted. The streets themselves have uneven sidewalks, and many restaurants have narrow doorways and possibly steps. Restaurants that do have wheelchair access are indicated in the listings pages of this guide. Also, the organizations that are listed on page 299 provide information for disabled travelers in Greece.

VEGETARIAN FOOD

GREEK CUISINE provides plenty of choice for vegetarians. Greeks enjoy such a variety of dishes for each course that it is easy to order just vegetable dishes for first and main courses in traditional restaurants, tavernas or *kafeneía*. Vegetable dishes are substantial, inexpensive, imaginatively prepared, and satisfying.

Vegans may have more of a problem, for there are few places in Greece catering to special diets. However, since Greek cooking relies little on dairy products, it is possible to follow a vegan diet almost anywhere in Greece.

PICNICS

THE BEST TIME to picnic in Greece is in spring, when the countryside is at its most beautiful and the weather is not too hot. The traditional seasonal foods, such as Lenten olive oil bread, sweet Easter bread, pies filled with wild greens, fresh cheese, and young retsina wine, all make perfect fare for picnics. Summer is the ideal time for eating at the beach. The best foods for summer snacks are peaches and figs, yogurt and cheese, and tomatoes, various breads, and olives.

The Classic Greek Menu

THE TRADITIONAL FIRST COURSE is a selection of *mezédes*, or snacks; these can also be eaten in *ouzerí*, or bars, throughout the day. Meat or fish dishes follow next, usually served with a salad. The wine list tends to be simple, and coffee and cakes are generally consumed after the meal in a nearby pastry shop. In rural areas traditional dishes can be chosen straight from the kitchen.

Mezédes are both a first course and a snack with wine or other drinks.

Taramosaláta *is a purée of salted mullet roe and breadcrumbs or potato. Traditionally a dish for Lent, it is now on every taverna menu.*

Souvlákia *are tiny chunks of pork, flavored with lemon, herbs, and olive oil, grilled on skewers. Here they are served with* **tzatzíki**, *a refreshing mixture of creamy yogurt, cucumber, garlic, and mint.*

Olives

Fish are at their best around the coast and on the islands.

Melitzanosaláta and revythosaláta *are both purées. Melitzanosaláta, left, is grilled eggplant and herbs; and* revythosaláta, *right, is chickpeas, coriander, and garlic.*

Melitzánes imám baïldí *are eggplants filled with a ragoût of onions, tomatoes, and herbs.* **Dolmádes** *(bottom) are parcels of grape leaves tightly stuffed with currants, pine nuts, and rice.*

Fried squid

ΜΕΖΕΣ
Mezés

Ελιές
Eliés

Ταραμοσαλάτα
Taramosaláta

Τζατζίκι
Tzatzíki

Σουβλάκια
Souvlákia

Ρεβυθοσαλάτα
Revythosaláta

Μελιτζανοσαλάτα
Melitzanosaláta

Ντολμάδες
Ntolmádes

Μελιτζάνες ιμάμ μπαïλντί
Melitzánes imám baïldí

Χωριάτικη σαλάτα
Choriátiki saláta

ΨΑΡΙΑ
Psária

Πλακί
Plakí

Σχάρας
Scháras

Τηγανιτά καλαμάρια
Tiganitá kalamária

Choriátiki saláta, *Greek salad, combines tomatoes, cucumbers, onions, herbs, capers, and feta cheese.*

Scháras *means "from the grill." This summer dish of grilled swordfish is served with a salad of bitter greens.*

Psária plakí *is a whole fish baked in an open dish with carrots, leeks, and potatoes in a tomato, fennel, and olive oil sauce.*

BREAD IN GREECE

Bread is considered by Greeks to be the staff of life and is served at every meal. Village bakers vary the bread each day with flavorings of currants, herbs, wild greens, or cheese. The many Orthodox festivals are celebrated with special breads.

Olive rolls with herbs   **Pita bread, unleavened**

Paximádia (twice-baked bread)   *Koulourákia* (sweet or plain rolls)   *Tsouréki* (festival bread loaf)

ΚΡΕΑΣ
Kréas

Μουσακάς
Mousakás

Κεφτέδες
Keftédes

Χοιρινό σουβλάκι
Choirinó souvláki

Κλέφτικο
Kléftiko

ΛΑΧΑΝΙΚΑ ΚΑΙ ΣΑΛΑΤΙΚΑ
Lachaniká kai salatiká

Μελιτζάνες και κολοκυθάκια τηγανιτά
Melitzánes kai kolokythákia tiganitá

Αγκινάρες α λα πολίτα
Agkináres a la políta

Σπαράγγια σαλάτα
Sparangia saláta

ΓΛΥΚΑ
Glyká

Φρέσκα φρούτα
Fréska froúta

Σύκα στο φούρνο με μαυροδάφνη
Sýka sto foúrno me mavrodáfni

Γιαούρτι και μέλι
Giaoúrti kai méli

Meat is more readily available on the mainland than the islands.

Kebabs of grilled pork

Vegetables and salads often use wild produce.

Fried eggplants and zucchini

Artichokes with potatoes, dill, lemon, and oil

Asparagus in olive oil and lemon

Desserts are simple affairs of pastry, fruit, or yogurt.

Fresh fruit varies according to what is in season.

Mousakás *is made of layers of fried eggplant and potato slices, spicy minced meat, and savory bechamel sauce, topped with cheese.*

Keftédes *are meat patties, well flavored with herbs, coriander, and cumin, and fried in olive oil. They are served here with saffron rice.*

Sýka sto foúrno me Mavrodáfni *are fresh figs baked in Mavrodaphne wine sauce, served as a dessert or sweet treat. The sauce, of wine, spices, and honey, is flavored with orange-flower water.*

Giaoúrti kai méli *(yogurt with honey) is the most wonderful snack in Greece, served in specialty "milk shops," to be eaten there or taken home.*

Kléftiko *is usually goat meat wrapped in parchment paper and cooked so that the juices and flavors are sealed in.*

What to Eat in Athens and the Peloponnese

Slices of melon

ANCIENT GREECE regarded cooking as both a science and an art. In Athens, and through Attica and the Peloponnese, you still find the ingredients that inspired the chefs of antiquity and, later, the cuisine of the Ottoman Empire with its highly flavored meat dishes. The simplicity of Greek cooking and its reliance on fresh raw materials are what make it distinctive.

Fresh fruit and vegetable market in Argos

ATHENS

The capital is a city of immigrants from the countryside, the islands, and the shores of the eastern Mediterranean. Its diversity is reflected in the markets and the cuisine.

Sparángia kai agináres *is lightly boiled wild asparagus and artichoke hearts in an olive oil and lemon juice sauce, a typical early spring* mezés.

Avgotarácho *is the smoked and salted roe of the gray mullet. It is a rare and expensive treat.*

Souvlákia *are chunks of pork or lamb, marinated in lemon juice and herbs, then grilled on a skewer. Here it is served with a yellow saffron pilaf.*

Kotópoulo riganáto *is chicken slowly roasted on a spit or grill, glistening with olive oil and pungent with oregano, accompanied here by okra.*

Mprizóles *is a thin beef or pork steak basted with olive oil and lemon juice. Here it is served with a chopped salad.*

Riváni

Pistachios in filo pastry

Sweet pastries *filled with nuts and honey, syrup-drenched cakes, pies, doughnuts, and* glyká *(sweet fruits) are mainly eaten in cafés.*

Loukoumádes

Mpougátsa

Katéïfi   Glyká

Sweets *such as nougat,* pastéli *(honey-sesame candy),* loukoúmia *(yeast doughnuts in syrup), and* chalvás *(halva, or sweetmeats) have been a part of Athens street life since the days of Aristotle. They are sold in small shops or stalls.*

Coffee *in Greece is traditionally made from very finely ground beans boiled up with water in a long handled* mpríki *(coffee pot) and drunk from a tiny cup. It is served in cafés rather than tavernas.*

THE PELOPONNESE

Ingredients here are as varied as the terrain: fish from the sea and, from the mountains, sheep, goat, and game. From the hills come several varieties of cheese, olives, and honey.

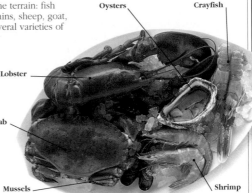

Oysters
Crayfish
Lobster
Crab
Mussels
Shrimp

Fakés is a warm or cold vegetable side dish of green lentils, black olives, lemon juice, fresh herbs, and olive oil. It is also served as a mezés, or as a main course with cheese and bread.

Shellfish and crustaceans, especially lobster and crab, are the prize catch of the Mediterranean. Delicious straight from the sea, they are traditionally char-grilled or pan-fried, sprinkled with fresh herbs, sea salt, olive oil, and lemon juice.

OLIVES AND OLIVE OIL IN GREEK COOKING

Greece produces the largest variety of olives in the world and is also a major exporter. Greek olives can be brine-cured, dry-cured in rock salt, oil-cured, or water-cured, methods that have been used for thousands of years. Olives are also pressed to extract rich olive oil. The best quality olive oil, extra-virgin, is made by pressing just-ripe olives only.

Throúmpes   Ionian green   Nafplíou

Kalamátas   Cracked green   Amfissas

Extra-virgin oil from the Máni

Can of blended olive oil for everyday use

Arní me vótana is a country casserole of lamb on the bone, herbs, and early summer vegetables: beans, carrots, tomatoes, and potatoes.

Choriátiko choirinó is a pork chop marinated in olive oil, lemon juice, sea salt, and oregano, then grilled. It is often served with a salad of chórta (wild greens).

Sýka Mavrodáfni is a dessert of dried figs that are simmered in Mavrodaphne wine and spices, and served with slices of mature kefalotýri cheese.

Kaïmáki is a very thick cream. It is served with sweet pastries and occasionally rice puddings or, as here, with walnuts drenched in honey.

What to Eat in Central and Northern Greece

MAINLAND GREECE, with its long and checkered history, is a place where regional food boundaries are blurred and a variety of cooking traditions coexist. The meat and fruit dishes of Thessaloníki reveal a Jewish influence; the spices, sausages, and oven cooking of Ioánnina stem from Ottoman times; and a love of sheep's cheese, pies, and offal came to Métsovo and the Epirus mountains with the Vlachs from Romania.

Fresh local produce in Thessaloníki bazaar

CENTRAL AND WESTERN GREECE

The regional specialties of cheese, pies, grilled or spit-roasted game, and offal are often flavored with local mountain herbs.

Spicy meat pie

Chórta (wild greens) coil pie

Olive pie

Leek pie

Píttes, *or pies, are a specialty of Epirus. Fillings range from game or offal to cheese and vegetables, often combined with rice or pasta.*

Saganáki *is a mezés or light lunch of kaséri or kefalotýri cheese, cut in slices, fried in olive oil, and served with lemon.*

Skordaliá me psári kapnistó, *found in inland areas, is a mezés of smoked fish with a garlic and walnut sauce and sharp, cracked green olives.*

Fasoláda *is an oven-baked dish of large white kidney beans, vegetables, herbs, and olive oil. It is one of Greece's staple dishes.*

Spetsofái *is made by quickly sautéeing slices of spicy country sausage with herbs and vegetables.*

Bourthéto *is a western coast specialty. Small fish are baked in an open dish and covered in a thick, spicy tomato sauce.*

Glykó kástano *is a chestnut pudding with honey and orange-blossom flavoring.*

Výssino, *a sweet snack made from morello cherries in a thick syrup, is served with slices of aged kaséri cheese.*

GREEK CHEESES

Greece produces sheep's, cow's and goat's cheeses. Each type of cheese is made according to local traditions and usually named by taste and texture, not place of origin.

Feta in olive oil

Métsovo   *Kefalotýri*   *Graviéra*   *Kaséri*

NORTHERN GREECE

The spicy food of the North is the legacy of the 1922 Greek immigrants from Asia Minor. The Balkan influence is obvious in pickles, walnuts, and yogurt.

Pasatémpo *means "to pass the time" – the purpose of this dish of lightly roasted sunflower and pumpkin seeds and pistachio nuts.*

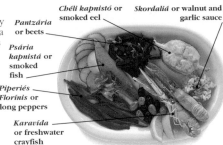

Chéli kapnistó or smoked eel

Skordaliá or walnut and garlic sauce

Pantzária or beets

Psária kapnistá or smoked fish

Piperiés Florínis or long peppers

Karavída or freshwater crayfish

This regional platter of mezédes *is made up of small traditional dishes of contrasting colors, textures, and flavors.*

Pigeon *or other small game birds are served grilled with* fáva *(yellow lentil purée) and purslane salad.*

Soutzoukákia, *a specialty of Thrace and Macedonia, are meat patties flavored with coriander, pepper, and cumin.*

Tas **kebab**, *a country dish of slowly casseroled goat, kid, mutton, or beef, is so tender it can be cut with a fork.*

Gemistá *are vegetables stuffed with rice, pine nuts, and herbs and slowly oven baked.*

Damáskina, *prunes, are filled with* kaïmáki *cream in a honey and Mavrodaphne wine syrup.*

Filo pies *are pastries filled with chopped pistachios, cinnamon, and honey.*

WHAT TO DRINK IN GREECE

Wine has been part of Greek cultural life from the earliest times. It is usually served with food. Major wine-producing areas include Attica, Macedonia, and the Peloponnese. Mavrodaphne is a fortified dessert wine produced in Pátra. Asprolíthi is a dry white wine. Both are examples of excellent modern wines. Traditional Greek specialties include *tsípouro*, distilled from the stems, pits, and skins of crushed grapes; retsina, which is wine flavored with pine resin *(see p147)*; and the strong, anise-flavored spirit, ouzo.

Asprolíthi wine

Mavrodaphne wine

Ouzo

Tsípouro

Choosing a Restaurant

THE RESTAURANTS in this guide have been selected across a wide range of price categories for their good value, traditional food, and interesting location. This chart lists the restaurants by area, starting with Athens. Use the color-coded thumb tabs, which indicate the areas covered on each page, to guide you to the relevant section of the chart.

	AIR-CONDITIONING	OUTDOOR TABLES	LIVE ENTERTAINMENT	LOCAL WINES

ATHENS

ACROPOLIS: *Strofí* ⓓⓓ
Rovértou Gkálli 25, 11742. **Map** 5 C3. ⓒ *01 921 4130.*
The rooftop views of the Acropolis attract a constant stream of diners.
The menu features all the mainstays of a Greek taverna including fried
zucchini, octopus, and roast lamb. ● *lunch; Sun.* 🗐 ● ▨ ▨

EXARCHEIA: *Mpármpa Giánnis* ⓓ
Emmanouíl Mpenáki 94, 10681. **Map** 2 F3. ⓒ *01 330 0185.*
This popular taverna offers such dishes as octopus and pasta, baked cod and
tomatoes, and seasonal cooked vegetables. ● *Sun evening; Aug.* ▨ ▨

EXARCHEIA: *Kostogánnis* ⓓⓓ
Zaími 37, 10682. **Map** 2 F2. ⓒ *01 821 2496.*
The entrance to this restaurant, within easy reach of the National
Archaeological Museum, is past an enticing buffet display of shellfish
and marinated fish platters. ● *lunch; Sun; Aug.* ● ▨ ▨

EXARCHEIA: *Oasis* ⓓⓓ
Valtetsíou 44, 10681. **Map** 2 F3. ⓒ *01 330 1369.*
Set in a beautiful garden, this taverna offers wonderful dishes such as
baked mackerel and melt-in-the-mouth roast suckling pig. ● ▨ ▨

KOLONAKI: *Dimókritos* ⓓⓓ
Dimokrítou 23, 10673. **Map** 3 A5. ⓒ *01 361 3588.*
The excellent food in this stylish taverna includes cuttlefish cooked in red
wine, tongue with lemon sauce, and a wide range of appetizers. ● *Sun; Aug.* ● ▨

KOLONAKI: *Filíppou* ⓓⓓ
Xenokrátous 19, 10675. **Map** 3 C5. ⓒ *01 721 6390.*
This Kolonáki favorite offers all the standard taverna fare. Roast chicken
with lemon potatoes and *dolmádes* are particularly good. ● *Sun; Aug 15.* ▨ ▨

KOLONAKI: *Lykóvrysi* ⓓⓓ
Plateía Kolonakíou, 10673. **Map** 3 B5. ⓒ *01 361 6712.*
A popular meeting place, the Lykóvrysi serves a few Greek dishes like
fasouláda (bean soup) alongside traditional international dishes. ● ▨

KOLONAKI: *To Kafeneío* ⓓⓓ
Loukianoú 26, 10675. **Map** 3 B5. ⓒ *01 722 9056.*
Excellent *mezédes* are served at this upscale Kolonáki *mezedopoleío.* Also
featured are some of the better new-generation Greek wines. ● *Sun; Aug.* ● ▨

KOLONAKI: *Vivliothíki* ⓓⓓ
Plateía Filikís Etaireías 18, 10673. **Map** 3 A5. ⓒ *01 363 7897.*
The lunches at this chic, French-style brasserie include smoked
salmon, steak tartare, pasta, and salads. 🗐 ● ▨ ▨

KOLONAKI: *Dekaoktó* ⓓⓓⓓ
Souidías 51, 10676. **Map** 3 C5. ⓒ *01 723 5561.*
A dozen candlelit tables, seductive *mezédes,* perfectly grilled fish, and
a good wine list make for a romantic place to dine. 🗐 ● ▨

KOLONAKI: *The Food Company* ⓓⓓⓓ
Corner of Anagnostopoúlou & Dimokrítou, 10673. **Map** 3 A4. ⓒ *01 363 0373.*
Anyone in need of real sandwiches, bagels, and carrot cake should head to
this café run by two American women. ● *Aug 1–15.* ▨

KOLONAKI: *Dódeka Apostóloi* ⓓⓓⓓⓓ
Kanári 17, 10671. **Map** 3 A5. ⓒ *01 361 9358.*
Typical *mezédes* are served in the downstairs wine bar at lunch times while
in the evenings international cuisine is offered upstairs. ● *Sun; Jun–Sep.* 🗐 ● ▨

	AIR-CONDITIONING	OUTDOOR TABLES	LIVE ENTERTAINMENT	LOCAL WINES

Average prices for a three-course meal for one, including a half-bottle of house wine, tax, and service:
Ⓓ up to 3,000 Dr
ⒹⒹ 3–5,000 Dr
ⒹⒹⒹ 5–8,000 Dr
ⒹⒹⒹⒹ 8–11,000 Dr
ⒹⒹⒹⒹⒹ over 11,000 Dr.

AIR-CONDITIONING
Restaurant with air-conditioning.

OUTDOOR TABLES
Tables for eating outdoors, often with a good view.

LIVE ENTERTAINMENT
Dancing or live music performances on various days of the week.

LOCAL WINES
A specialized selection of local Greek wines.

KOLONAKI: *Kíku*   ⒹⒹⒹ   ● · · ▨
Dimokrítou 12, 10673. **Map** 3 A5. ☎ *01 364 7033.*
The city's finest Japanese restaurant has all the ingredients you would expect: understated décor, perfect *sushi* and *sashimi*. ● *lunch; Sun; mid-Jul–mid-Aug.* ✎

LYKAVITTOS HILL: *Al Convento*   ⒹⒹⒹ   ●
Anapíron Polémou 4–6, 11521. **Map** 4 D4. ☎ *01 723 9163.*
One of the city's better Italian restaurants, the food includes old favorites such as spaghetti *al vongole* and *carbonara* as well as *carpaccio*, arugula, and parmesan. ● *lunch; Sun.* ✎

LYKAVITTOS HILL: *Senor Frog*   ⒹⒹⒹⒹ   ●
Anapíron Polémou 10, 11521. **Map** 3 B5. ☎ *01 722 4524.*
Drink margaritas and sample the city's best Mexican food, especially the baked stuffed crab and *fajitas,* in this popular restaurant. ● *lunch; Mon; Jun 15–20.* ✎

MAKRYGIANNI: *Socrates' Prison*   ⒹⒹ   ● ▨ · ▨
Mitsaíon 20, 11742. **Map** 6 D3. ☎ *01 922 3434.*
Close to the Herodes Atticus theater, this popular taverna offers mainly Greek cuisine. The house wine is excellent. ● *lunch; Sun; Aug 10–31.* ✎

MONASTIRAKI: *Sigálas*   Ⓓ   · ▨
Plateía Monastirakíou 2, 10555. **Map** 2 D5. ☎ *01 321 3036.*
Wine barrels and colorful murals decorate this long-established taverna that still offers classic Greek dishes such as stuffed tomatoes and *mousakás.* ✎

MONASTIRAKI: *Thanásis*   Ⓓ   ●
Mitropóleos 69, 10555. **Map** 6 D1. ☎ *01 324 4705.*
This is a favorite spot for some of the best and least expensive grilled food in the city. Try the kebabs of spiced meat, onions, tomato, and parsley, wrapped in grilled pita bread. ● *Jan 1, Easter Sun, Dec 25.*

MONASTIRAKI: *Cafe Avissynia*   ⒹⒹ   ● ▨ ● ▨
Plateía Avissynías, 10555. **Map** 5 C1. ☎ *01 321 7047.*
Tables are always packed for the accordionist and singer who perform every weekend. During the week, when the café is quieter, is a better time to sample the unusual Macedonian dishes. ● *Aug.* ✎

MONASTIRAKI: *Oinodíki*   ⒹⒹⒹ   ● ▨ · ▨
Plateía Avissynías, 10555. **Map** 5 C1. ☎ *01 321 5465.*
This tiny wine bar offers one of the best wine lists in the city and a limited selection of *mezédes* to complement the wines. ● *Jul–Aug.* ✎

MONASTIRAKI: *Koutí*   ⒹⒹⒹⒹ   ● ▨
Adrianoú 23, 10555. **Map** 6 D1. ☎ *01 321 2836.*
Set in a well-restored 19th-century house overlooking the ancient Agora, this restaurant serves fresh Mediterranean food. ● *Mon evening; Aug.* ✎

OMONOIA: *Andréas*   ⒹⒹ   · ▨ · ▨
Themistokléous 18, 10678. **Map** 2 E3. ☎ *01 382 1522.*
Set in a small alley off Themistokléous, this *ouzerí* specializes in seafood such as octopus, shellfish, anchovies, and fried squid. ● *Sat evening; Sun; Aug 1–20.*

OMONOIA: *Athinaikón*   ⒹⒹ   ● · · ▨
Themistokléous 2, 10678. **Map** 2 E3. ☎ *01 383 8485.*
This old establishment serves a wide range of well-executed and delicious fish and meat *mezédes*. Meals are accompanied by carafes of ouzo and wine. ● *Sun; Aug.*

OMONOIA: *Néon*   ⒹⒹ   ●
Dórou 1, 10431. **Map** 2 E3. ☎ *01 523 6409.*
All-day eating at this self-service chain restaurant includes a salad bar, fresh pasta, grilled meats, and typical oven-baked Greek dishes.

For key to symbols see back flap

<table>
<tr><td>

Average prices for a three-course meal for one, including a half-bottle of house wine, tax, and service:
Ⓓ up to 3,000 Dr
ⒹⒹ 3–5,000 Dr
ⒹⒹⒹ 5–8,000 Dr
ⒹⒹⒹⒹ 8–11,000 Dr
ⒹⒹⒹⒹⒹ over 11,000 Dr.

</td><td>

AIR-CONDITIONING
Restaurant with air-conditioning.

OUTDOOR TABLES
Tables for eating outdoors, often with a good view.

LIVE ENTERTAINMENT
Dancing or live music performances on various days of the week.

LOCAL WINES
A specialized selection of local Greek wines.

</td></tr>
</table>

		AIR-CONDITIONING	OUTDOOR TABLES	LIVE ENTERTAINMENT	LOCAL WINES
PANGRATI: *Kallimármaron* Efforíonos 13, 11636. **Map** 7 B2. **℃** *01 701 9727.* Situated behind the Panathenaic stadium, this relaxed restaurant provides hearty Greek cooking. Try the unusual *kókoras* (cockerel) with pasta or wild boar and garlic sauce. ● *Sun evening; mid–Aug 31.* 🗐	ⒹⒹ		▣		▣
PANGRATI: *Mánesis* Márkou Mousoúrou 3, 11636. **Map** 7 A4. **℃** *01 922 7684.* A lovely garden and dishes such as baked shrimp and lamb make this taverna very popular in the summer. ● *lunch; Aug 10–20.*	ⒹⒹ	●	▣		▣
PANGRATI: *Spondí* Pýrronos 5, 11636. **Map** 7 B4. **℃** *01 726 4021.* This restaurant, in a restored Neo-Classical house, serves food with Greek and Pacific influences. Dishes include steamed grouper. ● *lunch; Mon; Aug.* 🗐	ⒹⒹⒹⒹ	●	▣		▣
PLAKA: *O Damígos* Kydathinaíon 41, 10558. **Map** 6 E2. **℃** *01 322 5084.* This basement taverna specializes in salt cod and garlic sauce, chunky French fries and salad. The chilled retsina is excellent. ● *Jun–Sep.*	Ⓓ				▣
PLAKA: *To Geráni* Tripódon 14, 10557. **Map** 6 E2. **℃** *01 324 7605.* A popular restaurant set in a Neo-Classical house with balcony seating and walls crowded with Greek ephemera. Try the sausages flambéed in ouzo and *saganáki* (fried cheese).	Ⓓ	●	▣		
PLAKA: *Byzantinó* Kydathinaíon 18, 10558. **Map** 6 E2. **℃** *01 322 7368.* Excellent daily specials such as the *chtapódi krasáto* (octopus) and baked vegetable dishes entice the locals to this old-fashioned taverna. 🗐	ⒹⒹ	●	▣		
PLAKA: *Eden* Lysíou 12, off Mnisikléous,10556. **Map** 6 E1. **℃** *01 324 8858.* Housed in a Neo-Classical building with modern interior, this is Athens' oldest vegetarian restaurant. Food is made with organically grown produce. ● *Tue.* 🗐	ⒹⒹ	●			
PLAKA: *Symposion* Mnisikléous 246, 10556. **Map** 6 D1. **℃** *01 325 4940.* This lively *ouzerí* serves traditional Greek food such as *dolmádes* as well as grills and spinach and cheese pies. Retsina is served from the barrel. 🗐	ⒹⒹ	●	▣	●	▣
PLAKA: *Tsekoúras* Corner of Tripódon & Epichármou 2, 10558. **Map** 6 E2. **℃** *01 323 3710.* Distinguished by its indoor fig tree, this inexpensive and cheerful taverna serves delicious fava beans, stewed snails, salads, and grills. ● *lunch; Aug.*	ⒹⒹ				▣
PLAKA: *Xynoú* Géronta 4, 10558. **Map** 6 E2. **℃** *01 322 1065.* Favored by the old Athenian aristocracy who enjoy the simple setting and food. Unsophisticated murals and a strolling trio of guitarists add to the charm of this simple taverna. ● *lunch; Sat, Sun; Jul.*	ⒹⒹ		▣	●	▣
PLAKA: *Dáfni* Lysikrátous 4, 10557. **Map** 6 E2. **℃** *01 322 7971.* Garish frescoes adorn the walls of this converted Neo-Classical mansion. Stick to the simple dishes, such as swordfish or *keftédes* (pork or beef meatballs). ● *lunch; Nov–Apr: Sun.* 🗐	ⒹⒹⒹⒹ	●	▣	●	▣
PSYRRI: *I Palaiá Agorá* Plateía Theátrou 2, 10552. **Map** 1 C4. **℃** *01 321 1115.* Set in a whitewashed courtyard with green-painted wine barrels, this decent taverna offers dishes such as *plakí* (baked fish). ● *Tue, Wed evening.*	Ⓓ		▣	●	▣

PSYRRI: *Plateía Iróon*
Karaïskáki 34, 10554. **Map** 1 C5. **(** *01 321 1915.*
Good food and drink along with *rempétika* music contribute to the
noisy, amiable atmosphere of this small café.

PSYRRI: *Tavérna tou Psyrrí*
Aischýlou 12, 10554. **Map** 2 D5. **(** *01 321 4923.*
With an owner from the Cycladic island of Náxos, the food in this taverna
relies heavily on the island's delicious vegetables, meat, and fish. End the
meal with a slice of Náxos *graviéra* cheese. ● *Sun evening; Aug 15–20.*

PSYRRI: *To Díporto*
Sokrátous 9, 10552. **Map** 2 D4. **(** *01 321 1463.*
This archetypal taverna, hidden beneath an olive shop, serves a few delicious
dishes each day such as *revíthia* (chickpeas), *fasouláda* (bean soup), grilled
sardines, and always a meat stew. ● *Sun; Easter day; Dec 25.*

PSYRRI: *I Stoá toun Athanáton*
Evripídou 63, 10554. **Map** 2 D4. **(** *01 325 1513.*
Tucked away in an alley, this old taverna has been serving warming
beef stews, grills, and soups for many years. Birds in a large cage and
faded Aegean photographs amuse the clientele. ● *Aug.*

PSYRRI: *Vitrína*
Navárchou Apostóli 7, 10554. **Map** 1 C5. **(** *01 321 1200.*
Stuffed chicken with eggplant and herbs, and lamb with red wine,
and cardamom sauce are among the more successful innovative
dishes at this modern-style restaurant. ● *Tue–Sat lunch; Mon; Aug.*

SYNTAGMA: *Apótsos*
Panepistimíou 10, 10671. **Map** 2 F5. **(** *01 363 7046.*
A famous lunch-time haunt serving some fine *mezédes* to a distinguished
clientele of businessmen, politicians, and writers. ● *evening; Sun; Aug.*

SYNTAGMA: *Ideal*
Panepistimíou 46, 10678. **Map** 2 E3. **(** *01 330 3000.*
Since 1922, this much-loved institution has been serving excellent Greek and
international cuisine. Specials include milk-fed veal with eggplant, stuffed
zucchini, and *agkináres a la políta* (artichokes in lemon juice). ● *Sun.*

SYNTAGMA: *Kentrikón*
Kolokotróni 3, 10562. **Map** 2 E5. **(** *01 323 2482.*
This quiet, understated restaurant offers a wide spectrum of Greek dishes,
such as lamb in lemon sauce, pilafs, and grilled liver. ● *evening; Sat, Sun.*

SYNTAGMA: *Strofiliá*
Plateía Karítsi, 10561. **Map** 2 E5. **(** *01 323 4803.*
Named after the owner's excellent wine made in Attica, this bar offers a wide
range of wines by the glass and a few interesting *mezédes*. ● *Jun–mid-Sep.*

SYNTAGMA: *Delfoí*
Níkis 13, 10557. **Map** 6 F1. **(** *01 323 4869.*
This discreet restaurant offers a large selection of fine grills, slow-
baked stews, and a variety of salads. ● *Sun.*

SYNTAGMA: *GB Corner*
Hotel Grande Bretagne, Plateía Syntágmatos, 10563. **Map** 6 F1. **(** *01 331 4444.*
This is a long-established restaurant serving *bauté* Greek and international
food. The service is impeccable.

THISEIO: *Iródeion*
Apostólou Pávlou 29, 11851. **Map** 5 B1. **(** *01 346 1585*
Unusual *mezédes* such as fried chicken breast and stuffed *kalámari* are served at
this traditional *mezedopoleío*. A warm atmosphere and Acropolis views.

THISEIO: *Ta Vrachákia*
Corner of Ortynaíon & Pnýkos, 11851. **Map** 5 B2. **(** *01 346 6783.*
A fine view of the Acropolis is the main reason for dining at this simple grill
house. Salads, meats, and french fries are the main fare. ● *lunch.*

THISEIO: *Pil Poul*
Corner of Apostólou Pávlou & Poulopoúlou, 11851. **Map** 5 B1. **(** *01 342 3665.*
Fashionable Mediterranean cooking and views of the Acropolis draw the
crowds to this busy and expensive restaurant. ● *Sun.*

Average prices for a three-course meal for one, including a half-bottle of house wine, tax, and service:

Ⓓ up to 3,000 Dr
ⒹⒹ 3–5,000 Dr
ⒹⒹⒹ 5–8,000 Dr
ⒹⒹⒹⒹ 8–11,000 Dr
ⒹⒹⒹⒹⒹ over 11,000 Dr.

AIR-CONDITIONING
Restaurant with air-conditioning.

OUTDOOR TABLES
Tables for eating outdoors, often with a good view.

LIVE ENTERTAINMENT
Dancing or live music performances on various days of the week.

LOCAL WINES
A specialized selection of local Greek wines.

	AIR-CONDITIONING	OUTDOOR TABLES	LIVE ENTERTAINMENT	LOCAL WINES
AROUND ATHENS				
ANAVYSOS: *Vláchos* Ⓓ		■		■
GLYFADA: *O Tzórtzis* ⒹⒹ	●	■		■
KALLITHEA: *Valentína* ⒹⒹ		■		
KIFISIA: *O Mpókaris* ⒹⒹ	●	■		■
KOROPI: *To Alsos* ⒹⒹ		■		
MAROUSI: *Altamíra* ⒹⒹⒹ	●	■		
MOUNT PARNITHA: *O Vláchos* Ⓓ				■
PIRAEUS: *Alli Skála* ⒹⒹ	●	■		■
PIRAEUS: *Vasílenas* ⒹⒹ		■		■
PIRAEUS: *Kóllias* ⒹⒹⒹ	●	■	●	■
PIRAEUS: *Dourámbeis* ⒹⒹⒹⒹ	●	■		■

ANAVYSOS: *Vláchos*   Ⓓ
Leofóros Anavýsou, 19013. **Road map** D4. 📞 *0291 54669.*
Meat grills, dips such as *tzatzíki* (yogurt and cucumber) and other standard Greek fare can be enjoyed at this traditional taverna with a wooden interior. The vine-covered patio is a pleasant place to dine during the summer.

GLYFADA: *O Tzórtzis*   ⒹⒹ
Konstantinoupóleos 4, 16675. **Road map** D4. 📞 *01 894 6020.*
Situated in Glyfáda, 2 km (1 mile) north of Vouliágmeni, this classic taverna survives amid Glyfáda's blaring fast-food joints. *Biftéki* (hamburgers), chicken, and fried zucchini are some of the specialties.

KALLITHEA: *Valentína*   ⒹⒹ
Lykoúrgou 235, 17675. **Road map** D4. 📞 *01 943 1871.*
In the area of Kallithéa, 2 km (1 mile) southwest of the Acropolis, this tiny taverna with its ethnic Pontian cuisine and chilled vodka is popular with Russian diners. Food includes pickles, breads, and stuffed cabbage leaves. 🗒

KIFISIA: *O Mpókaris*   ⒹⒹ
Acharnón & Sokrátous 17, 14561. **Road map** D4. 📞 *01 801 2589.*
This famed garden taverna specializes in grills, *stifádo* (sausage stew) and traditional aromatic pies. Try the house rosé and white wines which are excellent. ● *Mon–Sat lunch; Aug.*

KOROPI: *To Alsos*   ⒹⒹ
Leofóros Lavríou 21, 19400. **Road map** D4. 📞 *01 664 2714.*
Situated in Koropí, 6 km (4 miles) south of Paianía, this grill-house offers perfectly roasted lamb and pork, served with large helpings of salads and vegetables, in a quiet garden setting.

MAROUSI: *Altamíra*   ⒹⒹⒹ
Perikléous 28, 15122. **Road map** D4. 📞 *01 612 8841.*
Mexican, Arabic, and Asian cuisines meet in a mad culinary mix at this popular restaurant in Maroúsi, 15 km (9 miles) north of Athens. ● *lunch; Sun; Aug 1–15.* 🗒

MOUNT PARNITHA: *O Vláchos*   Ⓓ
Leofóros Párnithos, Párnitha, 13671. **Road map** D4. 📞 *01 246 3762*
Situated in Párnitha, in the foothills of Mount Párnitha, this atmospheric taverna serves traditional Greek cuisine. Specialties are their meat grills.

PIRAEUS: *Alli Skála*   ⒹⒹ
Serífou 57, Kamínia, 18541. **Road map** D4. 📞 *01 482 7722.*
Real home cooking and a courtyard filled with banana trees distinguish this elegant restaurant. The food is outstanding and includes cuttlefish, organ dishes, and stuffed peppers with caper leaves. ● *lunch.*

PIRAEUS: *Vasílenas*   ⒹⒹ
Aitolikoú 72, 18545. **Road map** D4. 📞 *01 461 2457.*
This restaurant offers a perfect introduction to Greek cuisine, with 16 dishes brought to the table in succession. ● *lunch; Sun; Aug 1–20.*

PIRAEUS: *Kóllias*   ⒹⒹⒹ
Stratigoú Plastíra 3, Taboúria, 18756. **Road map** D4. 📞 *01 462 9620.*
In typically Aegean surroundings, superb fish and appetizers such as *garidósoupa* (prawn and tomato soup) are available. ● *Sun; Aug 1–15.* 🗒

PIRAEUS: *Dourámbeis*   ⒹⒹⒹⒹ
Aktí Dilavéri 29, 18533. **Road map** D4. 📞 *01 412 2092.*
Opened in 1932, this is arguably the best fish restaurant in Piraeus. All the fish comes from the islands of Ios, Náxos, and Páros, and is served with delicious salads. ● *Aug.* 🗒

PIRAEUS: *Varoúlko* ⒹⒹⒹⒹ
Deligiórgi 14, 18533. **Road map** D4. **[** *01 411 2043.*
Reservations are necessary at this backstreet restaurant. The innovative
chef, Leftéris Lázarou, prepares such dishes as shrimp and artichokes,
seafood *dolmádes*, and mussel and lentil salad. ● *lunch; Sun; Aug.* 🍴

VARI: *Ta Vláchika* ⒹⒹ
Leofóros Váris 35, 16672. **Road map** D4. **[** *01 895 6141.*
One of the best of the many meat restaurants in Vári, 2 km (1 mile) north of
Vouliagméni, Ta Vláchika specializes in spit-roast kid, lamb, and suckling pig.
Try the oven-roasted goat and *kokorétsi* (piquant heart and liver sausage).

VARKIZA: *Esplanade* ⒹⒹⒹ
Leofóros Poseidónos 16, 16672. **Road map** D4. **[** *01 897 1760.*
An old-fashioned waterfront café that offers Greek and international
dishes, as well as a patisserie, ice creams, and drinks. 🍴

VOULIAGMENI: *Lámpros* ⒹⒹⒹⒹ
Leofóros Poseidónos 20, 16671. **Road map** D4. **[** *01 896 0144.*
Located at the water's edge since 1889, this famed restaurant has
a variety of seafood, salads, and meat dishes. A good wine list
complements the freshly grilled mullet and sea bream. ● *Sun evening.*

THE PELOPONNESE

ANCIENT CORINTH: *Archontikó* ⒹⒹ
On shore road, 20100. **Road map** C4. **[** *0741 27968.*
A family-run concern where the *mezédes* such as *sieftalíes* (charcoal-grilled
minced pork sausages) are more daring than the main courses. Fair-sized
portions are accompanied by excellent house rosé. ● *lunch; Easter period.*

ANDRITSAINA: *O Giorgís* Ⓓ
Main square, 27061. **Road map** C4. **[** *0626 22004.*
Situated near the temple of Bassae, this well-respected, tree-shaded
taverna produces standard oven-cooked food.

GEROLIMENAS: *Akrogiáli* Ⓓ
Town beach, 23071. **Road map** C5. **[** *0733 54204.*
The ground-floor restaurant of this modern, 1970s hotel is a veritable
oasis when touring the Inner Máni. The restaurant specializes in
fish dishes, but meat grills are also available.

GYTHEIO: *I Kózia* Ⓓ
Vasiléos Pávlou 13, 23200. **Road map** C5. **[** *0733 24086.*
An exception among the tourist-orientated tavernas along the
waterfront in Gýtheio, the Kózia often has a small crowd at the
front admiring its arresting display of fish on ice. 🍴

GYTHEIO: *O Kóstas* Ⓓ
Konstantínou Sachíni, 23200. **Road map** C5. **[** *0733 22084.*
This basic taverna offers good Greek cuisine such as veal *stifádo.*
Vegetarian dishes include fresh *fasolákia* (green beans).

KALAMATA: *I Kríni* Ⓓ
Evangelistrías 40, 24101. **Road map** C5. **[** *0721 24474.*
An old family-run taverna offering fresh fish of the day and good home
cooking. Enjoy the atmospheric *rempétika* music. ● *lunch; Sun.*

KARDAMYLI: *Léla's* ⒹⒹ
Off main square, near the old factory, 24040. **Road map** D5. **[** *0721 73541.*
The food at one of the oldest tavernas in Kardamýli, 34 km (21 miles) south of
Kalamáta, has remained largely unaffected. Greek oven dishes with German
draught beer are offered as well as ocean views and impromptu music.

KORINTHOS: *Anaxagóras* Ⓓ
Agíou Nikoláou 31, 20100. **Road map** C4. **[** *0741 26933.*
Situated in Kórinthos, 6 km (4 miles) northeast of ancient Corinth, this local
favorite offers a mix of seafood, meat, and *mezédes* as well as a limited range
of oven dishes such as baked eggplant.

KORONI: *Kagkelários* Ⓓ
Waterfront, 24004. **Road map** C5. **[** *0725 22648.*
Of four adjacent dockside eateries, this has the most imaginative menu.
Mussels, sea urchins, shrimp, and small local fish are reasonably priced. 🍴

For key to symbols see back flap

Average prices for a three-course meal for one, including a half-bottle of house wine, tax, and service:
Ⓓ up to 3,000 Dr
ⒹⒹ 3–5,000 Dr
ⒹⒹⒹ 5–8,000 Dr
ⒹⒹⒹⒹ 8–11,000 Dr
ⒹⒹⒹⒹⒹ over 11,000 Dr.

AIR-CONDITIONING
Restaurant with air-conditioning.

OUTDOOR TABLES
Tables for eating outdoors, often with a good view.

LIVE ENTERTAINMENT
Dancing or live music performances on various days of the week.

LOCAL WINES
A specialized selection of local Greek wines.

		AIR-CONDITIONING	OUTDOOR TABLES	LIVE ENTERTAINMENT	LOCAL WINES
METHONI: *I Klimatariá* Plateía Polytechníou, 24006. **Road map** B5. Ⓒ *0723 31544.* Regarded as one of the best restaurants for its gourmet preparation of Greek dishes, the menu includes a wide variety of vegetarian dishes. ⬤ *Nov–mid-May.* ▨	Ⓓ	●	▣		▣
MONEMVASIA: *I Matoúla* Main through road, 23070. **Road map** C5. Ⓒ *0732 61660.* For many decades this was the only taverna in Monemvasía. All traditional dishes can be enjoyed under a giant fig tree in the garden. ⬤ *Oct–Mar: Mon–Wed.*	Ⓓ		▣		
NAFPLIO: *Omorfi Póli* Corner of Kotsonopoúlou 1 & Vassilísis Olgas, 21100. **Road map** C4. Ⓒ *0752 25944.* A varied menu of Greek casseroles and grills with generous portions. Booking is necessary, since there are only 15 indoor tables. ⬤ *lunch.* ▨	Ⓓ		▣		▣
NAFPLIO: *O Vasílis* Staïkopoúlou 22, 21100. **Road map** C4. Ⓒ *0752 25334.* Of all the competing restaurants along Staïkopoúlou, this is one of the oldest and the best for hearty Greek food. ⬤ *Oct–Mar: Tue; Nov 15–30.* ▨	Ⓓ	●	▣	●	▣
NAFPLIO: *Ta Fanária* Corner of Staïkopoúlou 13 & Soútsou, 21100. **Road map** C4. Ⓒ *0752 27141.* This long-running favorite offers seating under grapevines. It is best visited at lunch when dishes, including good *mousaká*, emerge fresh from the oven. There is also good bulk retsina from Mégara. ⬤ *Nov 15–30.* ▨	Ⓓ		▣		▣
NAFPLIO: *Zormpás* Staïkopoúlou 30, 21100. **Road map** C4 Ⓒ *0752 25319.* This family-run taverna prepares all the standard Greek dishes. Try the delicious homemade fish soup or the octopus. ▨	Ⓓ	●	▣		
NEOS MYSTRAS: *O Mystrás* Main square, 23100. **Road map** C5. Ⓒ *0731 20047.* This traditional taverna in Néos Mystrás, 1 km (0.5 miles) east of the Byzantine site of Mystrás, serves mountainous portions of the best vegetable stews in the Peloponnese, as well as olives and meat grills. ⬤ *Nov–Mar.*	Ⓓ		▣		▣
OLYMPIA: *Dionysos* Praxitélous Kordíli, 27065. **Road map** B4. Ⓒ *0624 22032.* Lamb *frikasse* (egg and lemon sauce) and other Greek specialties can be enjoyed under the great plane tree of this taverna in Olympia, 500 m (1,600 ft) east of ancient Olympia. ⬤ *Dec 15–Jan 30.*	Ⓓ		▣		▣
OLYMPIA: *Kladaíos* Behind railroad station, 27065. **Road map** B4. Ⓒ *0624 23322.* Situated in Olympia, 500 m (1,600 ft) east of ancient Olympia, this popular restaurant is highly regarded for its *mezédes*. It is beautifully situated overlooking the river. Seating here is limited so arrive early to be sure of a place. ⬤ *lunch.*	Ⓓ		▣		▣
PATRA: *Lavýrinthos* Poukevil 44, 26223. **Road map** C4. Ⓒ *061 226436.* This taverna offers unusual interpretations of regular Greek dishes. Food is accompanied by wine from the barrels decorating the taverna. ⬤ *Sun.*	Ⓓ				▣
PYLOS: *O Grigóris* Georgíou Krasánou, 24001. **Road map** C5. Ⓒ *0723 22621.* During the summer, tasty oven casseroles are served in the rear garden. Charcoal-grilled fish is available on request. ⬤ *Easter period; Oct.*	Ⓓ		▣		▣
SPARTI: *Elysé* Konstantínou Palaiológou 113, 23100. **Road map** C5. Ⓒ *0731 29896.* This elegant restaurant with pastel-pink decor offers a good range of traditional Greek oven casseroles and grills. ▨	Ⓓ		▣		▣

CENTRAL AND WESTERN GREECE

AGIOS IOANNIS: *Ostria*   ⓓ ● ▦   ▦
On shore road, 37012. **Road map** D3. 📞 *0426 31331.*
Situated in Agios Ioánnis, 25 km (16 miles) north of Miliés, this restaurant serves
mouthwatering examples of typical Pílio dishes such as rabbit stew *(kounéli
kokkinistó)* and wild greens pie *(chortópita).* ● *Tue, Wed, Thu lunch; Nov–Mar.*

ARACHOVA: *Karathanásis*   ⓓ   ▦   ▦
Delfón 56, 32004. **Road map** C3. 📞 *0267 31360.*
A family-run taverna in the heart of Aráchova, 11 km (8 miles) east of ancient
Delphi, offering simple grills and stews with fresh bread. ● *Easter day.*

ARACHOVA: *O Sákis*   ⓓ ● ▦   ▦
Delfón 51, 32004. **Road map** C3. 📞 *0267 31984.*
This restaurant in Aráchova, 11 km (8 miles) east of ancient Delphi,
serves "mountain" food staples such as beef, chicken, pasta, goat, and
pork. The salads are ample and liberally sprinkled with herbs. ● *Jul–Aug.*

IOANNINA: *Kípos*   ⓓ ● ▦   ▦
Karaïskáki 20, 45444. **Road map** B2. 📞 *0651 78287.*
This pleasant taverna stands out for its fresh approach to traditional
Greek dishes, flavoring the ever-popular pork and lamb with
traditional herbs and spices. ● *lunch; Easter period, Aug 12–28.*

IOANNINA: *Própodes*   ⓓ ● ▦
Nisí, 45500. **Road map** B2. 📞 *0651 81803.*
A good island restaurant, well worth the short boat trip to eat there in the
evening. Eel and crayfish from the local lake are available as well as
trout from fish farms in the mountains. 🥗

IOANNINA: *To Manteío*   ⓓ ● ▦   ▦
Plateía Neomártyros Georgíou 15, 45221 **Road map** B2. 📞 *0651 25452.*
Enjoy charcoal-grilled meats and *souvláki* on the vine-canopied terrace of
this taverna. Fruit or halva are on the house. ● *Easter day, Jul 26–27, Dec 25.*

KALAMPAKA: *Metéora*   ⓓ   ▦
Plateía Dimarcheíou, 42200. **Road map** B2. 📞 *0432 22316.*
Wholesome Greek food prepared by the owner's wife and the usual menu
of salads, *mousakás*, and grills can be enjoyed here. ● *mid-Nov mid-Mar.*

KALAMPAKA: *O Kípos tou Ilía*   ⓓ ● ▦ ● ▦
At entrance to village, 42200. **Road map** B2. 📞 *0432 23216.*
Set in a traditional old house with a fireplace for winter dining, this restaurant
offers good Greek cuisine at reasonable prices. There is a large choice of
appetizers and salads as well as homemade deserts. ● *Nov–Apr: Mon.*

KASTRAKI: *Metéora*   ⓓ   ▦   ▦
On Kastráki–Metéora road, 42200. **Road map** B2. 📞 *0437 22285.*
Close to the Metéora rocks, this simple taverna is set in an old house and
serves traditional Greek cuisine. All food is freshly made and there is a fire
in winter as well as a garden for the summer months. ● *main public hols.*

KASTRAKI: *Parádeisos*   ⓓ   ▦   ▦
On the main road to the Metéora, 42200. **Road map** B2. 📞 *0432 22723.*
This modern grill-house, within close proximity to Metéora, offers all the
standard Greek fare. There is a beautiful, flower-filled garden.

MAKRINITSA: *Pántheon*   ⓓ   ▦   ▦
Main square, 37011. **Road map** D3. 📞 *0421 99324.*
Views over Vólos, 14 km (9 miles) north, would be reason enough to sit
here, but locals also drive up here to sample Pílio cooking, such as the
spicy sausage, pepper, and tomato stew known as *spetzofái.*

METSOVO: *Athínai*   ⓓ   ▦   ▦
Main square, 44200. **Road map** B2. 📞 *0656 41332.*
The menu in this traditionally decorated, family-run taverna includes game
dishes in season but also vegetarian specialties such as leek pie and bean soup.

METSOVO: *Galaxías*   ⓓ   ▦   ▦
Main square, 44200. **Road map** B2. 📞 *0656 41123.*
Housed in a traditional stone building with wooden ceilings and a veranda
overlooking the square, the menu features regional cuisine including
kokorétsi (grilled organ kebab) and beef cooked in a clay pot. 🥗

For key to symbols see back flap

<table>
<tr><td colspan="4">

Average prices for a three-course meal for one, including a half-bottle of house wine, tax, and service:
ⓓ up to 3,000 Dr
ⓓⓓ 3–5,000 Dr
ⓓⓓⓓ 5–8,000 Dr
ⓓⓓⓓⓓ 8–11,000 Dr
ⓓⓓⓓⓓⓓ over 11,000 Dr.

</td></tr>
</table>

AIR-CONDITIONING
Restaurant with air-conditioning.

OUTDOOR TABLES
Tables for eating outdoors, often with a good view.

LIVE ENTERTAINMENT
Dancing or live music performances on various days of the week.

LOCAL WINES
A specialized selection of local Greek wines.

	AIR-CONDITIONING	OUTDOOR TABLES	LIVE ENTERTAINMENT	LOCAL WINES
METSOVO: *To Metsovítiko Salóni* ⓓ Tosítsa, next to post office, 44200. **Road map** B2. 📞 0656 42142. A stylish restaurant decorated in Métsovo mountain style, with rugs and wall hangings. The menu features Métsovo specialties such as *spetzofái*, with seasonal game dishes and the local red wine, *katói*.		▪	●	▪
MILIES: *Paliós Stathmós* ⓓ Old railroad station, 37010. **Road map** D3. 📞 0423 86425. This stylish restaurant–guesthouse has an Italian chef who produces delightful food, such as beef in lemon sauce, in the equally delightful setting of the old railroad station. ● *Mon; Nov.*		▪		▪
MONODENDRI: *Kateerína's Art* ⓓⓓ By Víkos Gorge, 44010. **Road map** B2. 📞 0653 61233. Housed in a typical grand Zagorian house near the Víkos Gorge, this restaurant offers many Zagorian specialties such as *alevrópita* (a rich cheese pie) and traditional mountain game dishes in season.		▪	●	▪
PARGA: *Floísvos* ⓓ Mavrogénous 10, 48060. **Road map** B3. 📞 0684 31624. The menu of this restaurant may offer few surprises but the food is reliable, a good value for the money, and enhanced by stunning views of the Ionian coastline. ● *mid-Oct–May.*	●	▪	●	▪
PARGA: *Tzímas* ⓓ Anexartisías 63, 48060. **Road map** B3. 📞 0684 31251. One of several restaurants enjoying lovely views of the Ionian sea, this waterfront taverna offers fresh fish of the day as well as all the standard traditional Greek dishes. ● *Nov–Mar.*	●	▪		
PARGA: *Vílla Noúli* ⓓ Sarakiníka, 48060. **Road map** B3. 📞 0684 35239. Fresh fish is a specialty at this waterfront restaurant. Daily specials vary but expect to see snapper, mullet, tuna, and swordfish. ● *Nov–Mar.*		▪	●	

NORTHERN GREECE

	AIR-CONDITIONING	OUTDOOR TABLES	LIVE ENTERTAINMENT	LOCAL WINES
ALEXANDROUPOLI: *Klimatariá* ⓓ Polytechníou 18, 68100. **Road map** E1. 📞 0551 26288. This restaurant is noted for its large menu, which covers all the basic Greek dishes such as *mousakás* and stuffed peppers as well as fresh fish and regional specialties such as *katsikáki* (baked goat). 🍴	●	▪		▪
ALEXANDROUPOLI: *Neráïda* ⓓ Kýprou 5, 68100. **Road map** E1. 📞 0551 22867. One of several eating places around Plateía Kýprou, this stylish restaurant is a popular choice and specializes in seafood.		▪	●	▪
KASTORIA: *Omónoia* ⓓ Mitropóleos 97, 52100. **Road map** B2. 📞 0467 23964. This busy restaurant, situated on a small square in the upper town has a changing menu. It serves all the regular dishes as well as some vegetarian options like bean stew. The fish soup is strong and filling.		▪		▪
KAVALA: *Michalákis* ⓓ Kassándrou 1, 65403. **Road map** D1. 📞 051 221185. This pleasant taverna offers meat and typical Greek dishes, such as stuffed tomatoes. Fresh fish is also featured on the menu.	●	▪		▪
KAVALA: *Pános Zafíra* ⓓ Karaolí Dimitríou 20, 65302. **Road map** D1. 📞 051 227978. Famous for its seafood, this restaurant offers less common dishes such as *gávroi* (fresh anchovies). 🍴		▪		▪

LITOCHORO: *Damaskiniá* ⓓ
Vasiléos Konstantínou 4, 60200. **Road map** C2. ▐ *0352 81247.*
Situated in Litóchoro, 21 km (13 miles) south of Katerína, this lively taverna
offers good home-cooked Greek fare. Meals include grilled fish and stews.

NEA FOKAIA: *Kostís* ⓓⓓⓓ
At traffic lights, 63077. **Road map** D2. ▐ *0374 81379.*
Situated in Néa Fókaia, 17 km (11 miles) south of Néa Moudaniá, this
restaurant transforms basic dishes such as feta with the addition of onions
and red peppers. Cod in batter with *skordaliá* (garlic sauce) is a specialty. 🍲

NEOS MARMARAS: *Ta Péfka* ⓓ
Waterfront, 63081. **Road map** D2. ▐ *0375 71763.*
Set among pine trees in Néos Marmarás, 52 km (30 miles) southeast of Néa
Moudaniá, this restaurant serves unusual dishes such as *mýdia saganáki*
(mussels in red sauce) and octopus *mezédes.* ● *Nov–Dec.* 🍲

PEFKOCHORI: *Toronéos* ⓓ
Pefkochóri beach, 63085. **Road map** D2. ▐ *0374 61495.*
Basic Greek staples are enhanced by specialties such as stuffed squid
or fried pumpkin in this welcoming taverna in Pefkochóri, 42 km
(26 miles) south of Néa Moudaniá. ● *Oct 20–Apr 20.* 🍲

THESSALONIKI: *Agorá* ⓓ
Kapodistríou 5, 54625. **Road map** C2. ▐ *031 532428.*
Backstreet family *ouzerí* offering good Greek cuisine. Salads are generous
and meat and fish dishes deliciously grilled. ● *Sun; Jul 26–Aug 19.* 🍲

THESSALONIKI: *Stratís* ⓓ
Leofóros Níkis 19, 54623. **Road map** C2. ▐ *031 279353.*
This restaurant serves traditional favorites such as *mousaká* as well as
generous salads. There is also a wide range of imported wines and beers. 🍲

THESSALONIKI: *Ta Koumparákia* ⓓ
Egnatía 140, 54622. **Road map** C2. ▐ *031 271905.*
This simple Greek grill, with its friendly service and good simple food
make it a reliable and popular choice. ● *Christmas day, Easter day, May 1.*

THESSALONIKI: *Ta Spáta* ⓓ
Aristotélous 28, 54623. **Road map** C2. ▐ *031 277412.*
This grill-house is almost always busy and specializes in spit-roasted
chicken. It also serves hearty peasant salads.

THESSALONIKI: *Aristotélous* ⓓⓓ
Aristotélous 8, 54623. **Road map** C2. ▐ *031 233195.*
A smart, lively *ouzerí* serving some unusual food such as spicy feta and
pepper dip, or cuttlefish stuffed with feta. ● *Sun evening; Jul 20–Aug 20.*

THESSALONIKI: *Chamádrakas* ⓓⓓ
Manoúli Gagíli 13, 55132. **Road map** C2. ▐ *031 447943.*
Choose your own lobster at this family-run, seafront taverna. There is a large
selection of Greek cuisine as well as home-produced wine. ● *Jan 1.* 🍲

THESSALONIKI: *Prigkiponísia* ⓓⓓ
Krítis 60, 54646. **Road map** C2. ▐ *031 427151.*
This spacious taverna, with conservatory and mezzanine level, offers a wide
selection of *mezédes* as well as specialties such as lamb with eggplant.

THESSALONIKI: *Zéfyros* ⓓⓓ
Leofóros Níkis 13, 54623. **Road map** C2. ▐ *031 279933.*
This restaurant offers European and Middle Eastern as well as Greek cuisine.
Unusual combinations include prunes in bacon. ● *Jul 10–15, Aug 15–20.*

THESSALONIKI: *Ta Nisiá* ⓓⓓⓓ
Proxénou Koromilá 13, 54623. **Road map** C2. ▐ *031 285991.*
A popular spot, this taverna specializes in fresh fish and game dishes.
Imaginative combinations such as shrimp and bacon, and a good dessert
menu are offered. The walnut pie is a regular feature. ● *Sun.* 🍲

XORTIATIS: *Plátanos* ⓓ
Agía Paraskevís 1, 57010. **Road map** D2. ▐ *031 349260.*
Situated in Xortiátis village, 18 km (11 miles) east of Thessaloníki, this taverna
is worth the visit for its local specialties such as *teingerosarmás* (oven-baked
lamb innards) and *exochikó* (pork baked in tomatoes). ● *Easter day.*

For key to symbols see back flap

SURVIVAL
GUIDE

PRACTICAL INFORMATION

REECE'S APPEAL is both cultural and hedonistic. Its physical beauty, hot climate, and warm seas, together with the easy-going outlook of its people, are all conducive to a relaxed vacation. It does pay, however, to know something about the nuts and bolts of Greek life to avoid unnecessary frustrations – when to visit, what to bring, how to get around, and what to do if

Soldier in ceremonial dress

things go wrong. Greece is no longer the cheap vacation destination it once was, though public transportation, car rental, dining, and hotel accommodations are still relatively inexpensive compared with most other European countries. Tourist information is available through the many EOT offices (see p300), which offer plenty of advice on the practical aspects of your stay.

WHEN TO VISIT

TOURIST SEASON in Greece – late June to early September – is the hottest (see p49) and most expensive time to visit, as well as being very crowded. December to March are the coldest and wettest months everywhere, with reduced public transportation, and many hotels and restaurants closed for the winter.

Skiing in Greece is possible from January to April, with around 20 mainland resorts to choose from (see p310).

Spring (late April–May) is one of the loveliest times to visit – the weather is sunny but not yet debilitatingly hot, there are relatively few tourists around, and the countryside is ablaze with brightly colored wildflowers and fresh, brilliant greenery (see pp22–3).

WHAT TO BRING

MOST OF LIFE'S comforts are available in Greece, although it is advisable to take a good map of the area in which you intend to stay (see p319), an AC adaptor for

your electrical gadgetry (see p301), sunglasses and a sun hat, mosquito repellent, any medical supplies you might need, and a high factor (15 and up) sunscreen.

Apart from swimwear, light clothing is all you need for most of the year, although a sweater or light jacket for the evening is also recommended, and is essential in May and October. During winter and spring rainwear should be taken, as well as warm clothes. Many religious buildings have dress codes that should always be adhered to (see p301).

ΕΛΕΓΧΟΣ ΔΙΑΒΑΤΗΡΙΩΝ
PASSPORT CONTROL

Passport control sign at Athens airport

VISA REQUIREMENTS

VISITORS FROM EU countries, the US, Canada, Australia, and New Zealand need only a valid passport for entry to Greece (no visa is required), and may stay for a period of up to 90 days. For longer stays a resident's permit must be

obtained from the **Aliens' Bureau** in Athens, or the local police in remoter areas.

Any non-EU citizens planning to work or study in Greece should contact their local Greek consulate a few months in advance about visas and work permits.

CUSTOMS

VISITORS ENTERING Greece from within the EU are no longer subject to any customs controls or other formalities. Limits for duty-paid goods have been similarly relaxed in recent years, though anything valuable should be recorded in your passport upon entry if it is to be reexported. Visitors coming from non-EU countries may be subject to the occasional spot check on arrival in Greece.

The unauthorized export of antiquities and archaeological artifacts from Greece is treated as a serious offense, and penalties range from hefty fines to prison sentences.

Any prescription drugs that are brought into the country should be accompanied by a copy of the prescription for the purposes of the customs authorities (see pp302–3).

Restrictions on the import and export of money are covered on page 305.

EU and non-EU visitors may bring in and export the following quantities of duty-free goods: 200 cigarettes or 100 cigarillos or 50 cigars or 250 grams of tobacco (18 years or over); 1 liter spirits and 2 liters wine or liqueurs (18 years or over); 50 grams of perfume and 250 ml cologne.

Visitors on the beach in high summer

◁ **The attractive harbor of Paralía Astros, south of Náfplio**

A family arriving at Athens airport

TRAVELING WITH CHILDREN

CHILDREN ARE much loved by the Greeks and welcome just about everywhere. Baby-sitting facilities are provided by most hotels on request, though you should check this before you register (see p261).

Discounts of up to 50 percent are offered on most public transportation for children aged 10 and under, but in some cases it is 8 and under.

Swimming in the sea is generally safe for kids, but keep a close eye on them as lifeguards are rare in Greece. Also be aware of the hazards of overexposure to the sun and dehydration.

WOMEN TRAVELERS

GREECE IS A VERY SAFE country and local communities are generally welcoming. Foreign women traveling alone are usually treated with respect, especially if dressed modestly (see p301). However, as elsewhere, hitchhiking alone in Greece carries potential risks and is not advisable.

STUDENT AND YOUTH TRAVELERS

WITHIN Greece itself, no discounts are offered on ferry, bus, or train travel, except to students actually studying in Greece. However, there are plenty of deals available getting to Greece, especially during the off-season. There are scores of agencies for student and youth travel, including **STA Travel**. IYHF (International Youth Hostel Federation) membership cards are rarely asked for in Greek hostels, but to be on the safe side it is worth joining before setting off.

Most state-run museums and archaeological sites are free to EU students with a valid International Student Identity Card (ISIC); non-EU students with an ISIC card are usually entitled to a 50 percent reduction. There are no youth discounts on these entrance fees, but occasional discounts are possible with a "Go 25" card which can be obtained from any STA office by travelers who are under 26.

International student identity card

FACILITIES FOR THE DISABLED

THERE ARE FEW facilities in Greece for assisting the disabled, so careful planning is essential – sights that have wheelchair access are indicated at the beginning of each entry in this guide. **The Society for the Advancement of Travel for the Handicapped (SATH)**, publishes a quarterly magazine, *ACCESS to Travel*, which focuses on destinations, attractions, accommodations, transportation, and other information useful to people with disabilities.

A sign directing access for wheelchairs at Athens airport

Vacation Essentials

The EOT's Greek tourism emblem

F OR A CAREFREE vacation in Greece, it is best to adopt the philosophy *sigá, sigá* (slowly, slowly). Within this principle is the ritual of the afternoon siesta, a practice that should be taken seriously, particularly during the hottest months when it is almost a physiological necessity. Almost everything closes for a few hours after lunch, reopening later in the day when the air cools and Greece comes to life again. The stores reopen their doors, the restaurants start filling up, and, at seaside locales, practically everyone partakes in the *vólta*, or evening stroll – a delightful Greek institution.

TOURIST INFORMATION

T OURIST INFORMATION is available in many towns and villages in Greece, either in the form of government-run **EOT** offices (Ellinikós Organismós Tourismoú, or National Tourist Organization of Greece), municipally run tourist offices, the local tourist police *(see p302)*, or privately owned travel agencies. The EOT publishes an array of tourist literature, including maps, brochures, and leaflets on transportation and accommodations – be aware though that not all of their information is up-to-date. The addresses and phone numbers of the EOT, municipal tourist offices, and the tourist police are listed throughout this guide.

GREEK TIME

G REECE IS NORMALLY 2 hours ahead of Britain (GMT), 1 hour ahead of European countries on Central European Time (such as France), 7 hours ahead of New York, 10 hours ahead of Los Angeles, and 8 hours behind Sydney.

Clocks go forward one hour to Greek daylight savings on the last Sunday in March and back again on the last Sunday in September. This can make the time difference an extra hour either way during April and October when the change may be out of synch with other countries – the cause of many a missed flight or ferry!

EOT office in the center of Athens

OPENING HOURS

O PENING HOURS tend to be vague in Greece, varying from day to day, season to season, and place to place. It is therefore advisable to use the times given in this book as rough guidelines only and to check with local information centers for accurate times.

State-run museums and archaeological sites generally are open from around 8am to 3pm (the major ones staying open as late as 7pm in the summer months). Mondays and main public holidays *(see p48)* are the usual closing days. Locally run and private museums may be closed on additional

A *periptero*, or kiosk, with a wide array of papers and periodicals

public holidays and on local festival days. Monasteries and convents are open during daylight hours, but may close for a few hours in the afternoon.

Opening times for stores are covered on page 308, pharmacies on page 303, banks on page 304, post offices on page 307, and OTE (telephone) offices on page 306.

Most shops and offices are closed on public holidays and local festival days, with the exception of some shops within tourist resorts. Major local festivals are included in the Visitors' Checklists in each main town entry in this guide.

ADMISSION CHARGES

M OST STATE-RUN museums and archaeological sites charge between 500 Dr and 2,000 Dr entrance fee. Discounts are available, however, ranging from around 25 percent for EU citizens age 60 years and over (use your passport as proof of age) to 50 percent for non-EU students armed with an international student identity card (ISIC) *(see p299)*.

Though most museums and sites are closed on public holidays, the ones that do remain open are free of charge.

EVENTS

T HE TWO English-language papers *Athens News* and the weekly *Greek Times* both have What's On columns, the latter listing events all over Greece and also those of special interest to children. *Athenscope* is the main Athens English-language listings magazine, while *The Athenian* gives a summary of cultural goings-on. Entertainment in Athens is covered in this guide on pages 118–21. A list of Greek festivals and cultural events is given on pages 44–8, but it is worth asking your nearest tourist office about what's happening locally. Other forms of entertainment include the outdoor cinema in summer, which is very popular with the Greeks; most films are in English with Greek subtitles. There are also

A sign about dress codes at a monastery in Metéora, central Greece

bars, discos, and nightclubs in the resorts, as well as tavernas and *kafeneía* (coffee shops), found in every village and often the center of social life.

RELIGION

GREECE IS ALMOST entirely Greek Orthodox. The symbols and rituals of the religion are deeply rooted in Greek culture and are visible everywhere. Saints' days are celebrated throughout Greece *(see p48)*, sometimes on a local scale and sometimes across the entire country.

The largest religious minority are the Muslims of Thrace, though they constitute less than 2 percent of the country's total population. Places
of worship for other religions are mostly situated within Athens and its environs.

A Greek priest

ETIQUETTE

LIKE ANYWHERE ELSE, common courtesy and respect is appreciated in Greece, so try speaking a few words of the language, even if your vocabulary only extends as far as the basics *(see pp348–52)*.

Though formal attire is rarely needed, modest clothing (trousers for men and skirts for women) is *de rigueur* for visits to churches and monasteries.

Topless sunbathing is generally tolerated, but nude bathing is officially restricted to a few designated beaches.

In restaurants, the service charge is always included in the check, but tips are still appreciated – the custom is to

leave between 10 and 15 percent. Public toilet attendants should also be tipped. Taxi drivers do not expect a tip, but they are not averse to them either; likewise hotel porters and chambermaids.

PHOTOGRAPHY

PHOTOGRAPHIC FILM is readily available in Greece, although it is often quite expensive in tourist areas and close to the major sights.

Taking photographs inside churches and monasteries is officially forbidden; inside museums photography is usually permitted, but flashes and tripods are often not. In most cases where a still camera is allowed, a video camera will also be fine, but you may have to pay an extra fee. At sites, museums, or religious buildings it is best to get permission before using a camera, as rules vary.

ELECTRICAL APPLIANCES

Typical two-pin plug, as used throughout Greece

GREECE, LIKE OTHER European countries, runs on 220 volts/50 Hz AC. Plugs have two round pins, or three

round pins for appliances that need to be grounded. Adaptors, which are available in most Greek supermarkets, are required for British electrical appliances, and transformers are needed for North American equipment.

CONVERSION CHART

GREECE USES the metric system, with two exceptions: sea distances are expressed in nautical miles and land is measured in *strémmata*, the equivalent of about a quarter of an acre.

US Standard to Metric
1 inch = 2.54 centimeters
1 foot = 30 centimeters
1 mile = 1.6 kilometers
1 ounce = 28 grams
1 pound = 454 grams
1 US quart = 0.947 liter
1 US gallon = 3.6 liters

Metric to US Imperial
1 millimeter = 0.04 inch
1 centimeter = 0.4 inch
1 meter = 3 feet 3 inches
1 kilometer = 0.6 mile
1 gram = 0.04 ounce
1 kilogram = 2.2 pounds
1 liter = 1.1 US quarts

Personal Health and Security

GREECE IS ONE of the safest European countries to visit, with a time-honored tradition of honesty that still survives despite the onslaught of mass tourism. But, like traveling anywhere else, it is still advisable to take out a comprehensive travel insurance policy. One place where danger is ever present, however, is on the road. Driving is a volatile matter in Greece, and it now has the highest accident rate in Europe. Considerable caution is recommended for drivers and pedestrians.

Fire department emblem

PERSONAL SECURITY

THE CRIME RATE in Greece is very low compared with other European countries. Nevertheless, a few precautions are worth taking, like keeping cars and hotel rooms locked, watching your handbag in public, and not keeping all your documents together in one place. If you do have anything stolen, contact the police or tourist police.

POLICE

GREECE'S POLICE are split into three forces: the regular police, the port police, and the tourist police. The tourist police are the most useful for vacationers, combining normal police duties with tourist advice. Should you suffer a theft, lose your passport, or have cause to complain about shops, restaurants, tour guides, or taxi drivers, your case should first be made to them. As every tourist police office claims to have at least one English speaker, they can act as interpreters if the case needs to involve the local police. Their offices also offer maps, brochures, and advice on finding accommodations.

LEGAL ASSISTANCE FOR TOURISTS

EUROPEAN CONSUMERS' associations together with the European Commission have created a program, known as **EKPIZO**, to inform tourists of their rights. Its aim is specifically to help vacationers who experience problems

A policeman giving directions to tourists

with hotels, campsites, travel agencies, and so forth. They will furnish tourists with the relevant information and, if necessary, arrange legal advice from lawyers in English, French, or German. Contact the main Athens branch for their local telephone numbers.

MEDICAL TREATMENT AND INSURANCE

VISITORS from the US should check with their insurance companies before leaving home to be sure they are covered if medical care is needed. Many medical facilities will require you to pay for your treatment in full at time of service: be aware that public health facilities are limited in Greece and private clinics are expensive. In some cases, insurance companies require you to provide an official translation before they will reimburse you. Travelers may wish to take out additional, private travel insurance for the cost of any emergency care, doctors' fees, and repatriation.

Not all policies, for instance, will cover you for activities of a "dangerous" nature, such as motorcycling and trekking, and only some will cover you for ambulances and emergency flights home. Paying for your flight with a credit card such as Visa or American Express may also provide some limited travel insurance, including reimbursement of your air fare if the agent goes bankrupt.

HEALTH PRECAUTIONS

IT COSTS LITTLE or nothing to take a few sensible precautions when traveling abroad, and certain measures are essential if vacationing in the extreme heat of summer. The most obvious thing to avoid is overexposure to the sun, particularly for the fairskinned: wear a hat and good-quality sunglasses, as well as a high-factor sunscreen. If you do burn, aloe vera lotion is soothing. Heat stroke is a real hazard for which medical attention should be sought immediately, while heat exhaustion and dehydration (made worse by alcohol consumption) are also serious.

Be sure to drink plenty of water, even if you don't feel thirsty, and if in any doubt invest in a package of electrolyte pills (a mixture of potassium salts and glucose) available at any Greek pharmacy, to avoid dehydration and replace lost minerals.

Port policeman's uniform   **City policeman's uniform**

An ambulance with the emergency number emblazoned on its side

Fire engine

Police car

Always go prepared with an adequate supply of any medication you may need while away, as well as a copy of the prescription with the generic name of the drug – this is useful not only in case you run out, but also for the purposes of customs when you enter the country. Pain relievers containing codeine, available in some European countries, are in fact illegal in Greece.

Tap water in Greece is generally safe to drink, but in remote communities it is a good precaution to check with the locals. Bottled spring water is for sale throughout the country and often has the advantage of being chilled.

However tempting the sea may look, swimming immediately after a meal is not recommended as stomach cramps can be a problem.

Underwater hazards to be aware of are weaver fish, jellyfish, and sea urchins. The latter are not uncommon and are extremely unpleasant if stepped on. If you do, the spine will need to be extracted using olive oil and a sterilized needle. Jellyfish stings can be relieved by vinegar, baking soda, or various other remedies sold at Greek pharmacies. Though rare, the weaver fish has a powerful sting, causing extreme pain. The immediate treatment is to immerse the affected area in very hot water to dilute the venom's strength.

No inoculations are required for visitors to Greece, though tetanus and typhoid boosters may be recommended by your doctor.

PHARMACIES

GREEK PHARMACISTS are highly qualified and can not only advise on minor ailments, but also dispense medication not usually available over the counter back home. Their premises, *farmakeía*, are identified by a red or green cross on a white background. Pharmacies are open from 8:30am to 2pm, but are usually closed in the afternoon and on Saturday mornings.

Pharmacy sign

However, in larger towns there is usually a rotation system to maintain a service from 7:30am to 2pm and from 5:30 to 10pm. Details are posted in pharmacy windows, both in Greek and English.

EMERGENCY SERVICES

IN CASE OF EMERGENCIES the appropriate services to call are listed in the directory below. For accidents or other medical emergencies, a 24-hour ambulance service operates within Athens. Outside Athens, in rural towns, and on the islands, it is unlikely that ambulances will be on 24-hour call. If necessary, patients can be transferred from local ESY (Greek National Health Service) hospitals or clinics to a main ESY hospital in Athens by ambulance or helicopter.

A complete list of ESY hospitals, private hospitals, and clinics is available from the tourist police.

DIRECTORY

NATIONWIDE EMERGENCY NUMBERS

Police
(100.

Ambulance
(166.

Fire
(199.

Road assistance
(174.

Coastguard patrol
(108.

ATHENS EMERGENCY NUMBERS

Tourist police
(171.

Doctors
(105 (2pm –7am).

Pharmacies
For information on 24-hour pharmacies:
(107 (central Athens).
(102 (suburbs).

Poison control center
(01 779 3777.

EKPIZO BUREAU

Athens branch
Valtetsiou 43–45,
10681 Athens.
(01 330 0673.

Banking and Local Currency

Eurocheque logo

CHANGING MONEY is straightforward in Greece and does not pose any special problems. If there is no bank where you are staying, there will probably be a post office, and even in the smallest towns and resorts you can expect to find a car rental firm or travel agency that will oblige by changing cash and travelers' checks – albeit with a sizable commission. The larger towns and tourist centers all have the usual banking facilities, including an increasing number of cash machines (ATMs).

National Bank of Greece ATM

BANKING HOURS

ALL BANKS ARE OPEN from 8am to 2pm Monday to Thursday, and from 8am to 1:30pm on Friday. In the larger cities and tourist resorts there is usually at least one bank that reopens its exchange desk for a few hours in the evening and on Saturday mornings during the summer season.

Cash machines, although seldom found outside the major towns and resorts, are in operation 24 hours a day. All banks are closed on public holidays *(see p48)* and may also be closed on any local festival days.

BANKS AND EXCHANGE FACILITIES

THERE ARE BANKS in all major towns and resorts, as well as exchange facilities at post offices (which tend to charge lower commissions and are found in the more remote areas of Greece), travel agents, hotels, tourist offices, and car rental agencies. Always take your passport with you when cashing travelers' checks, and check exchange rates and commission charges

beforehand, as they vary greatly. In major towns and tourist areas you may find a foreign exchange machine for changing money at any time of day or night. These operate in several languages, as do the ATMs.

CARDS AND CHECKS

VISA, MASTERCARD (Access), American Express, and Diners Club are the most widely accepted credit cards in Greece. They are the most convenient way to pay for plane tickets, international ferry journeys, car rentals, most hotels, and larger purchases. Cheaper tavernas, shops, and hotels as a rule do not accept credit cards.

Bank of Greece logo

You can get a cash advance on a foreign credit card at some banks, though the minimum amount is 15,000 Dr, and you will need to take your passport with you as proof of identity. A credit card can be used for withdrawing local currency at cash machines. Either at a bank or an ATM, a 1.5 percent processing charge is usually levied (2.5 percent for Visa).

Cirrus and Plus debit card systems operate in Greece. Cash can be obtained using the Cirrus system at National Bank of Greece ATMs and the Plus system at Commercial Bank ATMs.

Travelers' checks are the safest way to carry large sums of money. They are

refundable if lost or stolen, though the process can be time-consuming. American Express and Thomas Cook are the best-known brands of travelers' checks in Greece. They usually incur two sets of commissions: one when you buy them (1–1.5 percent) and another when you cash them. Rates for the latter vary considerably, so shop around before changing your money.

Travelers' checks can be cashed at most post offices *(see p307)* – an important thing to remember if you are traveling to a rural area or remote island.

Eurocheques are available only to holders of a European bank account and are issued in the form of a checkbook. They are honored at banks and post offices throughout Greece, as well as many hotels, shops, and travel agencies. There is no commission charged when cashing Eurocheques, though there is an annual fee of about $12 for holding a European account and a fee of about two percent for each check used. Fees are debited directly from the account.

Visitors changing money at a foreign exchange bureau

Foreign exchange machine

CURRENCY

THE GREEK UNIT of currency is the drachma (Dr), and denominations in widest circulation are notes of 100, 500, 1,000, 5,000, and 10,000 Dr, and coins of 5, 10, 20, 50, and 100; a 200 Dr coin has now also been introduced. No more than 100,000 drachmas in cash may be brought into, or taken out of, Greece. There is no limit on foreign currency and travelers' checks being imported, but anything over the value of 600,000 Dr in cash should be declared on entry, in case it needs to be re-exported. Foreign currency over 6,200,000 Dr must be transferred through a bank.

DIRECTORY

To report a lost or stolen credit card, ask for the US operator and request the following collect numbers from Greece:

Mastercard
[303-278-8000.

American Express
[910-668-5110.

Diners Club
[303-799-1504.

Visa
[410-581-9994.

To report lost or stolen travelers' checks, ask for the US operator and request the following collect from Greece:

American Express
[801-964-6665.

Call these numbers directly from Greece:

Thomas Cook/ Mastercard
[00 800 4128366.

Thomas Cook/Visa
[00 800 44 128455.

Coins
These are the coins in widest circulation throughout Greece. They are shown at their actual size.

100 Dr

50 Dr

20 Dr

10 Dr

5 Dr

Bank Notes
The most commonly used bills are in denominations of 100 to 10,000 drachmas. The bills are all of equal size, but each denomination is a different color and carries a portrait of a historical or mythological figure.

10,000 drachmas

5,000 drachmas

1,000 drachmas

500 drachmas

100 drachmas

Communications

Post office logo

THE GREEK NATIONAL telephone company is the OTE (Organismós Tilepikoinonión Elládos). Telecommunications have improved dramatically in recent years, and now there are direct lines to all major countries. These are often better than local lines, but the rates are among the highest in Europe. Greek mail is reasonably reliable and efficient, especially from the larger towns and resorts; faxes are also easy to send and receive. The Greeks are avid newspaper readers, and in addition to a vast array of Greek publications, there are also some excellent English-language papers and magazines.

TELEPHONES AND FAXES

PUBLIC TELEPHONES can be found in many locales – hotel lobbies, telephone booths, street kiosks, or the local OTE office. Long-distance calls are best made in a telephone booth using a phonecard – available at any kiosk in denominations of 100, 500, and 1,000 units. Alternatively, they can be made at a metered phone in an OTE office, where you can also make collect calls. OTE offices are open daily from 7am to 10pm or midnight in the larger towns; or until around 3pm in smaller communities. Charges are variable, but in general local calls are cheap, out-of-town domestic calls are surprisingly expensive, and long-distance calls are extortionate. You can call the operator first for specific rates, as well as information about peak and off-peak times, which vary depending on the country you are phoning.

Ship-to-shore and shore-to-ship calls can be made through INMARSAT; for information on this service call the marine operator from Greece at 158.

Faxes can be sent from OTE offices, a few city post offices, and some car rental and travel agencies, though expect to pay a heavy surcharge wherever you go. The easiest way to receive a fax is to become friendly with your nearest car rental or travel agency – both will usually oblige and keep faxes aside for you – otherwise the OTE office is the place to go.

RADIO AND TV

WITH THREE state-owned radio services and a plethora of local stations, the airwaves are positively jammed in Greece, and reception is not always dependable. There are many Greek music stations to listen to, as well as classical music stations such as ETA 3, one of the three state-run stations, which can be heard at 95.6 FM. Daily news summaries are broadcast in English, French, and German, and with a shortwave radio you will be able to pick up the BBC World Service in most parts of Greece. Its frequency varies, but in the Greater Athens area it can be heard at 107.1 FM. There is another English station, Superstar, at 93.4 FM.

Greek TV is broadcast by two state-run and several privately-run stations, plus a host of cable and satellite stations from across Europe. Most stations are a mix of foreign soap operas, game shows, sports, and movies, foreign films tending to be subtitled rather than dubbed.

ET1, one of the two state-run channels, transmits news summaries in English each day at 6pm, and satellite stations CNN and Euronews televise news in English around the clock. Guides for television programs are published in all the English-language papers and magazines.

A public phone

USING A PHONECARD TELEPHONE IN GREECE

1 Lift the receiver and wait for a dial tone.

2 Insert the phonecard.

3 The screen will display the number of units available, then tell you to enter the telephone number.

4 Enter the number and wait to be connected.

5 If the card runs out in mid-call, it will reemerge; remove and insert another.

7 Replace the receiver after your call. When the card reemerges, remove it.

6 If you want to make another call, do not replace the receiver; simply press the follow-on call button and dial.

500-unit telephone card

100-unit telephone card

Red mailbox for express mail | **Yellow mailbox for all other mail**

NEWSPAPERS AND MAGAZINES

THE TRUSTY corner *períptera* (kiosks), bookstores in larger towns, and tourist shops in the resorts often sell day-old foreign newspapers and magazines, though the mark-up is substantial. Much cheaper, and also widely available, are the English-language papers published in Athens. *Athens News* is printed every day except Monday, and the *Greek Times* comes out each week. There is also the *Athenian*, a monthly magazine available in most resorts as well as the capital. These publications are all excellent sources of information on local entertainment, festivals and cultural goings-on, while also providing coverage of domestic and international news.

Stamp machine

Popular Greek language newspapers are *Eleftherotypía*, *Eléftheros Týpos*, and *Ta Néa*.

POST

GREEK POST offices *(tachydromeía)* are generally open from 7:30am to 2pm Monday to Friday, with some main branches staying open as late as 8pm (main branches occasionally open for a few hours on weekends). All post offices are closed on public holidays *(see p48)*. Those with an "Exchange" sign will change money in addition to the usual services.

Mailboxes are usually bright yellow; those with two slots are marked *esoterikó*, meaning domestic, and *exoterikó*, meaning overseas. Bright red mailboxes are reserved for express mail, both domestic and overseas. Express is a little more expensive, but cuts delivery time by a few days.

Stamps *(grammatósima)* can be bought over the counter at post offices and also at *períptera*, the latter usually charging a ten percent commission. Airmail letters to most European countries take three to six days, and anywhere from five days to a week or more to North America, Australia, and New Zealand. If you are sending postcards, allow additional time for reaching any destination.

The *poste restante* system – whereby mail can be sent to, and picked up from, a post office – is widely used in Greece. Mail should be clearly marked "Poste Restante," with the recipient's last name underlined so that it gets filed in the right place. A passport or some other proof of identity is needed when collecting the mail, which is kept for a maximum of 30 days before being returned to the sender.

If you are sending a parcel from Greece to a non-EU country, do not seal it before going to the post office. The contents will need to be inspected by security before it is sent, and if the package is sealed they will unwrap it.

The main post offices in the center of Athens are indicated on the Street Finder map, at Plateía Syntágmatos, Tritís Septemvríou, and on Aiólou.

DIRECTORY

Domestic Calls
- 151 *(domestic operator)*.
- 131 *(directory assistance for local calls anywhere in Greece)*.
- 132 *(directory assistance for nonlocal calls within Greece)*.

International Calls
- 161 *(international operator and directory assistance)*.
- 162 *(international directory assistance if calling from Athens)*.

International Calls from Greece
Dial 00, the country code (a list is given below), the local area code (minus the initial 0), and then the number itself.
Australia 61.
Ireland 353.
New Zealand 64.
UK 44.
US & Canada 1.

International Calls to Greece from Abroad
Dial the international access code (a list is given below), 30 (country code), the area code minus initial 0, and then the number itself.
Australia 0011.
Ireland 016.
UK & New Zealand 00.
US & Canada 011.

Athenians reading newspapers on a clothes line at a street kiosk

Shopping in Greece

SHOPPING IN GREECE can be entertaining, particularly when you buy directly from the producer. In smaller villages, embroiderers, lace makers, and potters can often be seen at work. Most other goods in Greece have been imported and carry a heavy markup. For information on shopping in Athens see pages 114–17.

Souvenir shop window in Párga, central Greece

VAT AND TAX-FREE SHOPPING

ALMOST ALWAYS included in the price, FPA *(Fóros Prostitheménis Axías)* – the equivalent of VAT (sales tax) – is about 18 percent in Greece.

Visitors from outside the EU staying less than three months may claim this money back on purchases over 40,000 Dr. A "Tax-Free Check" form must be completed in the store, a copy of which is then given to the customs authorities on departure. You may be asked to show your receipt or goods as proof of purchase.

OPENING HOURS

ALLOWING FOR plenty of exceptions, shops and boutiques are generally open on Monday, Wednesday, and Saturday from 9am to 2:30pm, and on Tuesday, Thursday, and Friday from 9am to 1:30pm and 5pm to 8pm. Department stores remain open Monday to Friday from 9am to 8pm and Saturday from 9am to 3pm. Supermarkets, found in all but the smallest communities, are often family-run and open long hours, typically Monday to Saturday from 8 or 9am to 9 or 10pm. Sunday shopping is possible in most tourist resorts and also in some of the

suburban shopping malls in Athens. The corner *períptero* (street kiosk), found in nearly every town, is open from around 7am to 11pm or midnight, selling everything from aspirin to ice cream, as well as bus tickets and phonecards.

"Brettos" distillery and liquor store, in Athens

MARKETS

MOST TOWNS in Greece have their weekly street market *(laïkí agorá)*, a colorful selection of fresh fruits and vegetables, herbs, fish, meat, and poultry – often juxtaposed with shoes and

We refund your VAT **TAX FREE Club** MEMBER OF

Tax-free shop symbol

underwear, fabrics, household items, and sundry electronic equipment. In the larger cities, the street markets are in a different area each day, usually opening early and packing up by about 2pm, in time for the siesta. Prices are generally cheaper than in the supermarkets, and a certain amount of bargaining is also acceptable, at least for non-perishables. This guide gives market days in the information under each town entry.

In Athens, there is a famous Sunday-morning flea market around Plateía Monastirakíou and its radiating streets that should not be missed if you are in the city *(see p87)*.

FOOD AND DRINK

CULINARY DELIGHTS to look out for in Greece include honey, olives, olive oil, pistachios, herbs, and spices. There are also various cheeses, including feta, and the sweet breads and cookies of the *zacharoplasteío* (cake and pastry shop). Greece is also renowned for several drinks, including ouzo (an anise-flavored spirit), retsina (a resinated wine), brandy, and the firewater *tsípouro*.

SIZE CHART							
Women's dresses, coats and skirts							
Greek	44	46	48	50	52	54	(size)
GB/Australian	10	12	14	16	18	20	(size)
US	8	10	12	14	16	18	(size)
Men's suits							
Greek	44	46	48	50	52	54	56	(size)
GB/US	34	36	38	40	42	44	46	(inches)
Australian	87	92	97	102	107	112	117	(cm)
Women's shoes							
Greek	36	37	38	39	40	41	(size)
GB	3	4	5	6	7	8	(size)
US/Australian	5	6	7	8	9	10	(size)
Men's shoes							
Greek	40	41	42	43	44	45	(size)
GB/Australian	7	7 ½	8	9	10	11	(size)
US	7 ½	8	8 ½	9 ½	10 ½	11 ½	(size)

What to Buy in Greece

TRADITIONAL handicrafts, though not particularly cheap, do offer the most genuinely Greek souvenirs. Handicrafts cover a range of items from finely wrought gold reproductions of ancient pendants to rustic pots, wooden spoons, and handmade sandals. Some of the country's best ceramics can be found in the markets and shops of Athens' northern suburb Maroúsi. Brightly colored embroidery and wall-hangings are produced in many villages throughout Greece, where they are often seen hanging out for

Rugs for sale at Aráchova

sale, along with thick *flokáti* rugs, which are handwoven from sheep or goat's wool. These are made mainly in the Píndos Mountains and can also be found at Aráchova, near Delphi *(see p221)*. In the small, rural communities, crafts are often cottage industries, earning the family a large chunk of its annual income. Here, there is room to engage in some haggling over the price. The *Shopping in Athens* section, on pages 114–17, indicates places within the capital where traditional crafts may be bought.

Gold jewelry *is sold in larger towns or cities. Modern designs are found in jewelers such as Lalaounis, and reproductions of ancient designs in museum gift shops.*

Icons *are generally sold in shops and monasteries. They range from very small portraits to substantial pictures. Some of the most beautiful, and expensive, use only age-old traditional techniques and materials.*

Ornate utensils, *such as these wooden spoons, are found in traditional craft shops. As here, they are often hand-carved into the shapes of figures and produced from the rich-textured wood of the native olive tree.*

Komboloí *or worry beads, are a traditional sight in Greece; the beads are counted as a way to relax. They are sold in souvenir shops and jewelers.*

Kitchenware *is found in most markets and in specialty shops. This copper coffee pot* (mpríki) *is used for making Greek coffee.*

Leather goods *are sold throughout Greece. The bags, backpacks, and sandals make useful and good-value souvenirs.*

Ornamental ceramics *come in many shapes and finishes. Traditional earthenware, often simple, functional, and unglazed, is frequently for sale by the roads on the outskirts of Athens and the larger towns.*

Special Interest Vacations and Outdoor Activities

MANY ORGANIZED TOURS and courses cater to the special interests of visitors to Greece. You can follow in the footsteps of the apostle Paul or visit ancient archaeological sites with a learned academic as your guide; you can improve your writing skills, draw wildflowers, or paint the Greek landscape. Sailing and windsurfing vacations are available, as well as walking tours and botanical and birdwatching expeditions. Many vacations are offered with food and accommodations included in the price.

Mountain walker

the Píndos range in central Greece (see p206). **Trekking Hellas** arranges walking tours in these regions, as well as a tour to the remote mountain areas of Agrafa and Stereá, offering a harsh landscape to explore at the southern end of the Píndos range. *The Mountains of Greece: A Walker's Guide* (Cicerone Press) is a good source of information.

Visitors on a tour of the ancient remains at Olympia (see pp170–72)

ARCHAEOLOGICAL TOURS

FOR THOSE interested in Greece's ancient past, a tour to some of the famous archaeological sites can make a fascinating and memorable vacation. You can choose from an array of destinations and itineraries, all guided by qualified archaeologists. As well as visiting ancient ruins, many tours also take in Venetian fortresses, Byzantine churches and frescoes, museums and monasteries en route to the archaeological sites.

WRITING AND PAINTING

WITH ITS vivid landscape and renowned quality of light, Greece is an inspirational destination for artistic endeavor. Courses in creative writing, and drawing and painting, are available at all levels and are conducted by professional tutors, well established in their craft. The Metropolitan Museum of Art in New York organizes tours that highlight painting and art history, as does the Smithsonian in Washington., DC. "Greece Your Way" tours, organized by **Guaranteed Travel,** will

put together a specialized package focusing on any aspect of interest in both mainland Greece and throughout the Islands.

NATURE TOURS

MUCH OF the Greek countryside is rich in birdlife and noted for its spring flowers. The shorelines are also good for wildlife. Several tour operaters, such as **F-Zein**, **Metro Tours**, and **Pharos Travel and Tourism**, offer personalized ecotour packages that specialize in the botany, horticulture, or geology of mainland Greece. The **Hellenic Ornithological Society** can be contacted for advice on bird-watching in Greece.

WALKING

GREECE IS A PARADISE for walkers, particularly in the spring when the countryside is at its greenest, the wild flowers are in bloom, and the sun is not yet too hot.
The best locations for walking are in the mountain ranges of the Taÿgetos in the Peloponnese (see p195) and

SKIING

THERE ARE several ski centers throughout the mainland, including some within easy reach of Athens – the closest being Mount Parnassus, near Delphi (see p221). Depending on snow conditions, the season runs from the start of January to the end of April.
Costs are low compared with other European resorts, though facilities are quite basic. For more information on skiing in Greece, contact the **Hellenic Skiing Federation**, or pick up a copy of the EOT's booklet entitled *Mountain Refuges and Ski Centres*; it is free from tourist offices and describes all the major ski centers.

WATER SPORTS

WITH ITS extensive and varied coastline, warm weather, and crystal clear seas, it is not surprising that so many water-lovers are attracted to Greece. Facilities

Vacationers learning the skills of windsurfing in coastal waters

Vacationers sailing off the Greek mainland coast

for water sports are numerous: everything from windsurfing and water-skiing to jet-skiing and parasailing is available in the larger resorts, and many of the places that rent equipment will also provide training.

Inland, kayaking, white-water rafting, and canoeing holidays are organized by **Trekking Hellas**.

SCUBA AND SNORKELING

THE AMAZINGLY clear waters of the Mediterranean reveal a world of submarine life and ancient archaeological remains.

Snorkeling can be enjoyed almost anywhere along the coast, though scuba diving is restricted. Greece is highly protective of its antiquities,

and it is forbidden to remove them or even to photograph them. A list of places where oxygen equipment may be used is available from the Greek Tourist Office (EOT) *(see p300)*, or write to the **Department of Underwater Archaeology** in Athens.

SAILING VACATIONS

SAILING VACATIONS can be booked through charter companies either in Greece or abroad. The season runs from April to late October, and itineraries range from a few days to several weeks.

Charters fall into four main categories. Bareboat charter, without a skipper or crew, is available to anyone with sailing experience (most

charter companies require at least two crew members to have a basic skipper's licence). Crewed charters range from the modest services of a paid skipper, assistant, or cook to fully crewed yachts. Chartering a yacht as part of a flotilla – typically in a group of 6 to 12 yachts – provides the opportunity of independent sailing with the support of a lead boat contactable by radio. **Sunsail** and **Thomas Cook** offer this kind of holiday, as well as a combined vacation mixing cruiser sailing with shore-based dinghy sailing and windsurfing. Contact the **Hellenic Yachting Federation** for details.

CRUISES AND BOAT TRIPS

GREECE'S UNIQUE combination of natural beauty and fascinating history makes a cruise both relaxing and stimulating. Running from April to October, a variety of options are available, ranging from the luxury of a large liner, accompanied by guest speakers, to inexpensive short cruises and boat trips. The former can be booked through **Hellenic Holidays** or any of the other companies listed while the latter are organized locally and best booked at a travel agent on the spot.

DIRECTORY

Department of Underwater Archaeology
Kallispéri 30,
11742 Athens.
(01 924 7249.

F-Zein Ltd
132 Syngrou Ave.,
Athens.
(011-301-92 16285.
FAX 011-301-922-9995.

Guaranteed Travel
83 South Street,
Morristown,
NJ 07960.
(201-540-1770.
FAX 201-540-8602.

Hellenic Holidays
1501 Broadway,
Suite 1601,
New York,
NY 10036.
(212-944-8388.

Hellenic Ornithological Society
Emmanouíl Mpenáki 53,
10681 Athens.
(01 381 1271.

Hellenic Professional and Bareboat Yacht Owners' Association
Office A8,
Marína Zéas,
18536 Piraeus.
(01 452 6335.

Hellenic Skiing Federation
Karagiórgi Servías 7,
10563 Athens.
(01 323 4412.

Hellenic Water-ski Federation
Leofóros Possidónos,
16777 Athens.
(01 894 7413.

Hellenic Yachting Federation
Possidónos 55,
Piraeus.
(01 930 4825.

Metro Tours
484 Lowell St.,
Peabody, MA 01960.
(800-221-2810.

Pharos Travel and Tourism
230 W. 31st Street,
New York, NY 10001.
(800-999-5511.
FAX 212-736-3921.

Raymond & Whitcomb
400 Madison Ave.,
New York, NY 10017.
(212-759-3960.
(800-245-9005
(outside NY)

Smithsonian Institution
1000 Jefferson Dr. SW,
Washington, DC 20560.

Trekking Hellas
Filellínon 7,
10557 Athens.
(01 323 4548.

TRAVEL INFORMATION

RELIABLY HOT, SUNNY WEATHER makes Greece an extremely popular destination for vacationers, particularly from the colder parts of North America. During high season (May to October) there are countless flights, bringing millions to the shores of Greece. For those with more time, it is also possible to reach Greece from Europe by car, rail, and bus. Traveling on the Greek mainland is easy enough. There is an extensive bus network reaching even the tiniest communities, with frequent

Olympic Airways passenger airplane

services on all major routes. Greece's rail network is skeletal by comparison, and, aside from the intercity expresses, service is much slower. Traveling around by car offers the most flexibility, allowing the visitor to dictate the pace and to reach places that are not accessible by public transportation. However, road conditions are variable, and in remoter parts can be rough, pot-holed, and dangerous *(see p320)*. Some of the larger centers and popular tourist destinations can also be visited by plane from Athens and Thessaloníki.

GETTING TO GREECE BY AIR

THE MAIN AIRLINES operating direct scheduled flights from the US to Athens and Thessaloníki are **Olympic Airways** (the Greek national airline), **Delta**, and **TWA**. One advantage of Olympic Airways is that, if flying to Athens, you land at the west terminal *(see p314)*, which means there is no need to change terminals if you want a connecting domestic flight.

From Europe, there are around 20 international airports in Greece that can be reached directly. On the mainland, only Athens and Thessaloníki handle scheduled flights. The other mainland international airports – Préveza, Kalamáta and Kavála – can be reached directly only by charter

flights. From outside Europe, all scheduled flights to Greece arrive in Athens, and only a few airlines offer direct flights – most will require changing planes, and often airlines, at a connecting European city. Direct daily flights from London are offered by Olympic, **British Airways**, and **Virgin Airways**.

From Australia, Olympic Airways operates flights out of Sydney, Brisbane, and Melbourne. These generally necessitate a stopover in Southeast Asia or Europe, but there are two direct flights a week from Australia, leaving from Melbourne and Sydney. Flights from New Zealand are also via Melbourne or Sydney. Other carriers with services from Australasian cities to Athens include **Qantas**, **Singapore Airlines**, **KLM**, and **Gulf Air**.

Travellers with duty-free goods

Check-in desk at Athens airport's West Terminal

A new airport at Spárta, 25 km (15 miles) east of Athens, is under construction, but, as yet, there is no completion date.

CHARTERS AND PACKAGE DEALS

CHARTER FLIGHTS to Greece are nearly all from within Europe, and mostly operate between May and October. Tickets are sold by travel agencies either as part of an all-inclusive package tour or as a flight-only deal.

Although they tend to be the cheapest flights available, charters do carry certain restrictions: departure dates cannot be changed once booked, and there are usually minimum and maximum limits to one's stay (typically between three days and a month). And if you plan to visit Turkey from Greece, bear in mind that charter passengers can do so only for a day trip; staying any longer will forfeit the return ticket for your flight home from Greece.

International passengers arriving at Athens' East Terminal

Booking agency in Athens

FLIGHT TIMES

FLYING TO ATHENS from New York takes about 10 hours, although a nondirect flight can take more than 12. From Los Angeles the journey's duration totals from 17 to 19 hours, depending on the European connection. The flight from London or Amsterdam is around 3.5 hours; from Paris and Berlin about 3 hours (it is a little quicker from Berlin). From Madrid it takes just over 4 hours, from Rome a little under 2 hours, and from Sydney or Melbourne, via Bangkok, it is a 19-hour flight.

AIR FARES

FARES TO GREECE are generally at their highest from June to September, but how much you pay will depend more on the type of ticket you decide to purchase. Charters are usually the least expensive option during the tourist season, although discounted scheduled flights are also common and worth considering for longer visits or during the low season, when there are not very many charters available. Reasonable savings can also be made by booking an APEX (Advance Purchase Excursion) ticket well in advance but, like charters, these are subject to minimum and maximum limits to one's stay and other restrictions. Travelers on a budget will often be able to find bargain flights through travel agents advertising in the newspapers, and inexpensive, last-minute deals are also advertised on the Internet. Whoever you book through, be sure that the company is a fully bonded and licensed member of ASTA (American Society of Travel Agents) or an equivalent authority – this will guarantee that you can get home should the company go bankrupt during your stay; it

Departure gates symbol

also should guarantee that you receive compensation. Note that domestic flights in Greece are subject to an airport tax, which is explained on page 314.

FLIGHT CONNECTIONS WITHIN GREECE

Kaváia

Thessaloníki

Alexandroúpoli

Kastoriá

Kozáni

Corfu

Ioánnina

Límnos

Skiáthos

Skýros

Lésvos

Préveza

Kefalloniá

Chíos

Sámos

Zákynthos

Ikaría

Syros   Mýkonos

Leros

Kalamáta

Páros

Náxos

Kos

Mílos

Santoríni

Astypálaia

Rhodes

Kýthira

Kastellórizo

Kárpathos

Crete (Chaniá)

Kásos

Crete (Irákleio)   Crete (Siteía)

KEY

✈ International airport

☒ Domestic airport

— Air route

m = 200km

Flight Connections in Greece

Olympic
logo

A THENS AIRPORT has two main terminals (East and West) and an additional terminal for charter flights. As well as having the largest number of international flights, Athens also has the most connecting services to other parts of Greece. Nearly all of these depart from the West terminal, so unless you arrive on an Olympic flight you will need to change terminals. Thessaloníki also handles scheduled flights, but only from within Europe. Greece's other international airports are served by charters only, mostly from the UK, Germany, the Netherlands, and Scandinavia.

Interior of the West (Olympic) terminal at Athens airport

DOMESTIC FLIGHTS

G REECE'S DOMESTIC airline network is extensive. **Olympic Airways** and its affiliate, **Olympic Aviation**, operate most domestic flights, though there are also a number of private companies, such as **Air Greece**, **Aegean** Aviation, and **Interjet**, providing services between Athens and some of the major island destinations. Fares for domestic flights are at least double the equivalent bus journey or deck-class ferry trip. Tickets and timetables for Olympic flights can be obtained from any Olympic Airways office in Greece or abroad, as well as from most major travel agencies. Reservations are essential in tourist season.

Olympic Airways operates direct flights from Athens to eight mainland towns, including Thessaloníki, Ioánnina, and Alexandroúpoli, and to over two dozen islands.

ATHENS AIRPORT MAIN TERMINALS

The East terminal is the main one for international flights. Domestic and all Olympic Airways flights leave from the West terminal. The two are connected by bus.

KEY

▨ Public access	▢ Passport control
▨ Check-in	▨ Baggage reclaim
▢ Passengers only	▢ No access
▨ Customs	▢ Boarding pass control

WEST TERMINAL

Car rental
International arrivals
International departures
Hotel reservations
Domestic departures
Domestic arrivals
Tickets
Banks and currency
To departure lounge
International departures

EAST TERMINAL

Car rental
International departures
Tickets
Banks
International arrivals
Bank of Greece

There are a number of inter-island services available during the summer, and about a dozen of these operate year round *(see p313).*

An airport departure tax is charged on domestic flights. There are two rates of tax: one for flights up to a distance of 430 air miles, and a double tariff for longer journeys.

TRANSPORT FROM ATHENS AIRPORT

F ROM ATHENS AIRPORT the most convenient way of getting to the city center is by taxi. There are stands outside the terminal buildings, and fares are low – less than in any other European city.

The journey time may vary greatly, depending on traffic congestion; when the roads are fairly clear, it takes about 30 minutes.

Alternatively, the express bus 091 *(see p325)* runs from the West (Olympic Airways), East, and Charter terminals to Plateía Syntágmatos in the center of Athens. Buses

depart every half hour from 5am to midnight, and every hour after midnight.

A second express bus (19) runs from the airport terminals to Plateía Karaïskáki at the port of Piraeus. Departures are about every 50 minutes between 5am and midnight, with four departures between midnight and 5am.

One of the smaller planes in Olympic's fleet, for short-haul flights

---

DIRECTORY

ATHENS AIRPORT

Athens West Terminal
Flight information:
01 936 3363.

Athens East Terminal
Flight information:
01 969 4111.

OLYMPIC AIRWAYS

Arrivals and Departures
01 936 3363.
144.

Athens Office
Syngroú 96,
11741 Athens.
01 926 9111.
01 966 6666
(reservations).

Thessaloníki Office
Kountouriótou 3,
Thessaloníki.
031 230240.

OTHER AIRLINES

Air Canada
Othonos 10,
10557 Athens.
01 322 3206.

Air France
Karageórgi Servias 4,
10562 Athens.
01 323 8507.

British Airways
Othonos 10,
10557 Athens.
01 325 0602.
Thessaloníki:
0312 42005.

Delta Airlines
Othonos 4,
10557 Athens.
01 331 1673.

Gulf Air
Nikis 30,
10557 Athens.
01 322 9544.

KLM
Vouliagménis 41,
16675 Athens.
01 988 0177.

Qantas
Nikodímou 2,
10564 Athens.
01 303 9063.

Singapore Airlines
Xenofóntos 9,
10557 Athens.
01 323 9111.

TWA
Xenofontos 8,
10557 Athens.
01 322 6451.

United Airlines
Syngroú 5, 11743 Athens.
01 924 2645.

Virgin Airways
Tziréon 8–10,
11742 Athens.
01 924 9100
(reservations).

PRIVATE AIRLINES (FOR DOMESTIC TRAVEL)

Aegean Aviation
East Terminal,
Athens Airport,
16603 Athens
01 995 0325.

Air Greece
Filellínon 22,
10557 Athens.
01 324 4457.

Interjet
Syngroú 350,
17680 Athens.
01 930 2151.

KAL Aviation
Vasiléos Konstantínou 26,
11635 Athens.
01 723 9971.

Olympic Aviation
01 938 4149.
01 936 3565 *(or via Olympic Airways).*

TRAVEL AGENCIES IN ATHENS

American Express Travel Services
Ermoú 2,
10563 Athens.
01 324 4975.

Ginis Vacances
3rd floor,
Ermoú 23–25,
10563 Athens.
01 325 0401.

Hellenic Holidays
Lékka 3–5, Syntágmatos,
10563 Athens.
01 323 7800.

International Student and Youth Travel Service
2nd floor, Nikis 11,
10557 Athens.
01 323 3767.

Manos Travel
Panepistimíou 39,
10564 Athens.
01 325 0711.

OLYMPIC AIRWAYS OFFICES ABROAD

Australia
37–49 Pitt Street,
Suite 303, Level 3,
Underwood House,
Royal Exchange,
Sydney, NSW 2001.
(2) 251 2044.

Canada
80 Bloor Street,
Suite 500, Toronto,
Ontario M5S F2V1.
(416) 964 7137.

UK
11 Conduit Street,
London W1R OLP.
0171-409 2400.
0171-409 3400
(ticket office).

US
645 Fifth Avenue,
New York, NY 10022.
(212) 735-0200.

Traveling by Train

Greek railroad's OSE logo

GREECE'S RAIL NETWORK is limited to the mainland, and the system is fairly skeletal by European standards. With the exception of intercity express trains, service tends to be slow. In compensation, non-express tickets are very inexpensive (much less than buses in fact), and some lines are pleasurable in themselves, traveling as they do through rugged and beautiful countryside. Fast and efficient intercity trains operate on some of the major lines, though tickets for these trains are more expensive. An overnight sleeper service is also available on the Athens–Thessaloníki and Thessaloníki–Alexandroúpoli routes.

via Belgrade; the line via Alexandroúpoli splits, going to Sofia and Istanbul; and the line to Flórina continues to Skopje. Intercity express trains run from Athens to Thessaloníki, Alexandroúpoli, Vólos, and Kozáni; and from Pireaus to Pátra, Kyparissía, and Thessaloníki. From Thessaloníki express trains run to Kozáni, Alexandroúpoli, and Vólos.

First- and second-class coaches of a non-express train

TRAVELING TO GREECE BY TRAIN

TRAVELING TO GREECE by train is expensive, but may be useful if you wish to make stopovers en route. From London to Athens, the main route takes about three and a half days. The journey is through France, Switzerland, and Italy, then by ferry from the Adriatic ports of Bari or Brindisi, via the Greek island of Corfu, to the port of Pátra, and finally on to Athens.

The other route is through the region of the former Yugoslavia, and does not necessitate a ferry crossing. The train travels overland via Budapest in Hungary, on to Belgrade and Skopje to arrive in Greece at Thessaloníki.

TRAVELING AROUND GREECE BY TRAIN

GREECE'S RAIL NETWORK is run by the state-owned **OSE** (Organismós Sidirodrómon Elládos), and Athens forms the hub of the system. A north-bound line from Lárissis station links Athens and Thessaloníki, with branch lines to Chalkída (Evvoia);

Vólos; Kardítsa, Tríkala, and Kalampáka; and Edessa and Kozáni. The southern narrow-gauge railroad runs from Athens' Peloponnísou station to towns in the Peloponnese, linking Athens to Kalamáta via Pátra and Pýrgos, or via Argos and Trípoli. Some routes are extremely picturesque, two of the best being the rack-and-pinion line between Diakoftó and Kalávryta in the Peloponnese (*see p168*), and the elevated section of line between Leivadiá and Lamía in central Greece.

From Thessaloníki there are three lines. The Polýkastro line continues to Budapest,

TRAIN TICKETS

TRAIN TICKETS can be bought at any OSE office or railroad station, plus some authorized travel agencies. It is worth getting your ticket – and reserving a seat at no extra charge – several days in advance, especially in summer when there are often more passengers than seats. A 50 percent surcharge is levied for tickets issued on the train.

There are three basic types of ticket: first class, second class, and intercity express. The first two are at most half the price of the equivalent bus journey, though service tends to be slower; tickets for intercity express trains are more costly but worth it for the time they save. A 20 percent reduction is offered on all round-trips, and a 30 percent discount for groups of six or more.

The Greek Railpass (sold by travel agents in North America) offers an easy, economical, and scenic way to travel from place to place in Greece. The pass allows the user 3, 5, or 10 days

Athens' Lárissis station, for trains to northern Greece

Peloponnísou station ticket window

of unlimited rail travel within a specified period. If traveling to Greece from England, InterRail and Eurail passes are both honored in Greece.

TRAIN STATIONS IN ATHENS

ATHENS HAS two train stations, virtually next door to each other, about a 15-minute walk northwest of Plateía Omonoías. Lárissis station, on Deligiánni, serves northern Greece (Thessaloníki, Vólos, and Lárisa), the Balkans, Turkey, and western Europe.

Additionally, tickets for OSE buses abroad are sold here, and there are baggage storage facilities. Peloponnísou station is a five-minute walk to the south over a metal bridge that crosses the railroad tracks. This serves trains for the Peloponnese, including Pátra, which is the main port for ferries to Italy. Trolleybus No. 1 from Plateía Syntágmatos passes close to Lárissis station. Alternatively, there are always taxis to be found in Athens, and fares are inexpensive compared with most other European cities.

The distinctive front end of an intercity express train

GREEK RAIL NETWORK

Sofia
Kastaniés
Ístanbul
Belgrade
Sofia
Skopje
Sidirókastro
Xánthi
Sérres
Dráma
Komotiní
Polýkastro
Kilkís
Féres
Flórina
Edessa
Alexandroúpoli
Amýntaio
Thessaloníki
Véroia
Kozáni
Kateríni
Litóchoro
Kalampáka
Lárisa
Tríkala
Kardítsa
Vólos
Lamía
Leivadiá
Chalkída
Pátra
Aígio
Thebes
Diakoftó
Xylókastro
Kyllíni
Kalávryta
Corinth
Piraéus
ATHENS
Pýrgos
Olympía
Argos
Tripoli
Náfplio
Megalópoli
Kyparissía
Kalamáta

KEY

— Principal rail routes

0 kilometers   200

0 miles   100

DIRECTORY

OSE OFFICES

Athens
Sína 6.
℡ 01 362 4402.
Karólou 1 (information).
℡ 01 522 4563.

Thessaloníki
Aristotélous 18.
℡ 0312 39174.

Lárisa
Velí 14.
℡ 0412 22201.

Vólos
Iásonos 42.
℡ 0421 25759.

RECORDED INFORMATION

℡ 145 (departures from Athens to other Greek destinations).
℡ 147 (departures from Athens to international destinations).

RAILROAD STATIONS

Athens
Lárissis station.
℡ 01 823 7000.
Peloponnísou station.
℡ 01 513 1601.

Thessaloníki
℡ 031 517517.

Pátra
℡ 061 221311.

Lárisa
℡ 041 236250.

Vólos
℡ 0421 23712.

RAIL TRAVEL FROM THE UK

British Rail International
Victoria Station,
London SW1V 1JY.
℡ 0171-834 2345.

Eurotrain
52 Grosvenor Gardens,
London SW1W OAG.
℡ 0171-730 8518.

Wasteels
Victoria Station,
London SW1V 1JY.
℡ 0171- 834 7066.

Traveling by Road

Road sign to port

Tʀᴀᴠᴇʟɪɴɢ ᴀʀᴏᴜɴᴅ ɢʀᴇᴇᴄᴇ by car gives you the flexibility to explore at your own pace. There are express highways between Athens, Thessaloníki, Vólos, and Pátra that are very fast, though tolls are charged for their use. The maps in this guide categorize the roads into four groups, from the express routes in blue to unpaved roads in yellow *(see back flap)*. The road system is continually being upgraded, and most routes are now surfaced.

You have priority

You have right of way

Do not use car horn

Wild animals crossing

Hairpin turn ahead

Traffic circle ahead

Tʀᴀᴠᴇʟɪɴɢ ᴛᴏ Gʀᴇᴇᴄᴇ ʙʏ Cᴀʀ

Bᴇᴄᴀᴜsᴇ ᴏғ ᴘᴏʟɪᴛɪᴄᴀʟ upheaval in the former Yugoslavia, the most direct overland routes to Greece are currently not recommended. Automobile organizations such as the ELPA (the Automobile and Touring Club of Greece) can offer advice on routes and regulations. It is worth asking their advice on insurance needs and any special regulations for countries en route.

You will need to take a valid national driver's licence, vehicle registration and insurance papers (at least liability), and a green card (international certificate of insurance). **ELPA** (the Automobile and Touring Club of Greece) also offers information on driving in Greece.

Rᴜʟᴇs ᴏғ ᴛʜᴇ Rᴏᴀᴅ

Dʀɪᴠɪɴɢ ɪs ᴏɴ the right in Greece, and road signs conform to European norms. There may be exceptions on small rural back roads, where the names of villages are often marked in Greek only.

The speed limit on national highways is 120 km/h (75 mph) for cars; on country roads it is 90 km/h (55 mph) and in towns 50 km/h (30 mph). The speed limit on national highways for motorcycles up to 100 cc is 70 km/h (45 mph), and 90 km/h (55 mph) for larger motorcycles.

Although usually ignored, the use of seatbelts in cars is required by law, and children under the age of ten are not allowed to sit in the front seat. Parking and speeding tickets must be paid at the local police station or your car rental agency.

Cᴀʀ Rᴇɴᴛᴀʟ

Tʜᴇʀᴇ ᴀʀᴇ sᴄᴏʀᴇs of car rental agencies in every tourist resort and major town, offering a full range of cars and four-wheel-drive vehicles.

A line of mopeds for rent

An express recovery vehicle

International companies such as **Budget**, **Avis**, **Hertz**, and **InterRent-Europcar** tend to be more expensive than their local counterparts, though the latter are generally as reliable.

The car rental agency should have an agreement with an emergency towing company, such as **Express**, **Hellas**, or the **InterAmerican Towing Company** in the event of a vehicle breakdown. Also, be sure to check the insurance policy cover: liability is required by law, but personal accident insurance is strongly recommended. A valid national driver's licence that has been held for at least one year is needed, and there is a minimum age requirement, ranging from 21 to 25 years.

Sign for car rental

Mᴏᴛᴏʀᴄʏᴄʟᴇ, Mᴏᴘᴇᴅ, ᴀɴᴅ Bɪᴄʏᴄʟᴇ Hɪʀᴇ

Mᴏᴛᴏʀᴄʏᴄʟᴇs ᴀɴᴅ ᴍᴏᴘᴇᴅs are readily available for rent in all the tourist resorts. Mopeds are ideal for short distances on fairly flat terrain, but for travel in more remote or mountainous areas a motorcycle is essential.

Whatever you decide to rent, make sure that the vehicle is in good condition before you set out, and that you have adequate insurance cover; also check whether your own travel insurance covers you for motorcycle accidents (many do not).

Speeding in Greece is penalized by fines, drunk driving laws are strict, and helmets are compulsory.

Though less widely available, bicycles can be rented in some tourist resorts.

Rack of bicycles for rent at a coastal resort

The hot weather and tough terrain make cycling extremely hard work, but, on the positive side, bikes can be transported free on most Greek ferries and buses, and for a small fee on trains.

GAS STATIONS

GASOLINE STATIONS are plentiful in towns, though in rural areas they are few and far between – always set out with a full tank to be on the safe side. Fuel is sold by the liter, and the price is very high by american standards. There are usually either three or four grades available: super (95 octane), unleaded, super unleaded and diesel, which is confusingly called *petrélaio* in Greece.

Unleaded and super gas

Filling stations set their own working hours in Greece. Generally they are open seven days a week, from around 7am or 8am to between 7pm and 10pm. Some stations in the larger towns remain open 24 hours a day.

TAXIS

TAXIS PROVIDE a reasonably priced way of making short trips around Greece. All taxis are metered, but for longer journeys a price can usually be negotiated *per diem* or per trip. Also, drivers are generally amenable to

Δράμα
Drama 36
Θεσσαλονίκη
Thessaloniki 161

Dual-language road sign, found on most routes

dropping you off somewhere and returning to pick you up a few hours later.

In Athens taxis are plentiful and can simply be hailed. In smaller towns it is best to find one at a taxi stand, which is likely to be either in the center or by the bus or train station. Most rural villages have at least one taxi, and the best place to arrange for one is at the local *kafeneío* (café). In Greece taxis are often shared with other passengers; each pays for their part of the journey. Although taxis are metered, it is worth getting a rough idea of the price before setting out. Tipping is not expected, but it never goes amiss.

HITCHHIKING

GREECE IS A RELATIVELY safe place for hitchhiking but, like anywhere else, there are potential risks. Women especially are advised against hitching alone.

If you do hitchhike, finding a ride is usually easier in the less populated, rural areas, than on busy roads heading out from major towns and cities.

MAPS

NOT TOO MUCH reliance should be given to maps issued by local travel agents and car rental agencies. Visitors intending to do much motoring are advised to bring the GeoCenter regional road maps (1:300,000 range) or the single-sheet Freytag & Berndt maps (1:650,000), both are more widely available abroad than within Greece itself.

Traveling by Bus

G REECE'S BUS SYSTEM is operated by KTEL (Koinó Tameío Eispráxeon Leoforeíon), a syndicate of privately run companies. The network is comprehensive in that it provides every community with services of some sort. In rural villages this may be once a day or, in more remote places, once or twice a week. Services between the larger centers are frequent and efficient. Time permitting, bus travel is a good way of experiencing the country.

International buses also connect Greece with the rest of Europe, though fares do not compare well with charter flights during the summer vacation season.

EUROPEAN BUS SERVICES TO GREECE

B US JOURNEYS from London to Athens take three or four days and are not as cheap as a bargain air fare. However, if you are not in a hurry, it is cheaper than taking the train.

Eurolines is a very reliable company, with a huge network of European destinations. Its coaches have reclining seats, toilets, and washing facilities, and there are frequent short stops en route. Single or round-trip tickets (the latter open-ended for up to six months) can be booked at any Eurolines office in person, or by telephone using a credit card.

Olympic Bus leaves every Friday (and Tuesday in high season) from the Brunswick Center, near Russell Square in London. It goes via Belgium and Italy, crossing to Greece on the Brindisi–Pátra ferry. For Australians this is preferable to the route across France, as no visa is required for passage through Belgium.

UK COACH OFFICES

Eurolines
52 Grosvenor Gardens, Victoria, London SW1.
█ 0171-730 8235.

Olympic Bus
70 Brunswick Centre, London WC1.
█ 0171-837 9141.

TRAVELING IN GREECE BY BUS

T HE GREEK bus system is extensive, with services to even the remotest destinations and frequent express

Domestic bus, run by KTEL

coaches on all the major routes. Large centers, such as Athens, usually have more than one terminal, and each serves a different set of destinations.

Ticket sales are computerized for all major routes, with reserved seating on modern, air-conditioned coaches. It pays to buy your ticket at least 20 minutes before the bus is scheduled to depart, since seats often get sold out on popular routes, and Greek buses have a habit of leaving a few minutes early.

In the villages of the countryside, the local *kafeneío* (café) often serves as the bus station. You can usually buy your ticket from the proprietor of the *kafeneío*, who may also have a timetable. Otherwise it is possible to buy a ticket when you board.

KTEL logo

BUS TOURS

I N THE RESORT AREAS, travel agents offer a wide range of excursions on air-conditioned buses accompanied by qualified guides. These include trips to major archaeological and historical sites, other towns and seaside resorts, popular beaches, and specially organized events. Depending on the destination, some bus tours leave very early in the morning, so they are best booked a day in advance.

BUS SERVICES FROM ATHENS

F ROM ATHENS there are frequent bus services to all the larger mainland towns, apart from those in Thrace, which are served by buses from Thessaloníki. Athens' Terminal A is situated 4 km (2.5 miles) northeast of the city center at Kifisoú 10 *(see p325).* The terminal serves Epirus, Macedonia, the Peloponnese, and the Ionian islands of Corfu, Kefalloniá, Lefkáda, and Zákynthos (ferry crossings are included in the price of the ticket). It takes 7.5 hours to Thessaloníki, and 7 hours to the port of Párga.

Terminal B is at Liosíon 260, north of Agios Nikólaos metro station, but most easily reached by taxi. It serves most destinations in central Greece, including Delphi, which takes 3 hours, and Vólos, which takes 6.

Buses to destinations around Attica, including Soúnio, Lávrio, Rafína, and Marathónas, leave from the Mavrommataíon bus terminal in Athens, a short walk north from the National Archaeological Museum on the corner of Leofóros Alexándras and 28 Oktovríou (Patisíon).

Eurolines international bus

Traveling by Sea

Greek catamaran

GREECE HAS ALWAYS been a nation of seafarers, and with its hundreds of islands and thousands of miles of coastline, the sea plays an important part in the life and history of the country. Today, it is a major source of revenue for Greece, with millions of tourists descending each year for seaside holidays in the Mediterranean and Aegean. The Greek mainland and islands are linked by a vast network of ferries, hydrofoils, and catamarans.

TRAVELING TO GREECE BY SEA

THERE ARE REGULAR year-round ferry crossings from the Italian ports of Ancona, Bari, and Brindisi to the Greek

Passengers on the walkways of a car ferry leaving dock

ports of Igoumenítsa in Epirus and Pátra in the Peloponnese, plus summer sailings from Venice, Trieste, and Otranto. Trip times and fares vary considerably, depending on time of year, point of embarkation, ferry company, type of ticket, and discounts (for students, youths, or railcard holders). Dozens of shipping lines cover the Italy–Greece routes, so it is best to shop around. In summer, reservations are advisable, especially if you are transporting a car or want a cabin.

GREEK FERRY SERVICE

THE GREEK FERRY SERVICE is good, though notoriously flexible with regard to schedules and departure times. From the smaller ports, your only

Dane Sea Lines funnel

concern will be getting a ferry that leaves on the day, and for the destination, that you want. Check the timetable on arrival for frequency and times of services, as schedules are changed each week.

Matters get more complicated from Piraeus, Greece's busiest port. Each of the many competing companies have agents at the dockside. Tickets and bookings (essential in tourist season) should be made through them, or at a travel agency.

Greece also has a network of hydrofoils and catamarans. They are twice as fast as ferries and, as a consequence, twice as expensive. As well as serving the islands, many stop at ports along the mainland coast. Most depart from Rafina, but those going to the Peloponnese coast depart from Piraeus, nearly all from Zea port. Advanced booking is usually essential.

The Greek tourist office's weekly schedules can serve as a useful guideline for all departures, and some of the English-language papers also print summer sailings.

If you are traveling out of season, expect all services to be significantly reduced and some routes to be suspended.

PIRAEUS PORT MAP

Piraeus is the largest and most important port in Greece. This map shows the layout of the main harbor and gives an indication of where you are likely to find ferries to various destinations.

KEY TO DEPARTURE POINTS

- ▇ Argo-Saronic islands
- ▇ Northeast Aegean islands
- ▇ Dodecanese
- ▇ Cyclades
- ▇ Crete
- ▢ International ferries
- ▇ Hydrofoils and catamarans

For key to symbols see back flap

Getting Around Athens

Trolleybus stop sign

THE SIGHTS OF ATHENS' city center are closely packed, and almost everything of interest can be reached on foot. This is the best way of sightseeing, especially in view of the appalling traffic congestion, which can make both public and private transport slow and inefficient. The expansion of the metro system should go some way to relieve these traffic problems but, until its completion, the bus and trolleybus network provides the majority of public transit in the capital for Athenians and visitors alike. Taxis are an alternative and, with the lowest tariffs of any EU capital, are worth considering even for longer journeys.

Orange and white regional bus for the Attica area

One of the large fleet of blue and white buses

BUS SERVICES IN ATHENS

ATHENS IS SERVED by an extensive bus network. Bus journeys are inexpensive, but can be slow and uncomfortably crowded, particularly in the city center and during rush hours; the worst times are from 7am to 8:30am, 2pm to 3:30pm, and 7:30pm to 9pm.

Tickets can be bought individually or in a book of ten, but either way, they must be purchased in advance from a *períptero* (street kiosk), a transit booth, or certain other designated places. The brown, red, and white logo, with the words *eisitíria edó*, indicates where you can buy bus tickets. The same ticket can be used on any bus or trolleybus, and must be stamped in a special ticket machine to cancel it when you board. There is a penalty fine for not stamping your ticket. Tickets are valid for one ride only, regardless of the distance and, within the central area, are not transferable from one vehicle to another.

Athens bus ticket booth

USEFUL ROUTES IN ATHENS

Metro stations at Kerameikós, Plateía Syntágmatos, and the National Gallery of Art are due to be in operation by 1998, though excavations may delay their opening.

Plateía Omonoías
M

National Archaeological Museum

M Kerameikós

National Historical Museum

National Gallery of Art
M

KEY
— Bus A5
— Bus 230
— Trolley bus 1
— Trolley bus 3
— Trolley bus 7
— Trolley bus 8
— Trolley bus 9
— Minibus 60
— Minibus 100
M Metro

M
Ancient Agora

Plateía Syntágmatos M

Lykavittós Hill

Acropolis

Benáki Museum

Museum of Cycladic Art

Pláka

ΜΟΝΑΣΤΗΡΙΟΝ
Monastirion

Monastiráki metro sign

ATHENS BUS NETWORKS

THERE ARE FOUR principal bus networks serving greater Athens and the Attica region. They are individually color coded: blue and white, red, orange and white, and green. Blue and white buses run an extensive network of over 300 routes in greater Athens, connecting districts to each other and to central Athens. A small complementary network of minibuses with red stop signs also operates, but in the central area only.

Orange and white buses serve the Attica area *(see pp142–3)*. On these you pay the conductor and, as distances are greater, fares are more expensive as well. The two terminals for orange and white buses are both situated on Mavrommataíon, by Pedío tou Areos (Areos Park). Though you can board at any designated orange stop, usually you cannot get off until you are outside the city area. These buses are less frequent than the blue and white service, and on some routes buses stop running in the early evening.

Green express buses, the fourth category, travel between central Athens and Piraeus. Numbers 040 and 049 are very frequent – about every 6 minutes – running from Athinas, by Plateía Omonoías, to various stops in Piraeus, including Plateía Karaïskáki, at the main harbor.

TROLLEYBUSES IN ATHENS

COMPLEMENTING the bus system is a network of trolleybuses, which are color coded yellow. There are about 19 trolleybus routes criss-crossing the city center. They provide a good way of getting around the sights of central Athens. All routes pass the Pláka area, but route 3 is useful for getting to the National Archaeological Museum from Plateía Syntágmatos, and route 1 links Lárissis railroad station with Plateía Omonoías and Plateía Syntágmatos, the heart of Athens' city center.

Front view of an Athens trolleybus

ATHENS' METRO

THE METRO is a fast and reliable means of transport in Athens. However, its usefulness is limited by the fact that, currently, there is just one line. It runs from Kifisiá in the north to Piraeus in the south, with central stations at Thiseío, Monastiráki, Omónoia, and Victoria. The majority of the line is overland and only runs underground between Attikí and Monastiráki stations through the city center. The line is used mainly by commuters, but can be useful for tourists, especially to reach the port of Piraeus.

Metro tickets

The ticket price increases a little if the journey passes through Omónoia station in either direction. Tickets can be bought at any metro station and must be validated before entering the train – there are machines for this purpose at the entrances to all platforms. Trains run every five minutes, and operate from 5am to midnight.

Expansion of Athens' metro is now under way, with two additional lines and 18 new stations scheduled to open by the end of 1998. The routes will extend the network diagonally from northwest to southeast, and laterally from east to west, with connecting points at Omónoia and Monastiráki. These lines will be 20 m (66 ft) underground, in order to avoid material of archaeological interest. The excavations that have begun as a result of the expansion project are currently impeding the metro lines' development, however, and the projected opening date is very likely to be delayed, possibly by several years.

Piraeus metro station

DRIVING IN ATHENS

D RIVING IN ATHENS can be a nerve-racking experience, especially if you are not accustomed to the Greek way of driving. Many streets in the center are pedestrianized, and there are also plenty of one-way streets, so you need to plan routes carefully. Finding a parking space can also be very difficult. Despite appearances to the contrary, parking in front of a no-parking sign or on a single yellow line is illegal. There are parking meters and pay-and-display machines, as well as underground lots, though they fill up quickly.

In an attempt to reduce dangerously high air pollution levels, there is an "odd-even" driving system in effect. Cars with an odd number at the end of their licence plates can enter the central grid (*daktýlio*) only on dates with an odd number, and cars with an even number on their plates are allowed only on even dates. The rule does not apply to foreign cars but, if possible, avoid taking your car into the city center.

Parking meter in Athens

No parking on odd-numbered days of the month

No parking on even-numbered days of the month

Yellow Athens Taxi

ATHENIAN TAXIS

S WARMS OF YELLOW taxis can be seen cruising around Athens at most times of the day or night. However, trying to persuade one to stop for you can be difficult, especially from 2pm to 3pm when taxi drivers change shifts. Then, they will pick you up only if you happen to be going in a convenient direction for them.

To hail a taxi, stand on the edge of the pavement and shout out your destination to any cab that slows down. If a cab's "TAXI" sign is lit up then it is definitely for hire (but often a taxi is also for hire when the sign is not lit). It is also common practice for drivers to pick up extra passengers along the way, so do not ignore the occupied cabs. If you are not the first passenger, take note of the meter reading immediately: there is no fare-sharing, so you should be charged only for your portion of the journey (or the minimum fare of 200 Dr, whichever is greater).

Athenian taxis are extremely cheap by European standards – depending on traffic, you should not have to pay more than 700 Dr to go anywhere in the downtown area, and between 1,000 Dr and 1,700 Dr from the center to Piraeus or the airport. Double fares come into effect between midnight and 5am, and for journeys that exceed certain distances from the city center. There are also small surcharges for extra pieces of luggage weighing over 10 kg (22 lbs), and for trips from the airport, ferry, or railroad terminals. Taxi fares are increased around the Christmas holiday and during Easter.

For a small extra charge, you can make a phone call to a radio taxi company and arrange for a car to pick you up at an appointed place and time. Radio taxis are plentiful in the Athens area. Listed below are the telephone numbers of a few companies:

Express
[01 993 4812.

Kosmos
[01 420 0042.

Hellas
[01 645 7000.

WALKING

T HE CENTER OF ATHENS is very compact, and almost all major sights and museums are to be found within a 20- or 25-minute walk of Plateía Syntágmatos, which is generally regarded as the city's center. This is worth bearing in mind, particularly when traffic is congested, all buses are full, and no taxi will stop. Athens is still one of the safest European cities to walk around in, but, as in any sizeable metropolis, it pays to be vigilant, especially at night.

Sign for a pedestrianized area

Visitors to Athens walking up the Areopagos

ATHENS TRANSIT LINKS

THE HUB OF ATHENS' city transit is the area around Plateía Syntágmatos and Plateía Omonoías. From this central area trolleybuses or buses can be taken to the airport, the harbor at Piraeus, Athens' two train stations, and its domestic and international bus terminals.

Bus 091 provides a service that links the city center with the airport's East, West, and Charter terminals. Buses 040 and 049 link the harbor at Piraeus with the city center at Syntágmatos and Omonoías. The metro also extends to Piraeus harbor. Piraeus is linked directly to the airport: bus 19 goes from Piraeus to all the airport terminals, and also operates a limited service throughout the night.

Trolleybus route 1 goes past Lárissis train station (with the Peloponnísou station a short walk away), while bus 024 goes to bus terminal B, on Liosíou, and bus 051 to bus terminal A, on Kifisoú.

Though more expensive than public transit, the most convenient way of getting to and from these destinations is by taxi. The journey times vary greatly but, if traffic is light, from the city center to the airport takes between 25 and 30 minutes; the trip from the city center to Piraeus takes about 30 to 40 minutes; and the trip from Piraeus to the airport also takes in the region of 30 to 40 minutes.

Bus from the port of Piraeus to Athens' city center

ATHENS TRANSIT LINKS

Achárnes

Thessaloníki

024

Agios Eleuthérios

Bus Terminal B

Ancient Eleusis
Ancient Corinth

E94

ATHINON

Monastery of Dafní

Káto Patísia

Agios Nikólaos

Sepólia M

051

Bus Terminal A

Attikí

Mavrommataíon Bus Terminal

Lárissa

Peloponnísou & Lárissis

Deligiánni

Victoria

091, 051, 024, 049

Soúnio
Rafína
Lávrio

ATHINON

KIFISOU

Kerameikós

Omónoia

Akadimías

Evangelismós

Syntagma

Ancient Eleusis

PIREOS

Thiseío

Monastiráki

M

Pétralona

040, 091

Pérama

Eleftheríou Venizélou-Távros

Kallithéa

PIREOS

Olympeíon

Néos Kósmos

Análatos

ANDREA

SINGROU

Agios Ioánnis M

Dáfni

M

19, 049, 040

Moscháto M

Piraeus

Fáliro

VOULIAGMENIS

KEY

Central Athens

Greater Athens

Airport terminal

Metro station

Bus terminal

Railroad station

- - Major bus route

Divided highway

Major road

Minor road

Kalamáki

POSIDONOS

Saronic
Gulf

19, 091

West Air Terminal

East Air Terminal

Charter Terminal

19, 091

Koropí

General Index

Acknowledgments

DORLING KINDERSLEY would like to thank the following people whose contributions and assistance have made the preparation of this book possible.

MAIN CONTRIBUTORS

MARC DUBIN is an American expatriate who divides his time between London and Sámos. Since 1978 he has traveled in every province of Greece. He has written or contributed to numerous guides to Greece.

MIKE GERRARD is a travel writer and broadcaster who has written several guides to various parts of Greece, where he has been visiting annually since 1964.

ANDY HARRIS is a travel and food journalist based in Athens. He is the author of *A Taste of the Aegean*.

TANYA TSIKAS is a Canadian writer and travel guide editor. Married to a Greek, she has spent time in Crete and currently lives in Oxford.

ADDITIONAL ILLUSTRATIONS

Richard Bonson, Louise Boulton, Gary Cross, Kevin Goold, Roger Hutchins, Claire Littlejohn.

DESIGN AND EDITORIAL ASSISTANCE

Hilary Bird, Elspeth Collier, Catherine Day, Jim Evoy, Emily Hatchwell, Leanne Hogbin, Kim Inglis, Lorien Kite, Felicity Laughton, Andreas Michael, Ella Milroy, Lisa Minsky, Robert Mitchell, Jennifer Mussett, Tamsin Pender, Jake Reimann, Simon Ryder, Rita Selvaggio, Claire Stewart, Claire Tennant-Scull, Amanda Tomeh.

DORLING KINDERSLEY would also like to thank the following for their assistance: The Greek Wine Bureau, Odysea.

DK PUBLISHING would like to thank Alexis Theodorcopoulos, Frederick Jones, Christopher Barford, and Phoebe Todd-Naylor for moral support.

ADDITIONAL RESEARCH

Anna Antoniou, Anastasia Caramanis, Magda Dimouti, Shirley Durant, Panos Gotsi, Zoi Groummouti, Peter Millett, Tasos Schizas, Garifalia Tsiola.

ADDITIONAL PHOTOGRAPHY

Stephen Bere, John Heseltine, Steven Ling, Clive Streeter, Jerry Young.

ARTWORK REFERENCE

Ideal Photo S.A., The Image Bank, Tony Stone Worldwide.

PHOTOGRAPHY PERMISSIONS

DORLING KINDERSLEY would like to thank the following for their assistance and kind permission to photograph at their establishments:

Ali Pasha Museum, Ioannina; City of Athens Museum; Museum of Greek Folk Art, Athens; V Kyriazopoulos Ceramic Collection; Kavala Modern Art Gallery; National Gallery of Art, Athens; National War Museum, Athens; Nicholas P Goulandris Foundation Museum of Cycladic and Ancient Art, Athens; Theatrical Museum, Athens; University of Athens Museum; Polygnotos Vagis Museum, Thassos. Also all other cathedrals, churches, museums, hotels, restaurants, shops, galleries, and sights too numerous to thank individually.

PICTURE CREDITS

t = top; tl = top left; tlc = top left center; tc = top center; trc = top right center; tr = top right; cla = center left above; ca = center above; cra = center right above; cl = center left; c = center; cr = center right; clb = center left below; cb = center below; crb = center right below; bl = bottom left; b = bottom; bc = bottom center; bcl = bottom center left; br = bottom right; bottom right above = bra; bottom right below = brb; d= detail.

Every effort has been made to trace the copyright holders. DORLING KINDERSLEY apologizes for any unintentional omissions and would be pleased, in such cases, to add an acknowledgment in future editions.

Works of art have been reproduced with the permission of the following copyright holders: Vorres Museum *Water Nymph* (1995) Apostolos Petridis.

The publisher would like to thank the following individuals, companies and picture libraries for permission to reproduce their photographs:

AISA ARCHIVO ICONGRAFICO, Barcelona: Museo Archeologique Bari 57tr; Museo Archeologique Florence 54tl; AKG, London: 173t, 259; Antiquario Palatino 53bl; *Bilder aus dem Altherthume*, Heinrich Leutemann 228c;

British Museum 95br; Edward Dodwell 87cr; Erich Lessing Akademie der Bildenden Künste, Vienna 54c; Musée du Louvre 53tl; National Archeological Museum, Athens 26–7(d), 27t; Staatliche Kunstsammlungen, Albertinum, Dresden 31crb; Liebighaus, Frankfurt/Main 33c; Museum Narodowe, Warsaw 145b; Staatliche Antikensammlungen und Glyptotek, München 4, 52b; Mykonos Museum 55t; ALLSPORT: Mike Hewitt 120t; ANCIENT ART AND ARCHITECTURE: 29cl, 30t, 34t, 34ca, 35cl, 37t, 56cb, 56b(d), 246cb, 254c; ANTIKENMUSEUM BASEL UND SAMMLUNG LUDWIG: 60–1, 185br(d); APERION: John Hios 184c; Kamarias Tsigamos 118c; APOLLO EDITIONS: 185t; ARGYROPOULOS PHOTO PRESS: 45t, 45ca, 47t, 47cb, 47b, 48cb; CENTRE FOR ASIA MINOR STUDIES: Museum of Greek Popular Musical Instruments Fivos Anoyianakis Collection 104t.

BENAKI MUSEUM: 25b, 36ca, 39t, 39c, 41ca, 65br, 78–9 all; PAUL BERNARD: 33t; BIBLIOTHEQUE NATIONAL, Paris: Caoursin folio 175 38–9(d); BODLEIAN LIBRARY, Oxford: MS Canon Misc 378, 170v, 34cb; BRIDGEMAN ART LIBRARY, London: Birmingham City Museums and Art Galleries *Pheidias Completing the Parthenon Frieze,* Sir Lawrence Alma-Tadema 58t; Bradford Art Galleries and Museums *The Golden Fleece* (c.1904), Herbert James Draper 220br; British Museum, London *Cup, Tondo, with Scene of Huntsmen Returning Home* 29cr, *Black-necked Amphora, Depicting Boxers and Wrestlers* (c.550–525 BC) Nidosthenes 173cra; Fitzwilliam Museum, University of Cambridge *Figurine of Demosthenes,* Enoch Wood of Burslem (c.1790) (lead glazed earthenware) 57tl; Giraudon, Louvre, Paris *Alexander the Great,* portrait head (3rd century BC) Greek (marble) 32tr; House of Masks, Delos *Mosaic of Dionysus Riding a Leopard* (c.AD 180) 35t; Guildhall Art Library *Clytemnestra,* John Collier 179c; Louvre, Paris *Double Bust of Aristophanes and Sophocles* (15th century) 56t; National Archaeological Museum, Athens *Bronze Statue of Poseidon* (c.460–450 BC) photo Bernard Cox 52ca; Private Collection *Two-tiered Icon of the Virgin and Child and Two Saints, Cretan School* (15th century) 38cl; © THE BRITISH MUSEUM: 26clb, 27cb, 28t, 30cb, 31clb, 53tr(d), 53br, 55c(d), 60tl, 61tl, 61tr, 97b, 173cla(d), 185bl.

CAMERA PRESS, London: ANAG 43tl, 43bl(d); Wim Swaan 62–3, 243t; JEAN LOUP CHARMET: Bibliotheque des Artes Decoratifs 24(d); BRUCE COLEMAN LTD: Udo Hirsch 236b; Dr Eckart Pott 257c; Hans Reinhard 22t, 23cla, 206b.

C M DIXON PHOTO RESOURCES: 27ca; Staatliche Antikensammlung und Glyptotek, München 32tr; MARC DUBIN: 17t, 21bca, 169t, 206t, 208cr, 253t, 253br.

ECOLE NATIONALE SUPERIEURE DES BEAUX ARTS, Paris: *Delphes Restauration du Sanctuaire Envoi Tournaire* (1894) 30–1; EKDOTIKI ATHINON: 19br, 26crb; ELIA: 186c; ET ARCHIVE: British Museum 185c; National Archaeology Museum, Naples 32ca; MARY EVANS PICTURE LIBRARY: 241b.

FERENS ART GALLERY: Hull City Museums and Art Galleries and Archives *Electra at the Tomb of Agamennon* (1869), Lord Frederick Leighton 55b; FOLK ART MUSEUM, Athens: 110t, 110b.

GIRAUDON, Paris: Laruros Versailles Chateau *Le Batille de Navarin,* Louis Ambroise Garneray 200t; Louvre, Paris 60c, *Scene de Massacres de Scio,* Delacroix 40ca(d); Musee Nationale Gustave Moreau *Hesiode et Les Muses* Gustave Moreau 56ca; Musee d'Art Catalan, Barcelona 95bra; National Portrait Gallery, London *Portrait of George Gordon Byron,* Thomas Phillips (1813) 149tr(d); NICHOLAS P GOULANDRIS FOUNDATION MUSEUM OF CYCLADIC AND ANCIENT GREEK ART: 65tr, 74–5 all.

ROBERT HARDING PICTURE LIBRARY: David Beatty 44br; N A Callow 263t; Tony Gervis 44cla, 44bl; Photri 314t; Adam Woolfitt 46c; HELIO PHOTO: 254b; HELLENIC POST SERVICE: 43cla; MICHAEL HOLFORD: British Museum 32cb, 52t; HULTON GETTY COLLECTION: 41cb(d); Central Press Photo 42clb(d); HUTCHISON LIBRARY: Hilly Janes 98t.

IDEAL PHOTO SA: T Dassios 45br, 175t, 232, 252t, 252bl, 252br, 253cl, 262b; C. Vergas 48b,178b; IMAGES COLOUR LIBRARY: 99b; IMPACT PHOTOS: Caroline Penn 45bl.

KOSTOS KONTOS: 26cr, 42cra, 42cla, 45crb, 119b, 120b, 140, 152tl, 153tl, 153ca, 153b, 170t, 175c, 178c, 184t, 189tr, 303t, 315t. ILIAS LALAOUNIS: 309cla.

MAGNUM PHOTOS LTD: Constantine Manos 44t; MANSELL COLLECTION: 52–3; MUNICIPAL ART GALLERY OF ATHENS: *Despinis TK* Mitarakis Yannis 88t.

NATIONAL GALLERY OF VICTORIA, Melbourne: Felton Bequest (1956) *Greek by the Inscriptions Painter Challidian* 54b; NATIONAL HISTORICAL MUSEUM, Athens: 38t, 40t, 40–1(d), 41t, 42b, 173clb, 188cl(d), 194c; NATIONAL TOURIST ORGANISATION OF GREECE: George Boutos 46b; NATURAL IMAGE: Bob Gibbons 23crb, 23bl; Peter Wilson 237cr; NATURE PHOTOGRAPHERS: S C Bisserot 236c; Brinsley Burbridge 23clb, 23br; N A Callow 22b; Andrew Cleave 23bc, 237b; Peter Craig Cooper 237cl; Paul Sterry 23t, 23cra, 225cr; ANTONIS NICOLOPOULOS: 311t.

OLYMPIC AIRWAYS: 312t; ORONOZ ARCHIVO FOTOGRAFICO: 211b; Biblioteca National Madrid *Invasions Bulgares Historia Matriksiscronica FIIIV* 36cb(d); Charlottenberg, Berlin 53tr; El Escorial, Madrid *Battle Lepanto Cambiaso Luca* 38cr(d); Museo Julia 53cl(d); Musee Louvre 60b; Museo Vaticano 61bl, 221tr.

ROMYLOS PARISIS: 14t, 104b, 136–7, 218b; City of Athens Museum 40cb; PICTURES: 12, 14b, 44crb, 310c; POPPERFOTO: 42crb, 43cra, 43br, 98b, 180t, 262t; MICHALIS PORNALIS: 218c, 219cb, 219b; PRIVATE COLLECTIONS: 5t, 216t, 217t, 217b.

REX FEATURES: 15c; Argyropoulos/Sipa 48t; Sipa/C.Brown 43tr.

SCALA, Florence: Gallerie degli Uffizi 28b; Museo Archeologico, Firenze 29t; Museo Mandralisca Cefalu 30ca; Museo Nationale Tarquinia 61br; Museo de Villa Giulia 28–9, 60tr; SPATHARIO SHADOW THEATRE MUSEUM: 151c; SPECTRUM COLOUR LIBRARY: 244b; MARIA STEFOSSI: 118b; THEODOROS-PATROKLOS STELLAKIS: 154b; CARMEL STEWART: 279c; TONY STONE IMAGES: Aperion 152tl(d).

TAP SERVICE ARCHAEOLOGICAL RECEIPTS FUND HELLENIC REPUBLIC MINISTRY OF CULTURE: A Epharat of Antiquities 43cb, 58b, 94bl, 94br, 95t, 95c, 96b, 98c, 99cr, 100t, 100c; Acropolis Museum 96t, 97t, 97c; Ancient Corinth Archaeological Museum 166c; B Epharat of Antiquities 82, 141b, 144 all, 146c, 146bl, 146br, 147tl, 147c, 148c, 148b; Byzantine Museum, Athens 67t, 76 all; D Epharat of Antiquities 139c, 139bl, 162–3 all, 164–5, 167bl, 177b, 178t, 179t, 179b, 180c, 181c; Delphi Archaeological Museum 50–1, 228t, 230tl, 231t, 231b; E Epharat of Antiquities 174cb; Elefis Archaeological Museum 156b; 11th Epharat of Byzantine Antiquities 237tr; 5th Epharat of Byzantine Antiquities 19tl, 19cl, 37c, 190–1, 192t, 192b; 1st Epharat of Byzantine Antiquities 139cra, 152c, 153cb, 222–3 all; I Epharat of Antiquities 138ca, 205t, 226–7, 228b, 229c, 230tr, 230b; IB Epharat of Antiquities 211t, 212c; IO Epharat of Antiquities 256c; IST Epharat of Antiquities 241c; Keramikos Archaeological Museum 89t, 89cr, 89br, 91t, 91car; Marathon Archaeological Museum 145c; National Archeological Museum, Athens 3c, 26t, 28tr, 65tl, 68t, 68c, 68b, 69t, 69c, 69b, 70–1 all, 99t, 155t, 157cr; 9th Epharat of Byzantine Antiquities 248c, 248b; Pireaus Archaeological Museum 155t; 2nd Epharat of Byzantine Antiquities 19tr; 6th Epharat of Byzantine Antiquities 13t, 19cr; 7th Epharat of Byzantine Antiquities 19bl, 218tl, 219ca; Thebes Archaeological Museum 221t; Thessaloníki Archaeological Museum 31t, 139t, 233t, 242b(d), 244t, 246t, 246ca, 246b, 247tl, 247tr, 247c, 247b, 244tl; Γ Epharat of Antiquities 88c, 88b, 89cl, 89bl, 90t, 90b, 91cla, 91cb, 91b, 156t, 156c, 157cl, 157bl, 157bc, 157br; Z Epharat of Antiquities 138ca, 170c, 170b, 171t, 171b, 172 all, 201c, 201b, 310bl; TRIP PHOTOGRAPHIC LIBRARY: Marc Dubin 250–1; YANNIS TSAROUHIS FOUNDATION: Private Collection *Barber Shop in Marousi* (1947) 42tr.

WADSWORTH ATHENEUM, Hartford Connecticut: T Pierpont Morgan Collection 189b; WERNER FORMAN ARCHIVE: 36t; Alan Williams: 49t; PETER WILSON: 59bl, 92–3, 94t, 100b, 106–7, 214–5, 216c; WOODFIN CAMP & ASSOCIATES: John Marmaras 254t; ADAM WOOLFITT 45clb.

Front Endpaper: all special photography except Rt IDEAL PHOTO SA: T Dassios and Rbl KOSTOS KONTOS (d).

Jacket: all special photography except KOSTOS KONTOS: front cra(d); NATURAL IMAGE: Bob Gibbons front br; PETER WILSON: front cra.

Phrase Book

HERE IS NO universally accepted system for representing the modern Greek language in the Roman alphabet. The system of transliteration adopted in this guide is the one used by the Greek Government. Though not yet fully applied throughout Greece, most of the street and place names have been transliterated according to this system. For Classical names this guide uses the k, os, on, and f spelling, in keeping with the modern system of transliteration. In a few cases, such as Socrates and Philoppapus, the more familiar Latin form has been used. Classical names are left unaccented. Where a well-known English form of a name exists, such as Athens or Corinth, this has been used. Variations in transliteration are given in the index.

GUIDELINES FOR PRONUNCIATION

The accent over Greek and transliterated words indicates the stressed syllable. In this guide the accent is not written over capital letters nor over monosyllables, except for question words and the conjunction ή (meaning "or"). In the right-hand "Pronunciation" column below, the syllable to stress is given in bold type.

On the following pages, the English is given in the left-hand column with the Greek and its transliteration in the middle column. The right-hand column provides a literal system of pronounciation and indicates the stressed syllable in bold.

THE GREEK ALPHABET

Α α	A a	**a**rm
Β β	V v	**v**ote
Γ γ	G g	**y**ear (when followed by e and i sounds) **n**o (when followed by ξ or γ)
Δ δ	D d	**th**at
Ε ε	E e	**e**gg
Ζ ζ	Z z	**z**oo
Η η	I i	**k**eep
Θ θ	Th th	**th**ink
Ι ι	I i	**k**eep
Κ κ	K k	**k**id
Λ λ	L l	**l**and
Μ μ	M m	**m**an
Ν ν	N n	**n**o
Ξ ξ	X x	ta**x**i
Ο ο	O o	**f**ox
Π π	P p	**p**ort
Ρ ρ	R r	**r**oom
Σ σ	S s	**s**orry (zero when followed by μ)
ς	s	(used at end of word)
Τ τ	T t	**t**ea
Υ υ	Y y	k**ee**p
Φ φ	F f	**f**ish
Χ χ	Ch ch	lo**ch** in most cases, but **h**e when followed by a, e, or i sounds
Ψ ψ	Ps ps	ma**ps**
Ω ω	O o	**f**ox

COMBINATIONS OF LETTERS

In Greek there are two-letter vowels that are pronounced as one sound:

Αι αι	Ai ai	**e**gg
Ει ει	Ei ei	k**ee**p
Οι οι	Oi oi	k**ee**p
Ου ου	Ou ou	l**u**te

There are also some two-letter consonants that are pronounced as one sound:

Μπ μπ	Mp mp	**b**ut, sometimes nu**mb**er in the middle of a word
Ντ ντ	Nt nt	**d**esk, sometimes u**nd**er in the middle of a word
Γκ γκ	Gk gk	**g**o, sometimes bi**ng**o in the middle of a word
Γξ γξ	nx	a**nx**iety
Τζ τζ	Tz tz	han**ds**
Τσ τσ	Ts ts	i**t's**
Γγ γγ	Gg gg	bi**ng**o

IN AN EMERGENCY

Help!	Βοήθεια! Voitheia	vo-**ee**-theea
Stop!	Σταματήστε! Stamatiste	sta-ma-t**ee**-steh
Call a doctor!	Φωνάξτε ένα γιατρό Fonáxte éna giatró	fo-n**ak**-steh e-na ya-**tro**
Call an ambulance/ the police/the fire department!	Καλέστε το ασθενοφόρο/την αστυνομία/την πυροσβεστική Kaléste to asthenoforo/tin astynomia/tin pyrosvestiki	ka-**le**-steh to as-the- no-**fo**-ro/teen a-sti- no-**mia**/teen pee-ro- zve-stee-k**ee**
Where is the nearest telephone/hospital/ pharmacy?	Πού είναι το πλησιέστερο τηλέφωνο/νοσοκο- μείο/φαρμακείο; Poú einai to plisiés- tero tiléfono/ nosoko- meio/farmakeio?	p**oo** ee-ne to plee- see-**e**-ste-ro tee-**le**- pho-no/no-so-ko- me**e**-o/far-ma-ke**e**-o

COMMUNICATION ESSENTIALS

Yes	Ναι Nai	neh
No	Οχι Ochi	**o**-chee
Please	Παρακαλώ Parakaló	pa-ra-ka-**lo**
Thank you	Ευχαριστώ Efcharistó	ef-cha-ree-**sto**
You are welcome	Παρακαλώ Parakaló	pa-ra-ka-**lo**
OK/alright	Εντάξει Entáxei	en-**dak**-zee
Excuse me	Με συγχωρείτε Me synchoreite	me seen-cho-r**ee**-teh
Hello	Γειά σας Geiá sas	ye**e**a sas
Goodbye	Αντίο Antío	an-de**e**-o
Good morning	Καλημέρα Kaliméra	ka-lee-**me**-ra
Good night	Καληνύχτα Kalinýchta	ka-lee-ne**e**ch-ta
Morning	Πρωί Proí	pro-e**e**
Afternoon	Απόγευμα Apógevma	a-**po**-yev-ma
Evening	Βράδυ Vrádi	vrath-i
This morning	Σήμερα το πρωί Simera to proi	se**e**-me-ra to pro-e**e**
Yesterday	Χθές Chthés	chthes
Today	Σήμερα Simera	se**e**-me-ra
Tomorrow	Αύριο Avrio	**av**-ree-o
Here	Εδώ Edó	ed-**o**
There	Εκεί Ekei	e-k**ee**
What?	Τι; Ti?	tee
Why?	Γιατί; Giatí?	ya-te**e**
Where?	Πού; Poú?	p**oo**
How?	Πώς; Pós?	pos
Wait!	Περίμενε! Perimene!	pe-re**e**-me-nch

USEFUL PHRASES

How are you?	Τί κάνεις; Ti káneis?	tee ka-nees
Very well, thank you	Πολύ καλά, ευχαριστώ Poly kalá, efcharistó	po-lee ka-la, ef-cha-ree-sto
How do you do?	Πώς είστε; Pós eíste?	pos ces-te
Pleased to meet you	Χαίρω πολύ Chairo polý	che-ro po-lee
What is your name?	Πώς λέγεστε; Pós légeste?	pos le-ye-ste
Where is/are...?	Πού είναι; Poú eínai?	poo ce-ne
How far is it to...?	Πόσο απέχει...; Póso apéchei...?	po-so a-pe-chee
How do I get to?	Πώς μπορώ να πάω...; Pós mporó na páo...?	pos bo-ro-na pa-o
Do you speak English?	Μιλάτε Αγγλικά; Miláte Angliká?	mee-la-te an-glee-ka
I understand	Καταλαβαίνω Katalavaino	ka-ta-la-ve-no
I don't understand	Δεν καταλαβαίνω Den katalavaino	then ka-ta-la-ve-no
Could you speak slowly?	Μιλάτε λίγο πιο αργά παρακαλώ; Miláte ligo pio argá parakaló?	mee-la-te lee-go pyo ar-ga pa-ra-ka-lo
I'm sorry	Με συγχωρείτε Me synchoreite	me seen-cho-ree teh
Does anyone have a key?	Έχει κανένας κλειδί; Echei kanénas kleidi?	e-chee ka-ne-nas klee-dee

USEFUL WORDS

big	Μεγάλο Megálo	me-ga-lo
small	Μικρό Mikró	mi-kro
hot	Ζεστό Zestó	zes-to
cold	Κρύο Krýo	kree-o
good	Καλό Kaló	ka-lo
bad	Κακό Kakó	ka ko
enough	Αρκετά Arketá	ai-ke-ta
well	Καλά Kalá	ka-la
open	Ανοιχτά Anoichtá	a-neech-ta
closed	Κλειστά Kleistá	klee-sta
left	Αριστερα Aristerá	a-ree-ste-ra
right	Δεξιά Dexiá	dek-see-a
straight ahead	Ευθεία Eftheia	ef-thee-a
between	Ανάμεσα / Μεταξύ Anámesa / Metaxý	a-na-me-sa/me-tak-see
on the corner of...	Στη γωνία του... Sti gonia tou...	stee go-nee-a too
near	Κοντά Kontá	kon-da
far	Μακριά Makriá	ma-kree-a
up	Επάνω Epáno	e-pa-no
down	Κάτω Káto	ka-to
early	Νωρίς Norís	no-rees
late	Αργά Argá	ar-ga
entrance	Η είσοδος I eísodos	ee ce-so-thos
exit	Η έξοδος I éxodos	ee e-kso-dos
toilet	Οι τουαλέτες /WC Oi toualétes / WC	ee too-a-le-tes
occupied/engaged	Κατειλημμένη Kateilimméni	ka-tee-lee-me-nee

unoccupied/vacant	Ελεύθερη Eléftheri	e-lef-the-ree
free/no charge	Δωρεάν Doreán	tho-re-an
in/out	Μέσα /Έξω Mésa/ Exo	me-sa/ek-so

MAKING A TELEPHONE CALL

Where is the nearest public telephone ?	Πού βρίσκεται ο πλησιέστερος τηλεφωνικός θάλαμος; Poú vrísketai o plisiésteros tilefonikós thálamos?	poo vrees-ke-teh o plee-see-e-ste-ros tee-le-fo-ni-kos tha-la-mos
I would like to place a long-distance call	Θα ήθελα να κάνω ένα υπεραστικό τηλεφώνημα Tha ithela na káno éna yperastikó tilefónima	tha ec-the-la na ka-no e-na ee-pe-ra-sti-ko tee-le-fo-nee-ma
I would like to call collect	Θα ήθελα να χρεώσω το τηλεφώνημα στον παραλήπτη Tha ithela na chreóso to tilefónima ston paralipti	tha ce-the-la na chre-o-so to tee-le-fo-nee-ma ston pa-ra-lep-tee
I will try again later	Θα ξανατηλεφωνήσω αργότερα Tha xanatilefoniso argótera	tha ksa-na-tee-le-fo-ni-so ar-go-te-ra
Can I leave a message?	Μπορείτε να του αφήσετε ένα μήνυμα; Mporeite na tou afisete éna minyma?	bo-ree-te na too a-fee-se-tch e-na mee-nee-ma
Could you speak up a little please?	Μιλάτε δυνατότερα, παρακαλώ; Miláte dynatótera, parakaló	mee-la-teh dee-na-to-te-ra, pa-ra-ka-lo
Local call	Τοπικό τηλεφώνημα Topikó tilefónima	to-pi-ko tee-le-fo-nee-ma
Hold on	Περιμένετε Periménete	pe-ri-me-ne-tch
OTE telephone office	Ο ΟΤΕ / Το τηλεφωνείο O OTE / To tilefoneio	o O-TE / To tee-le-fo-nee-o
Phone booth/kiosk	Ο τηλεφωνικός θάλαμος; O tilefonikós thálamos	o tee-le-fo-ni-kos tha-la-mos
Phone card	Η τηλεκάρτα I tilekárta	ee tee-le-kar-ta

SHOPPING

How much does this cost?	Πόσο κάνει; Póso kánei?	po-so ka-nee
I would like...	Θα ήθελα... Tha ithela...	tha ce-the-la
Do you have...?	Έχετε...; Echete...?	e-che-teh
I am just looking	Απλώς κοιτάω Aplós koitáo	a-plos kee-ta-o
Do you take credit cards/travelers' checks?	Δέχεστε πιστωτικές κάρτες/travelers' checks; Décheste pistotikés kártes/travelers' checks?	the-ches-teh pee-sto-tee-kes kar-tes/ travelers' checks
What time do you open/close?	Ποτέ ανοίγετε/ κλείνετε; Póte anoigete/ kleinete?	po-teh a-nee-ye-teh/ klee-ne-tch
Can you ship this overseas?	Μπορείτε να το στείλετε στο εξωτερικό; Mporeite na to steilete sto exoterikó?	bo-ree-teh na to stee-le-teh sto e-xo-te-ree ko
This one	Αυτό εδώ Aftó edó	af-to e-do
That one	Εκείνο Ekeino	e-kce-no

expensive	Ακριβό Ακρινό	a-kree-vo
cheap	Φθηνό Fthinó	fthee-no
size	Το μέγεθος Το mégethos	ta me-ge-thos
white	Λευκό Lefkó	lef-ko
black	Μαύρο Μάvro	mav-ro
red	Κόκκινο Kókkino	ko-kee-no
yellow	Κίτρινο Kitrino	kee-tree-no
green	Πράσινο Prásino	pra-see-no
blue	Μπλε Mple	bleh

TYPES OF STORE

antique shop	Μαγαζί με αντίκες Magazí me antíkes	ma-ga-zee me an-dee-kes
bakery	Ο φούρνος Ο foúrnos	o foor-nos
bank	Η τράπεζα Ι trápeza	ee tra-pe-za
bazaar	Το παζάρι Το pazári	to pa-za-ree
bookstore	Το βιβλιοπωλείο Το vivliopoleío	to vee-vlee-o-po-lee-o
butcher	Το κρεωπολείο Το kreopoleío	to kre-o-po-lee-o
cake shop	Το ζαχαροπλαστείο Το zacharoplasteío	to za-cha-ro-pla-stee-o
cheese shop	Μαγαζί με αλλαντικά Magazí me allantiká	ma-ga-zee me a-lan-dee-ka
department store	Πολυκάταστημα Polykatástima	Po-lee-ka-ta-stee-ma
fish market	Το ιχθυοπωλείο/ ψαράδικο Το ichthyopoleío/ psarádiko	to eech-thee-o-po-lee-o /psa-rá-dee-ko
greengrocer	Το μανάβικο Το manáviko	to ma-na-vee-ko
hairdresser	Το κομμωτήριο Το kommotírio	to ko-mo-tee-ree-o
kiosk	Το περίπτερο Το períptero	to pe-reep-te-ro
leather shop	Μαγαζί με δερμάτινα είδη Magazí me dermátina eídi	ma-ga-zee me ther-ma-tee-na ee-thee
street market	Η λαϊκή αγορά Ι laïkí agorá	ee la-ee-kee a-go-ra
newsstand	Ο εφημεριδοπώλης Ο efimeridopólis	O e-fee-me-ree-tho-po-lees
pharmacy	Το φαρμακείο Το farmakeío	to far-ma-kee-o
post office	Το ταχυδρομείο Το tachydromeío	to ta-chee-thro-mee-o
shoe store	Κατάστημα υποδημάτων Katástima ypodimáton	ka-ta-stee-ma ee-po-dee-ma-ton
souvenir shop	Μαγαζί με "souvenir" Magazi me "souvenir"	ma-ga-zee meh "souvenir"
supermarket	Σουπερμάρκετ/ Υπεραγορά "Supermarket"/ Yperagorá	"Supermarket" / ee-per-a-go-ra
tobacconist	Είδη καπνις Eídi kapnis	Ee-thee kap-nees
travel agent	Το ταξειδιωτικό γραφείο Το taxeidiotikó grafeío	to tak-see-thy-o-tee-ko gra-fee-o

SIGHTSEEING

tourist information	Ο ΕΟΤ Ο ΕΟΤ	o E-OT
tourist police	Η τουριστική αστυνομία Ι touristikí astynomía	ee too-rees-tee-kee a-stee-no-mee-a
archaeological	αρχαιολογικός archaiologikós	ar-che-o lo yee-kos

art gallery	Η γκαλερί Ι gkaleri	ee ga-le-ree
beach	Η παραλία Ι paralia	ee pa-ra-lee-a
Byzantine	βιζαντινός vyzantinós	vee-zan-dee-nos
castle	Το κάστρο Το kástro	to ka-stro
cathedral	Η μητρόπολη Ι mitrópoli	ee mee-tro-po-lee
cave	Το σπήλαιο Το spílaio	to spee-le-o
church	Η εκκλησία Ι ekklisía	ee e-klee-see-a
folk art	λαϊκή τέχνη laïkí téchni	la-ee-kee tech-nee
fountain	Το συντριβάνι Το syntriváni	to seen-dree-va-nee
hill	Ο λόφος Ο lófos	o lo-fos
historical	ιστορικός istorikós	ee-sto-ree-kos
island	Το νησί Το nisi	to nee-see
lake	Η λίμνη Ι límni	ee leem-nee
library	Η βιβλιοθήκη Ι vivliothiki	ee veev-lee-o-thee-kee
mansion	Η έπαυλις Ι épavlis	ee e-pav-lees
monastery	Μονή moni	mo-ni
mountain	Το βουνό Το vounó	to voo-no
municipal	δημοτικός dimotikós	thee-mo-tee-kos
museum	Το μουσείο Το mouseío	to moo-see-o
national	εθνικός ethnikós	eth-nee-kos
park	Το πάρκο Το párko	to par-ko
garden	Ο κήπος Ο kipos	o kee-pos
gorge	Το φαράγγι Το farángi	to fa-ran-gee
grave of…	Ο τάφος του… Ο táfos tou…	o ta-fos too
river	Το ποτάμι Το potámi	to po-ta-mee
road	Ο δρόμος Ο drómos	o thro-mos
saint	άγιος/άγιοι/αγία/ αγίες ágios/ágioi/agía/agies	a-yee-os/a-yee-ee/a-yee-a/a-yee-es
spring	Η πηγή Ι pigi	ee pee-yee
square	Η πλατεία Ι plateía	ee pla-tee-a
stadium	Το στάδιο Το stádio	to sta-thee-o
statue	Το άγαλμα Το ágalma	to a-gal-ma
theater	Το θέατρο Το théatro	to the-a-tro
town hall	Το δημαρχείο Το dimarcheío	To thee-mar-chee-o
closed on public holidays	κλειστό τις αργίες kleistó tis argies	klee-sto tees aryee-es

TRANSPORTATION

When does the… leave?	Πότε φεύγει το…; Póte févgei to…?	po-teh fev-yee to…
Where is the bus stop?	Πού είναι η στάση του λεωφορείου; Poú eínai i stási tou leoforeíou?	poo ee-neh ee sta-see too le-o-fo-ree-oo
Is there a bus to…?	Υπάρχει λεωφορείο για…; Ypárchei leoforeío gia…?	ee-par-chee le-o-fo-ree-o yia…
ticket office	Εκδοτήρια εισιτηρίων Ekdotiria eisitirion	Ek-tho-tee-reea ee-see-tee-ree-on
round-trip ticket	Εισιτήριο με επιστροφή Eisitirio me epistrofi	ee-see-tee-ree-o meh e-pee-stro-fee
one-way ticket	Απλό εισιτήριο Apló eisitirio	a-plo ee-see-tee-reeo

bus station	Ο σταθμός λεωφορείων Ο stathmós leoforeíon	o stath-mos leo-fo-ree-on
bus ticket	Εισητήριο λεωφορειου Eisitírio leoforeíou	ee-see-tee-ree-o leo-fo-ree-oo
trolleybus	Το τρόλλευ Το trólley	to tro-le-ee
port	Το λιμάνι Το limáni	to lee-ma-nee
train/metro	Το τρένο Το tréno	to tre-no
railroad station	σιδηροδρομικός σταθμός sidirodromikós stathmós	see-thee-ro-thro-mee-kos stath-mos
moped	Το μοτοποδήλατο / το μηχανάκι Το motopodílato / Το michanáki	to mo-to-po-thee-la-to/to mee-cha-na-kee
bicycle	Το ποδήλατο Το podílato	to po-thee-la-to
taxi	Το ταξί Το taxi	to tak-see
airport	Το αεροδρόμιο Το aerodrómio	to a-e-ro-thro-mee-o
ferry	Το φερρυπότ Το ferympot	to fe-ree-bot
hydrofoil	Το δελφίνι / Το υδροπτέρυγο Το delfíni / Το ydroptérygo	to del-fee-nee / To ee-throp-te-ree-go
catamaran	Το καταμαράν Το katamarán	to catamaran
for rent	Ενοικιάζονται Enoikiázontai	e-nee-kya-zon-deh

STAYING IN A HOTEL

Do you have a vacant room?	Εχετε δωμάτια; Echete domátia?	e-che-teh tho-ma-tee-a
double room with double bed	Δίκλινο με διπλό κρεββάτι Díklino me dipló krevváti	thee-klee-no meh thee-plo kre va tee
room with twin beds	Δίκλινο με μονά κρεββάτια Díklino me moná krevvátia	thee-klee-no meh mo-na kre-vat-ya
single room	Μονόκλινο Monóklino	mo-no-klee-no
room with a bath	Δώμάτιο με μπάνιο Domátio me mpánio	tho-ma-tee-o meh ban-yo
shower	Το ντουζ Το douz	To dooz
porter	Ο πορτιέρης Ο portiéris	o por-tye-rees
key	Το κλειδί Το kleidí	to klee-dee
I have a reservation	Εχω κάνει κράτηση Echo kánei krátisi	e-cho ka-nee kra-tee-see
room with a sea view/balcony	Δωμάτιο με θέα στή θάλασσα/μπαλκόνι Domátio me théa sti thálassa/mpalkóni	tho-ma-tee-o meh the-a stee tha-la-sa/bal-ko-nee
Does the price include breakfast?	Το πρωινό συμπεριλαμβάνεται στην τιμή; Το proinó symperi- lamvánetai stin timí?	to pro-ce-no seem-be-ree-lam-va-ne-teh steen tee-mee

EATING OUT

Do you have a table?	Εχετε τραπέζι; Echete trapézi?	e-che-te tra-pe-zee
I want to reserve a table	Θέλω να κρατήσω ένα τραπέζι Thélo na kratiso éna trapézi	the-lo na kra-tce-so e-na tra-pe-zee
The check, please	Τον λογαριασμό, παρακαλώ Τοn logariazmó parakaló	ton lo-gar-yas-mo pa-ra-ka-lo
I am a vegetarian	Είμαι χορτοφάγος Eímai chortofágos	ce-meh chor-to-fa-gos
What is fresh today?	Τί φρέσκο έχετε σήμερα; Τί frésko échete simera?	tce fres-ko e-che-teh see-me-ra?

waiter/waitress	Κύριε / Γκαρσόν / Κυρία (female) Kýrie/Garson"/Kyría	Kee-ree-eh/Gar-son/Kee-ree-a
menu	Ο κατάλογος Ο katálogos	o ka-ta-lo-gos
cover charge	Το κουβέρ Το "couvert"	to koo-ver
wine list	Ο κατάλογος με τα οινοπνευματώδη Ο katálogos me ta oinopnevmatódi	o ka-ta-lo-gos meh ta o-no-pnev-ma-to-thee
glass	Το ποτήρι Το potíri	to po-tce-ree
bottle	Το μπουκάλι Το mpoukáli	to bou-ka-lee
knife	Το μαχαίρι Το machairi	to ma-che-ree
fork	Το πηρούνι Το piroúni	to pee-roo-nee
spoon	Το κουτάλι Το koutáli	to koo-ta-lee
breakfast	Το πρωινό Το proinó	to pro-ce-no
lunch	Το μεσημεριανό Το mesimerianó	to me-see-mer-ya-no
dinner	Το δείπνο Το deípno	to theep-no
main course	Το κυρίως γεύμα Το kyrios gévma	to kee-ree-os yev-ma
starter/first course	Τα ορεκτικά Τα orektiká	ta o-rek-tee-ka
dessert	Το γλυκό Το glykó	to ylee-ko
dish of the day	Το πιάτο της ημέρας Το piáto tis iméras	to pya-to tees ee-me-ras
bar	Το μπαρ Το "bar"	To bar
taverna	Η ταβέρνα Ι tavérna	ee ta-ver-na
café	Το καφενείο Το kafeneío	to ka-fe-nee-o
fish taverna	Η ψαροταβέρνα Ι psarotavérna	ee psa-ro-ta-ver-na
grill house	Η ψησταριά Ι psistariá	ee psee-sta-rya
wine shop	Το οινοπωλείο Το oinopoleío	to ee-no-po-lce-o
dairy shop	Το γαλακτοπωλείο Το galaktopoleío	to ga-lak-to-po-lce-o
restaurant	Το εστιατόριο Το estiatório	to e-stee-a-to-ree-o
ouzeri	Το ουζερί Το ouzeri	to oo-ze-ree
meze shop	Το μεζεδοπωλείο Το mezedopoleío	To me-ze-do-po-lce-o
take-out kebabs	Το σουβλατζίδικο Το souvlatzidiko	To soo-vlat-zee-dee-ko
rare	Ελάχιστα ψημένο Eláchista psiméno	e-lach-ees-ta psee-me-no
medium	Μέτρια ψημένο Métria psiméno	met-ree-a psee-me no
well done	Καλοψημένο Kalopsiméno	ka-lo-psee-me-no

BASIC FOOD AND DRINK

coffee	Ο καφές Ο Kafés	o ka-fes
with milk	με γάλα me gála	me ga-la
black coffee	σκέτος skétos	ske-tos
without sugar	χωρίς ζάχαρη choris záchari	cho-rees za-cha-ree
medium sweet	μέτριος métrios	me-tree-os
very sweet	γλυκύς glykýs	glee-kees
tea	τσάι tsái	tsa-ee
hot chocolate	ζεστή σοκολάτα zesti sokoláta	ze-stee so-ko-la-ta
wine	κρασί krasí	kra-see
red	κόκκινο kókkino	ko-kee-no
white	λευκό lefkó	lef-ko
rosé	ροζέ rozé	ro-ze

raki	Το ρακί / Το raki	to ra-kee
ouzo	Το ούζο / Το oúzo	to oo-zo
retsina	Η ρετσίνα / I retsina	ee ret-see-na
water	Το νερό / Το neró	to ne-ro
octopus	Το χταπόδι / Το chtapódi	to chta-po-dee
fish	Το ψάρι / Το psári	to psa-ree
cheese	Το τυρί / Το tyrí	to tee-ree
halloumi	Το χαλούμι / Το chaloúmi	to cha-loo-mee
feta	Η φέτα / I féta	ee fe-ta
bread	Το ψωμί / Το psomí	to pso-mee
bean soup	Η φασολάδα / I fasoláda	ee fa-so-la-da
hummus	Το χούμους / Το houmous	to choo-moos
halva	Ο χαλβάς / Ο chalvás	o chal-vas
meat kebabs	Ο γύρος / Ο gýros	o yee-ros
Turkish delight	Το λουκούμι / Το loukoúmi	to loo-koo-mee
baklava	Ο μπακλαβάς / Ο mpaklavás	o bak-la-vas
klephtiko	Το κλέφτικο / Το kléftiko	to klef-tee-ko

NUMBERS

1	ένα / éna	e-na
2	δύο / dýo	thee-o
3	τρία / tría	tree-a
4	τέσσερα / téssera	te-se-ra
5	πέντε / pénte	pen-deh
6	έξι / éxi	ek-si
7	επτά / eptá	ep-ta
8	οχτώ / ochtó	och-to
9	εννέα / ennéa	e-ne-a
10	δέκα / déka	the-ka
11	έντεκα / énteka	en-de-ka
12	δώδεκα / dódeka	tho-the-ka
13	δεκατρία / dekatría	the-ka-tree-a
14	δεκατέσσερα / dekatéssera	the-ka-te-se-ra
15	δεκαπέντε / dekapénte	the-ka-pen-de
16	δεκαέξι / dekaéxi	the-ka-ek-si
17	δεκαεπτά / dekaeptá	the-ka-ep-ta
18	δεκαοχτώ / dekaochtó	the-ka-och-to
19	δεκαεννέα / dekaennéa	the-ka-e-ne-a
20	είκοσι / eíkosi	ee-ko-see
21	εικοσιένα / eikosiéna	ee-ko-see-e-na
30	τριάντα / triánta	tree-an-da
40	σαράντα / saránta	sa-ran-da
50	πενήντα / peninta	pe-neen-da
60	εξήντα / exinta	ek-seen-da
70	εβδομήντα / evdominta	ev-tho-meen-da

80	ογδόντα / ogdónta	og-thon-da
90	εννενήντα / enneninta	e-ne-neen-da
100	εκατό / ekató	e-ka-to
200	διακόσια / diakósia	thya-kos-ya
1,000	χίλια / chília	cheel-ya
2,000	δύο χιλιάδες / d´yo chiliádes	thee-o cheel-ya-thes
1,000,000	ένα εκατομμύριο / éna ekatomm´yrio	e-na e-ka-to-mee-ree-o

TIME, DAYS, AND DATES

one minute	ένα λεπτό / éna leptó	e-na lep-to
one hour	μία ώρα / mia óra	mee-a o-ra
half an hour	μισή ώρα / misí óra	mee-see o-ra
quarter of an hour	ένα τέταρτο / éna tétarto	e-na te-tar-to
half past one	μία και μισή / mía kai misí	mee-a keh mee-see
quarter past one	μία και τέταρτο / mia kai tétarto	mee-a keh te-tar-to
ten past one	μία και δέκα / mia kai déka	mee-a keh the-ka
quarter to two	δύο παρά τέταρτο / d´yo pará tétarto	thee-o pa-ra te-tar-to
ten to two	δύο παρά δέκα / d´yo pará déka	thee-o pa-ra the-ka
a day	μία μέρα / mia méra	mee-a me-ra
a week	μία εβδομάδα / mia evdomáda	mee-a ev-tho-ma-tha
a month	ένας μήνας / énas minas	e-nas mee-nas
a year	ένας χρόνος / énas chrónos	e-nas chro-nos
Monday	Δευτέρα / Deftéra	thef-te-ra
Tuesday	Τρίτη / Triti	tree-tee
Wednesday	Τετάρτη / Tetárti	te-tar-tee
Thursday	Πέμπτη / Pémpti	pemp-tee
Friday	Παρασκευή / Paraskeví	pa-ras-ke-vee
Saturday	Σάββατο / Savváto	sa-va-to
Sunday	Κυριακή / Kyriaki	keer-ee-a-kee
January	Ιανουάριος / Ianouários	ee-a-noo-a-ree-os
February	Φεβρουάριος / Fevrouários	fev-roo-a-ree-os
March	Μάρτιος / Mártios	mar-tee-os
April	Απρίλιος / Aprílios	a-pree-lee-os
May	Μάιος / Máios	ma-ee-os
June	Ιούνιος / Ioúnios	ee-oo-nee-os
July	Ιούλιος / Ioúlios	ee-oo-lee-os
August	Αύγουστος / Avgoustos	av-goo-stos
September	Σεπτέμβριος / Septémvrios	sep-tem-vree-os
October	Οκτώβριος / Októvrios	ok-to-vree-os
November	Νοέμβριος / Noémvrios	no-em-vree-os
December	Δεκέμβριος / Dekémvrios	the-kem-vree-os